HANDBOOKS

W9-BRW-013

VERMONT

MICHAEL BLANDING & ALEXANDRA HALL

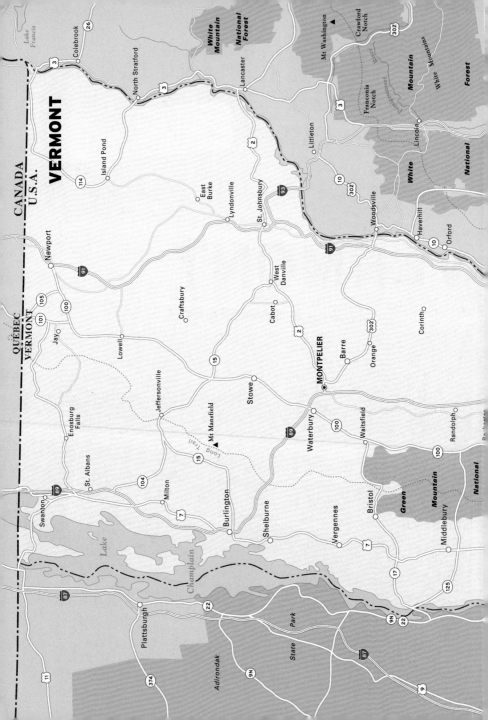

Contents

Discover Vermont

"I love Vermont because of her hills and valleys, her scenery, and invigorating climate," President and native Vermonter Calvin Coolidge once said. "But most of all because of her indomitable people." That description barely begins to describe the determination of those living in the Green Mountain State – or the beauty of the land itself. With its mountains that draw skiers by the thousands in winter and scent the land with pine in the summer, and its historic towns filled with a vibrant mixture of artists, farmers, and other independent spirits, Vermont may be geographically small, but it makes an unquestionably big impression.

Independence is in Vermont's blood. An independent republic from 1777-1791, it played a key role in the American Revolution and was settled by pioneers who created the New England town meeting (which still exists in almost all of Vermont's 237 towns). In the years since, the left-leaning state has been the first to abolish slavery and legalize civil unions (and gay marriage by an act of the Legislature).

But while politics may have helped shape Vermont's character, it's the landscape that truly defines it. The Green Mountains for which the state is named serve as its backbone, spreading forests and pastoral valleys from the Northeast Kingdom down to its southernmost points. To the northwest, Lake Champlain is abutted by New York and Quebec province – both

of which exert their various cultural influences across the border. And to the east sits the Connecticut River Valley, home to several of the state's larger towns. Everywhere in between, you'll find country that sets the standard for quaintness: villages teeming with church steeples, gazebos, and traditional architecture, not to mention big swaths of cow-dotted farmland punctuated by covered bridges.

Those farms, in addition to sustaining the state's tradition of family-run dairies, have made Vermont a major source for gourmet specialty foods. The state's reputation as a cheese mecca has skyrocketed in recent years as has its production: The state currently makes about 125 million pounds of cheese each year. It is also the world's biggest supplier of maple syrup, a fact that should surprise no one who has witnessed the land's other magnificent draw: an abundance of trees, which, come autumn, delight with a fiery mosaic of color.

It's all enough to assure visitors that there truly is no other state like Vermont – something the natives have believed from the very start.

Planning Your Trip

► WHERE TO GO

Southern Green Mountains

Within southern Vermont is a roller-coaster jumble of forested slopes and hidden valleys that are home to picture-postcard villages and maple farms. Signs for cheese shops and maple syrup are legion on the roadsides. Come shop at the outlet stores in Manchester, see the sights in historic Bennington, or peruse the art galleries in funky Brattleboro.

Along Route 4

U.S. Highway 4 slices across the middle of the state, separating the two halves of the Green Mountain National Forest. Along this corridor are many of the state's main centers of civilization: Rutland, once a center for marble production in the country; Woodstock, a quintessential New England town; and in the middle of the route, the "Beast of the East," the ski resort of Killington.

Champlain Valley

Buttressed on one side by mountains and shored up on the other by the coastline

IF YOU HAVE . . .

skiing Stowe Mountain Resort

- **A WEEKEND:** Visit the Southern Green Mountains, basing yourself in Brattleboro.
- **FIVE DAYS:** Add a road trip along Route 4 from Quechee to Killington.
- **A WEEK:** Add an excursion to Waterbury and Stowe in the Northern Green Mountains.
- **TWO WEEKS:** Add Burlington, the Lake Champlain Islands, and a trip to the Northeast Kingdom.

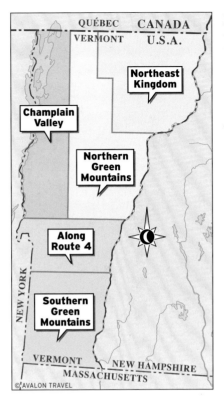

QUÉBEC CANADA
VERMONT U.S.A.

Northeast Kingdom

Champlain Valley

Northern Green Mountains

Along Route 4

NEW YORK

Southern Green Mountains

VERMONT
MASSACHUSETTS NEW HAMPSHIRE

© AVALON TRAVEL

holds two of the state's oldest and most attractive settlements: the delightful college town of Middlebury and the "big city" of Burlington, situated on the shores of Lake Champlain.

Northern Green Mountains

As you travel northward, the mountains get bigger and woollier, culminating with the soaring slopes of Mount Mansfield just outside the alpine village of Stowe. This part of the state is an outdoors-lover's dream. On the edge of the mountains is the state capital, Montpelier, and Vermont's number-one tourist attraction—the ice cream factory that made Ben & Jerry's a household name (and, for some, an addiction).

Northeast Kingdom

Those who scratch beneath the surface of this stark landscape often come away proclaiming that this is their favorite part of the state, prizing it for its majestic beauty. This region is also home to some of the state's most famous gustatory attractions, including Cabot Creamery and Maple Grove Farms, as well as the cherished biking and cross-country skiing terrain of the Kingdom Trails Network.

of North America's sixth largest lake, this broad valley, dotted with farms and dairies,

▶ WHEN TO GO

Almost every season beckons with something attractive. We say "almost" because, with its chilly temperatures and rainfall, spring is rightfully known as "mud season." And while there's still plenty to do indoors, Vermont is definitely at its best when the great outdoors are involved.

That's why, with its mountains, abundance of snow, and plethora of resorts, Vermont is a skier's Valhalla come winter. If there's any downside to visiting during this season (besides the average temperatures

hitting the low 20s), it's only that everyone else has the same idea. Ski resorts and towns get congested and expensive.

In summer, those same mountains abound with excellent hiking and biking, and the state's deep woods are a field day for hunters, anglers, and bird-watchers. The days are sunny and temperatures tend to hover in the mid-70s. The countryside yields an abundance of farm-fresh produce and artisanal cheeses. As for the crowds? They're at a minimum, so visitors can enjoy

picturesque Peacham

the landscape and towns minus any long lines.

Peak travel is in autumn, particularly in late September and October when the foliage is at its most dramatic and students are pouring into area colleges. Fall foliage season may be Vermont's shining moment every year— and what a moment it is, when the state's famed and glorious foliage takes center stage and draws leaf peepers by the hundreds of thousands. And with the crowds, prices tend to rise. Still, if the tourist rush can be avoided, there are few places in the world that celebrate fall so well, with a plethora of farmstands, harvest festivals, and mountains decked out in all of their autumn raiment. If leaf peeping isn't your thing, however, you can save money by traveling in late August or early September, when the summer humidity has dissipated but hotel prices haven't yet skyrocketed.

Explore Vermont

▶ THE BEST OF VERMONT

The best way to explore Vermont is to get in a car and hit the back roads, stopping at country stores and maple sugar farms nestled in Green Mountain valleys. This two-week tour takes in a mix of Vermont's prime attractions in an easygoing circle around the state.

Day 1

Start in Brattleboro. Spend the day exploring Brattleboro's artsy attractions, including the Brattleboro Museum & Art Center and the Estey Organ Museum, and leave enough time for shopping on quirky Main Street. Time your visit to correspond to the first Friday night of the month to experience Brattleboro's Gallery Walk and soak in the creative spirit of the city.

Day 2

From Brattleboro head north along winding Route 30, stopping for a stroll around Newfane's village green before taking the turn north onto Route 35 to Grafton (45 min.). Here, take a tour of the Grafton Village Cheese Company and the town's small Nature Museum before a meal and stay at the historic Grafton Inn.

Day 3

Head west on Routes 121 and 11, then north on Route 100 to Weston (30 min.), where you'll need at least an hour to really explore the phenomenon that is the Vermont Country Store. After lunch, continue north along scenic Route 100 to Plymouth (35 min.) to stand

Grafton Village Cheese Company

in the company of greatness at the President Calvin Coolidge State Historic Site. Push on north along 100A and east on Route 4 to spend the night at the Woodstock Inn & Resort in Woodstock (25 min.).

Day 4

Spend the morning with Vermont's star bovines at Woodstock's Billings Farm & Museum. (For a true treat, time your visit with the farm's Cow Appreciation Day.) Then take in the scenic drive north along Route 12, east on Route 107, and then north along Route 100, ending up in the Mad River Valley town of Warren (90 min.). Spend the afternoon exploring The Warren Store and the picturesque village center or take advantage of the many recreational opportunities with a hike up Camel's Hump or Mount Ellen, a bike ride through town, or a wild canoe ride on the Mad or Winooski River.

Day 5

Head north along Route 100 to Waterbury (30 min.) for a morning tour of the Ben & Jerry's Factory. (It's never too early for Chunky Monkey!) Then it's off to the big city! Drive west along I-89 to the big ol' college town of Burlington (45 min.). Spend the morning strolling among the shops on Church Street before heading to the waterfront in the afternoon for a visit to the ECHO Lake Aquarium and Science Center or Lake Champlain Maritime Museum. Tonight, take in a show at the Flynn Center for the Performing Arts.

Day 6

Push on south down Route 7 to Middlebury (1 hr.), where you can get a morning tour of Middlebury College's pristine gray granite campus. After lunch, head east along Route 125 to commune with Vermont's favorite adopted son via a hike along the meditative Robert Frost Interpretive Trail.

Continue south down Route 7 to the covered bridge capital of Proctor (35 min.), visiting the paean to all things European, Wilson Castle. Stop for lunch in nearby Rutland (15 min.) and then drive to sophisticated Manchester (50 min.) for an afternoon of outlet shopping.

Day 7

Spend the morning driving up the Mount Equinox Skyline Drive for a beautiful view of the Green Mountains. Then head south down Route 7 to Bennington (40 min.), where you can check out the Bennington Battle Monument and the distinctive folk art of Grandma Moses at the Bennington Museum before spending the night in Bennington.

Day 8

Spend your last day tracing the meandering Route 9 east over the Green Mountains to the *Back to the Future* downtown of Wilmington and the quirky college town of Marlboro. If you haven't yet gotten your farm fix, take a detour up Route 100 to visit Adams Family Farm for a sleigh ride or hayride before spending one last night in Brattleboro.

COVERED BRIDGES

Warren Bridge crosses the Mad River.

Bridges in Vermont were covered to protect the roadway and supports from the ravages of New England weather. The covers were relatively easy to replace compared with the supports driven into the river bottoms. Originally, there were more than 600 covered bridges in Vermont; two-thirds of them were destroyed in the disastrous flood of 1927. Dozens more were simply not replaced when their covers became damaged or rotted.

While Pennsylvania is the state with the largest number of surviving covered bridges, Vermont and New Hampshire have long fought over which of the states can lay claim to being the "covered bridge capital of New England." Actually, Vermont blows New Hampshire out of the water, with 106 surviving covered bridges compared to the Granite State's 54. If it's any consolation, however, New Hampshire can lay claim to having the longest covered bridge, the 450-foot Cornish-Windsor Bridge over the Connecticut River. (That's the Windsor-Cornish Bridge to Vermonters.) Because the official boundary between the states is the west bank of the river, nearly the entire bridge is firmly within New Hampshire state territory.

· **Number of Covered Bridges in Vermont:** 106

· **Oldest Bridge in Vermont:** Pulp Mill Covered Bridge in Middlebury, dating from 1820 (page 133)

· **Oldest Continuously Operating Bridge in Vermont:** Great Eddy Bridge in Waitsfield, dating from 1833 (page 167)

· **Longest Bridge in Vermont:** Scott Covered Bridge, north of Brattleboro–277 feet long (page 36)

· **Most Camera-Friendly Bridge Near Norman Rockwell's Home:** Bridge at the Green in Arlington (page 48)

· **Longest Bridge not Technically in Vermont:** Windsor-Cornish Bridge in Cornish, New Hampshire (page 72)

· **Town with the Most Covered Bridges in the United States:** Montgomery, Vermont, with six covered bridges (page 211)

· **Place Where You Can See Two Bridges at Once Spanning Different Sections of the Same Road:** Cox Brook Road in Northfield (page 150)

· **Best Place to Learn About Covered Bridges:** Covered Bridge Museum in Bennington (page 45)

▶ LEAF PEEPING

The term may evoke comical images of tourists sneaking up on unsuspecting fallen leaves to ogle them, but come autumn in Vermont, "leaf peeping" is serious business. It's the basis for the state's second-biggest tourist season, drawing visitors in droves from around the country, and often the globe, to witness the glorious color palette of fall. Trees begin to change color in mid-September and the show lasts through mid-to-late October, progressing north to south through the state.

But taking on the leaves can also mean taking on a crush of tourists. Make reservations in advance and check the season's progress online before you travel. We've also tried to include some quieter places that take you off the beaten path where you can actually enjoy nature's presentation.

Day 1

Start in Montpelier. Get acquainted with the state's history at the Vermont Historical Society Museum and splurge on dinner at La Brioche Bakery. Spend the night at Inn at Montpelier.

Day 2

From Montpelier, take I-89 west to follow Route 100 north to Stowe. Mount Mansfield's peak lures skiers in winter, but in fall it's all about the lush foliage across its slopes. No visit to Stowe is complete without a trip to the Trapp Family Lodge, the ski chalet built by the real-life von Trapps, whose story leapt to screen in *The Sound of Music*. The chalet also offers overnight accommodations.

Day 3

The next day, follow the foliage south on Route 100 to the Mad River Valley, stopping for lunch at The Warren Store and for a gambol around the Saturday afternoon

east Montpelier

HISTORICAL REVOLUTION

Retrace the steps of some of Vermont's most famous explorers—from Samuel de Champlain to the wild Green Mountain Boys—in a tour of history, Vermont-style.

- **Ethan Allen Homestead:** In Burlington, you can learn about Vermont's greatest—and most flawed—hero.

- **Bennington Battle Monument:** A 306-foot memorial pays homage to the first winning battle of the American Revolution, complete with a diorama of the conflict inside and artifacts in the neighboring museum.

- **Hubbardton Battlefield State Historic Site:** The Green Mountain Boys, under Seth Warner, held off British general Johnnie Burgoyne here in a heroic rear guard action.

- **Lake Champlain Maritime Museum:** This museum in Vergennes tells the surprising tale of Benedict Arnold's early Revolutionary War heroics against the British navy—before he turned traitor. Then, take a tour of the lake to see the site of the Battle of Valcour Island, where Arnold daringly escaped the Brits.

- **Mount Independence State Historic Site:** Hike along the Revolutionary battleworks and see where the Americans prepared their defenses against the British.

- **St. Alban's:** This pretty town was the unlikely site of Vermont's one and only Civil War battle.

- **St. Anne's Shrine: See** the site of Fort St. Anne, where Samuel de Champlain "discovered" Vermont in 1609 and where Jesuit priests still hold mass.

Waitsfield Farmers' Market on the Mad River Green. Spend the night in Warren at Round Barn Farm.

Day 4

From the Mad River Valley, follow Route 100 south to Hancock, then cut west across the mountains on Route 73 through Middlebury Gap, oohing and aahing at the foliage. Continue to Middlebury for a tour of the small but impressive Middlebury College Museum of Art or the quaint Vermont Folklife Center. Stay overnight at the Swift House Inn.

Day 5

From Middlebury, Route 7 continues south to Rutland, which offers a taste of America's great small-town memorialist at the Norman Rockwell Museum. Try to time your visit for the Proctor Fall Festival in late September. Bed down for the night at the Inn at Rutland.

Day 6

The next day, head south on Route 7, where the sophisticated outlet town of Manchester lies quietly in the Southern Green Mountains. Spend the morning touring the exhibits at the Southern Vermont Art Center or the Victorian furnishings at Abraham Lincoln's son's former estate of Hildene. At night, the romantic The Reluctant Panther Inn & Restaurant offers a place to stay, while the on-site restaurant includes views of Mount Equinox.

Day 7

Today, head south on Route 7A, making a detour in Shaftsbury (15 min.) to visit the Robert Frost Stone House Museum, former home of its namesake poet. The surroundings are a perfect foil to Frost's love of the outdoors, and the poems that exemplified them: The house sits on seven acres filled

skiers at Sugarbush

with stone walls, birches and apple trees, none of which are more vibrant than during foliage season.

From Shaftsbury, it's a three-hour drive north to return to Montpelier, or to the airport in South Burlington.

▶ SKIING AT ITS PEAK

For many visitors, winter is the best time to see Vermont. Twinkling Christmas lights on the pine trees at quaint country inns call to mind a Norman Rockwell version of the season. But enough of that—the real reason you come to the Green Mountain State in the winter is to strap on some sticks or a board and get up on that fresh powder. Here's a primer on finding slopes for every desire.

Big and Bad

For many skiers in the East, the sport starts and ends with Killington, the biggest, baddest mountain in these parts. Or make that mountains—with six peaks to choose from, Killington literally has something for everyone, including careening double diamonds, twisting glades, and family-friendly cruisers.

For a slightly less crowded experience, many skiers head north to Sugarbush, which is second only to Killington in number and variety of trails; it boasts a large amount of natural snowfall thanks to the storms that come in from Lake Champlain.

"Uncrowded" doesn't describe Mount Snow, the rowdy party mountain in the southern part of the state, but it does have the most accessible big mountain skiing around, making it a favorite of day-trippers from New York and southern New England.

OPEN UP AND SAY SPA

the Stoweflake Mountain Resort and Spa

Regular visitors to the area call it "the Stowe response"—the sense of relaxation that sets in after a few days spent in the bucolic area. Whether it occurs as a result of all the spas clustered in the vicinity or because so many spas have clustered to accommodate the already relaxed population is the kind of chicken-and-egg question to which there is no answer. Best to leave the pondering to someone else and submit yourself to a massage at one of the following excellent (and often elegant) Stowe-area facilities:

- **Evergreen Healing Arts Center** (4285 Mountain Rd., 802/253-7118)

- **Golden Eagle Resort and Spa** (511 Mountain Rd., 802/253-4811, www. goldeneagleresort.com/spa.html)

- **Stoweflake Mountain Resort and Spa** (1746 Mountain Rd., 802/253-7355, www. stoweflake.com/spa.aspx)

- **Topnotch Resort and Spa** (4000 Mountain Rd., 802/253-8585, www. topnotchresort.com)

Skiers' Mountains

You know the type—those who eschew the latest moisture-wicking jackets and snowboards for a beat-up old parka and the same skis they've had since high school. In Vermont, purists like this flock to Mad River Glen, an unapologetically ugly and demanding pile of rock in Waitsfield, where half the trails are double diamond and the motto is "Ski It If You Can."

Somewhat more forgiving is nearby Stowe Mountain Resort, which hugs the slopes of Vermont's highest peak, Mount Mansfield, and has resisted the runaway development of some mountains we won't name to work with the surrounding community and keep alive the true alpine village.

Those *really* wanting to get away from it all go all the way to the Canadian border to Jay Peak, which boasts the most snowfall of any mountain in Vermont and gives skiers plenty of elbow room with which to enjoy all that powder.

Crowd-Pleasers

Winning the prize for best all-around resort is Stratton Mountain, which offers a good balance of big mountain skiing and accessibility. It's particularly popular with snowboarders—after all, the sport was invented here, and Stratton claims no fewer than five terrain parks for the sport.

Nearby, Okemo wins accolades for its skier-friendly atmosphere and a good balance of difficult trails and programs for kids and families.

Family Fun

Parents can't do much better than Smugglers' Notch, which offers a money-back guarantee if any member of the family doesn't have a good time. Small chance of that, as three mountains, kids' and teens' programs, and an indoor activity center provide plenty to put a smile on the face of even the most recalcitrant youngster.

In southern Vermont, Bromley Mountain markets itself as a resort for the whole family, with nearly 50 trails for all abilities and a ski school for kids featuring mascot Clyde Catamount.

Next door to Killington, pint-sized Pico Mountain offers inviting terrain for beginners and intermediate skiers, along with lift privileges at its big brother for the experts in the family.

Off the Groomed Trail

The best deal in Vermont skiing is undoubtedly the Middlebury College Snow Bowl, the official course for Middlebury College's alpine team. Free from crowds and affordable at $30 for adults, it nevertheless offers plenty of challenging terrain.

Similarly off the beaten track is Burke Mountain, a much larger mountain with 50 trails hidden in the Northeast Kingdom. It's usually buried under snow, which it gets some 250 inches of annually. Yet despite that, and despite some truly challenging upper-mountain slopes that could hold their own with any mountain in the East, it is a virtual ghost town during the week.

▶ INTO THE GREEN MOUNTAINS

There is a reason the state of Vermont is named after its primary physical feature. Everywhere you look, it seems, the Green Mountains beckon picturesquely from the horizon, practically begging you to test your mettle on their slopes. This weeklong jaunt is custom-made for the outdoors traveler.

Day 1

Start your tour in Burlington. On your first day, take a guided kayak tour of Lake Champlain, reveling in the unique vantage of the islands from the open water. (Or, if you are trained in scuba diving, opt instead for an underwater tour of the shipwrecks at the Lake Champlain Underwater Historic Preserves.)

Day 2

The next day, head south down Route 7 to Middlebury, then head into the Moosalamoo Recreation Area, 20,000 acres of pristine Green Mountain wilderness that is the state's best-kept secret. Park on Route 53 near Branbury State Park and hike the North

VERMONT WITH KIDS

sitting on the dock of Lake Champlain

Vermont is a ideal for families, with lots of candy factories, farm animals, and old historic museums.

- **Adams Family Farm:** This friendly farm in Wilmington specializes in sleigh rides and hayrides through the fields (page 40).

- **Ben & Jerry's Factory:** The one can't-miss attraction of any Vermont family vacation (page 163).

- **ECHO Lake Aquarium and Science Center:** Located on Burlington's waterfront, kids are guaranteed to get wet as they learn about frogs, snakes, and the resident sea monster, Champ (page 103).

- **Fairbanks Museum & Planetarium:** This treasure trove of mummies, dinosaur fossils, stuffed animals, and Civil War memorabilia, also includes an interactive weather center for budding meteorologists (page 190).

- **Lake Champlain Chocolates:** See how chocolate is made and then enjoy some truffles and bonbons afterwards (page 106).

- **Morgan Horse Farm:** At the University of Vermont's farm, little ones can pet and ride the stallions and mares (page 132).

- **Morse Farm Maple Sugarworks:** Kids can learn how maple syrup is made and harvested, then try maple ice cream and candy at the gift shop (page 160).

- **Neighborly Farms:** Neighborly prides itself on its organic cheese-making, with 50 Holsteins and farmers who just love to show kids how milk turns into cheddar or feta (page 150).

- **The Retreat Farm:** This working farm in Brattleboro also has a petting barn that encourages junior farmers to feed and groom the animals (page 26).

- **Vermont Toy & Train Museum:** Case after case of toys from yesteryear will bring back memories, but there are also toys from today for kids to play with (page 74).

Branch Trail two miles in to stay overnight at Moosalamoo Campground. Keep your eyes peeled for moose!

Day 3

Hike back to the parking area, and then drive north along Route 17 through the breathtaking Appalachian Gap, then north along Route 100 through the Mad River Valley to Stowe (90 min.). Reacquaint yourself with civilization with a stroll through the village in preparation for a more taxing workout tomorrow.

Day 4

Today, it's up early to tackle the highest mountain in the state, hiking Mount Mansfield for a panoramic view of the mountains all around. At night, nurse sore muscles with a cocktail at one of Stowe's many après-ski pubs.

Day 5

Give your legs a rest and your arms a workout with a paddle down the scenic Winooski River in the Lamoille Valley, chockablock with typical Vermont scenery of red barns and cows. Or for a bit more adventure, head to Green River Reservoir where you can paddle in to one of its unique wilderness campsites, accessible only by car top boat, and spend your nights listening to the calls of the loons.

Day 6

Today, head into Vermont's wild Northeast Kingdom with a drive north up Route 100, east on Route 15, east on U.S. Highway 2, and north on U.S. Highway 5 to East Burke. There, rent yourself a mountain bike and set out on the Kingdom Trails Network, 100 miles of pristine country landscape just crying out for two-wheeled exploration.

Day 7

Spend another day on your bike, tackling the death-defying slopes of Burke Mountain. Or stretch your legs on a hike up Mount Hor to commune with peregrine falcons with a view over the lovely Lake Willoughby. At night, splurge on a massage in preparation for tomorrow's trip home.

mountain biking on the Kingdom Trails Network

SOUTHERN GREEN MOUNTAINS

The easy access to the southern part of Vermont means that license plates from New York and Massachusetts often outnumber the green-and-white plates of the locals. The winding roads of the Green Mountain foothills can get especially crowded on weekends around foliage season (mid-Sept.–mid-Oct.) and during school vacations in ski season. Why go farther north, skiers ask, when mountains like Stratton, Mount Snow, and Okemo offer challenging trails just a couple hours' drive from Boston?

The three major towns of southern Vermont each have their own distinctive personalities. Brattleboro exudes an artsy, crunchy-granola vibe that wafts from galleries and shops ready-made for browsing.

Bennington is a working-class town living off its history as the site of a major battle during the Revolutionary War. Manchester, on the other hand, is anything but struggling. Buoyed by its designer clothing outlets and luxury spas, this is where the New York set comes to get away and play.

In between these relative metropolises are the storybook villages that epitomize New England in the minds of many people. One of the best ways to see this part of the state is just to get in the car and drive. You are sure to come across that perfect gazebo on the town green; a country store packed with homemade fudge and handicrafts; or a maple syrup farm offering tours with the purchase of a jug.

HIGHLIGHTS

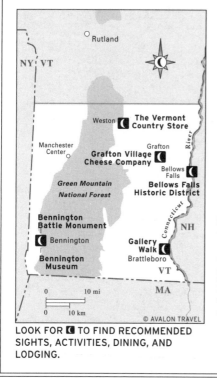

Gallery Walk: If you aren't lucky enough to live in an artists' colony, visiting this monthly festival in Brattleboro is the next best thing (page 24).

Bellows Falls Historic District: This walking tour of American architectural history includes examples of every major home style (page 32).

Grafton Village Cheese Company: You "cheddar" stop here for demonstrations of Vermont's best cheese-making (page 34).

Bennington Battle Monument: The first American victory on the battlefield is celebrated at this Revolutionary War landmark (page 44).

Bennington Museum: In addition to battle artifacts, this museum features a peerless collection of folk art by Grandma Moses (page 44).

The Vermont Country Store: Quaint it ain't, but this gargantuan store does provide authentic Vermont one-stop shopping (page 57).

LOOK FOR ◖ TO FIND RECOMMENDED SIGHTS, ACTIVITIES, DINING, AND LODGING.

Unlike in the more northerly parts of the state, lodgings and restaurants in this area tend to stay open year-round, making it a nice place to visit in the winter (though be warned that the whole area shuts down during the month of March, otherwise known in these parts as "mud season"). Of course, the region really comes into its own in fall, when the foliage does its annual color dance on the back roads, and country inns often jack up their prices as well. For many shopaholics, a trip to the region begins, stays, and ends in Manchester. Full days of shopping at deeply discounted designer outlets and luxury inns have made the place a destination that can easily fill an enthusiast's vacation.

PLANNING YOUR TIME

You could easily breeze through southern Vermont in a couple of days, but to really appreciate the area, a leisurely week of cruising the back roads or the ski slopes is more like it. You're best off basing yourself in Brattleboro, the pint-sized cultural mecca that beguiles tourists. Try to time your trip to take in the monthly **Gallery Walk** on the first Friday of the month, when the town really displays its artistic talents. While in Brattleboro, you

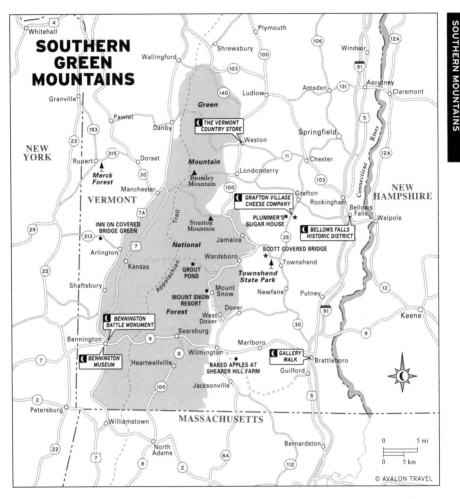

can take a few leisurely days to explore the historic homes of nearby **Bellows Falls,** the cheese-making operation at **Grafton Village Cheese Company,** and the quintessentially Vermont **Vermont Country Store.** Unlike in Brattleboro, there's not much to see in down-beat Bennington, but it's worth making a day trip to the city to see the Revolutionary War–era **Bennington Battle Monument** and accompanying **Bennington Museum.**

Brattleboro

The southeastern corner of Vermont is characterized by the gentle foothills of the Green Mountains as they descend in wave upon wave down to the Connecticut River Valley. Starting in 1724, this was the first part of Vermont to be founded—late compared to the rest of New England. The first permanent settlement in the state was at Fort Dummer, an outpost for protecting the fertile Connecticut River Valley from the Native American peoples to the north. The fort grew steadily from a vibrant trading post to a solid base of manufacturing, eventually becoming the city of Brattleboro. In the mid-19th century, it became known as a therapeutic center, famed for a "water cure" that drew some of the country's most prominent citizens for plunges in its ice-cold springs. Later, it became the "Organ Capital of the Country" for its Estey Organ Company.

Nowadays, few places make art as much a part of daily life as Brattleboro, which has reinvented itself in recent years as a mecca for painters and artisans. During its monthly Gallery Walk, shops and restaurants showcase local work, which is then left on the walls to inspire patrons in the following weeks. (Don't be surprised if after dinner you find yourself asking for a painting with your doggie bag.) The artistic sensibility of the town extends to its politics, earning it a reputation as one of the most progressive towns in Vermont. This is the kind of place where shops advertise "Breastfed Babies Welcome" on their windows and sell organic hemp clothing inside. Instead of a supermarket, it has a food co-op, where you can choose from 300 kinds of cheese and sign a petition against genetically modified foods on your way out the door. The town's mercantile past has even given its brick downtown a quasi-urban feel that harmonizes with its cosmopolitan leanings.

SIGHTS
◖ Gallery Walk

Snow or shine, crowds throng the center of town on the first Friday of every month for the Gallery Walk (802/257-2616, www.gallerywalk.org, 5:30–8:30 P.M., free), Brattleboro's signature social event. Try to time your visit to coincide with Gallery Walk, as no other experience will give you a better feel for the spirit of the town. The streets take on a festival atmosphere as neighbors catch up on news and pore over the latest creations of their friends while noshing on vittles and red wine. A free map and guide available online will help you plan your attack on the fifty-some venues, which are mostly concentrated on Elliot and Main Streets.

Be sure to check out William Hays's landscapes and portraits (both human and canine) at the **Artist's Loft Gallery** (103 Main St., 802/257-5181, www.theartistsloft.com). The best one-stop shopping is the **River Gallery School of Art** (32 Main St., 802/257-1577, www.rivergalleryschool.org, 9:30 A.M.–5 P.M. daily, nights and weekends when classes are in session), which usually features many different artists, along with refreshments, in its large and well-lit space. Another sure bet is the **In-Sight Photography Project** (45 Flat St., 802/251-9960, www.insight-photography.org, 10 A.M.–6 P.M. Mon.–Fri.), which gets cameras into the hands of local youth, often with arresting results. Also worth checking out: **Gallery in the Woods** (145 Main St., 802/257-4777, www.galleryinthewoods.com, noon–5 P.M. Thurs.–Sun.), which has a prominent location on Main Street.

Brattleboro Museum & Art Center

In 2004, an exhibit of never-before-seen Andy Warhol paintings put the Brattleboro Museum

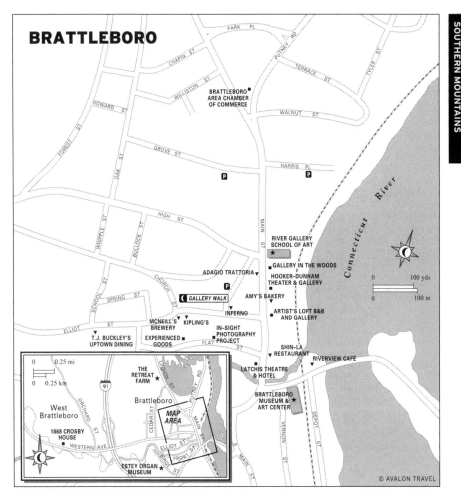

& Art Center (10 Vernon St., 802/257-0124, www.brattleboromuseum.org, 11 A.M.–5 P.M. Thurs.–Mon., $8 adults, $6 seniors, $4 students, children under 6 free) on the art map. Its shows are rarely so impressive, but the center is worth a look for its unusual location in a renovated train depot as well as for its provocative exhibitions of contemporary American art, often featuring leading artists from around New England. On the first Friday of the month, the galleries and gift shop stay open until 8:30 P.M., with free admission after 5:30 P.M.

Estey Organ Museum

Harkening back to the past, Estey Organ Museum (108 Birge St., 802/246-8366, www. esteyorganmuseum.org, 2–4 P.M. Sat.–Sun. June–Sept., $5), celebrates Brattleboro's century-long history as home to the largest reed organ–making factory in the world. The Estey Organ Company once employed more than

The Retreat Farm in Brattleboro

500 people and produced half a million organs; its former engine house now displays reed, pipe, and electronic versions along with exhibits on the history of the craft.

Rudyard Kipling's House

In 1892, Brattleboro gained a brief fame as the home of writer Rudyard Kipling, whose new bride was a native of the area. The author wrote *Captains Courageous* and *The Jungle Book* at his palatial home, Naulakha (Hindi for "jewel beyond price"), and may have lived there longer if it hadn't been for a feud with his neighbor and brother-in-law Beatty Balestier. Eventually the tiff grew so heated that Balestier forced Kipling's bicycle off the road with his carriage, instigating one of the country's first celebrity trials. Embarrassed by the publicity, Kipling escaped back to England instead of showing up in court. Kipling's former home is not open to the general public, but it can be rented out for groups of up to eight through the United

Kingdom's **Landmark Trust** (707 Kipling Rd., Dummerston, 802/254-6868, www.landmark-trustusa.com, $140–425 per night, 3-night minimum). The home still contains the author's original furniture, down to the billiard table in the attic.

The Retreat Farm

On the outskirts of town, The Retreat Farm (350 Linden St., 802/257-2240, www.theretreatfarm.com, 10 A.M.–4 P.M. Wed.–Sat., noon–4 P.M. Sun. late May–Oct., $6 adults, $5 children under 12) has a family-friendly petting zoo showcasing dozens of animals, both familiar (rabbits, goats) and exotic (emus, llamas). It's a cut above ordinary petting zoos, in both mission and execution, since the 475-acre plot is still a working farm owned by The Windham Foundation, a private foundation dedicated to preserving Vermont's rural traditions. Perhaps because of that, the big barn housing the animals is particularly interactive for children, providing not only food to feed the animals, but also brushes and scratchers to help care for them. Another section with farm implements allows budding MacDonalds to play at being farmer for a day. For kids and grown-ups alike, the foundation recently revitalized a network of hiking trails accessible year-round from behind the farm as well as from other points of entry around town; they've also opened a satellite outlet of the popular Grafton Village Cheese Company (also owned by the foundation) next to the farm.

ENTERTAINMENT AND EVENTS
Nightlife

Brattleboro's **Inferno** (19 Elliot St., 802/258-6529, www.gotoinferno.com, 4 P.M.–1 A.M. Sun.–Thurs., 4 P.M.–2 A.M. Fri.–Sat.) is the area's prime gathering spot for karaoke, trivia nights, and local blues, rock, and folk music.

Just as popular is the "7 Delicious Sins" drink menu and long list of craft beers.

Just watching the crowd at **Kipling's** (78 Elliot St., 802/257-4848, 11 A.M.–8 P.M. Mon.–Tues., 11 A.M.–2 A.M. Wed.–Fri., 3 P.M.–2 A.M. Sat.) is entertainment enough; around since the 1930s, the pub pulls in seemingly every walk of life from town and serves a slew of beer on tap. Another great place to cure what "ales" you is **McNeill's Brewery** (90 Elliot St., 802/254-2553, www.mcneillsbrewery.com, 4 P.M.–2 A.M. Mon.–Thurs., 1 P.M.–2 A.M. Fri.– Sun.), which lures connoisseurs from as far as England for its specialty house-made bitters and lagers.

The Arts

The landmark art deco building that houses the **Latchis Theatre** (50 Main St., 802/254-6300, www.latchis.com, $8 adults, $6 children and seniors, $6 matinees) is as much a part of the show as anything on the screen. Its 750-seat main theater has an iridescent mural of the zodiac on the ceiling and frolicking Greeks along the walls. Three movie theaters show a mix of first-run and independent films. The 1938 building is also a hotel.

On the other end of the spectrum, patrons of the **Hooker-Dunham Theater & Gallery** (139 Main St., 802/254-9276, www.hookerdunham. org, events $5–20, gallery admission free) will be forgiven for thinking they've been buried alive in a funky crypt-like performance space that showcases art-house films, folk and chamber music, and avant-garde theater.

Events

Each June, the cows take over for the **Strolling of the Heifers** (www.strollingoftheheifers.org, early June), a recently inaugurated festival to celebrate the area's agrarian history and draw attention to the challenges faced by local farmers. In an opening parade, the pride of the pastures saunter down the street, followed by cow floats and kids in cow costumes. During the day, a Dairy Fest scoops out free ice cream, cheese tasting, and a "celebrity" milking contest. Events recently added to the celebration include a Green Expo, showcasing environmentally sustainable products and lifestyles, and a fiercely competitive Grilled Cheese Cook-off, pitting professional and amateur chefs against each other for the coveted Golden Spatula. At a community contra dance in the evening, attendees party until the you-know-whats come home.

SHOPPING

Part of the pleasure of visiting Brattleboro is strolling along its main streets and poking around the eclectic mix of shops, which are anything but cookie-cutter.

Clothing and Accessories

Do well while doing good at **Experienced Goods Thrift Shop** (77 Flat St., 802/254-5200, www.brattleborohospice.org, 10 A.M.–5:30 P.M. Tues.–Sat.), two rooms of used clothing, books, and bric-a-brac at rock-bottom prices; proceeds from sales support the Brattleboro Hospice. **Life's Little Luxuries by Linda** (2 Elliot St., 802/258-9999, www.luxuriesbylinda. com, 10 A.M.–6 P.M. Mon. and Wed.–Sat., 11 A.M.–5 P.M. Sun., Dec. hours may vary) carries a full selection of lingerie and jewelry to put you in the mood. The clothing at **Boomerang** (12 Elliot St., 802/257-6911, www.boomerangvermont.com, 10 A.M.–6 P.M. Mon.–Thurs., 10 A.M.–7 P.M. Fri., 10 A.M.–6 P.M. Sat., 11 A.M.–5 P.M. Sun.) is both used and faux-vintage, and it covers every style from the past five decades.

Books

Books tower from floor to ceiling at **Brattleboro Books** (36 Elliot St., 802/257-7777, http://brattleborobooks.com, 10 A.M.–6 P.M. Mon.–Sat.,

11 A.M.–5 P.M. Sun.), an independent store with the best selection in town.

Housewares

Verde for Garden & Home (133 Main St., 802/258-3908, www.verdeforgardenandhome.com, 9:30 A.M.–6 P.M. Mon.–Thurs., 9:30 A.M.–7 P.M. Fri., 9:30 A.M.–6 P.M. Sat., 11 A.M.–5 P.M. Sun.) carries pillows, garden statuary, and intelligent children's books. A large, if overpriced, selection of antiques from Brattleboro's past can be found at **Twice Upon a Time** (63 Main St., 802/254-2261, www.twicetime.com, 10 A.M.–6 P.M. Mon.–Sat., 11 A.M.–6 P.M. Sun.), located in a former two-story department store. **A Candle in the Night** (181 Main St., 802/257-0471, www.acandleinthenight.com, 10 A.M.–6 P.M. Mon.–Sat., noon–5 P.M. Sun.) is the kind of store that dreams are made of; in addition to a huge selection of Oriental rugs, it carries imported antique furniture pieces from India, many of which are on a truly mammoth scale.

Gifts

You can find one-of-a-kind gifts at **Vermont Artisan Designs & Gallery** (106 Main St., 802/257-7044, www.vtartisans.com, 10 A.M.–6 P.M. Mon.–Thurs. and Sat., 10 A.M.–8 P.M. Fri., 10 A.M.–5 P.M. Sun.), which features pottery, furniture, and other crafts made by artisans from across the state.

FOOD

The town's unofficial meeting hall is **Amy's Bakery Arts Cafe** (113 Main St., 802/251-1071, 8 A.M.–6 P.M. Mon.–Sat., 9 A.M.–5 P.M. Sun., $6.50–10), where locals catch up over freshly baked bread, pastries, and coffee at tables overlooking the Connecticut River. A closer view of the water can be had at **Riverview Cafe** (36 Bridge St., 802/254-9841, www.riverviewcafe.com, 8 A.M.–3 P.M. Mon., Thurs., and Sun., 8 A.M.–9 P.M. Fri.–Sat., $10–30), where

kayakers and blue herons sometimes join diners at river level. The menu of sandwiches, pasta, and grilled main courses emphasizes fresh ingredients from local farms.

The best meal in town—and one of the best in Vermont—can be found at **❰ T. J. Buckley's Uptown Dining** (132 Elliot St., 802/257-4922, www.tjbuckleys.com, 6–10 P.M. Wed.–Sun., $35 prix fixe), a renovated 1927 Worcester diner car with an open kitchen and just five tables. Chef-owner Michael Fuller prepares a handful of options nightly. All of them feature bold flavor combinations, such as venison with eggplant caponata, truffle oil, and fresh currants; and melt-in-your-mouth quail with duck leg confit and root vegetables.

Landlocked Vermont might be the last place you'd expect to find good sushi, but the fish is fresh and expertly prepared at **Shin-La Restaurant and Sushi Bar** (57 Main St., 802/257-5226, 11 A.M.–9 P.M. Mon.–Fri., 11 A.M.–9:30 P.M. Sat.–Sun., $9–18), a fixture in town. It also offers Korean barbecue and noodle dishes.

SPORTS AND RECREATION
Hiking and Camping

The actual grounds of Fort Dummer are now underwater, flooded when a dam was built along the Connecticut River. The area around it, however, has been preserved as **Fort Dummer State Park** (517 Old Guilford Rd., 802/254-2610, www.vtstateparks.com/htm/fortdummer.cfm, mid-May–Labor Day, campsites $16–25). The 217-acre retreat that contains a mile and a half of gentle hiking trails through a densely wooded oak forest is home to squirrels, deer, wild turkey, and ruffed grouse. The campground has 50 wooded tent sites, as well as 10 more secluded lean-tos to accommodate overnight camping. The campground has hot showers and a dumping station, but no hookups.

HOW TO SPOT A COW

© MICHAEL MCDONALD/123RF.COM

Cows are so integral to the Vermont landscape, it's tough to imagine a typically beautiful vista in the state that isn't dotted with one or two of the lumbering grazers. But they're also just as key to Vermont's culture. The state produces an average of 2.5 billion pounds of milk every year—mostly through private family dairy farms that proudly refuse to give their cows BGH (that's bovine growth hormones, which are used elsewhere in the industry). The farmers believe they are detrimental to both the cows and the milk. Some Vermont farms have even devised ways of using cow manure to solve their energy prob-lems; working with the local power companies, several hundred farms currently use the methane from cow manure to generate electricity.

Here's a quick cheat sheet for identifying the next cow you see:

- **Dutch Belted:** black or brown with white belts
- **Guernsey:** fawn with white splotches
- **Highland:** reddish-brown with white horns and shaggy coat
- **Holstein:** black with white splotches
- **Jersey:** fawn all over

Boating

Canoes and kayaks can be rented from the **Vermont Canoe Touring Center** (451 Putney Rd., 802/257-5008, kayak: $20 for 2 hours, $30 for 4 hours, $40 for a full day; canoe: $25 for 2 hours, $35 for 4 hours, $45 for a full day; appointments required) at the intersection of the Connecticut and West Rivers. The stretch of the Connecticut above Vernon dam is wide and pleasant, with some small islands along the way for paddlers to get out and explore; the West River is smaller but similarly peaceful, though it can also offer some great class II and III whitewater in the early spring when the snow melts, or on one of a few release dates from the upstream dam each year.

ACCOMMODATIONS

The smell of buttered popcorn fills the lobby of the **Latchis Hotel** (50 Main St., 802/254-6300, www.latchis.com, $80–210), an unusual art deco theater-hotel. Period details like terrazzo floors and chrome fixtures transport guests back to the 1930s. The rooms themselves are a bit run-down, but the central location and historic-cool ambience more than make up the difference.

Named after the wife of the Revolutionary War general, the friendly **Molly Stark Motel** (829 Marlboro Rd., 802/254-2440, $45–75) has basic rooms on the road toward Marlboro and Mount Snow, and it's pet-friendly.

Romance practically runs from the faucets at **The 1868 Crosby House** (175 Western Ave., 802/257-7145, www.crosbyhouse.com, $150–180). Three individual rooms each have queen-size beds and fireplaces; the largest has a double-whirlpool bath. Fans of Merchant Ivory films will love the special afternoon tea at which the innkeepers lay out a selection of gloves and hats for guests, along with feathers and other accessories for decorating.

Despite the confusing name—which has led some guests to look for the wrong street address—**Forty Putney Road** (192 Putney Rd., 800/941-2413, www.fortyputneyroad.com, $159–329), an inn at 192 Putney Road, couldn't be cuter. The pristine white house (formerly a doctor's home) is surrounded by specimen trees and meticulous gardens outside, and filled with serenely decorated rooms evocative of the Provencal and English countryside. A full gourmet breakfast is included.

There is no easier way for an outsider to feel part of the community than to stay at **The Artist's Loft B&B and Gallery** (103 Main St., 802/257-5181, www.theartistsloft.com, $158–188), located among the galleries along Main

Street. Artists Patricia Long and William Hays rent out a suite with an inspirational view of the river; guests are invited to observe the artists at work and shoot the breeze in the adjoining studio and gallery.

INFORMATION AND SERVICES

The **Brattleboro Area Chamber of Commerce** (180 Main St., 802/254-4565, www.brattleborochamber.org) runs a visitors center downtown.

The area's premier hospital is **Brattleboro Memorial Hospital** (17 Belmont Ave., 802/257-0341, www.bmhvt.org/). For pharmacy needs, there's **Rite-Aid Pharmacy** (499 Canal St., 802/257-4204, 8 A.M.–9 P.M. Mon.–Sat., 9 A.M.–5 P.M. Sun., pharmacy 9 A.M.–9 P.M. Mon.–Fri., 9 A.M.–6 P.M. Sat., 9 A.M.–5 P.M. Sun.), which also offers faxing services, and **Walgreens** (476 Canal St., 802/254-5633, 8 A.M.–10 P.M. daily, pharmacy 8 A.M.–10 P.M. Mon.–Fri., 9 A.M.–6 P.M. Sat.–Sun.). For non-medical emergencies, contact the **Brattleboro Police** (230 Main St., 802/257-7946).

Banks are found all over the downtown area, particularly on Main Street. ATMs are plentiful around retail stores, in and around hotels, and in convenience stores. Free Internet access (with purchase) is offered at **Twilight Tea Lounge** (41 Main St., 802/254-8887, www.twilighttealounge.com, noon–8 P.M. Tues.–Thurs., noon–9 P.M. Fri.–Sat., noon–8 P.M. Sun.) and at **Mocha Joe's Cafe** (82 Main St., 802/257-5637, www.mochajoes.com, 7 A.M.–8 P.M. Mon.–Thurs., 7 A.M.–10 P.M. Fri., 7:30 A.M.–10 P.M. Sat., 7:30 A.M.–8 P.M. Sun.).

GETTING THERE AND AROUND

To get to Brattleboro from Boston (115 mi., 2 hr. 15 min.), take Route 2 west to Greenfield, then I-91 north to exit 1. From Hartford (85 mi., 1 hr. 30 min.) and Springfield (60 mi., 1 hr.), Brattleboro is a straight shot north up I-91 to exit 1. From Manchester, New Hampshire (80 mi., 1 hr. 40 min.), take I-93 and I-89 to exit 5, then head west along Route 9 to the Vermont border.

From Burlington, **Amtrak** trains (800/872-7245, www.amtrak.com) stop at **Brattleboro Train Station** (10 Vernon Rd.) once daily.

Buses with **Greyhound Bus Lines** (800/642-3133, www.greyhound.com) run to Brattleboro from Boston and New York, stopping at the **Vermont Transit Terminal** (Rtes. 5 and 9, 802/254-6066).

Brattleboro's municipal bus service, the **BeeLine** (802/254-4541), offers routes throughout downtown and outlying areas.

North of Brattleboro

North of Brattleboro, the gentle foothills of the Green Mountains hold a half-dozen small villages tucked into their forested valleys. Red barns and trim white houses line the winding roads, often with brooks tracing alongside their paths. The heart of this area is the village of **Grafton,** painstakingly preserved by a private foundation that owns much of the town. A walking tour of the village is a nice way to slow down an afternoon. Grafton is also renowned for its cheese-making company, which has contributed to the state's reputation for sharp and creamy cheddars. The surrounding towns, meanwhile, have their own attractions: the immaculate town green in **Newfane,** a basket maker and music festival in **Putney,** and a teddy bear company in **Townshend.**

PUTNEY TO BELLOWS FALLS

No fewer than six schools grace the bucolic town of Putney, which earned its fortunes from paper mills that grew along Sackett's Brook in the 1900s. Now it is better known for its boarding school, The Putney School, as well as its concentration of artists and musicians, who gather for an annual music series every summer. A bit farther up the interstate, the town of Rockingham is known by the name of Bellows Falls, the town's main village, whose brick Italianate clock tower is visible from miles around. The relative narrowness of the Connecticut River here made it a natural place

for a bridge in the mid-1800s. It soon became a crossroads and market town, and, with the construction of the railroad a hundred years later, a center of industry for companies like the Vermont Farm Machine Company, which produced dairy equipment, and the Bellows Falls Cooperative Creamery, which processed cow milk, both of which made town residents very rich indeed. Though its heyday has long passed, Bellows Falls retains a Victorian-era downtown full of independent shops and restaurants. Route 5 runs directly through Putney and Bellows Falls and is a great alternative scenic road to the big interstate.

Sights

A time warp back to the days when Bellows Falls was a railroad center, the **Green Mountain Flyer** (54 Depot St., Bellows Falls, 802/463-3069, www.rails-vt.com, May–Oct., $19 adult, $15 children 3–12, children under 3 free) offers trips along the Connecticut River north to Chester, taking in picturesque views of two covered bridges and a natural gorge.

A bit hokey, but fun for the kids, is **Santa's Land USA** (635 Bellows Falls Rd., Putney, 802/387-5550, www.santasland.com, 10 A.M.–5 P.M. Sat.–Mon. July–early Sept.; 10 A.M.–5 P.M. Sat.–Sun. Oct.–Dec., $10 adults, $10 children 3–15, $10 seniors, children under 2 free), which bills itself as St. Nick's Green Mountain summer home. In an amusement park that has been going strong for more than 50 years, the little ones will thrill to a polar train, iceberg slide, petting zoo with real reindeer (and camels?), and of course, visits with the jolly old man himself.

◖ Bellows Falls Historic District

Bellows Falls is unique in having examples of homes of just about every architectural style in New England—including Federal, Greek Revival, Gothic Revival, Italianate, Second Empire, Stick, Shingle, Queen Anne, Colonial Revival, Dutch Colonial Revival—and pretty stellar examples at that. The town produces a self-guided walking tour to the Bellows Falls Historic District (802/463-3964, www.rockbf. org). Highlights include the Second Empire **Wyman & Almira Flint House Masonic Temple** (61 Westminster St.) and the curious Greek Revival/Queen Anne–hybrid **Babbitt Tenement House** (11 South St.). Homes are private and not open for tours, but a walking tour of their exteriors is a more than pleasant way to pass an afternoon.

Events

Every summer, 40 top chamber music students gather in Putney to study and perform with acclaimed instructors at the appropriately named **Yellow Barn Music School and Festival** (63 Main St., Putney, 802/387-6637, www.yellowbarn.org, late June–early Aug.). The sounds of violin and piano fill up the eaves of Yellow Barn Concert Hall for a magical five weeks of music.

Shopping

Picnic baskets, step baskets, Shaker reproduction baskets, Nantucket lightship baskets, and every other conceivable form of wicker carrying apparatus can be found at the somewhat overblown **Basketville** (8 Bellows Falls Rd., Putney, 802/387-5509, www.basketville. com, 9 A.M.–6 P.M. Mon.–Sun.) in downtown Putney. What started here as a family

business more than 100 years ago has grown into a giant emporium, usually crowded with tourists. Less known but no less impressive, **Vermont Botanical** (1126 S. Valley Rd., Putney, 802/387-2474, www.vermontbotanical.com, hours vary) is a labor of love of artist Maggie Lake, who takes Vermont wildflowers, jack-in-the-pulpits, and fiddlehead ferns and presses them in frames of bird's-eye maple. The results, which can be viewed in an on-site studio, are surprisingly painterly.

Find all manner of gifts at **Coyote Moon** (22 Rockingham St., Bellows Falls, 802/463-9559, 10 A.M.–5 P.M. Mon–Sat.), a treasure trove of handmade jewelry, sweaters made by local weavers, and imported home furnishings. Then there's the mother lode of its retail genre, **Vermont Country Store** (1292 Rockingham Rd., Bellows Falls, 802/463-2224, www.vermontcountrystore.com, 8:30 A.M.–6 P.M. daily). Known far and wide for its catalog business, the store is far more impressive in person—the bustling multifloored spot is crammed with everything from insulated curtains and Parisian perfumes to miniature music boxes and pumpkin rolls made that morning. Beware, however: the place tends to get incredibly crowded, so if you're planning on browsing or buying at a leisurely pace, it's best to get here before the lunchtime rush.

Food

A blue school bus along with a few scattered picnic tables is all that you'll find at the outdoor **Curtis' BBQ** (7 Putney Landing Rd., Putney, 802/387-5474, www.curtisbbqvt.com, 11 A.M.–7 P.M. Wed.–Sun., Apr.–Oct., $7–25), which bills itself as the "ninth wonder of the world" and rarely disappoints. Run by transplanted Georgian Curtis Tuffs, this is where to get your fix of Southern-style pork ribs and grilled chicken, slathered with a tangy special sauce. (Just don't tell Curtis's pet Vietnamese potbellied pig what you are eating.)

The level of care that goes into dishes at the **Putney Inn** (57 Putney Landing Rd., Putney, 800/653-5517, www.putneyinn. com, 11:30 A.M.–3 P.M. and 5–9 P.M. Mon.– Thurs., 11:30 A.M.–3:30 P.M. and 5–9:30 P.M. Fri., 8–10:30 A.M., 11:30 A.M.–3:30 P.M., and 5–9:30 P.M. Sat., 8–11 A.M. and noon–9 P.M. Sun., $6–29) is hard to come by these days. The quiet-but-comfortable dining room is a mecca for inn guests and locals, who arrive daily for the lovingly conceived plates of maple-glazed pork and burgers made of grass-fed Vermont beef.

Information and Services

The **Great Falls Region Chamber of Commerce** (17 Depot St., Bellows Falls, 802/463-4280, www.gfrcc.org) operates a visitors center stocked with brochures, educational exhibits, and enthusiastic staff. It's adjacent to the railway station. Pharmacy services can be found at **Rite-Aid Pharmacy** (112 Rockingham St., Bellows Falls, 802/463-9910, 8 A.M.–9 P.M. Mon.–Sat., 9 A.M.–5 P.M. Sun., pharmacy 9 A.M.–9 P.M. Mon.–Fri., 9 A.M.–6 P.M. Sat., 9 A.M.–5 P.M. Sun.) or **Greater Falls Pharmacy** (78 Atkinson St., Bellows Falls, 802/460-2634, 8:30 A.M.–5:30 P.M. Mon.–Fri., 9 A.M.–5 P.M. Sat.). ATMs are available at several locations in downtown Putney and Bellows Falls, including at branches of **Chittenden Bank** (58 Main St., Putney or 25 The Square, Bellows Falls). Free Wi-Fi Internet access is available in the cafe at **Village Square Booksellers** (32 The Square, Bellows Falls, 802/463-9404).

GRAFTON

What do you do when you want to ensure that a quaint Vermont village survives intact? Well, you buy it. At least that seems to be the course taken by New Jersey investment banker Dean Mathey, who was so besotted by the picturesque town of Grafton that he started a private foundation, the Windham Foundation, to help

© MICHAEL BLANDING

a covered bridge in Grafton

preserve the town. His foresight has created an unusual—and beautiful—anomaly in the region in which half of the buildings in this historic town center are owned and operated by the foundation, including the Grafton Village Cheese Company, and many private residences that have been restored to their 19th-century state. The foundation also owns and manages large tracts of undeveloped land, including miles of wooded cross-country trails and a large sheep farm that harkens back to Grafton's heyday as a woolen center.

◖ Grafton Village Cheese Company

No trip to Vermont is complete without sampling the state's justly famous cheddar cheeses. Better yet, see how the stuff is made at this cooperative company (533 Townshend Rd., 800/472-3866, www.graftonvillagecheese. com, 10 A.M.–5 P.M. daily), which revives more

than a century of cheese-making in the village. Through a viewing window, visitors can see workers literally "cheddaring," or turning, blocks of soft curd. Each day the factory churns out more than 5,000 pounds of cheddar, made from the milk of Jersey cows on surrounding farms. A small store allows you buy samples aged up to six years—though unless you like your cheese crumbly and acidic, three or four years is usually ideal.

Plummer's Sugar House

Vermont's other famous foodstuff can be found down the road at Plummer's Sugar House (2866 Townshend Rd., 802/843-2207, www.plummerssugarhouse.com, 8 A.M.–5 P.M. daily), where sugar from 4,000 trees is turned into maple syrup every February through April. The proprietors, John and Debe Plummer, are happy to give tours of the syrup-making process in exchange for a purchase.

clothbound cheddar at Grafton Village Cheese Company

CHEDDARING

It's been said that cheddar isn't merely a noun or an adjective, but also a verb. At least, that is, it's considered to be such in England and Vermont. In the latter, cheddaring began in the 1800s as a way for dairy farmers to use up extra milk. Today, it's more of a craft, practiced among small dairy farms as a labor of love (as well as, of course, a way to make a living). Vermont cheddar houses take enormous pride in their product, proclaiming it by far America's finest sharp cheese. And they take great pains to live up to that claim. Cheddaring starts with adding rennet to warm milk to curdle it into a custard-like consistency. They then cut it with mesh wires and allow the curd to drain off all the whey before it is milled, salted, pressed, and aged. And that last stage is where the majority of the flavor and refinement come in. The most sharp-flavored (and most expensive) cheddars are those that have been aged the longest. For some, the crumbly astringence of a four- or five-year aged cheddar is the height of perfection. For us, a three-year from Grafton Village provides just the right balance between cream and bite.

Nature Museum

Grafton is also home to a small Nature Museum (186 Townshend Rd., 802/843-2111, www.nature-museum.org, 10 A.M.–4 P.M. Thurs. and Sat.–Sun., $5 adults, $4 seniors and students, $3 children 3–12), $15 for families, which is filled with dioramas and stuffed examples of the local fauna. While some of the exhibits are a bit mangy, the museum is worth a look for its impressive catamount, the name for now-extinct mountain lions in these parts.

Shopping

Taking the wildly varied weather of Vermont as its inspiration, **Grafton Seasons** (217 Main St., 802/843-2499, www.graftonseasons.com, 9:30 A.M.–5:30 P.M. daily) fills its shelves with gifts and keepsakes that nod to each time of year. That means handblown glass candleholders by Simon Pearce sit next to Irish pottery, lots of clothing and toys, and of course, maple syrup.

Food

Most of the best restaurants in these parts double as country inns. The menu at the **Grafton Inn** (92 Main St., 802/843-2231, www.old-tavern.com, 6–9 P.M. daily, $19–32) is creative continental, emphasis on creative. The menu usually features at least one dish utilizing cheddar from the Grafton Village Cheese Company next door.

Grab some delicious made-to-order sandwiches at **Grafton Grocery Market** (162 Main St., 802/843-1196, 8 A.M.–6 P.M. Mon.–Sat., 8:30 A.M.–5 P.M. Sun., $5–9). The atmospheric deli also sells excellent cheeses, wines, and sweets—along with any other fixings you might need for a country picnic.

Information and Services

For more information on Grafton, contact **The Windham Foundation** (802/843-2211, www.windham-foundation.org), which owns and operates many of the town's attractions, including the Grafton Village Cheese Company.

In addition to the hospital in Brattleboro, area emergency health services are provided by **Grace Cottage Hospital** (185 Grafton Rd., Townshend, 802/365-7357, www.gracecottage.org). Pharmacy services can be found across the street at **Messenger Valley Pharmacy** (170 Rte. 30, Townshend, 802/365-4117, 8:30 A.M.–6 P.M. Mon.–Fri. and 9 A.M.–2 P.M. Sat.).

TOWNSHEND AND NEWFANE

Completing the loop of small towns north of Brattleboro are two villages that vie for status as archetypal Vermont villages. The farming community of Townshend, chartered in 1753,

© MICHAEL BLANDING

Grafton's congregational church

has served as the commercial heart of the area from its beginnings. It's now a good place to stop and refuel at the general store and restaurants, and take a moment to admire the quaint town center.

The neighboring village, chartered as the town of Fane (also in 1753), was prevented from holding its first town meeting for almost a decade because of the disruption of the French and Indian War. Rechartered in 1761 as Newfane, the town formed around an unusually wide town green, around which are now ranged a stunning collection of white clapboard buildings that are veritably blinding on a sunny day.

Sights

Learn everything you ever wanted to know about stuffed animals at the **Mary Meyer Museum of Stuffed Toys** (Rte. 30, 2 mi. north of Rte. 25, Townshend, 802/365-4160 or 888/758-2327, www.bigblackbear.com,

9:30 A.M.–5 P.M. Mon.–Fri.), a fun and informative museum at the site of a toy company that dates back to the 1930s. Kids will enjoy learning how their stuffed animals are made; parents should be warned, however, that they are unlikely to escape without a new addition to the menagerie.

Also in the area is the **Scott Covered Bridge** (Rte. 30, west of Townshend), which at 277 feet is the longest in Vermont (though not open to vehicle traffic). In all, seven covered bridges are scattered throughout the immediate vicinity, including the 118-foot-long **Williamsville Bridge** (Dover Rd., South Newfane).

Events

Held each year on the Saturday after Columbus Day, the **Townshend Pumpkin Festival** (802/365-7300, www.townshendvt.net) makes the most out of its namesake gourd with a carving contest, scarecrow decorating, and a costumed parade—not to mention all the apple cider and pumpkin pie you can stomach.

Shopping

Bring something meaty home from **Lawrence's Smoke Shop and Country Store** (653 Rte. 30, Townshend, 802/365-7372, www.lawrencessmokeshop.com, 9 A.M.–5 P.M. Mon.–Thurs., 9 A.M.–6 P.M. Fri.–Sun.), a jackpot for carnivores. Founded by Merrill and Norma Lawrence in 1964, it churns out intensely flavored cob-smoked bacon, hams, turkey, and specialty smoked sausages—many of which get bought as gifts but are eaten before they're ever wrapped.

Food

The **Four Columns Inn** (21 West St., Newfane, 802/365-7713, www.fourcolumnsinn.com, 5:30–8 P.M. daily with reservation, $27–38) is arguably better known for its four-star dining room than for its bedrooms. Celeb chef Greg Parks has been blending Asian, French, and New American cuisine for three decades. Among those who have enjoyed his fare are Mick Jagger, Tom Cruise, and Paul Newman.

Equally genteel supping is found at **Windham Hill Inn** (311 Lawrence Dr., West Townshend, 802/874-4080, www.windhamhill.com, 6–8:30 P.M. daily, $88 prix fixe), a dining room that's part rustication, part refinement. London-born Executive Chef Graham Gill is adept at whipping up superb specialties such as tea-smoked salmon with beet root risotto and parsnip-parmesan ravioli with wild mushroom ragout. If the Grand Marnier soufflé with orange hard sauce is on the menu, don't skip it. The wine line is equally extraordinary.

SPORTS AND RECREATION
Hiking and Camping

Located at the base of Bald Mountain, **Townshend State Park** (2755 State Forest Rd., Townshend, 802/365-7500, www.vtstateparks.com/htm/townshend.cfm, late May–early Sept.) was headquarters for the Civilian Conservation Corps during the Great Depression, which built a well-appointed campground with stone house, picnic area, and fire tower. The campground itself is heavily wooded, offering quiet seclusion to 30 tent sites and 4 lean-to sites ($16–25/night) that are located along the backside of a gently babbling brook. From the campsite, a steep trail leads up to the 1,700-foot summit of Bald Mountain, passing several waterfalls and scenic vistas along the way. The trail is nearly three miles round trip, and can be completed in approximately three hours.

Cross-Country Skiing

Grafton Ponds (783 Townshend Rd., Grafton, 802/843-2400, www.graftonponds.com, 9 A.M.–4 P.M. daily, $12–18 adults, $10 seniors and students, $5 youth, children under 5 free) is a skiing center featuring over 2,000 acres of rolling fields and woodlands. The park converts to a biking center during the warmer months, when it rents mountain bikes (half-day $15, full day $20).

ACCOMMODATIONS

Reasonably priced accommodations north of Brattleboro can be found at the **Putney Inn** (I-91, exit 4, Putney, 802/387-5517 www.putneyinn.com, $98–188). It has clean, basic rooms with quilts and flowered wallpaper, and a Vermont country breakfast is included in the rate.

Two of the buildings along Newfane's green are part of the ◖ **Four Columns Inn** (21 West St., Newfane, 802/254-2352, www.fourcolumnsinn.com, $195–400), an upscale bed-and-breakfast with 15 rooms. In some, the bathrooms are nearly as big as the bedrooms, complete with whirlpool tubs and gas fireplaces.

winter fun at Grafton Ponds

A bit stuffier, but no less luxurious, is Grafton's historic **Grafton Inn** (92 Main St., Grafton, 802/843-2231, www.old-tavern.com, $165–420), which enjoyed a reputation after the Civil War as a hangout for literary types including Rudyard Kipling, Daniel Webster, Ralph Waldo Emerson, and Oliver Wendell Holmes. Furnished with oil portraits of presidents, four-poster beds, and period pieces, history practically speaks from the walls.

GETTING THERE AND AROUND

From Brattleboro, drive up I-91 to exit 4 for Putney (12 mi., 15 min.) or exit 5 for Bellows Falls (25 mi., 30 min.). From Bellows Falls, take Route 121 to Grafton (12 mi., 25 min.). Continue south down Route 35 for Townshend (10 mi., 20 min.) then south down Route 30 for Newfane (5 mi., 10 min.). Complete the loop by continuing down Route 30 to Brattleboro (12 mi., 20 min.). Of course, the loop works just as well the other way.

The Molly Stark Trail

West of Brattleboro, Route 9 winds like a salamander through the southernmost peaks of the Green Mountains, dipping into creek beds forested with birch, beech, and sugar maple, and rising for stunning views of the surrounding hills. (The summit of Hogback Mountain is particularly worth pulling over for.) The route is known as the "Molly Stark Trail" after the wife of the New Hampshire general who became the hero of the Battle of Bennington during the Revolutionary War—a remarkable homage to a woman who never saw the route that bears her name.

MARLBORO

The small college town of Marlboro is little more than a blip on the map, consisting of a few old farmhouses gathered around an old town hall. That changes every summer, however, when it becomes home to a renowned classical music festival. With little more than 300 students, Marlboro College anchors the town with a distinctly counterculture vibe that bleeds over into the rest of the community.

Sights

Located atop Hogback Mountain, the **Southern Vermont Natural History Museum** (Rte. 9 at Hogback Mountain Scenic Overlook, 802/464-0048, www.vermontmuseum.org, 10 A.M.–5 P.M. daily late May–late Oct., 10 A.M.–5 P.M. Sat.–Sun. late Oct.–late May, $5 adults, $3 seniors, $2 children 5–12, children under 5 free) has more than 100 dioramas of stuffed New England fauna, including loons, black bears, and a mountain lion. In addition, it has a raptor center of very-much-alive hawks and owls and a woodland pond display of live turtles and frogs. In the summer months, the center also displays a working beehive.

Events

Founded by three musical families who relocated to Vermont more than 50 years ago, the **Marlboro Music Festival** (Marlboro College, 802/254-2394, www.marlboromusic.org, Sat.–Sun. mid-July–mid-Aug., $5–37) has since become the country's preeminent festival of chamber music. Masters and students play music together on the hilltop campus of tiny Marlboro College.

Food

Impressive traditional setting, impressive newfangled food; the historic **Colonel Williams Inn** (111 Staver Rd., 802/257-1093, www.colonelwilliamsinn.com, 5–8:30 P.M. daily, $32 prix fixe, four-course menu) settles guests into its handsome, traditional New England dining room and serves them fine Italian-inspired dishes. If the *agnello alla pecorara* (that's lamb with mushrooms) is available, don't pass it up. Ditto the hearty pork stew with artichokes.

WHO IS MOLLY STARK?

Route 9 between Brattleboro and Bennington is universally known as the Molly Stark Trail, after the wife of Revolutionary War general John Stark, hero of the Battle of Bennington. Stark is said to have marched along this route from New Hampshire across the state to the battlefield. Once there, he famously said: "We beat them today, or Molly Stark sleeps a widow tonight" (or something like that—the exact words are lost to history and faulty memory). Though Molly never even set foot on the trail herself, the name stuck, giving her imprimatur to schools, hospitals, parks, and lodgings along the way.

Fifth-generation farmer Bill Adams gives a tour at Adams Family Farm.

© MICHAEL BLANDING

WILMINGTON

Halfway between Brattleboro and Bennington, the unpretentious town of Wilmington has more worth stopping for. Unlike the ultra-quaint villages and overdeveloped ski resorts that surround it, Wilmington feels like the real deal, owing its atmosphere more to a 1950s-era vision of main street than the backwoods colonialism that pervades the rest of the region. An overflow of artists and craftspeople from Brattleboro fill the hills with galleries and scattered studios.

Wilmington's location in a valley along the Deerfield River has also made it susceptible to periodic flooding, sometimes with disastrous results. Downtown was inundated in the Great Flood of 1927, and again in 2011 when Hurricane Irene swept through the state. During the storm, Route 9 turned into a raging river, flooding businesses up to the second story, cutting off roads, and isolating the town for several days. After the storm passed, some

homes and businesses were found washed away across the valley, while others—including the town's iconic Dot's Restaurant—have taken months or years to rebuild.

Sights

Step into your very own Christmas card with a sleigh ride at **Adams Family Farm** (15 Higley Hill Rd., 802/464-3762, www.adamsfamily-farm.com, 11:30 A.M.–9 P.M. Tues.–Sun. mid-Dec.–mid-Mar., $20 adults, $10 children 4–12, children under 4 free). Drawn by Belgian draft horses, the sleighs travel through maple woods to a log cabin, where guests sip hot chocolate and listen to tunes from an old-fashioned player piano. In the summer (10 A.M.–5 P.M. Wed.–Sun., day pass $15 adults, $13 children 2–12, children under 2 free), fourth-generation hard-rock farmer Bill Adams exchanges horses for a sputtering 1959 John Deere for his entertaining tours of the farm, which has produced timber, maple syrup, sheep, and milk depending on Vermont's economic circumstances. The farm's latest economic driver is agritourism, run by fifth-generation farmers Kip and Tess (with sixth-generation Lauren an avid helper). A petting zoo offers a full complement of livestock to instantly turn visiting kids into walking renditions of Old MacDonald (a "baa baa" here, a "neigh neigh" there), and evening hay rides bringing guests to a bonfire pit for s'mores under the stars.

Shopping

Paper Moon Emporium (22 W. Main St., 802/464-5588) features antique signs, ski lodge paraphernalia, shaker jars, and seed boxes of the type that catalog stores make reproductions of.

In addition to its agriculture activities, **Adams Family Farm** (15 Higley Hill Rd., 802/464-3762, www.adamsfamilyfarm.com, hours vary by season) offers a slew of fun stuff to buy, including homemade jams and jellies, goat milk soaps, maple products, and hand-knit sweaters and hats.

Located on a back, back road in Wilmington, the **Art of Humor Gallery** (30 Not-A Rd., 802/464-5523, www.theartofhumor.com, 10 A.M.–5 P.M. Sat.–Sun. or by appt.) showcases the outlandish dogs, cats, cows, and plumber's cracks of pop cartoonist Skip Morrow.

For the purist, **Hundredth Monkey Holistic Store** (17 W. Main St., 802/464-4640, 10 A.M.–6 P.M. Mon. and Wed.–Sat., 11 A.M.–5 P.M. Sun.) carries not only organic foods, herbs, and astrology books, but that most quintessential of Vermont foodstuffs—organic maple syrup.

Hogback Mountain Gift Shop (7627 Rte. 9 E., 802/464-5494, 8:30 A.M.–6 P.M. Sun.–Thurs., 8:30 A.M.–7 P.M. Fri.–Sat.) is loved for its well-edited selection of clothes, stuffed animals, and cheeses.

Food

The heart of Wilmington, both physically and spiritually, has been **Dot's Restaurant** (3 E. Main St., 802/464-7284, www.dotsofvermont.com), a wood-paneled diner with historical photos lining the walls and local characters lining the barstools. Sadly, the restaurant was hard-hit by the flooding following Hurricane Irene in August 2011 and was forced to close. At time of publication, it was still shuttered while a fund-raising campaign by the state's historic preservation office continued to try and raise the necessary money to rebuild. (You can follow the progress online at www.rebuilddots.org.) With any luck, townies will soon again be lining up at 5 A.M. beneath the neon sign of this greasy spoon for healthy helpings of gossip along with their "Berry Berry Pancakes," a molten mess of blueberries, raspberries, and blackberries.

Despite the name, the taps at **Maple Leaf Brewery** (3 N. Main St., 802/464-9900, 3–10 P.M. Mon.–Thurs., noon–10:30 P.M. Fri.–Sun., $9–19) go beyond Molson to serve an ever-changing variety of microbrews. The pub also serves burgers and other entrees.

One of the best spots in town to watch the sunset across the Green Mountains is **Black Dog Tavern** (178 Route 9 East, 802/464-2135, 6–8 P.M. Tues.–Wed., 5:30–9 P.M. Thurs.–Sat., $7–16) in The White House Inn. Even with its abbreviated and casual menu of grass-fed burgers and BBQ duck wings, the place still rolls out elegance thanks to its mahogany bar, period chairs and sofas, and wood-burning stove.

Information and Services

The **Mount Snow Chamber of Commerce** (21 W. Main St., 877/887-6884, www.visitvermont.com, 8:30 A.M.–3:30 P.M. Mon., 8:30 A.M.–4:30 P.M. Tues.–Thurs., 10 A.M.–4 P.M. Sat.–Sun.) operates an information center in Wilmington on Route 9 just west of the traffic light. **Rite-Aid Pharmacy** (1 E. Main St., 802/464-7575, 8 A.M.–9 P.M. daily, pharmacy 9 A.M.–9 P.M. Mon.–Fri.,

9 A.M.–6 P.M. Sat., 9 A.M.–5 P.M. Sun.) is located right downtown, as are the ATMs at **Merchants Bank** (24 W. Main St., 802/464-8688, 8:30 A.M.–5 P.M. Mon.–Wed. and Fri., 8:30 A.M.–5:30 P.M. Thurs., 24-hour ATM) and **Chittenden Bank** (29 E. Main St.).

WEST DOVER AND MOUNT SNOW

More than 50 years ago, an ex-marine by the name of Walter Schoenknecht surveyed the slopes of Mount Pisgah and saw gold—in the form of winter visitors from around the region who would strap on skis and try out his new resort. From such humble beginnings grew Mount Snow—named not after the wintry white stuff but after farmer Reuben Snow, who once tilled the base of the mount that has grown to be the 800-pound gorilla of southern Vermont ski resorts. The little town of West Dover is little more than a footnote to the runaway development of the resort, and it includes a historic district of Greek Revival buildings in the town center. Meanwhile, in the shadow of the mountain, faux-Tyrolean hotels and restaurants are littered along the scenic twists and turns of Route 100.

Shopping

Take to the aisles of **Mountain Riders Snowboard & Bike Shop** (Mount Snow Access Rd., West Dover, 802/464-2222, www.mtnridersvt.com, 10 A.M.–5 P.M. daily) and then take to the slopes; the store has everything you'll need to go downhill in style, from boards to skis and the waterproof gear to don while riding it all.

Tucked into the hills along Route 100 north of West Dover are a number of artist studios. One of the most unique is **Hot Glass Works** (3819 Main St. Rte. 30, Jamaica, 802/874-4436, www.hotglassworks.net, 11 A.M.–5 P.M. daily). All items in this studio showroom are stamped "HOT"—meaning "Hank or Toby," the quirky husband-and-wife team who pour their creative spirits into colored glass coins, bowls, hummingbird feeders, and whatever else strikes their fancy.

Food

Tucked into a friendly inn looking out to the looming Mount Snow and warmed by brick fireplaces, **1846 Restaurant & Tavern at the West Dover Inn** (108 Rte. 100, West Dover, 802/464-5207, www.westdoverinn.com, 5–9 P.M. Mon.–Fri., noon–9 P.M. Sat.–Sun., $11–32) charms with handmade ravioli and breads, fresh local ingredients, and an intimate little tavern next door.

Information and Services

For more info on the area, contact the **Mount Snow Chamber of Commerce** (877/887-6884, www.visitvermont.com) or stop by its visitors center in Wilmington (on Rte. 9 just west of the traffic light). ATM machines are located at **Chittenden Bank** (2 Mountain Park Plz., West Dover). Wi-Fi Internet is available at **The Perfect Cup** (Rte. 100, 0.5 mile south of Mt. Snow, West Dover).

SPORTS AND RECREATION
Skiing

An object lesson in capitalism run amok can be found at **Mount Snow Resort** (39 Mount Snow Rd., West Dover, 800/245-7669, www.mountsnow.com, 9 A.M.–4 P.M. Mon.–Fri., 8 A.M.–4 P.M. Sat.–Sun., $75–85 adults, $58–67 young adults, $45–52 seniors and children age 6–18), which is chaotic, expensive, and often overcrowded. The resort's proximity to New York (a three- or four-hour drive depending on traffic) has given it a reputation for being favored by rowdy out-of-towners. If you enjoy skiing in a party atmosphere, however, the mountain's four faces will give you plenty to tackle, especially for intermediate skiers. The best bet is to get away from the main lodge as quickly as possible and head for the more out-of-the-way chairlifts, such as the steeper North Face.

ACCOMMODATIONS

If you plan on skiing at Mount Snow but don't want to stay at the resort, you can get package rates on lift tickets along with lodging at the historic **Old Red Mill Inn** (18 Rte. 100 N./Rte. 9, Wilmington, 802/464-3700 or 877/732-6455, www.oldredmill.com, $50–110). Cheap doesn't mean chintzy at this authentic ski-lodge style B&B with warm, friendly staff and a wraparound fireplace in the lobby. Located in the center of Wilmington in a real converted old lumber mill, the inn also offers a tavern menu of New England cuisine.

Baked apples and ice cream with breakfast are just the start of the Vermont hospitality at ◖ **Baked Apples at Shearer Hill Farm** (Shearer Hill Rd., 802/464-3253 or 800/437-3104, www.shearerhillfarm.com, $115), where gregarious innkeepers Patti and Bill Pusey have taken a former farm and car junkyard and

transformed it into a quiet retreat several miles back from the highway. The bed-and-breakfast features plush king-size beds along with fields of Hereford cows, potatoes, and wildflowers.

You can't get much more elegant than the **White House** (178 Rte. 9 E., Wilmington, 802/464-2135 or 866/774-2135, www.whitehouseinn.com, $150–340), a hilltop Victorian mansion with enough terraces, fireplaces, and whirlpools to melt even the most obstinate honeymooner.

GETTING THERE AND AROUND

From Brattleboro, drive west on Route 9 for Marlboro (10 mi., 20 min.) and Wilmington (20 mi., 30 min.). To drive to West Dover, take Route 100 north from Wilmington (6 mi., 9 min.). The **Deerfield Valley Transit Association** (802/464-8487, www.moover.com) operates the MOOver!, a Holstein-patterned bus offering free rides between Wilmington, West Dover, Brattleboro, Mount Snow, and other nearby locations.

Bennington to Manchester

The Green Mountain National Forest is divided into two parts by a valley in the middle of Vermont, where Route 4 cuts across the state. The southern branch of the forest is the larger of the two sections, but that is mitigated by the fact that the peaks here are smaller and the valleys more populated. The backbone of southern Vermont is Route 7, which runs from the historic (if run-down) town of Bennington up along the mountain ridges to the posh community of Manchester, which seems to get another big designer outlet store every time you turn around.

BENNINGTON

In the southeastern corner of the state, the large town of Bennington is perhaps best

known for the Revolutionary War battle that shares its name. Ironic, then, that the actual battle took place eight miles farther west over the New York border. (The clash is named for the storehouses in Bennington that were the object of the British troops.) In more recent years, Bennington has become better known for the small liberal arts college that is one of the artsiest (and most expensive) colleges in the country.

Despite these promising attributes, the town declined in recent decades due to a lack of industry, and the old brick downtown became depressed and uninviting. It's only in the past decade that Bennington has been looking up, taking a page from nearby Vermont towns to accentuate the art and culture generated by the college. That's a good thing, since both the town and its surrounding villages have a number of attractions worth a visit, including those paying homage to famous Vermonters Robert Frost and Grandma Moses.

◖ Bennington Battle Monument

It's hard to miss the 306-foot-tall limestone obelisk (15 Monument Cir., 802/447-0550, http://historicsites.vermont.gov/bennington, 9 A.M.–5 P.M. daily mid-Apr.–Oct., $2 adults, $1 children) that towers over the town like a half-size version of the Washington Monument. Inside is a diorama of the second engagement of the Battle of Bennington, along with an elevator that takes visitors two-thirds of the way up for a knockout view of the Green Mountains, the Berkshires, and the Taconic Range (in Vermont, Massachusetts, and New York, respectively). Appropriately heroic statues of the battle's heroes, colonels John Stark and

© VERMONTVACATION.COM/STEPHEN GOODHUE

Bennington Battle Monument

Seth Warner, stand on the monument grounds, along with a gift shop located on the actual site of the storehouse the British had hoped to capture.

◖ Bennington Museum

If you haven't had enough of the battle, you can learn even more at this underrated museum (75 Main St., 802/447-1571, www.benningtonmuseum.org, 10 A.M.–5 P.M. daily July–Oct., 10 A.M.–5 P.M. Thurs.–Tues. Feb.–June and Nov.–Dec., $10 adults, $9 students and seniors, under 18 free), which has a room explaining troop movements and displaying rifles and other Revolutionary War paraphernalia.

The museum's other big draw is the Grandma Moses gallery, which includes two dozen framed paintings by the famous New England folk artist, along with her painting desk (itself painted on) and chair. Anna Mary Robertson Moses lived in Bennington for eight years, from 1927 to 1935, and developed a simple (some might say simplistic) style that captured the past times of rural America—harvests, mills, sleigh rides, and ice skating—during a time when the United States was undergoing rapid industrialization. The museum also has several worthwhile galleries of 18th- and 19th-century furniture, pottery, and portrait paintings.

Bennington Potters

The first pottery in Bennington was made by a Revolutionary War veteran in 1793. Since then, the town has become famous for its earthenware, a tradition that is carried on at Bennington Potters (324 County St., 802/447-7531 or 800/205-8033, www.benningtonpotters.com, 9:30 A.M.–6 P.M. Mon.–Sat., 10 A.M.–5 P.M. Sun.), which is equal parts outlet store and museum. You can browse several rooms of mugs, bowls, and plates made in the company's distinctive "speckleware" patterns,

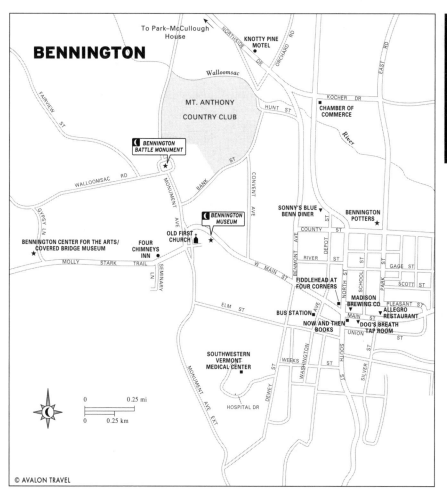

© AVALON TRAVEL

then watch artisans at work spinning clay in the potters' yard.

Old First Church

Robert Frost once wrote, "One could do worse than be a swinger of birches." It's fitting that his final resting place should be under a small grove of birches behind Bennington's Old First Church (1 Monument Cir., 802/447-1223, www.oldfirstchurchbenn.org, 10 A.M.–noon and 1–4 P.M. Sat., 1–4 P.M. Sun. late May–July; 10 A.M.–noon and 1–4 P.M. Mon.–Sat., 1–4 P.M. Sun. July–mid-Oct., donations welcome). In addition to Frost's grave, the cemetery also contains those of American, British, and Hessian soldiers killed at the Battle of Bennington.

Covered Bridge Museum

It was only a matter of time before someone

decided to dedicate an entire museum to that cult tourist phenom, the covered bridge. Enter the Covered Bridge Museum (Rte. 9 at Gypsy Ln., 802/442-7158, http://thebennington. org, 10 A.M.–5 P.M. Wed.–Mon., $9 adults, $8 students and seniors, $20 families, children under 12 free), which includes exhibits on bridge design and tools along with a light-up map showing the locations of all 100-some Vermont examples. No less than five are within a few minutes' drive of Bennington, including the dramatic **Chiselville Bridge** (E. Arlington Rd., off Rte. 7A, Sunderland), which spans a gorge over the Roaring Branch Brook. The museum is located in the **Bennington Center for the Arts** (44 Gypsy Ln., 802/442-7158, www. benningtoncenterforthearts.org, 10 A.M.–5 P.M. Wed.–Mon., $9 adults, $8 students and seniors, $20 families, children under 12 free), a large complex with displays of New England paintings and Native American arts.

Park-McCullough House

One of the most impressive Victorians in New England is the Park-McCullough House (1 Park St., 802/442-5441, www.parkmccullough. org, call for hours, May–Dec., $10 adults, $9 seniors, $7 students, children under 12 free), a Second Empire mansion filled with lavish antiques and period furniture. A separate carriage barn contains carriages, sleighs, and fire-fighting equipment.

Entertainment and Events

On August 16 of every year, Vermont celebrates its very own holiday, **Bennington Battle Day** (802/447-3311 or 800/229-0252, www.bennington.com), during which the town holds an annual parade along with battle reenactments on the monument grounds. A few weeks later, bring your breath mints to the **Southern Vermont Garlic and Herb Festival** (802/447-3311, www.lovegarlic.com), an annual Labor Day weekend celebration that offers up plenty

of piquant samples of garlic spreads, garlic jellies, garlic salsas, and even garlic ice cream (don't miss the tent with garlic margaritas) at a fairgrounds off Route 9 west of town. In between eating and not kissing, fairgoers can take in musical performances, face painting, and a hay maze.

Shopping

Every once in a while you stumble across a store so unique, you have no idea how to categorize it. Such a place is **Fiddlehead at Four Corners** (338 Main St., 802/447-1000, 10 A.M.–5 P.M. daily), a browser's dream of crafts and oddities in a huge old bank building. Recent finds here include limited-edition Dr. Seuss lithographs, framed animation cells from *The Simpsons,* and a "brew vault" full of antique light-up beer signs from the last 40 years.

More crafts can be found at the **Hawkins House Craftsmarket** (262 North St., 802/447-0488, www.hawkinshouse.net, 10 A.M.–6 P.M. Mon.–Sat., 11 A.M.–5:30 P.M. Sun.), including hooked rugs, blown glass, and jewelry from over 500 artisans. You can smell the dust at **Now and Then Books** (439 Main St., 2nd Fl., 802/442-5566, www.nowandthenbooksvt. com, noon–5 P.M. Sun.–Mon., 11:30 A.M.–5:30 P.M. Wed.–Sat., seasonal hours may vary), a warren of rooms piled eight feet high with books on every subject.

Food

If you don't know what to order at ◖ **Sonny's Blue Benn Diner** (314 North St./Rte. 7, 802/442-5140, 6 A.M.–5 P.M. Mon.–Tues., 6 A.M.–8 P.M. Wed.–Fri., 6 A.M.–4 P.M. Sat., 7 A.M.–4 P.M. Sun., $3–12), just look up. Every inch of wall space in this prefab 1940s diner car is covered with specials. Especially to-die-for are the waffles and French toast, topped with every imaginable combination of syrups, fruits, and nuts.

The authentic Italian at **Allegro Restaurant**

(520 Main St., 802/442-0990, www.allegroristorante.com, 5–9:30 P.M. daily, $6–21) has a huge local following, as evidenced by the oft-packed dining room. Settle in for the homemade specialty ravioli of the day or main courses such as diver scallops with lemon risotto.

The convivial **Madison Brewing Company** (428 Main St., 802/442-7397, www.madisonbrewingco.com, 11:30 A.M.–9:30 P.M. Sun–Thurs, 11:30 A.M.–10:30 P.M. Fri and Sat., $8–15) serves handcrafted beers with names like Old 76 Strong Ale and Suckerpond Blonde along with pub grub, steaks, and pasta.

Information and Services

The **Bennington Area Chamber of Commerce** (100 Veterans Memorial Dr., 802/447-3311, www.bennington.com) runs a visitors center in town. Emergency medical services are handled by **Southwestern Vermont Medical Center** (100 Hospital Dr., East Bennington, 802/442-6361, www.svhealthcare.org). For medications, **Extended Care Pharmacy** (207 North St., 802/442-4600) is located in the center of town, along with chain pharmacy **Rite-Aid Pharmacy** (194 North St., 802/442-2240, 8 A.M.–9 P.M. Mon.–Sat., 9 A.M.–6 P.M. Sun., pharmacy 9 A.M.–9 P.M. Mon.–Fri., 9 A.M.–6 P.M. Sat., 9 A.M.–5 P.M. Sun.). On the north side of town is **CVS Pharmacy** (8 Kocher Dr., 802/442-8369). For non-medical emergencies, contact **Bennington Police Department** (118 South St., 802/442-1030).

Several banks with ATM machines are located at the corner of Route 7 and Route 9, including **Chittenden Bank** (401 Main St.), **Sovereign Bank** (107 N. Side Rd.), and **Merchants Bank** (406 Main St., 802/442-8321, 8:30 A.M.–5 P.M. Mon.–Thurs., 8:30 A.M.–6 P.M. Fri.). Free Internet use is offered at the **Bennington Free Library** (101 Silver St., 802/442-9051, www.benningtonfreelibrary.org, 10 A.M.–7 P.M. Mon., 10 A.M.–5 P.M. Tues.–Wed. and Sat., 1–7 P.M. Thurs., 1–5 P.M. Fri.; also open 10 A.M.–1 P.M. Sat. in summer).

SHAFTSBURY AND ARLINGTON

Two of Vermont's most famous residents made their homes along the stretch of Route 7 between Bennington and Manchester. Poet Robert Frost moved to the town of Shaftsbury in 1920 after he had already achieved fame as a poet. He kept up a farm and orchard in the area for some 20 years until the untimely deaths of his wife and son. Just as Frost moved away, another chronicler of small-town New England, Norman Rockwell, was moving in. Rockwell lived in the neighboring town of Arlington from 1939 to 1953, producing some of his best-known paintings using his neighbors as models. The area hasn't changed much since Frost and Rockwell's time here; the highway veers around cliffs and mountainsides, skirting the unspoiled fringes of the state forest.

Sights

Robert Frost's trail can be followed to the **Robert Frost Stone House Museum** (121 Rte. 7A, Shaftsbury, 802/447-6200, www.frostfriends.org, 10 A.M.–5 P.M. Tues.–Sun. May–Nov, $5 adults, $2.50 students under 18, children under 6 free), where the poet lived for several years. Inside are changing exhibits dedicated to exploring Frost's life, along with a permanent exhibit dedicated to the poem "Stopping by Woods on a Snowy Evening," which he wrote at the dining room table here "on a hot June morning in 1922." On the grounds, you can amble among the stone walls and some of Frost's original apple trees.

Rockwell's former home, meanwhile, has been turned into a bed-and-breakfast. The **Inn on Covered Bridge Green** (3587 River Rd., Arlington, 802/375-9489, www.coveredbridgegreen.com) takes pride in advertising

Bridge at the Green, Arlington

that Rockwell painted in what is now its dining room and mixed paint in what is now its kitchen. Truth be told, little remains of the artist's time there. More impressive is the nearby covered **Bridge at the Green,** a brick-red number on Route 313 over the Batten Kill River that dates back to 1853 and is one of the most photographed bridges in the state.

Shopping

Feel moved to take on the mountains by hoof? **Trumbull Mountain Tack Shop** (969 Trumbull Hill Rd., Shaftsbury, 802/442-9672, www. trumbullmtn.com, 11 A.M.–5 P.M. Mon.–Sat., Sun. by appointment) will saddle you up properly or sell you a custom-made saddle that any of the equestrian ilk would be proud to take home. Take-home gifts of a more general sort are found in droves at **Wayside Country Store** (3307 Rte. 313, West Arlington, 802/375-2792, 4:30 A.M.–9 P.M. daily), the place to pick up everything you need for the drive (hot deli sandwiches and magazines) and everything you may ever need after you arrive home (fishing supplies, kerosene, and kids' toys).

There's a respectable amount of treasure to be unearthed at **Gristmill Antiques** (316 Old Mill Rd., East Arlington, 802/375-2500, 10:30 A.M.–5 P.M. Thurs.–Mon. May–June; 10:30 A.M.–5 P.M. daily July–Nov.), a well-kept shop housed in two buildings overlooking spectacular waterfalls. And if the kids (or you) are bummed about not seeing a bear in the Vermont woods, duck into **Village Peddler & Bearatorium** (261 Old Mill Rd., East Arlington, 802/375-6037, www.village-peddlervt.com, 10 A.M.–5 P.M. Mon–Sat., 11 A.M.–5 P.M. Sun., seasonal hours may vary) for a wee bit of consolation. The store, located in an erstwhile wagon shed, is home to the world's largest chocolate teddy bear. Or simply drown your sorrows in any of the house's maple syrup, maple candy, cheddar cheese, or honey.

Food

Restaurants are tough to come by in these parts, but **Chauncey's Family Dining** (5403 Rte. 7A, Arlington, 802/275-4190, http://chaunceysfamilydining.com, 7:30 A.M.–2:30 P.M. Sun.–Wed., 7:30 A.M.–8:30 P.M. Thurs.–Sat., $9–21) serves enough different kinds of food for 10 eateries. The family-friendly, rustic diner slings a mean corned beef hash, fiery chili, good ribs, and terrific breakfast items (like fluffy, enormous pancakes). The eager staff are usually more than happy to point out their favorite menu items.

MANCHESTER

If you've had your fill of maple syrup and cheddar cheese and could go for a hot latte and the *New York Times* crossword puzzle, then Manchester is your place. Vermont's Madison Avenue in the Mountains, the winding path of Route 7 is lined with outlet shops bearing the names of top designers such as Coach, Escada,

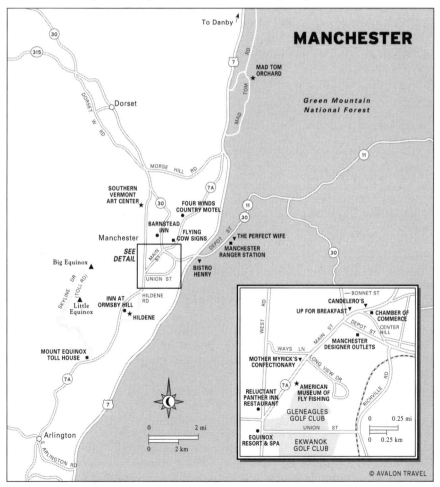

© AVALON TRAVEL

and Ralph Lauren. There's more to the town than shopping, however. Its location between the Taconic Range and Green Mountains makes it the perfect jumping-off point for outdoor pursuits.

Manchester began taking shape as a resort community in the 1850s, when Franklin Orvis began touting the Equinox House as one of the most fashionable hotels in Vermont. Located at the base of Mount Equinox, the highest peak in the Taconics, the hotel and the town drew moneyed guests from New York and Massachusetts to hike, ski, and fly-fish for trout in the Batten Kill River. Thanks to Franklin's brother Charles, the Orvis name is synonymous with fly-fishing, which is still avidly practiced in the area.

Sights

Among those who once made Manchester their summer home was Abraham Lincoln's son, Robert Todd Lincoln, who entertained guests at **Hildene** (1005 Hildene Rd., 802/362-1788, www.hildene.org, 9:30 A.M.–4:30 P.M. daily, $16 adults, $5 children 6–14, children under 6 free), a Georgian Revival mansion with grounds overlooking the Batten Kill River. Musical performances and craft fairs frequently take place on the grounds.

See how the masters cast and tied at the **American Museum of Fly Fishing** (4104 Main St./Rte. 7A, 802/362-3300, www.amff.com, 10 A.M.–4 P.M. Tue.–Sun., $5 adults, $3 children 5–14, $10 families, donations accepted). The quaint museum showcases flies tied by Mary Orvis Marbury and other originators of the sport, along with rods owned by such celebrities as Ernest Hemingway, Babe Ruth, and George H. W. Bush.

Few art museums are as beautifully situated as the **Southern Vermont Art Center** (930 Southern Vermont Arts Center Dr., 802/362-1405, www.svac.org, 10 A.M.–5 P.M. Tues.–Sat., noon–5 P.M. Sun., admission donations

$8 adults, $3 children, free Sun.), which has its wooded grounds on the flank of Mount Equinox. Inside, the center plays host to traveling art exhibitions, jazz and classical music concerts, and author readings.

For a closer look at the mountain (and a more distant view of the valley), take the **Mount Equinox Skyline Drive** (off Rte. 7A, 802/362-1115, www.equinoxmountain.com/skylinedrive, $15 car and driver, $5 per passenger, children under 10 free). The winding toll road climbs 3,800 feet to the summit for an unparalleled view of the surrounding peaks and sometimes sightings of eagles and peregrine falcons.

Spa

If Whole Foods were a spa, it would the **Equinox Resort and Spa** (3567 Main St. Rte. 7A, Manchester Village, 800/362-4747, www.equinoxresort.com, $115–220). The clean aesthetic focuses on bringing the Green Mountains inside with an emphasis on natural ingredients such as maple sugar, mineral clay, and wildflower essences, all sourced from Vermont. Not everything here is so local, however. Among the most decadent of treatments is an "autumn ritual" drawn from Egyptian roots incorporating chamomile and mineral gold in a top-to-tail massage and exfoliation.

Shopping

If you could afford it, you could spend a week shopping at all of the **Manchester Designer Outlets** (97 Depot St., 802/362-3736, www.manchesterdesigneroutlets.com, hours vary by store), which have some 30 factory outlet stores, including such top names as Giorgio Armani, Brooks Brothers, and Coach. The best stores are along Routes 11 and 30 (take a right after you hit the town center), conveniently grouped in several strip malls.

Peruse copper weathervanes and whimsical wooden animals at **Flying Cow Signs** (5073

Main St., 802/362-4927, www.flyingcowsigns. com, 10 A.M.–5 P.M. Mon.–Sat., closed Sun), which will make you a customized sign for your house starting at $65 and $9–11 per letter.

Finally, when you get hungry after all of the shopping, replenish your sugars at **Mother Myrick's Confectionary** (Rte. 7A, 888/669-7425, www.mothermyricks.com, 10 A.M.–5:30 P.M. daily), an old-fashioned candy shop carrying such mouthwatering classics as buttercrunch, truffles, and linzer torte, along with New England–specific recipes like maple-blueberry cheesecake.

Food

Vintage French posters fill the wall space of the large but intimate ◖ **Bistro Henry** (1942 Rte. 11/Rte. 30, 802/362-4982, www.bistro-henry.com, 5–9 P.M. Sun. and Tues.–Thurs., 5–9:30 P.M. Fri.–Sat., $25–32), founded by two transplanted Manhattan chefs. As the name suggests, the restaurant serves heavily Americanized bistro food, like grilled venison with lingonberry sauce and fettuccine with rabbit ("We only use the ugly ones, not the cute ones," says chef Henry). Henry's wife, Dina, makes desserts, including a Grand Marnier crème brûlée.

The food may be pretentious, but the atmosphere isn't at **The Perfect Wife** (2594 Depot St./Rte. 11/30, 802/362-2817, www.perfect-wife.com, restaurant 5–10 P.M. Mon.–Sat.; tavern 4 P.M.–close Mon.–Sat., $25–32), which feels more like a dinner party than a restaurant. Whether you have a perfect wife at home or not, you'll appreciate chef and "aspiring perfect wife" Amy Chamberlain's seared yellowfin tuna, coq au vin, and "howling wolf" vegetarian special.

You might not expect to find good Mexican food this far up in Vermont, but **Candelero's** (5103 Main St., 802/362-0836, www.can-deleros.net, 4–9 P.M. daily, 4–10 P.M. Fri.–Sat., $15–23) does a great job with creative

Southwestern cuisine, served in a brick Victorian house.

If the rooster motif at **Up for Breakfast** (4935 Main St./Rte. 7A, 802/362-4204, 7 A.M.–12:30 P.M. Mon.–Fri., 7 A.M.–1:30 P.M. Sat.–Sun., $8–12) doesn't open your eyes, the hearty meals here will. It's on the second floor overlooking Main Street. The "red flannel hash" and sourdough batard French toast are perfect for bulking up on carbs before hitting the hills or the slopes.

Information and Services

The **Manchester and the Mountains Chamber of Commerce** (5046 Main St., 800/362-4144, www.manchestervermont.net) runs a small information booth on the town green on Route 7A. Manchester has several pharmacies in the town center, including **Rite-Aid Pharmacy** (4993 Main St., Manchester Ctr., 802/362-2230, 8 A.M.–9 P.M. Mon.–Sat., 9 A.M.–6 P.M. Sun., pharmacy 9 A.M.–9 P.M. Mon.–Fri., 9 A.M.–6 P.M. Sat., 9 A.M.–5 P.M. Sun.).

Free Wi-Fi is available at **Spiral Press Cafe** (15 Bonnet St., 802/362-9944), right at the corner of Routes 15 and 30 and attached to Northshire Bookstore. In an emergency, contact the **Manchester Police Department** (6041 Main St., 802/362-2121).

NORTH OF MANCHESTER

A few miles north up the mountains from Manchester, the town of **Dorset** can rightly lay claim to being the birthplace of Vermont (though Windsor on the other side of the state might argue with it). During the days of disputed land claims, the leaders of the New Hampshire Grants met twice at a local tavern, signing the Articles of Association to declare themselves an independent territory. The association didn't last long, however, as the easterners declared their own independence a few years later. The pretty little town now has many fine examples of colonial buildings, as well as

Victorian homes from the era in the 1800s when it became a popular resort destination for New Yorkers seeking cool mountain air, and later for artists looking for bucolic scenes to grace their canvases. The town still fills each year with "summer people," as well as a disproportionate number of local artisans and furniture makers who have their studios in town.

The association with New York became rock-solid when marble was discovered in town, creating the first commercial marble quarry in America and supplying stone for the New York Public Library. Now some of the old quarries have taken on a second life as summer swimming holes. A bit farther north up Route 7, **Danby** was built literally and figuratively out of the trees all around it. Silas Lapham Griffith became Vermont's first millionaire on the strength of his sawmills, which at one point cut 50 million feet of timber a year. The town and those around it are filled with fine Victorian mansions from the days of the lumber and marble barons.

Sights

One of the better local historical museums in Vermont, the Dorset Historical Society's **Bley House Museum** (Rte. 30 at Kent Hill Rd., Dorset, 802/867-0331, www.dorsethistory. com, 10 A.M.–4 P.M. Wed.–Sat., 10 A.M.–2 P.M. Sat. mid-Apr.–Nov. 30, 10 A.M.–noon Wed., 10 A.M.–2 P.M. Thurs.–Sat. Dec.–mid-Apr., donations welcome) oozes evidence of the care and hard work of its volunteer curators. Exhibitions include a collection of coins—minted in nearby Rupert—from the days when Vermont was an independent republic (1776–1791), as well as artifacts relating to the marble, stoneware, and textile industries and several fine examples of paintings from the days in the early 20th century when the town was an artists' community. The historical society also provides a tape for a self-guided walking tour of many of the historic homes in the village, including the Dorset Inn,

which was built on the site of Kent Tavern, where the Republic of Vermont was arguably born.

Some thought Tom Smith crazy when he decided to restore his father's old mountainside apple orchard a bit over a decade ago. But he persisted, and the fruits of his labor can be seen (and picked) at **Mad Tom Orchard** (2615 Mad Tom Rd., East Dorset, 802/366-8107, www.madtomorchard.com, 9 A.M.–5:30 P.M. Tues.–Sun. in July, Sept., and Oct.). Guests can pluck McIntosh and Cortland apples from venerable 60-year-old trees (Tom provides a pole to pick those high on top) and hunt among the raspberry bushes with a view of the mountains all around.

Entertainment and Events

"Summer people" and year-rounders alike fill the aisles for the **Dorset Theatre Festival** (104 Cheney Rd., Dorset, 802/867-2223 Sept.–May or 802/867-5777 June–Aug., www.dorsettheatrefestival.org), an acclaimed summer stock festival that has been producing both classics (Tennessee Williams, Oscar Wilde) and new playwrights for 30 years. During the rest of the year, the playhouse gets turned back to the **Dorset Players** (802/867-5777 www.dorsetplayers.org), the amateur theater troupe that built the playhouse in the 1920s and performs excellent theater in its own right.

Shopping

Family-run for six generations, **H. N. Williams Shop** (2732 Rte. 30, Dorset, 802/867-5353, www.hnwilliams.com, 7:30 A.M.–6 P.M. Mon.–Fri., 7:30 A.M.–5 P.M. Sat., 8 A.M.–4 P.M. Sun.) began in 1840 as a harness shop. These days it's full of equally practical merchandise like dog treats, women's and men's clothing, footwear, hardware, and handmade quilts. Fill your home with one-of-a-kind pieces from **Dorset Custom Furniture** (23 Goodwood Ln., Dorset, 802/867-5541, www.dorsetcustomfurniture. com, 9 A.M.–4 P.M. Mon.–Fri.), and you'll never have to worry about suffering the fate of national manufacturer addicts. Everything from dining and coffee tables to desks to beds—made to your specifications—is here.

Food

It doesn't get much more historical in atmosphere than in the dining room of **Barrows House** (3156 Rte. 30, Dorset, 802/867-4455, www.barrowshouse.com, 5–9 P.M. Tues.–Sat., $24–34). The green walls are hand-painted with a mural of Dorset Historical Landmarks, so you're literally surrounded by the village's highlights. The menu does its part to outshine them, however, with specials like baked haddock with a cracker crumb and parmesan and hazelnut encrusted pork loin.

Information and Services

For more info, stop by the **Dorset Village Public Library** (Corner of Rte. 30 and Church St., 802/867-5774, www.dorsetlibraryinfo.org, 11 A.M.–5 P.M. Mon.–Fri., 10 A.M.–3 P.M. Sat.) or contact the **Dorset Chamber of Commerce** (802/867-2450, www.dorsetvt.com). An ATM machine is located at **Berkshire Bank** (23 Church St., Dorset, 802/867-2234).

SPORTS AND RECREATION

The **Equinox Resort** (3567 Main St./Rte. 7A, Manchester, 800/362-4747, www.equinoxresort.com, $314–469) offers several "upscale" outdoor activities. Perhaps the most impressive is the **British School of Falconry** (802/362-4780, www.equinoxresort.com/thingstodo/falconry, $115 per person for 45-minute lesson, $1,800 for four-day course), which, if you have the money to spend, will teach you how to hunt quail, pheasants, and other game birds with your very own Harris hawk. The school also offers archery and crossbow lessons ($90 per person for a 90-minute lesson) and year-round off-road driving on an 80-acre course ($225 per hour) through its affiliated **Land Rover**

Experience Driving School (802/362-0687, www.equinoxresort.com/thingstodo/driving). If you harbor images of chewing up mud and rock while you whiz around curves in your Land Rover, however, be forewarned that the driving school is more of an exercise in technology than skill—the truck does most of the work through its impressive array of dashboard settings that can take on snow, sand, mud, or any other terrain. Your job is to mostly keep your hands on the wheel and try not to scratch the paint job as you slowly maneuver through the course. If you are a gearhead, you'll love it; if not, you might find yourself wishing for a bit more control.

Hiking and Camping

Near Bennington is the start of the **Long Trail,** Vermont's predecessor to the Appalachian Trail, which wends its way along the spine of the Green Mountains from Massachusetts to the Canadian border. You can find information about day hikes along the trail as well as other hiking paths from the **Green Mountain Club** (802/244-7037, www.greenmountainclub.org). Guided trips near Bennington are offered by the **Bennington Chapter** (www.meetup.com/gmcbennington) of the club.

For the more adventurous, the Green Mountain Club maintains some 70 campsites along the Long Trail from Bennington to the Canadian border. Most of the sites are primitive in nature, accommodating anywhere from 8 to 20 people, and are first-come, first-serve, and free (some with a caretaker ask a small fee). All of the sites have a water source, and some are built out with lean-tos or fully enclosed lodges.

Hikers interested in venturing forth on the Long Trail would do well to pick up a copy of the *Long Trail Guide,* available in any bookshop or outdoor store in the area (and often at pharmacies and convenience stores as well), or through the GMC's website.

The **Green Mountain National Forest** (802/362-2307, www.fs.fed.us/r9/gmfl) operates several more campgrounds within the hills surrounding Bennington and Manchester. One of the best-kept secrets is the campground around **Grout Pond** (Forest Rd. 262, Stratton; get directions from the Manchester Ranger Station or download from the website), a semi-wilderness campground near Stratton Mountain between Arlington and West Wardsboro. The 1,600-acre recreation area is situated around a small pond that is used for canoeing and fishing. For those lucky enough to score it, there is a small cabin available on a first-come, first-serve basis with fireplace and woodstove. In addition, there are 6 other car-camping sites and 11 hike-in (or boat-in) sites, some with tent platforms and lean-tos, scattered at wide distances around the shore of the pond—at night, you'll barely know there is anyone else around you. There is no fee for any of the campsites, though donations are accepted for the upkeep of the area. More than 10 miles of trails meander through the surrounding woods.

For day hikers, the hills around Manchester and Bennington are filled with many more hiking trails, which start from several of the most popular sights. The **Manchester Ranger Station** (2538 Depot St./Rte. 11/30, Manchester, 802/362-2307, www.fs.fed.us/r9/gmfl) offers a free (if rudimentary) trail map of day hikes within Green Mountain National Forest that range from easy to difficult, with distances up to 11 miles. One popular day hike is the five-mile section of the Appalachian Trail that climbs Spruce Peak. Located off Route 15/30 near Peru, the trailhead rises and falls along an undulating ridge through hardwood forest, at one point crossing an abandoned old stagecoach route from Manchester. Eventually, the trail rises to the top of the peak with views of the town

of Manchester in the valley below, as well as picturesque views of Mount Equinox and its surrounding mountains.

If that whets your appetite to climb **Mount Equinox** itself, you can find a trail map at the tollhouse for Skyline Drive. Trails on the mountain vary, from a short hike up to a panoramic view of Manchester at Lookout Rock to a strenuous four-mile hike to the summit 3,848 feet above sea level. While grueling at times, the trail itself is a very pleasing one, climbing out from a dark forest of oak, maple, and birch into an alpine ecosystem scented with the sweet smell of balsam trees and occasionally graced with the presence of peregrine falcons and golden eagles. That's all a prelude to one of the best—if not the best—view in southern Vermont, surrounded on all sides by the green peaks of the Taconic Range. As a bonus, in between huffs and puffs you can feel vastly superior to the tenderfeet who failed to earn their view by taking the Skyline Drive to reach the top. If you are a tenderfoot yourself, a system of more gentle but no less pleasant trails is located at the **Equinox Preservation** (behind the Equinox Resort & Spa, 3567 Main St./Rte. 7A, Manchester, 800/362-4747, www.equinoxresort.com, $314–469). Park in the hotel parking lot and ask for a map at the concierge desk.

Skiing

In the winter months, Manchester becomes a playground for cross-country skiers, who have several trail systems to choose from. Several miles of groomed and tracked trails can be found at the **Hildene Touring Center** (Rte. 7A, Manchester, 802/362-1788, www.hildene.org, 9:30 A.M.–4 P.M. Dec.–mid-Mar., trail pass $16 adults, $5 youth, rental $15, lessons $30), where the estate's carriage barn is turned into a warming hut and rental shop. The sound of your own breathing will be all you hear at **Merck Forest** (Rte. 315, Rupert Mountain, 802/394-7836, www.merckforest.com, dawn–dusk daily, $25 camping, $50–90 cabins), a backcountry family farm and trail system on a remote stretch of the New York border.

The south-facing slopes of **Bromley Mountain** (3984 Rte. 11, Peru, 802/824-5522, www.winter.bromley.com, $65 weekend/$49 midweek adults, $55/$49 youth 13–17, $39/$39 youth 6–12, children under 6 free) make it one of Vermont's sunniest for downhill skiers. Although not as challenging as some of the bigger mountains nearby, at least Bromley lets you get a tan while you ski. It's also known for family programs, including a kids' ski school with animal friends Alex the Alligator and Clyde Catamount.

Snowmobiling

West of Manchester, **Equinox Snow Tours** (junction of Rte. 11 and Rte. 30, Winhall, 802/824-6628, www.vermontsnowmobile.com, $40–205 per person) offers tours through the national forest.

Fishing

The Equinox Resort & Spa (3567 Main St./Rte. 7A, Manchester, 800/362-4747, www.equinoxresort.com, $314–469) is also home to the **Orvis Fly Fishing School** (866/531-6213, $470 two-day course), which carries on the tradition of Frank Orvis by offering close instruction on snaring brook trout on the Batten Kill.

For a more flexible itinerary, contact **The Young Outdoor Company** (673 Crow Hill Rd., Arlington, 802/375-9313, bobyoung@together.net), whose proprietor, Bob Young, is a veteran instructor for the Orvis School and will instruct you in your choice of fly or spin fishing, with or without a boat.

Chartered bass fishing on nearby lakes is offered by **Green Mountain Fishing Guide Service** (593 Rte. 140, Tinmouth, 802/446-3375, http://greenmtnguide.com), whose bass master, Rod Start, has 25 years of experience on the fishing-tournament circuit.

Boating

If your vision of enjoying the river doesn't include a fishing rod, **BattenKill Canoe** (6328 Rte. 7A, Arlington, 802/362-2800, www.battenkill.com) rents canoes and leads package canoe tours with stays in country inns along the rivers.

Swimming

Dorset's history as a marble producer has benefited locals in the form of a huge man-made swimming pool at the **Dorset Marble Quarry** (Rte. 30 at Kelly Rd.). Though it can get crowded on hot days, the quarry has more than enough room for dozens of swimmers, along with cliffs for diving and cool human sculptures carved into the rock.

Horseback Riding

A few miles up Route 7, the **Chipman Stables** (Danby Four Corners, 802/293-5242, www.chipmanstables.com) takes visitors on guided horseback rides, as well as hayrides and sleigh rides depending on the season.

ACCOMMODATIONS
Under $100

Just down the hill from the Bennington Battle Monument, the **Knotty Pine Motel** (130 Northside Dr., Bennington, 802/442-5487, www.knottypinemotel.com, $65–98) offers exceptional value for a motel, with refrigerators, coffeemakers, and cable television in each of its spotless rooms.

Located in Manchester Center, the **Four Winds Country Motel** (7379 Rte. 7A, Manchester, 802/362-1105, http://fourwinds-manchester.com, $69–120) is a cut above the usual motel, with country furniture and antiques in the rooms.

$100-150

The current owner of the **Barnstead Inn** (349 Bonnet St., Manchester, 800/331-1619, www.

barnsteadinn.com, $135–250) used to sled down the hill beside the hay barn that has been converted into a bed-and-breakfast. The 14 individual rooms feature romantic touches like exposed beams and original antiques.

$150-250

Manchester's most romantic B&B, **◖ The Reluctant Panther Inn & Restaurant** (39 West Rd., Manchester, 802/362-2568, www.reluctantpanther.com, $179–759), was gutted by fire several years back. Owners Liz and Jerry Lavalley took the occasion to renovate with even more upscale amenities. Each room in the antique-filled home now has at least one fireplace (some have two) and a Jacuzzi-style tub (most large enough to fit two people). In addition, a carriage house and a pair of older buildings on the grounds feature wood-burning fireplaces and private porches. Despite the heavy emphasis on couples, some rooms do allow small dogs or small children. A restaurant on the premises offers a mix of upscale continental and American regional cuisine with a view of Mount Equinox. Panther or no, you'll be reluctant to leave.

Four chimneys really do project from the roof of **The Four Chimneys Inn** (21 West Rd./Rte. 9, Bennington, 802/447-3500, www.fourchimneys.com, rooms $195–299), a sprawling Revolutionary-era parsonage that has been converted to an upscale bed-and-breakfast. As might be expected, many of the rooms have fireplaces, including one with a real wood-burning hearth. The white-cloth dining room has French doors looking out on the grounds and serves a menu of refined New England cuisine, with specialties such as grilled apple cider salmon and mushroom and leek risotto.

More intimate, but no less luxurious, is **The Inn at Ormsby Hill** (1842 Main St./Rte. 7A, Manchester, 802/362-1163, www.ormsbyhill.

com, $240–425), a Revolutionary-era mansion named after a captain of the Green Mountain Boys. The inn, which underwent a renovation in 2008, prides itself on individual attention to guests and a lavish decor calling to mind an English drawing room (complete with carved mantelpieces and wood-beaded ceilings). Innkeeper Chris Sprague is an imaginative breakfast cook, along the lines of bacon-and-egg risotto and eggs Benedict bread pudding.

Over $250

Much has changed at the **Equinox Resort & Spa** (3567 Main St./Rte. 7A, Manchester, 800/362-4747, www.equinoxresort.com, $314–469) since Orvis's day. What hasn't changed is that this is still where those with money to burn receive the ultimate in luxury. The sprawling resort contains almost 200 rooms outfitted with plush furnishings, along with wooded grounds that stretch for 1,300 acres and include a luxury spa, a golf course, and a falconry school.

GETTING THERE AND AROUND

To get to Bennington, drive west along Route 9 from Brattleboro (40 mi., 1 hr.). Drive north up Route 7 from Bennington for Shaftsbury (10 mi., 15 min.), Arlington (15 mi., 25 min.), Manchester (25 mi., 40 min.), Dorset (30 mi., 45 min.), or Danby (35 mi., 50 min.).

Buses run by **Greyhound Bus Lines** (800/231-2222, www.greyhound.com) stop at **Bennington Bus Station** (126 Washington Ave., 802/442-4808). No buses or trains run to the Manchester area; the closest transit hub is Rutland, from which it's possible to take a free bus to Manchester with **Green Mountain Express** (802/447-0477), which also runs bus service within Manchester and to Bennington and other nearby locations.

Okemo Valley

Halfway between Brattleboro and Bennington, Route 100 is an alternative route northward (all the way to Canada if you choose). The twisting highway is on the short list of one of the most scenic in New England; if you drive on it a little, you'll quickly see why. In addition to stunning mountain scenery, the route is also home to the little fairy-tale village of Weston, with its picturesque town common and landmark Vermont Country Store. Heading northward, scenic Route 100 skirts around the base of Mount Okemo on its way through hills sprinkled with secluded mountain resorts.

WESTON

West of Manchester, Route 100 really takes flight through the heart of the Green Mountains, tracing ridges with panoramic views of the valleys below. Tucked into one of them, the tiny village of Weston might be the most scenic in all of Vermont, with a collection of lost-in-time houses and shops surrounding a perfect town green. In fact, the entire town is on the National Register of Historic Places. Despite its beauty, however, Weston might be just a quaint hamlet if not for the presence of the mother of all country stores, the Vermont Country Store, which draws tourists in fistfuls.

◖ The Vermont Country Store

Back in the day, when roads between villages were long and the snows would block mountain passes for months, the country store had to be all things to all people, packing foodstuffs, medicines, clothes, hardware, and everything else the family needed to prosper. Over time, stores specialized, and the country store literally fell by the wayside. That is, until it was revived by Vrest Orton, who opened the original restored country store (657 Main St.,

© MICHAEL BLANDING

The Vermont Country Store

802/824-3184, www.vermontcountrystore. com, 8:30 A.M.–6 P.M. daily, year-round) on Weston Common in 1946. The shop was so successful that it has spawned countless imitators and expanded many times over the past decades. Now the store is a Vermont vision of a country mall, with wood floorboards, rafters going back as long as a football field, and shelves packed with state-made products.

If you haven't yet found that perfect block of cheddar cheese or a tin of maple syrup, you'll find it here. But this is not just another tacky souvenir shop; the proprietors—still members of the Orton family—have gone out of their way to closely evoke the old-time rural character of the state, taking requests from customers to stock hard-to-find beauty products, medicinal balms, and rugged clothing items they remembered from yesteryear but despaired of ever finding again. Especially poignant for some customers are the children's toys and candy thought to have vanished long ago. For the true spirit of old-time Vermont, this is one-stop shopping.

Farrar-Mansur House Museum

Situated on the town common in Weston, the Federal-style Farrar-Mansur House Museum (Rte. 100, 802/824-8190, www.uvm.edu, 1–4 P.M. Sat.–Sun. late May–June, 1–4 P.M. daily July–early Sept., suggested donation $2) was originally built as a tavern at the turn of the 19th century. It is now filled with early American furnishings and portraits. Paintings in the parlor by Roy William, a student of John Singer Sargent, depict life in the town circa 1830.

Old Mill Museum

Run by the Weston Historical Society, the Old Mill Museum (Rte. 100, 802/824-8190, 1–4 P.M. Sat.–Sun. late May–June, 1–4 P.M. daily July–early Sept., suggested donation $2) displays proof that not everything in the town

was always so cute. Room after room is filled with rough-hewn farming and logging implements with which village folk carved out their lives. The building itself is an old sawmill, rebuilt after being burned in 1900.

Entertainment and Events

Party like it's 1499 at **Weston Priory** (58 Priory Hill Rd., 802/824-5409, www.westonpriory. org), a monastery set up on a steep hill on the way out of town, where Benedictine monks sing plainsong in a peaceful setting several times a day with wind and insects joining in for counterpoint. The public is invited to attend; praying is optional. The **Weston Playhouse Theatre Company** (703 Main St., 802/824-5288, www.westonplayhouse.org, late June–early Sept., $28–48) has been performing above-average community theater for 70 years. In addition to Broadway musicals and stage classics, the company performs a cabaret-style review nightly after each main performance.

The **Weston Antiques Show** (802/824-5307, www.westonantiquesshow.org) has been recognized as one of the best in New England. It takes place every year in the beginning of October, when the foliage is at its height.

Shopping

Lovers of year-round yuletide, take note: **Weston Village Christmas Shop** (660 Main St., 802/824-5477, www.westonvillagestore. com, 9 A.M.–5 P.M. daily) does its part to promote good tidings of comfort and joy with a store full of Christmas collectibles—everything from snow bubbles and outdoor decorations to some very cute ornaments. And what would Christmas be without candy? The store refuses to beg the question, instead offering enough maple candies, fudge, and lollipops to make any holiday sweet. And if you find yourself short on gifts (holiday or otherwise), turn in the direction of **West River Gallery** (614 Main St., 802/824-3250, www.westrivergallery.

com, 11 A.M.–5 P.M. Thurs.–Sun.). The craft store showcases excellent regional Vermont artists' work, including ceramic art and paintings. Meanwhile, the art-centric **Village Green Gallery** (661 Main St., 802/824-3669, www.thevillagegreengallery.com, 9:30 A.M.–5 P.M. Thurs.–Tues.) features photographs of snow, foliage, and fences that are a cut above the usual Vermont-made images, as well as furniture and crafts from Vermont artisans. Maybe that's because photographer and proprietor Nobu Fuji'i spent 30 years shooting modern architecture in Japan and brings a uniquely geometric eye to his shots.

Food

The spirit of Victorian New England is kept alive at the **Bryant House Restaurant** (Rte. 100, 802/824-6287, 11 A.M.–3:30 P.M. daily; dinner 4–9 P.M. Tues.–Sun., $13–20), next door to the Vermont Country Store. The bright red house is filled with antique light fixtures and furniture that surrounds diners as they savor gourmet salads and sandwiches. An adjoining barroom, adorned with mahogany wall paneling, serves key lime margaritas and apricot sours. Be forewarned, however, that on busy days at the store you can expect a wait of over an hour; a loudspeaker system next door ensures that you can shop while you wait.

SPRINGFIELD AND CHESTER

Along the Connecticut River, the area around Springfield is known as "precision valley" for its dominance in the machine tool industry during the 20th century. For a time, Yankee ingenuity was virtually synonymous with the name of Jones & Lamson, the Apple computer of its day, for the polished design of its tools that competitors could only hope to match. The company's success was due in large measure to two men who would become leading lights of the town and the state: designer and amateur astronomer James Hartness, who held more

than 120 patents and later became governor of Vermont, and his son-in-law Ralph Flanders, who later achieved fame as one of the few U.S. senators to challenge Joe McCarthy during his Communist witch hunt in the 1950s. The wealth of its industry made Springfield rich and populous, as evidenced by its rich supply of historic buildings overlooking a scenic 110-foot waterfall in the center of town.

On the way to Springfield from Route 100, Chester is another picture-perfect Vermont village with another picture-perfect town green. Growing up from an early stagecoach crossroads, the town achieved some success in the 19th century as a grist and textile mill center. On the green is an unusual stone church built with stone from local quarries, as well as an arts center that is a magnet to the concentration of artists and craftspeople in the area.

Sights

Built in 1785, the **Eureka Schoolhouse** (Rte. 11, east of Springfield, 802/828-3051, 11 A.M.–5 P.M. Wed.–Sun. June–Oct.) is Vermont's oldest one-room schoolhouse. In addition to serving as a visitors center for the area, the curious pyramidal building houses antique educational materials giving a sense of 19th-century pedagogy (hint: lots of memorization).

More impressive, architecturally speaking, is the stunning pillared mansion that houses the town's local historical society collection. It's almost as much of a draw as the high-quality displays at the **Miller Art Center** (9 Elm Hill St., Springfield, 802/885-2415, 11 A.M.–4 P.M. Thurs.–Fri., 11 A.M.–3 P.M. Sat. mid-May–mid-Oct., $3), which includes exhibits of pewter, pottery, antique children's toys, and photos and artifacts telling the story of Springfield's machine tool industry.

Located on Chester's town green, the **Chester Art Guild Gallery** (802/875-3767, 11 A.M.–4 P.M. Fri.–Sun. late May–mid-Oct.) holds regular exhibits of local artists as well as

A one-room schoolhouse hugs a curve near Chester.

© MICHAEL BLANDING

periodic local gallery walks and art sales on the lawn. Local artisans often also give "open studios"—brown-bag explanations of their techniques—at the nearby Old Academy Building.

Events

Like a beauty pageant for fruit, town elders pick the one perfect "official apple" to represent all others at the **Vermont Apple Festival & Craft Show** (Rte. 11, 802/885-2779, www.springfieldvt.com), held in Springfield each year on Columbus Day weekend. The event includes an apple pie contest with both traditional and nontraditional categories, as well as hand-pressed cider, animal exhibits, and a juried craft show.

Not to be outdone, Chester holds its own **Chester Fall Craft Fair** (on the green, 802/228-5830, www.okemovalleyvt.org, late Sept.) with several dozen local artisans showcasing their talents with jewelry, candles, dolls, bird houses, soaps, and other creative goods.

One of Vermont's most unusual celebrations occurs mostly at night. Among James Hartness's other gifts was a flair for constructing telescopes. The amateur astronomer collaborated with optician Russel Porter to construct the observatory in Mt. Palomar, California. Porter later instructed several Springfield townspeople in lens-making, and they established an astronomy and telescope-making club in a bright pink clubhouse named Stellafane, located on Breezy Hill. The legacy of that club lives on each year with the **Stellafane Convention** (www.stellafane.com, Aug.), a gathering of several thousand telescope makers and amateur astronomers who come to Springfield each year to compare optical inventions and—of course—go stargazing in neighboring fields. Members of the public are invited to join the fun and can even learn how to construct their own homemade telescopes in numerous workshops during the event.

Shopping

Do some one-stop shopping for the kiddies at **Village Children's Shop** (145 S. Main St., Chester, 802/875-3848, 10 A.M.–5 P.M. Mon.–Fri., 10 A.M.–3 P.M. Sat.). The store stocks an

THE ANIMATED SPRINGFIELD

Vermont is a picture-perfect place in more than one way, it seems: When it came time to choose the place to premiere *The Simpsons Movie* in 2007, a contest—Hometown Movie Challenge—was held, and Springfield, Vermont, beat out 13 other Springfields across the country. Over the course of *The Simpsons* television series' 18 seasons, the fictional Springfield's location has always remained a mystery. So over two days the Vermont town of 9,300 rallied its citizens and cameras, producing a film entry that garnered enough votes to win it the honor of hosting the movie opening at Main Street's Springfield Theater. The film begins with an opening sequence similar to the one on the show that then quickly morphs into Homer running through Springfield, Vermont, clumsily chasing a humongous doughnut through downtown. It ends with him leading everyone into the theater to watch the premiere.

impressive diversity of clothing, coats, shoes, and athletic wear for boys and girls, plus plenty of onesies and inordinately cuddly pajamas for babies. The toy selection is equally irresistible—filled with handmade wooden toys, oversized puzzles, and educational games.

Baubles for women—albeit of a less recreational sort—abound at **Forlie Ballou** (23 School St., Chester, 802/875-2090), a haven of specialty accessories from whipstitched leather bags and silk scarves to embroidered dresses, pretty sachets, and handmade soaps. Rather dress up your home than yourself? Take a peek into **Conrad Delia Windsor Chairs** (1300 Popple Dungeon Rd., Chester, 802/875-4219, www.popplefields.com, 10 A.M.–5 P.M. daily) and get a load of the handcrafted Windsor chairs made of pine, oak, ash, maple, and birch. (Chair-making classes are offered regularly.)

More local crafts can be found at **Gallery 103** (Rte. 103, Chester, 802/875-7400, www.gallery103.com, 10 A.M.–5 P.M. Wed.–Mon.), which is filled with the twisted metalwork of husband-and-wife team Payne and Elise Junker, along with homemade soaps and jewelry produced by other local artisans.

Food

Inexpensive and relaxed, **Heritage Deli & Bakery** (Calvin Coolidge Hwy., Rte. 103 S., Chester, 802/875-3550, www.heritagedelianddbakery.com, 7 A.M.–5 P.M. daily, $6–14) cooks up breakfasts, lunches, and dinners of overstuffed sandwiches like the Norman Rockwell, a tasty layering of turkey, garlic herb spread, and honey mustard on pumpernickel.

One of the homiest places for dinner is **Alice's Restaurant** (90 The Common., Chester, 802/875-3344, 11:30 A.M.–3 P.M. and 5–9 P.M. Wed.–Sat., 9 A.M.–3 P.M. Sun., $6–23). The extremely outgoing staff makes everyone feel welcome; tables are filled with a mix of date-night couples, skier families, and groups of friends. Dishes are nothing daring, but everything is hearty and homemade.

For healthy eating beginning to end, grab a table at **Moon Dog Cafe & Natural Foods** (287 S. Main St., Chester, 802/875-4966, www.moondogcafe.blogspot.com, 10 A.M.–6 P.M. Mon.–Sat., 10 A.M.–5 P.M. Sun., $6–14). There you'll find a bustling and friendly room filled with Vermont hipsters, families, and locals on lunch breaks digging into an organic menu of salads, soups, and sandwiches, or just kicking back and reading over coffee.

Information and Services

For more information on the area, stop by the **Eureka Schoolhouse visitors center** (Rte. 11, east of Springfield, 802/885-2779, 11 A.M.–5 P.M. daily late May–mid-Oct.)

or contact the **Springfield Chamber of Commerce** (802/885-2779, www.springfieldvt.com). Downtown Springfield is home to a half-dozen banks, including **Chittenden Bank** (6 Main St., 802/885-2175) and **Citizens Bank** (2 Chester Rd., Ste. 15, 802/885-5151, 9 A.M.–5 P.M. Mon.–Fri.), and several pharmacies, including **Rite-Aid Pharmacy** (2 Chester Rd., Ste. 25, 802/885-5311, 8 A.M.–9 P.M. Mon.–Sat., 9 A.M.–5 P.M. Sun., pharmacy 8 A.M.–8 P.M. Mon.–Fri., 9 A.M.–6 P.M. Sat., 9 A.M.–5 P.M. Sun.). Free Wi-Fi is on offer at the **Springfield Public Library** (43 Main St., 802/885-3108). For emergencies, contact the **police department** (201 Clinton St., 802/885-2113).

For Chester, the **Okemo Valley Regional Chamber of Commerce** (802/228-5830, www.okemovalleyvt.org) runs an information booth on the town green. Several banks are also available in downtown Chester, including **TD Banknorth** (326 Main St., 802/875-2151) and **Chittenden Bank** (57 Main St., 802/875-2127). Free Wi-Fi Internet access is available

at **Heritage Deli and Bakery** (642 Rte. 103 S., 802/875-3550).

LUDLOW AND PLYMOUTH

Situated at the base of Okemo, Ludlow isn't the prettiest of Vermont towns—mostly consisting of strip-mall motels and fast food catering to those on their way to the slopes. Outside the ski-resort crush, however, there is plenty of open farmland around the Black River. Former President Calvin Coolidge went to high school in Ludlow, but he was born a dozen miles up the valley in Plymouth, a sophisticated hamlet that saw a short boom of industry after a gold rush in the 1850s. Nowadays, it's more notable for its naturally wide valley between mountains, which allows visitors driving up Route 100 to see a more expansive view of the Green Mountains than hemmed-in valleys usually provide. In the face of such an awesome vista, it's easy to see why Cal was a man of so few words.

Sights

One of the best presidential historic sites in the country, the **President Calvin Coolidge State Historic Site** (3780 Rte. 100A, Plymouth Notch, 802/672-3773, http://historicsites.vermont.gov/coolidge, 9:30 A.M.–5 P.M. daily late May–mid-Oct., office exhibits only Mon.–Fri., $7.50 adults, $2 children 6–14, children under 6 free, $20 family pass) is situated on the grounds of the 30th president's boyhood home, a sprawling collection of houses, barns, and factories nobly situated in a mountain-ringed valley. The exhibits inside give a rare intimate look into the upbringing of the president known as "Silent Cal" for his lack of emotion, but who restored the dignity of the office during a time of widespread scandal.

Shopping

Brush up on your Vermont knowledge and lore at **The Booknook** (136 Main St., Ludlow,

President Calvin Coolidge State Historic Site

802/228-3238, www.thebooknookvt.com, hours vary seasonally), where Vermont authors are a specialty, or walk away with a title from the shop's selection of general fiction and best sellers. Local artists of a different sort produce all of the merchandise at **Silver Spoon Gallery** (44 Depot St., Ludlow, 802/228-4753, opening hours vary, call ahead). Pottery, silverware, paintings, and woven throw blankets are just some of the unique creations. **Green Mountain Sugarhouse** (820 Rte. 100 N., Ludlow, 800/643-9338, www.gmsh.com, 9 A.M.–6 P.M. daily) churns out sweets year-round, including maple syrup and a slew of candies.

Food

If you aren't careful, you may live up to the name of the **Pot Belly Pub & Restaurant** (130 Main St., Ludlow, 802/228-8989, www.thepotbelly.com, 11:30 A.M.–9:30 P.M. Sun.–Thurs., 11:30 A.M.–10:30 P.M. Fri.–Sat., $7–27), a convivial bar located at the foot of Mount Okemo that serves oversized burgers and hearty portions of barbecued ribs. When the skiers leave the slopes, a somewhat raucous bar scene ensues, often featuring live jazz or R&B. A private ski club has the best dining in Okemo Valley. You'll find it at **Bear Creek Mountain Club** (Rte. 100, Plymouth, 802/672-3811, www.hawkresort.com, 11 A.M.–6 P.M. daily, $18–32). Head in for the likes of lobster-stuffed ravioli and free-range chicken piccata. On weekends, live local bluegrass bands keep the vibe as good as the food.

Information and Services

For more information on the Okemo area, contact **Okemo Valley Regional Chamber of Commerce** (802/228-5830, www.okemovalleyvt.org), which runs information booths at the clock tower in Ludlow. **Chittenden Bank** (213 Main St., 802/228-8821, 9 A.M.–5 P.M. Mon.–Thurs., 9 A.M.–6 P.M. Fri.) has an ATM right downtown. Located in the same plaza is

a **Rite-Aid Pharmacy** (213 Main St., 802/228-8477, 8 A.M.–7 P.M. Mon.–Sat., 9 A.M.–5 P.M. Sun., pharmacy 8 A.M.–7 P.M. Mon.–Fri., 9 A.M.–6 P.M. Sat., 9 A.M.–5 P.M. Sun.). In the event of emergency, contact **Ludlow Police** (19 W. Hill St., 802/228-4411).

SPORTS AND RECREATION
Hiking and Camping

Created by the Civilian Conservation Corps in the 1930s, **Coolidge State Park** (855 Coolidge State Park Rd., Plymouth, 802/672-3612, www.vtstateparks.com, campsites $16–27) is one of the crown jewels of the Vermont park system. Built into the hillside overlooking Plymouth Notch, it features two loops of well-spaced, wooded campsites—one with 26 tent sites, the other with 36 lean-tos. Many of the sites are built on the hillside, with sweeping views over some 20,000 acres of the mostly undeveloped Coolidge State Forest. The park has several miles of hiking trails, including the relatively gentle ascent up Slack Hill, a three-mile round trip that leaves from the tent loop and is an ideal hike for families (don't expect expansive views from the summit, however, as the vista is mostly blocked by tree cover). Another trail of similar length and difficulty, the CCC trail, wends its way through hardwood forests and along streams filled with brook trout.

Skiing

The slopes at **Okemo Mountain Resort** (77 Okemo Ridge Rd., Ludlow, 800/786-5366, www.okemo.com, $39–77 adults, $35–67 youth and seniors 65–69, $29–52 children 7–12 and seniors 70 and over, children under 7 free) provide the perfect balance for families who want fun and accessible programs for the kids but still want reasonably challenging runs for mom and dad. The mountain has won a cult following for its refreshingly no-frills atmosphere and emphasis on customer service, which has gotten even better with the addition of a new, attractive slope-side village and base lodge. In recent years, however, the mountain has become overcrowded during peak periods. Also, diehards will be disappointed by its lack of really advanced terrain.

The 2,000-foot tall **Stratton Mountain** (5 Village Lodge Rd., Stratton Mountain, 800/787-2886, www.stratton.com, $76–87 adult, $67–75 youth, $59–65 children) is big-mountain skiing just a 2.5-hour drive from Boston. Accessibility doesn't come cheap though—weekend lift ticket prices are among the highest in New England. For snowboarders, at least, it's worth the price. The modern sport was invented by a Stratton bartender in the 1980s, and four terrain parks and the annual U.S. Open Snowboarding Championships continue to keep boarders busy.

ACCOMMODATIONS
Under $100

The **Colonial House Inn & Motel** (287 Rte. 100, Weston, 802/824-6286 or 800/639-5033, www.cohoinn.com, $55–120) combines the hospitality of a bed-and-breakfast with the prices of a motel. A rustic living room has a warm stove and plenty of comfy chairs, along with wireless Internet access for your laptop. The proprietors' baked pies were so popular that they created a separate business; pies are available for takeaway with advance notice.

$100-150

For a great deal, head to the **Salt Ash Inn** (4758 Rte. 100A/Jct. Rte. 100, Plymouth, 800/725-3223, www.saltashinnvt.com, $130–210). Just up from Calvin Coolidge's birthplace, new owners Karla and Naz Jenulevich have renovated this budget B&B with gas fireplaces and four-poster beds. The pair serve up local travel tips at an on-site bar.

Located in the former home of Vermont governor and machine tool baron James

Hartness, **⊠ Hartness House** (30 Orchard St., Springfield, 802/885-2115, www.hartnesshouse.com, $130–240) is a luxury bed-and-breakfast of 45 plush rooms decked out with all the modern amenities—four-poster beds, in-room DVD players, and wireless Internet. But that's far from the coolest feature of the property. That would be Hartness's private astronomy observatory, accessible through a secret 250-foot underground tunnel from the inn. Guests are afforded exclusive private tours of the five-room, underground apartment, which includes astronomical maps, telescope blueprints, and several antique telescopes, including two turn-of-the-20th-century telescopes still in working order.

$150-250

Right on the Weston town green, the **Inn at Weston** (630 Main St. Rte. 100, Weston, 802/824-6789, www.innweston.com, $185–325) offers romance in the form of queen featherbeds covered in country quilts, two-person whirlpool tubs, and in-room woodstoves. The innkeeper tends orchids in a greenhouse open for tours. The inn also features a dining room serving unusual contemporary cuisine such as seared diver scallops with vanilla infused butternut squash sauce and warm terrine of roasted eggplant, with Chocolate Frangelico crème brûlée for dessert.

GETTING THERE AND AROUND

To get to Weston, take Route 11 east from Manchester to Londonderry, then head north on scenic Route 100 (20 mi., 35 min.). Alternatively, continue from Londonderry east on Route 11 to Chester (15 mi., 20 min.) or Springfield (25 mi., 35 min.). From Weston, head north up Route 100 to Ludlow (10 mi., 15 min.) or Plymouth (25 mi., 35 min.). No public transportation serves the area.

ALONG ROUTE 4

Route 4 cuts across the center of the state like a belt tied tight around its waist, serving as a physical and mental dividing line between northern and southern Vermont. The route was already well established by the time the railroad line was laid across the state, connecting the crossroads of White River Junction with the burgeoning metropolis of Rutland. Now it is showing signs of wear, as every fall it bulges with crawling lines of leaf peepers looking for a quick cut across the state, and every winter it creeps with ski traffic eager to hit the slopes.

But there is a reason for the crowds, after all, as this thin and oft-congested ribbon of highway connects some of the state's prime attractions. The popular tourist lure of Woodstock maintains the perfect balance between the quaint, white-steepled Vermont of the picture postcards and the sophisticated quasi-urban mentality that makes Vermonters seem so enlightened. Farther down the highway, Killington serves as its foil, with an overbuilt riot of restaurants and motels climbing up to the peak of the state's most popular mountain for skiers. Rutland has seen better days since its 19th-century heyday, when it was one of the state's largest and most popular cities. Scratch beneath the rust, however, and you'll find a gorgeous Victorian downtown, surrounded by several stop-worthy tourist attractions in the surrounding valley.

HIGHLIGHTS

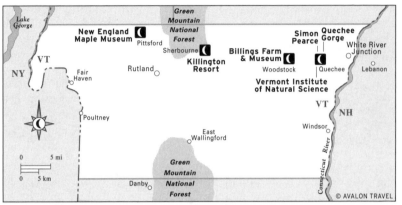

LOOK FOR █ TO FIND RECOMMENDED SIGHTS, ACTIVITIES, DINING, AND LODGING.

█ **Vermont Institute of Natural Science (VINS):** Get sized up by eagle eyes at this raptor rescue and nature center (page 73).

█ **Quechee Gorge:** The Grand Canyon it's not, but this deep river gorge is one of Vermont's most impressive natural features (page 74).

█ **Simon Pearce:** The kitchenware made here might be oh-so-upscale, but the glassblowing and pottery-making demos are absolutely hands-on (page 74).

█ **Billings Farm & Museum:** The farm that single-handedly saved Vermont's dairy industry now has exhibits about all aspects of agriculture (page 78).

█ **Killington Resort:** Love it or hate it, the six mountains of Killington provide the biggest and baddest skiing around (page 85).

█ **New England Maple Museum:** The "sappiest" museum in the world offers a fresh taste of the sweet stuff whether it's syrup season or not (page 92).

Finally, one of Vermont's quietest corners, the area around Lake Bomoseen and Lake St. Catherine, has been virtually undiscovered by tourists and is well worth a day or two spent ambling around farmstands and artisan shops or taking a boat out onto one of the lakes.

PLANNING YOUR TIME

Route 4 can serve as a day trip, splitting up a journey between the northern and southern part of the state, or it can be a route to spend several days exploring during winter or foliage season. From east to west, the first major stop

is Quechee, which holds several attractions particularly well suited to families, including the excellent **Vermont Institute of Natural Science,** the glassblowing and pottery-making exhibits at **Simon Pearce,** and the stunning natural wonder that is **Quechee Gorge.** Time your trip to include a morning hike to the bottom of the gorge then chill out at the other attractions during the afternoon. Quechee doesn't have the same variety of lodging—or the same charm—of neighboring Woodstock, so push on to the quaint shire town to spend the night.

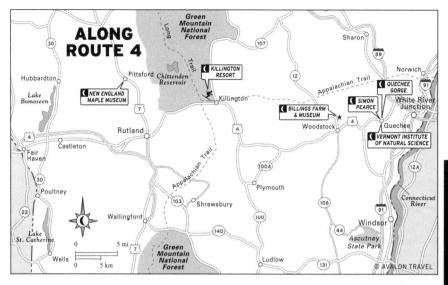

The next day, spend a half-day exploring **Billings Farm** or perusing the shops at Bridgewater Mill Marketplace. Depending on your appetite for skiing, Killington is either a stop you can spend a week at—thrilling to all of the terrain **Killington Resort** has to offer—or a place to drive quickly through to get away from the commercialism that has grown up around the mountain. While you may be tempted to drive through the industrial sprawl of Rutland as well, it's worth stopping for a day to take advantage of three excellent attractions: the **Vermont Marble Museum,** eclectic **Wilson Castle,** and the mandatory **New England Maple Museum**—not to mention the city's well-preserved Victorian downtown.

White River Junction Area

Situated at the confluence of the Connecticut River and two of northern New England's main thoroughfares—I-89 and I-91—White River Junction has always been something of a crossroads. By the late 1800s, it was the largest railroad center north of Boston, with 50 passenger trains and even more freight trains passing through daily, carrying stone, lumber, wool, and dairy products to Boston, New York, Montreal, or Burlington. As such, the town became the center of the Boston & Maine Railroad and an important hub for business and commerce well into the 20th century,

with a healthy collection of hotels and restaurants to cater to hungry and weary travelers.

While it lives up to its name, White River Junction is in fact only one village of the town of Hartford and has fewer than 3,000 inhabitants itself. It anchors a quasi-urban area that encompasses the nearby towns of Norwich to the north, Quechee to the west, and, across the river, its New Hampshire sister city, Lebanon. Within that radius is the college town of Hanover, home to northernmost Ivy League college Dartmouth. With its attractive town green and collection of funky shops it's practically an honorary Vermont village. A larger area, known as the "Upper Valley," stretches from Bellows Falls to the south all the way north to Fairlee.

WHITE RIVER JUNCTION

Despite its prominent location, White River Junction is a locale that most visitors to the state journey through, not to. After the decline of the railway, "WRJ" grew into an ugly industrial sprawl that didn't provide the most inviting introduction to the state. An economic base of manufacturing industries has provided steady employment to many neighboring residents, however, and recently the city's downtown has started to come back to life as artists seeking cheap rents have created lofts and studios, forming a residential community. That has given the town a funky vibe in some parts, and together with its inexpensive lodgings, makes it an easy and inexpensive stopover on your way to or from nearby Killington.

Sights

Located at the Amtrak passenger station in town, the **New England Transportation Museum** (100 Railroad Row, 802/291-9838, 9 A.M.–4 P.M. Nov.–May, 9 A.M.–5 P.M. May–Nov., donations accepted) displays exhibits relating to White River Junction's history as a railroad hub. Highlights are the "Old 494," a meticulously restored gleaming old steam engine, and an intricate model railroad that speeds by a Vermont scene complete with pine trees and moose. It's not especially riveting for adults, but it's guaranteed to be among any child's vacation highlights.

For more modern exhibits, stop by **Two Rivers Printmakers** (85 N. Main St., Ste. 160, 802/295-5901, www.tworiversprintmaking.com, open by appt.), one of the prime movers of the local art scene that regularly stages exhibits and events showcasing Upper Valley talent.

A museum of oddities as Lewis Carroll may

have invented it, the **Main Street Museum** (58 Bridge St., 802/356-2776, www.mainstreetmuseum.org, 1–6 P.M. Thurs.–Sun.) has only been around for a decade, but it takes its cues from the Wunderkammern, or "cabinets of curiosities," of Renaissance Europe, which gathered together sundry interesting and macabre artifacts from around the world to the amazement and delight of viewers. The museum's several rooms contain "a piece of wood from Strasbourg Cathedral," "an egg cup from a San Francisco Hotel in the Great Fire of 1907," "pressed poppies from Napoleon's Grave," and a thousand or so similar random artifacts ready-made to while away an afternoon. Sadly, the first floor of the museum was destroyed by water damage during Hurricane Irene in 2011. The second floor remained untouched and an enthusiastic team of volunteers has ensured the museum remains open as it rebuilds its collection.

Speaking of quirky, one of the more unusual accredited educational institutions in Vermont, the **Center for Cartoon Studies** (94 S. Main St., 802/295-3319, www.cartoonstudies.org, call for current exhibitions) bills itself as "America's only two-year cartooning program." Exhibit space on campus often showcases student work, and the school sometimes hosts visiting writers or cartoonists such as Myla Goldberg and Garry Trudeau.

Entertainment and Events

Lovers of serious theater (à la Arthur Miller's *The Price*), lighthearted productions (Terrence McNally's *The Full Monty*), and children's musicals (*Beauty and the Beast*) should investigate the ever-changing productions at **Northern Stage** (Briggs Opera House, 4 South Main St., 802/291-9009, www.northernstage.org). Considered one of the state's best, the company also stages many national and regional premieres.

Anyone with a three-year-old should take the

express train to **Glory Days of the Railroad Festival** (802/295-5036, www.vtglorydaysfestival.com, early Sept.), a one-day celebration of steamies, diesels, and engineers that brings model railroad enthusiasts young and old down to the train station museum for music and family-friendly attractions.

White River Indie Films (802/478-0191, www.wrif.org) stages a weeklong film festival each spring displaying films you won't see at your local multiplex, many made by Vermont filmmakers.

Shopping

Give your wardrobe a blast from the past at **Revolution** (26 N. Main St., 802/295-6487, www.revolutionvintage.com, 10 A.M.–7 P.M. Mon–Sat., noon–5 P.M. Sun.), modeled after urban thrift stores and packed with excellent-condition vintage-wear and creative reconstructed clothing, not to mention an espresso bar and a make-your-own T-shirt counter.

Take a love of landscapes and mix it with classic lighting and you've got **Lampscapes** (77 Gates St., 802/295-8044, www.lampscapes.com, 10 A.M.–5 P.M. Tues.–Sat.), a store filled to its brim with lamps that have been painted with one-of-a-kind designs by artist Ken Blaisdell.

Food

Laid-back and high-energy at once, **Tip Top Cafe** (85 N. Main St., 802/295-3312, www.tiptopcafevermont.com, 11:30 A.M.–2:30 P.M. and 5–9 P.M. Tues.–Sat., $7–20) is a great blend of bistro and coffeehouse. At lunchtime the sunny spot serves sandwiches and soups, and at night it brings the candlelight out alongside entrees like the house specialty, pork and ginger meatloaf.

For a dash of nightlife mixed into your supper, grab one of the coveted tables at **Elixir Restaurant and Lounge** (188 S. Main St., 802/281-7009, www.elixirrestaurant.com, 5–10 P.M. Tues.–Sat., $6–21). Along with its groovy vibe, the local hot spot doles out tasty bites like cocoa-dusted filet Mignon and delicious flatbreads piled up with garlic cream, tasso ham, radicchio, and stilton cheese.

Information and Services

For more information about White River Junction and the surrounding area, contact the **Upper Valley Chamber of Commerce** (802/295-6200, www.uppervalleychamber.com), which staffs an information booth (100 Railroad Row) at the railroad station in downtown White River Junction. WRJ has several pharmacies, including **Corner Drug** (213 Maple St., 802/295-2012). Banks clustered around the intersection of Routes U.S. 4 and 5 include **People's United Bank** (190 Maple St., 802/295-5701), **Mascoma Bank** (263 Maple St., 802/295-5456) and **Merchants Bank** (25 Ralph Lehman Dr., 802/295-2307, 9 A.M.–5 P.M. Mon.–Fri.). In emergencies, contact the **Town of Hartford police** (802/295-9425).

NORWICH AND HANOVER, NEW HAMPSHIRE

One of Vermont's oldest towns, Norwich was settled in 1765 by residents of Norwich, Connecticut, who ventured north to take advantage of the broadening New England frontier. A classic Vermont village, it is now better known as the site of two very different tourist attractions—the Montrose Museum of Science and the flagship store for King Arthur Flour.

Norwich bleeds across the river into its sister village of Hanover, founded the same year (1765) in what would later become New Hampshire. In terms of spirit, however, it's an honorary village of Vermont. Four years after the town was founded, Dartmouth College was established. Today, it's difficult to separate the two; the college is the town's main source of economy and attention, and the town is considered by the college to practically be an extension of its campus and an invaluable resource for its students (perhaps because it provides students something to do besides cow-tipping).

And indeed, there is plenty to do and see around town, from shopping to loafing around in the cafes on Main Street.

Sights

The collection at the excellent college art museum, **Hood Museum of Art** (6034 College St., Hanover, 603/646-2808, http://hoodmuseum.dartmouth.edu, 10 A.M.–5 P.M. Tues. and Thurs.–Sat., 10 A.M.–9 P.M. Wed., noon–5 P.M. Sun., free), begins with the building itself— an award-winning postmodern design by architects Charles Moore and Chad Floyd. The collection inside is like a survey course of the world's art, presenting European and American painting, sure, but also holding a particularly strong collection of art from less-familiar areas like the Near East and Africa. Among the highlights are a spectacular 9th-century bas-relief from an Assyrian palace and a collection of art from Indonesia and the South Pacific that is among the most important in the country.

An ambitious local enterprise with exhibits on wildlife, astronomy, and physics, the large **Montshire Museum of Science** (1 Montshire Rd./I-91 exit 13, Norwich, 802/649-2200, www.montshire.org, 10 A.M.–5 P.M. daily, $12 adults, $10 children 2–17, children under 2 free) is home to both a leaf-cutter ant colony and a 250-foot watercourse. Outdoors is a scale model of the solar system, along with several easy-grade nature trails.

Entertainment and Events

On campus, the **Spaulding Auditorium** (Dartmouth College, Hanover, 603/646-2422, http://hop.dartmouth.edu) at the Hopkins Center for the Arts is the place to catch plays, concerts, and dance shows put on by visiting artists as well as students.

Dartmouth's biggest event each year is **Winter Carnival** (603/646-3399, www.dartmouth.edu, early Feb.), a four-day celebration of the season with athletic (and not-so-athletic) competitions, giant snow sculptures, and hot chocolate–induced merriment.

Shopping

Go green—quite literally—with a little help from the stock at **Dartmouth Co-op** (21 S. Main St., Hanover, 800/643-2667, www.dartmouthcoop.com, 9:30 A.M.–6 P.M. Mon.–Sat., 11 A.M.–4 P.M. Sun.). Here, everything from golf hats and tote bags to sweatshirts and sleepwear comes emblazoned with the school's logo. All profits from the store go directly to the college.

Pick up everything you need to revamp your home—including design advice and services— at **C. Beston & Co.** (1 South St., Hanover, 603/653-0123, www.cbeston.com, 9:30 A.M.–5:30 P.M. Mon.–Fri., 9:30 A.M.–5 P.M. Sat.). Mostly, however, the store spotlights furnishings and accessories, from overstuffed chairs and painted benches to carved clocks and funky vases.

One could spend hours rifling through the aisles of **Left Bank Books** (9 S. Main St., Hanover, 603/643-4479, 9:30 A.M.–5:30 P.M. Mon.–Wed. and Sat., 9:30 A.M.–8 P.M. Thurs.–Fri., 11:30 A.M.–4 P.M. Sun.), which carries loads of fiction (classic and contemporary), poetry, how-tos, and kids' books. This is the place to stock up on all the books you need.

Food

Late-night cramming takes on new meaning at **Ramunto's Brick and Brew Pizzeria** (9 South St., Hanover, 603/643-9500, www.bricknbrew.com, 11 A.M.–midnight Mon.–Sat., noon–midnight Sun., $7–20), home to extra-greasy, thin-crust pies served on red-checked tablecloths. The house's special garlic or cinnamon knots are a snack beloved by students.

Head Chef Bruce MacLeod was classically trained in France and did stints all over the world before taking over the kitchen at **Carpenter & Main** (326 Main St., Norwich, 802/649-2922, www.carpenterandmain.com, 5:30–10 P.M. Wed.–Sat., 5:30–9 P.M. Sun., $11–31). His diverse background shows in the sophisticated menu, with offerings such as Moroccan lamb meatballs with spicy tomato glaze, duck confit with mustard vinaigrette, and wild bass with red pepper relish.

Snug in the corner of the Dartmouth green, the 99-seat Irish pub **Murphy's on the Green** (11 S. Main St., Hanover, 603/643-4075, http://murphysonthegreen.com, 11 A.M.–11 P.M. Mon.–Sat., 10 A.M.–10 P.M. Sun., $9–23) serves students and professors an inexpensive, better-than-average bar menu and lots of Irish-pub atmosphere. Sit in the beautiful back room (full of detailed wood wainscoting and 19th-century pews) and nosh on snacks like nachos and wings. Or, fill up on the very good Irish stew, fresh fish 'n' chips, or more wide-ranging options like fajitas.

The attractive, spot-lit dining room of **Mai Thai Cuisine** (44 S. Main St., Hanover, 603/643-9980, www.maithaicuisine.com, 11 A.M.–10 P.M. Mon.–Thurs., 11 A.M.–11 P.M. Fri.–Sat., $8–15) happily caters to both Thai-food neophytes (with well-known staples like pad Thai and spring rolls) and more adventurous eaters (with plates of *pla douk pad ped,* or catfish in spicy-sour sauce).

Information and Services

The **Hanover Area Chamber of Commerce** (603/643-3115, www.hanoverchamber.org) runs an information booth on the green. Free Wi-Fi is available at **Howe Library** (13 South St., Hanover, www.howelibrary.org, 10 A.M.–8 P.M. Mon.–Thurs., 10 A.M.–6 P.M. Fri., 10 A.M.–5 P.M. Sat., 1–5 P.M. Sun.). Pharmacies include **Eastman Pharmacy** (22 S. Main St., Hanover, 603/643-4112) and

CVS Pharmacy (79 S. Main St., Hanover, 603/643-3178, 24 hours daily, pharmacy 8 A.M.–10 P.M. Mon.–Fri., 9 A.M.–6 P.M. Sat.–Sun.). There's a **Bank of America** (63 S. Main St., Hanover, 603/643-1057) and a **Citizens Bank** (44 S. Main St., Hanover, 603/640-1150, 8:30 A.M.–5 P.M. Mon.–Fri., 9 A.M.–noon Sat.), along with a smattering of other banks with ATM machines. In an emergency, contact the **Hanover Police Department** (46 Lyme Rd., Hanover, 603/643-2222).

WINDSOR

Claiming to be no less than "the birthplace of Vermont," Windsor served as headquarters for the state militia during the time of the Revolutionary War. As the storm clouds of war swirled around Lake Champlain to the West, the leaders of New Connecticut (as the young territory was then called) gathered around a table in Elias West's tavern and hastily churned out a new state constitution based on that of Pennsylvania—with a few important changes such as abolishing slavery (the first state to do so) and granting of suffrage to men who did not hold property (though not, of course, to women). Somewhere in the course of negotiations, the delegates took the name of Vermont, a combination of the French words for "green" and "mountain"—and the rest, as they say, is history. The town center has retained its historic character, with many fine examples of Federal-style architecture well worth a stroll.

Historic Windsor Walking Tour

Windsor is justifiably proud of its place in the history of the republic, and Historic Windsor (802/674-6752, www.preservationworks.org) produces a walking tour brochure and (for those who still have portable tape players) a cassette describing the architectural and historical details of the buildings downtown.

ALONG ROUTE 4

© VERMONTVACATION.COM

Windsor-Cornish Bridge

A mandatory stop en route is **Old Constitution House** (16 N. Main St., 802/672-3773, http://historicsites.vermont.gov, 11 A.M.–5 P.M. Sat.–Sun. late May–mid-Oct., $2.50 adults, children 14 and under free), the tavern where the state constitution document was hammered out. The tavern has since been restored to its Revolutionary-era glory. A permanent exhibition looks at the state's struggle for statehood with period artifacts and decor.

Later in Windsor's history, the town took advantage of the swift-flowing Connecticut River to become a center of manufacturing. That era is preserved in the **American Precision Museum** (196 Main St., 802/674-5781, www.americanprecision.org, 10 A.M.–5 P.M. daily, late May–Oct., $7.50 adults, $4 students, children under 6 free, $19.50 family). If you've never thought about how people actually make the objects—from furniture to computer chips—that we use every day, you will after seeing the fascinating exhibits here, which include one of the world's largest collections of machine tools, as well as antique sewing machines, typewriters, rifles, and a "Machine Tool Hall of Fame" enshrining the ingenious inventors of modern manufacturing.

Windsor-Cornish Bridge

The granddaddy of Vermont covered bridges is actually in New Hampshire. That's because the state line is drawn on the *west* bank of the Connecticut River, thereby leaving all of the 450-foot Windsor-Cornish Bridge solidly on Granite State ground. No matter—the two spans over the Connecticut River are still a beaut. The longest covered bridge in the United States, it was built in 1866 on heavy spruce timber. Still open to traffic, it remains a testament to 19th-century engineering.

Events

Especially good times to visit the Harpoon

Brewery (802/674-5491, www.harpoonbrewery. com) are during the **Harpoon Championships of New England Barbecue** in late July—where you can discover how very well ale goes with ribs and grilled chicken—and **Harpoon Octoberfest** in early October, when the eponymous beer is released.

Food

The cuisines of both America and Africa sit side-by-side on the menu at **Mariam's Restaurant** (70 Main St., Windsor, 802/674-2662, www. mariamsrestaurant.com, 3–9 P.M. Mon.–Tues., 11 A.M.–9 P.M. Thurs.–Sat., $8–11), where you're as likely to find an order of chicken wings or nachos as you are plates of plantains or curried goat. There's also a nice selection of South African wines to round things off.

After filling your brain with history, fill your belly with a cold mug of New England's finest. The **Harpoon Brewery** (336 Ruth Carney Dr., 802/674-5491, www.harpoonbrewery. com, 10 A.M.–6 P.M. Sun.–Wed., 10 A.M.–9 P.M. Thurs.–Sat. May–Oct.; 10 A.M.–6 P.M. Sun. and Tues.–Wed., 10 A.M.–9 P.M. Thurs.–Sat. Nov.–Apr.) has won special acclaim for its India Pale Ale, giving Harpoon IPA a regular place on tap at most bars in New England. Just about everything the brewery makes, however, is a master in its class; other favorites are the Octoberfest and Munich Type Dark. The brewery is a bit stingy in its tastings, limiting visitors to four two-ounce samples per person. If you'd like more (and you will), you'll have to take a seat at the brewery's "beer garden," which serves sandwiches along with freshly poured pints.

Information and Services

For more information, contact the **Windsor/ Mt. Ascutney Chamber of Commerce** (802/674-5910). The regional hospital for the Upper Valley area, **Mount Ascutney Hospital and Health Center** (289 County Rd., 802/674-6711, www.mtascutneyhospital.org) handles both emergency and routine care. For pharmacy needs, turn to **Rite-Aid Pharmacy** (52 Main St., 802/674-2334). For banking needs, visit **People's United Bank** (50 N. Main St., 802/674-2131, 9 A.M.–5 P.M. Mon.–Fri.). Free public Wi-Fi is available at the **Windsor Public Library** (43 State St., 802/674-2556, http://windsorlibrary.org, 9 A.M.–8 P.M. Mon. and Wed., 9 A.M.–6 P.M. Fri., 9 A.M.–1 P.M. Sat.).

QUECHEE

As Route 4 winds its way along the Ottauquechee River into the heart of the state, it passes through a region beset by contrasts. On one hand is the natural beauty of the river, which reaches its peak at the stunning Quechee Gorge. On the other is the runaway development of condos and schlocky tourist shops of Quechee, which somewhat mars the tranquility. Even so, there is something endearing even about all the schlock, which seems more beholden to a retro era of car-touring and motor lodges than modern strip-mall development. Quechee is officially a village of the town of **Hartford,** so depending on the source you may find street addresses listed as either location.

◖ Vermont Institute of Natural Science

This museum (VINS, Rte. 4 just west of Quechee Gorge, 802/359-5000, www. vinsweb.org, 10 A.M.–4 P.M. daily Nov.–mid Apr.; 10 A.M.–5 P.M. daily mid-Apr.–mid-June; 10 A.M.–5:30 P.M. daily mid-June–Oct., $12 adults, $11 seniors, $10 children 4–17, children 3 and under free) is simple in its concept—an outdoor semicircle of cages underneath a large awning. But to call the feathery raptors inside the cages "birds" is like calling John Lennon "a musician." Over the years, VINS has made it its mission to rescue and rehabilitate birds of prey, including hawks, owls, and eagles, and display them for the education of visitors. Watching the raptors watch you is an unforgettable experience; behind the hooked beaks lie the deadly eyes of a killer. They become more accessible with the expert interpretation of the center's trained staff, who know the habits and quirks of the birds inside and out.

Try to time your visit with one of the raptor educational programs, held at 11 A.M., 1:30 P.M., and 3:30 P.M. daily, during which you can see these predators take flight. Of course, the other prime time to visit is during feedings, just before dusk. In addition to the raptor exhibits, VINS also has an hour-long interpretive nature trail and offers guided hikes into nearby Quechee Gorge.

◖ Quechee Gorge

It's not quite Vermont's answer to the Grand Canyon, no matter what some might say. And yet there's no denying that Quechee Gorge (Quechee State Park, 5800 Woodstock Rd.,

© MICHAEL BLANDING

Quechee Gorge

Hartford, 802/295-2990, www.vtstateparks. com) is a breathtaking natural wonder. Part of the appeal of the narrow, rocky canyon is the way it comes across Route 4 so suddenly, plunging 165 feet down into the Ottauquechee River racing below. The gorge was formed some 13,000 years ago, when waters from a glacial lake cut inch by inch through tough bedrock schist. While the view from the railroad bridge on the highway is spectacular, a more rewarding view can be had by taking a short hike down to the river.

◖ Simon Pearce

Town and Country readers from all over the East Coast make special trips just to buy glassware and pottery at Simon Pearce (1760 Main St., the Mill at Quechee, 802/295-2711, www.simonpearce.com, 10 A.M.–9 P.M. daily), which has crafted exquisite specimens of both for more than three decades. Located in an old mill building completely run by hydroelectric power, the studio is open to the public for demonstrations (call to confirm demonstration dates and times). In the downstairs area, potters spin Pearce's distinctive shapes, while glassblowers blow bubbles into glowing orange balls of 2,400-degree silica (the glassblowing room is a particularly popular place to spend time in winter). Also on display are pictures from the excavation of the mill pond and installation of a turbine brought from Nova Scotia in 1983. And then, of course, there are several levels where you can buy Pearce's designs yourself, including a healthy sampling of cut-rate "seconds" with minor imperfections. To find the Mill at Quechee (coming from I-89), cross Quechee Gorge and take a right at the first blinking light.

Vermont Toy & Train Museum

Just as impressive as the gorge next door, albeit in a completely different way, is this toy museum (Quechee Gorge Village, Rte.

© SIMON PEARCE

Simon Pearce

4, 802/295-1550, www.quecheegorge.com, 9:30 A.M.–5:30 P.M. daily, free), which has three complete model railroads and vintage toy train displays catering to the four-year-old in all of us. That's not the half of it, however. The real draw of this mini-museum is encapsulated in its slogan: "I had one of those!" Display after display exhibits vintage lunchboxes, dolls, robots, stuffed animals, and action figures from *Star Wars, Star Trek, Lost in Space, My Little Pony, Strawberry Shortcake,* and a dozen other galaxies you haven't inhabited in years. There's guaranteed to be at least one toy that sends you into spasms of reverie, if not a full-fledged nostalgia-fueled time warp back to an earlier, simpler time when a couple hunks of plastic and your imagination were all you needed for a great afternoon.

Events

Colored canvas lights up the sky above Quechee Gorge at the annual **Quechee Hot Air Balloon,** **Fine Arts, Craft & Music Festival** (802/295-7900, www.quecheeballoonfestival.com, June), a tradition for more than 25 years. The event features musical performances, kids' games, and—of course—rides "up, up, and away" in more than two dozen brightly colored balloons.

Shopping

Quechee's mix of high-end artisanal wares (such as Simon Pearce) and unabashedly kitschy shops (one gargantuan hall is dedicated entirely to Christmas) is an exercise in eclecticism. Highland charm pervades at **Scotland by the Yard** (8828 Woodstock Rd., Rte. 4, 802/295-5351, www.scotlandbytheyard.com, 10 A.M.–5 P.M. daily), where high-quality kilts of genuine Scottish worsted wool tartans (plus sporrans and vests to match) can be bought premade or custom-ordered. (Kilts are also sold for women and children, too.) Or pick up a few nonwearable Scottish accessories such as crests or pewter.

A full stable of country stores, antique shops, distilleries, art galleries, gift boutiques, and even a train museum are housed in **Quechee Gorge Village** (5573 East Woodstock Rd., 802/295-1550, www.quecheegorge.com, 9:30 A.M.–5:30 P.M. daily). Notably, the Vermont Antique Mall offers wall after wall of vintage glass, Civil War–era coins, and estate jewelry. With a locovore diner and Cabot Cheese shop to keep you from getting hungry while you shop, this center is a Vermont artisans' answer to the mass production of so many other malls.

Food

Dining options run as high and low (casual to quite spiffy) as the landscape around Quechee. Truly memorable meals can be found at **Simon Pearce Restaurant** (1760 Main St., 802/295-1470, www.simonpearce. com, 11:30 A.M.–5 P.M. and 6–9 P.M. Mon.–Sat., 11 A.M.–2:45 P.M. Sun., $10–24). Settle into the elegant and sunny room overlooking the rushing Ottauquechee River and its dam, and dig into plates of horseradish-crusted cod, crisp confit duck with orange sauce, and beef and Guinness stew with paprika potatoes. As part of the Simon Pearce building, the kitchen serves everything on pottery and glassware literally made downstairs.

Fans of **Firestone's** (Rte. 4 and Waterman Hill Rd., 802/295-1600, www.firestonesrestaurant.net, 11:30 A.M.–9 P.M. daily, 11:30 A.M.–10:30 P.M. Fri.–Sat., $7–23) drive all the way from Boston to enjoy the restaurant's enormous flatbread pizzas (cooked in a Canadian-style stone oven), unusually friendly atmosphere, and affable staff.

Information and Services

The racks at Quechee Gorge Village (Rte. 4, 802/295-1550, www.quecheegorge.com, 9:30 A.M.–5:30 P.M. daily) are stuffed with brochures on the town and surrounding area. For more information, contact the **Hartford Area Chamber of Commerce** (802/295-7900, www.hartfordvtchamber.com).

SPORTS AND RECREATION
Hiking and Camping

Hikers will find plenty of trails at **Ascutney State Park** (1826 Back Mountain Rd., Windsor, 802/674-2060, www.vtstateparks. com, mid-May–mid-Oct.). Two trails in particular leave from separate parking lots on Route 44 to climb the summit of 3,143-foot Mount Ascutney. The 3.2-mile Brownsville Trail makes a detour to an abandoned granite quarry, while the 2.7-mile Windsor Trail includes a small waterfall a mile into the hike. Both trails then include several viewing spots on their way up the mountain and join before the best views at the granite ledges of Brownsville Rock, a popular launching pad for both hawks and hang gliders. On the summit itself, there is also a fire tower that offers panoramic views of the surrounding mountains. Those not up for a strenuous hike can also drive up to the summit via the 3.7-mile Mount Ascutney Parkway. The park also has 49 campsites, including both tent sites and lean-tos ($16–25/night). The campsite has bathrooms and showers as well as a dump station for RVs, but no hookups. If possible, request one of the sites to the right of the entrance road, which tend to be more widely spaced and private.

West of West River Junction along Route 4, the **Quechee State Park** (5800 Woodstock Rd., Quechee, 802/295-2990, www.vtstateparks.com, late May–mid-Oct., campsites $16–27) also has some 50 campsites for overnight stays on the banks of the Ottauquechee River. The campsites here are larger, making them especially commodious to RVs. The campground also has a nice large field and play area for kids. Restrooms and showers are available, but no hookups.

Another nice day hike in the area is **Moose**

Mountain, located across the Connecticut River in Hanover. A favorite hike for Dartmouth students, the 1.7-mile trail to the 2,300-foot peak of South Moose Mountain is part of the Appalachian Trail. Several decades ago, an airplane crashed on the peak, and the summit was cleared of vegetation to facilitate helicopter landings to help clear the debris. Subsequently, a caterpillar infestation killed the remaining trees, leaving a bald and open view of downtown Hanover, Dartmouth College, and the surrounding Connecticut River Valley.

To find the trailhead, take East Wheelock Street from the Hanover green four miles to the village of Etna; turn left on Two Mile Road, right on Rudsboro Road, and left on the dirt Three Mile Road. There's a small dirt parking lot near the trailhead. The trail up to South Moose Mountain is a two-mile hike through a variety of terrain, including marshland and hemlocks. For a day hike, you can continue back down the way you came; for an overnight hike, you can proceed north another half-mile to the Moose Mountain Shelter, maintained by the **Dartmouth Outing Club** (603/646-2429, www.dartmouth.edu), which sleeps eight on a first-come, first-served basis, with a tent site for overflow. From there, a 1.5-mile loop takes you back to the parking area.

ACCOMMODATIONS
$100-150

With 30 guest rooms—each with private bathrooms, wireless Internet service, TVs, and phones, and many with queen-size or double beds—**Hotel Coolidge** (39 S. Main St., White River Junction, 802/295-3118, www.hotel-coolidge.com, $89–169) is one of the area's better deals. The hotel started as a junction house for the local railroad in the 1850s and, thanks to the decor, still retains much of that historic flavor. The hotel also dedicates one wing to a licensed youth hostel.

Ever since **Juniper Hill Inn** (153 Pembroke Rd., Windsor, 800/359-2541, www.juniperhillinn.com, $130–260) was featured on Gordon Ramsay's TV show *Hotel Hell*, it's gotten more than its share of buzz. But even though Ramsay's advice resulted in many improvements, the inn wasn't exactly falling apart before then. Built in 1902, the stately country home is a tasteful mix of four-poster beds and fireplaces with modern touches like CD players, bedside chocolates, and deep-soaking tubs.

The beautiful rooms at **The Quechee Inn at Marshland Farm** (1119 Quechee Main St., Quechee, 800/235-3133, www.quecheeinn.com, $109–259) are just part of the charm; the 18th-century farmhouse was once the home of Vermont's first lieutenant governor, Colonel Joseph Marsh. It still treats those who stay here like VIPs, with pretty, individually decorated rooms decked out with antiques, cable TV, and air-conditioning—and many with terrific views of the Ottauquechee River.

The Victorian **Norwich Inn** (325 Main St., Norwich, 802/649-1143, www.norwichinn.com, $140–230) opened in 1890 and has undergone several upgrades in the decades since. Today its 37 guest rooms and suites come stocked with all the modern necessities: TV, telephone, air conditioning, hairdryers, irons and ironing boards, and free wireless.

$150-250

Reminiscent of a Provencal estate, **Home Hill Inn** (703 River Rd., Plainfield, NH, 603/675-6165, www.homehillinn.com, $165–250) is an exquisite and romantic escape with only 12 guest rooms. Each is outfitted with tile or marble washrooms and crisp Frette linens, and many have fireplaces and private terraces. Dining in the butter-yellow dining room is a luxury indeed—dishes might include perfectly prepared organic roasted chicken, lamb loin with ratatouille, or beautiful plates of rare French cheeses.

ALONG ROUTE 4

Over $250

Facing the Dartmouth College green, **The Hanover Inn** (2 S. Main St., Hanover, 603/643-4300, www.hanoverinn.com, $259–309) is a study in country elegance: Guest rooms are furnished with handmade quilts and wingback chairs, the common areas have been recently renovated, and there are two acclaimed restaurants—the Daniel Webster Room (a crystal-laden fine dining room) and Zins (a warmly appointed, bustling wine bistro).

GETTING THERE AND AROUND

To drive to White River Junction from Boston, take I-93 to I-89. After crossing the Vermont border, take I-91 north to exit 11 (2 hrs. total). For Norwich and Hanover, take I-91 north from WRJ to exit 13 (5 mi., 10 min.). For Windsor, take I-91 south to exit 9, then Route 5 south (12 mi., 20 min.). For Quechee, head west on Route 4 (8 mi., 12 min.).

Amtrak (800/872-7245, www.amtrak.com) runs its Vermonter Service to White River Junction (100 Railroad Row) and Windsor (26 Depot Ave.). In summer months, the White River Flyer (800/707-3530, www.rails-vt.com) offers a round-trip train from WRJ to the Montshire Museum in Norwich.

Advance Transit (802/295-1824, www.advancetransit.com) runs regular free bus service around White River Junction, Norwich, Hanover, and Quechee. **Connecticut River Transit** (802/885-5165, www.crtransit.org) offers bus service between WRJ and Windsor.

Woodstock

Right off the bat, Woodstock looks different from most of the quaint villages in southern Vermont. The scale is grander, the houses more stately, and the downtown buildings more self-important. That's partly because shortly after the town was founded in 1765, it became the shire town for the county surrounding it, drawing a professional class of lawyers, doctors, teachers, and businesspeople who brought wealth and culture with them. Today, the town embodies both country-cute and upscale refinement, with an unparalleled village green surrounded by Victorian homes and a collection of upscale shops and galleries. Here, the restaurants all sport linen (or adorably retro marble tables), the inns all have bath amenities worth snagging, and the artists all have city agents. Even the year-round residents in Woodstock are usually ex-Manhattan performance artists or creative types who've come to live their lifelong dream of opening a patisserie, antiques shop, or country B&B.

Almost from its beginnings, the town has been a favorite tourist destination for visitors from Massachusetts and Connecticut. In 1793, Captain Israel Richardson built a tavern on the town green to serve the traffic from the stagecoach that passed through from Boston to Canada. That site is now occupied by the Woodstock Inn, which was founded in the 19th century to serve the growing tourist traffic from the railroad. In 1934, the first rope tow was installed on a pasture at the north end of town, ushering in a new era of winter sports for the moneyed set. That area survives as the modest ski area Suicide Six. Woodstock is also a good place to get in touch with Vermont's agricultural side, with a farm museum and cheesemaker in town.

SIGHTS
Billings Farm & Museum

Woodstock's most successful native son was Frederick Billings, a Vermonter who made it big

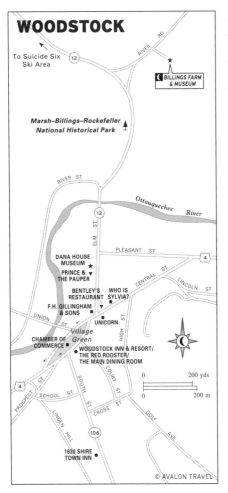

WOODSTOCK

To Suicide Six
Ski Area

RIVER RD

★ BILLINGS FARM
& MUSEUM

Marsh–Billings–Rockefeller
National Historical Park

RIVER ST

Ottauquechee River

ELM ST

PLEASANT ST

DANA HOUSE
MUSEUM ★
PRINCE &
THE PAUPER

BENTLEY'S   WHO IS
RESTAURANT   SYLVIA?

CENTRAL ST

LINCOLN ST

F.H. GILLINGHAM
& SONS

UNION ST

UNICORN

Village
Green

HIGH ST

CHAMBER OF
COMMERCE ■

WOODSTOCK INN & RESORT/
THE RED ROOSTER/
THE MAIN DINING ROOM

COURT ST

4

PROSPECT ST

SCHOOL ST

SOUTH ST

CROSS ST

GOLF AVE

LINDEN HILL

106

1830 SHIRE
TOWN INN ●

0   200 yds
0   200 m

© AVALON TRAVEL

ALONG ROUTE 4

$11 seniors, $6 children 5–15, $3 children 3–4, children under 3 free) afford visitors a chance to meet the descendants of those Jersey cows, who still produce milk in a working dairy farm. Exhibits and demonstrations explore typical Vermont farm life, including a period 19th-century farmhouse.

Next door, **Marsh-Billings-Rockefeller National Historical Park** (54 Elm St., 802/457-3368, www.nps.gov/mabi, late May–Oct., $8 adults, $4 seniors, children 15 and under free) is home to the mansion built by natural philosopher Charles Marsh during 1805–1807 and bought by Billings in 1861. The mansion, open for tours by advance reservation, has a Tiffany stained-glass window and an extensive collection of American landscape paintings. In 1934, Billings's granddaughter married Laurance Rockefeller and eventually donated the land to the National Park Service. Combination tickets ($17 adults, $15 youth 16–17, $13 seniors, May and October) include two-day admission to both Billings Farm and Marsh-Billings-Rockefeller National Historical Park.

Sugarbush Farm

More cows and other farm animals can be found at Sugarbush Farm (591 Sugarbush Farm Rd., 802/457-1757, www.sugarbushfarm.com, 8 A.M.–5 P.M. Mon.–Fri., 9 A.M.–5 P.M. Sat.–Sun.), which produces some of the best cheddar cheeses in Vermont. Set atop a scenic hilltop, the farm also produces maple syrup, mustards, and jams—all of which are free to sample. (Take a right across the covered bridge at the small village of Taftsville and follow the signs to the farm—call ahead for road conditions in winter and early spring.)

Dana House Museum

For a glimpse into Woodstock's nonagricultural past, visit the Dana House Museum (26 Elm St., 802/457-1822, www.woodstockhistorical. org, 1–5 P.M. Tues.–Sat., 11 A.M.–3 P.M. Sun.

as a lawyer in San Francisco during the Gold Rush. In the 1870s he returned to Woodstock determined to save the town's dying industry of dairy farming. He established a farm with cattle imported from the British isle of Jersey, putting into practice the most scientific practices of land management.

Today, the grounds of his farm (53 Elm St., 802/457-2355, www.billingsfarm.org, 10 A.M.–5 P.M. daily May–Oct., 10 A.M.–3:30 P.M. Sat.–Sun. Nov.–Feb., $12 adults,

the mansion at Marsh-Billings-Rockefeller National Historic Park

© MICHAEL BLANDING

June–late Oct., donations accepted), a Federal-style home once owned by a prosperous local dry goods merchant. Now a museum run by the Woodstock Historical Society, it contains period rooms full of fine china, antique furniture, kitchen instruments, and children's toys.

Thistle Hill Farm

For a taste of one of New England's most delicious organic cheeses, go straight to the source: Thistle Hill Farm (107 Clifford Rd., 802/457-9349, www.thistlehillfarm.org, hours vary). There they make the prize-winning Tarentaise, an aged, alpine raw-milk cheese, in copper vats in a cheese house just up the hill from the dairy barn. Visits are available by appointment, or you can just stop by to purchase their cheese.

Long Trail Brewing Company

Leave it to a Vermont brewery to pioneer "eco-brewing." Near Woodstock, the Long Trail Brewing Company (Rte. 4 and Rte. 100A,

Bridgewater Corners, 802/672-5011, www.longtrail.com, 10 A.M.–7 P.M. daily, free) uses heat capture, water treatment, and other green methods to reduce its footprint on the landscape—to the point of even feeding spent mash to Vermont dairy cows. You can learn about these innovations and sample its trademark Long Trail Ale and popular Blackbeary Wheat at the brewery's visitors center, along with samples of the new Brewmasters' series of rich-tasting, high-alcohol-content specialty beers.

EVENTS

Billings Farm sponsors many special events throughout the summer, including **Cow Appreciation Day** every July, which includes a judging of the Jerseys, ice cream and butter making, and (always gripping) dairy trivia, as well as a Harvest celebration in October with husking competitions and cider pressing. In August, the oh-so-modestly named **World's Greatest Book Sale and International Food**

downtown Woodstock

Fair brings rare and first-edition books alongside worldwide cuisine to the green.

SHOPPING
Downtown Woodstock

Billing itself as Vermont's oldest general store, **F. H. Gillingham & Sons** (16 Elm St., 802/457-2100, www.gillinghams.com, 8:30 A.M.–5 P.M. Mon.–Sat., 10 A.M.–4 P.M. Sun., seasonal hours may vary), founded in 1886, certainly looks the part: it's packed with locally made syrups, cheeses, and pottery, alongside more conventional grocery items. The eclectic **Unicorn** (15 Central St., 802/457-2480, www.unicornvt.com, 9:30 A.M.–5:30 P.M. Mon.–Fri., 9:30 A.M.–6 P.M. Sat., 10:30 A.M.–5 P.M. Sun.) specializes in bizarre and unusual gifts, from wooden kinetic sculptures to remote-controlled whoopee cushions.

Not your average vintage store, **Who Is Sylvia?** (26 Central St., 802/457-1110, 11 A.M.–5 P.M. Mon.–Tues., 10 A.M.–6 P.M. Thurs.–Sun.) stocks flapper dresses, pillbox hats, brocade jackets, and other hard-to-find items dating back more than a century. First among Woodstock's many galleries, the **Gallery on the Green** (1 The Green, 802/457-4956, www.galleryonthegreen.com, 10 A.M.–5 P.M. Mon., noon–5 P.M. Tues.–Thurs., noon–6 P.M. Fri., 10 A.M.–6 P.M. Sat., 10 A.M.–4 P.M. Sun.) showcases paintings and sculptures of local and visiting artists.

Bridgewater Mill Mall

On Route 4 between Woodstock and Killington is Vermont's version of a shopping mall. Don't expect to find Sears or Old Navy here—the three-story woolen mill, which opened in 1973, is filled with studio space for artisans and craftspeople. For example, a distant relation of Antarctic explorer Ernest Shackleton, Charles Shackleton, crafts simple but elegant Shaker and modern-style furniture at **Shackleton Thomas** (802/672-5175,

© THE WOODSTOCK INN & RESORT

A chef plates the first course at the Red Rooster, located in the Woodstock Inn & Resort.

www.shackletonthomas.com, 10 A.M.–5 P.M. Mon.–Sat., 11 A.M.–4 P.M. Sun.). President Clinton once commissioned him to fashion a "peace bowl" to present to the pope. Shackleton's partner, Miranda Thomas, complements his work with fired pottery lamps and bowls hand-carved with animal designs.

FOOD

The food may be fresh, but the ambience at **Bentley's Restaurant** (3 Elm St., 802/457-3232, www.bentleysrestaurant.com, 11:30 A.M.–9:30 P.M. Mon.–Thurs., 11:30 A.M.–10 P.M. Fri.–Sat., 11 A.M.–9:30 P.M. Sun., $10–27) is charmingly (and authentically) old. The casual gleaming bar brims with tassled lamps, velvet couches, palm fronds, and brocade bar stools, while the kitchen churns out hearty comfort foods like maple mustard chicken and linguine with seafood.

Sedate and sophisticated, **Prince & The Pauper** (24 Elm St., 802/457-1818, www.princeandpauper.com, 5–9 P.M. daily, $18–49) serves high-concept cosmopolitan dishes (don't miss the restaurant's signature Carre d'Agneau Royale) in a candlelit country setting—think high-backed wooden booths, exposed beams, and local art for sale on the wall. It's an ideal date setting, though it also successfully caters to families and groups.

Break out the dry cleaning for breakfast and lunch at **The Main Dining Room** (14 The Green, 800/448-7900, www.woodstockinn.com, $24–35) at the Woodstock Inn. The subtly grand space is where to find lovelies such as scallops with truffle vinaigrette followed by Grand Marnier soufflé glacé—not to mention a flat-out scrumptious (and epic) Sunday brunch.

Housed in the Woodstock Inn & Resort is the casually elegant **Red Rooster** (14 The Green, 800/448-7900, www.woodstockinn.com, 7 A.M.–10:30 P.M., noon–3 P.M., 5–9 P.M. daily, $24–35). The space was redesigned by New York designer Peter Guzy and features natural larch-wood walls that wrap around from floor to ceiling. A bubbling fountain in the center of the dining room reflects light from the skylight above. The food is also about relaxed refinement, thanks to creations such as grilled rib-eye with crab hash.

SPORTS AND RECREATION
Hiking

In addition to the exhibits at **Marsh-Billings-Rockefeller National Historical Park** (54 Elm St., 802/457-3368, www.nps.gov/mabi, 10 A.M.–5 P.M. daily late May–Oct. 31, $8 adults, $4 seniors, children 15 and under free), the preserve has 20 miles of carriage roads for walking, accessible from the park entrance on Route 12 and a parking lot on Prosper Road. The roads circle around the slopes of Mount Tom, which is forested with old-growth hemlock, beech, and sugar maples. Popular hikes include the loop around the mountain pond called the Pogue and the climb up the summit of Mount Tom, which lords over Woodstock and the river below. No mountain bicycles are allowed on the trails; in the winter, they are groomed for cross-country skiing.

Skiing

While it will never be confused with Vermont's larger ski resorts, **Suicide Six Ski Area** (802/457-6661, www.suicide6.com, lifts operate 9 A.M.–4 P.M. daily, $43–64 adults, $30–59 children) has two dozen or so trails ranging from beginner to double diamond. Now owned and operated by the Woodstock Inn, the resort has a double chairlift and a beginner's area with a J-bar lift. Guests of the Woodstock Inn ski for free on weekdays. Also affiliated with the inn, the **Woodstock Inn & Resort's Nordic Center** (Rte. 106/Cross St., 802/457-6674, www.woodstockinn.com, $18 adult, $12 child) has one of the best networks of cross-country-skiing trails in Vermont. More than 30 miles of trails marked easy, intermediate, and advanced weave up and around Woodstock's two mountains, Mount Tom and Mount Peg. The center also grooms trails for snowshoeing and winter hiking, and has skis and snowshoes for rent ($15 per person per day).

ACCOMMODATIONS

With the ambient cuteness quotient as high as it is in these parts, it should come as no shock to find so many well-kept inns and bed-and-breakfasts operating here. Prices tend to be a bit higher than in other areas, but then again, so are the service and settings.

Under $100

Bonus points for correctly spelling the **Ottauquechee Motor Lodge** (529 Rte. 4, 802/672-3404, www.ottauquechee.com, $59–160), which offers motel accommodations on a quiet stretch of Route 4 between Woodstock

and Bridgewater. The lodge is a cut above most motor lodges, with king-size beds and in-room refrigerators. And there's an added draw: the views of the surrounding mountains to the south.

$100-150

An 1830s farmhouse listed on the National Register, **The 1830 Shire Town Inn** (31 South St., 802/457-1830, www.1830shiretowninn.com, $85–160) offers an arguably perfect location for exploring Woodstock; the town's green is but a stone's throw from its white-picket-fenced facade, yet it's nestled on a quiet side street away from the bustle. Inside, the simple but well-kept rooms sport beamed ceilings and colorful quilts, and some have private porches. Breakfasts are individually prepared, homemade, and extra large.

$150-250

The present building of the **Woodstock Inn & Resort** (14 The Green, 802/457-1100 or 800/448-7900, www.woodstockinn.com, $235–620) dates from only 1892, but since 1793 the site it inhabits has been catering to tourists, who come as much for the recreational offerings as its 142 luxurious rooms. In summer, the property offers golf and tennis, while winter brings downhill and cross-country skiing. (And year-round, there's always the sparkling new 41,000-square-foot health and fitness center, complete with indoor pool, sauna, yoga room, and squash courts.) Recuperate afterwards next to the fireplace in your room (many, though not all, have them) or over afternoon tea in the alcove. Meals (particularly brunch) in the refined Main Dining Room are an epic and memorable affair.

Over $250

Ten miles outside of Woodstock, **Twin Farms** (Off Stage Rd., Barnard, 800/894-6327, www.twinfarms.com, $1,300–3,000) is an exquisite

ALONG ROUTE 4

© THE WOODSTOCK INN & RESORT

the Woodstock Inn & Resort

and ultra-romantic resort filled with seemingly every luxury you could ever need—and the individually outfitted rooms (with four-poster beds and fireplaces, whirlpool tubs, rare woods, museum art, and pastoral views) are just the beginning. The property caters to your every whim throughout the day, with everything from fresh-squeezed juices and on-property fly-fishing to salt body scrubs and a 26,000-bottle wine cellar. Note that the inn does not welcome children.

INFORMATION AND SERVICES

The **Woodstock Area Chamber of Commerce** (888/469-6378, www.woodstockvt.com) runs a welcome center (3 Mechanic St., 802/432-1100, 9 A.M.–5 P.M. daily) and an information booth (on the green). The well-stocked, independent **Woodstock Pharmacy** (19 Central St., 802/457-1306) is conveniently located in the center of town, as are the ATM machines at **People's United Bank** (2 The Green, 802/457-2660) and **Citizens Bank** (431 Woodstock Rd., 802/457-3666, 9 A.M.–5 P.M. Mon.–Fri.). The **Woodbridge Coffeehouse** (4374 Woodstock Rd. Rte. 4, 802/332-6075, www.woodbridgecoffeehouse.com) offers free Wi-Fi along with a selection of baked goods, sandwiches, and espresso drinks. In an emergency, contact the **Woodstock Police** (454 Rte. 4, 802/457-1420).

GETTING THERE

To get to Woodstock from Boston, take I-93 to Concord (70 mi., 1 hr. 15 min.), then I-89 to White River Junction (70 mi., 1 hr. 15 min.), before exiting onto Route 4 west for another 10 miles (20 min.). The total trip from Boston to Woodstock is about 150 miles (2 hr. 45 min.).

Killington

As Route 4 heads west, it climbs out of the Ottauquechee Valley and into the Green Mountains, where it skirts some of the highest peaks in the state—notably the downhill skiing empire known as Killington Resort. Long the most popular ski resort in the East, the mountain has more than enough terrain to challenge most skiers for a week. The peak of Mount Killington has always fascinated people. In 1763, Reverend Samuel Peters climbed to its summit and christened the area around it Verde-Mont after the lush green mountains all around. Its history as a resort, however, started in the 1950s, when 25-year-old entrepreneur Preston Lee Smith identified the mountain's location and amazing views (which reach to Maine on a clear day) as the perfect spot to realize his dream for a skiing empire. Opening Killington in 1958, Smith expanded ambitiously, opening lift after lift on neighboring peaks and making it one of the first mountains to install snow-making equipment to extend the season. (It's still known as the first resort to open and last to close each year.)

In subsequent years, Killington became a leader in the conglomeration that consumed many of the resorts in New England. The mountain's size and popularity led to runaway development on its flank—with the long, twisting Killington Road now a very un-Vermont stretch of hotels, restaurants, and nightclubs extending up to the summit. For some, it's a welcome bit of civilization (and fun) in the midst of the too-cutesy towns around it; for others it's a garish display better off in New Hampshire (which might explain why some Killington residents actually voted to secede from Vermont a few years ago and join its neighboring state to the east). In recent years, Killington has become more and more crowded, giving it the nickname "Beast of the East" in some circles. For the sheer difficulty and exhilaration of its terrain, however, it is arguably without equal east of the Rockies (only Sugarloaf in Maine compares), leading skiers to return year after year to test themselves on its slopes.

◖ KILLINGTON RESORT

The mountain that gives Killington its name is only one of six peaks that make up this massive ski resort (4763 Killington Rd., 800/621-6867, www.killington.com, $49–79 adults, $42–67 youth 13–18 and seniors, $34–55 youth 7–12), which together boast more than 200 trails. The main event is still Killington Peak, where most of the toughest trails start their descent. The peak is accessible from the express gondola from the K-1 Lodge at the top of Killington Road.

Quicker and more comfortable is the heated Skyeship gondola, which leaves from a base on Route 4 and whisks skiers up to the top of Skye Peak in 12 minutes. While that peak doesn't have the challenges of the main peak, it gives a longer ride down to the base. Popular with expert skiers, Bear Mountain is a steep peak loaded with double diamonds, including several tough glade-skiing trails.

Physically separate from Killington, the co-owned **Pico Mountain** (Rte. 4, 2 mi. west of Killington Rd., 866/667-7426, www.pico-mountain.com, $49–65 adults, $42–55 youth 13–18 and seniors, $34–46 children 7–12) is a quieter and less-crowded mountain with 50-some trails and a family-friendly reputation. On a busy weekend, however, both Killington and Pico get swamped—expect long waits in the lift lines and cattle herds in the cafeterias.

As might be expected, skiing is only the beginning of offerings at the resort, which

COURTESY OF KILLINGTON RESORT

snowboarding in Killington

stays open for outdoor recreation year-round. **Killington Snowmobile Tours** (802/422-2121, www.snowmobilevermont.com) offers one-hour gentle rides along groomed ski trails ($94 single/$119 double), as well as a more challenging two-hour backcountry ride through Calvin Coolidge State Forest ($149/$195). **Killington Snowshoe Tours** (800/767-7031, www.customtoursinc.com/killingtonsnowshoetours.htm) leads custom-designed backcountry tours for both beginners and advanced snowshoers.

In the summer months, Killington is famed for mountain biking on trails served by the same lifts that carry skiers in the winter. In fact, the resort produces a mountain biking map for its 45 miles of trails. Trail access is $30 for adults; a $65 pass is good for two days of trail access and unlimited rides on the lifts. The resort also rents bikes for use on its trails ($70 adult/day).

ENTERTAINMENT AND EVENTS

There's plenty to do around the slopes after the sun sets—provided your idea of fun revolves primarily around bars and clubs. One such example is **Outback Pizza/Tabu Nightclub** (2841 Killington Rd., 802/422-9885, http://outbackpizza.com, 5–10 P.M. Mon.–Thurs. and Sun., 5 P.M.–1 A.M. Fri.–Sat. in summer; opens at 3 P.M. in winter, $15–19), a convivial multi-level complex that's a bit like spring break in the mountains. Live bands (Thurs.–Sat. in winter) play from a stage in back, while guests crowd the tiny dance floor up front.

Meanwhile, 20-somethings looking to party, families, and snowboarders alike crowd **Pickle Barrel Night Club** (1741 Killington Rd., 802/422-3035, www.picklebarrelnightclub.com, Thurs.–Sun. Nov.–Apr.) for live concerts put on by bands from near and far, pub grub, and high-octane cocktails.

A popular dining spot by day, **Charity's** (8 Killington Rd., 802/422-3800) turns into a fun-but-genteel watering hole by night. Appointed with Tiffany-esque stained-glass pieces, its focal point is a central bar built in Italy in the 19th century and shipped to Killington three decades ago. Another popular retro spot is **Wally's** (2841 Killington Rd., 802/422-3177), which sports a chile pepper motif throughout its decor and in parts of its menu. Wally's most dedicated crowd isn't there to eat though, but rather to drink and socialize—mostly thanks to the friendliness of the bar staff.

Every summer, the hills are alive with the sounds of you-know-what, when the **Killington Music Festival** (802/773-4003, www.killingtonmusicfestival.org) stages its "Music in the Mountain" chamber-music concerts. The weekend after Labor Day, 1,000 motorcyclists invade town for the **Killington Classic Motorcycle Touring Rally** (518/798-7888, www.killingtonclassic.com). Events include a cycle rodeo and bike judging.

The **Killington Foliage Weekend** and **Brew Festival** (802/422-6237, www.killington.com) overlap in the town center and on the local slopes every year, getting underway in late September and early October. Family activities, from hayrides to gondola tours, are a highlight, as are the handcrafted brews served.

SHOPPING

This is ski country, say most visitors, not shopping country. And to that end, most of the retail you'll find is geared toward just that—gear. Ski shops are found at the base of every resort, but one of the best off-mountain is **Northern Ski Works** (2089 Killington Rd., next to the Wobbly Barn, 802/422-9675, www.northernski.com, 9 A.M.–6 P.M. daily, closed May–Sept.). It's where to head for all manner of equipment, from snowshoes and helmets to boards and, of course, skis.

Pick up crafty gifts, foods like jams, and moccasins at **Bill's Country Store** (2319 Rte. 4, 802/773-9313, www.billscountrystore.com, 8 A.M.–7 P.M. Mon.–Sat., 10 A.M.–5 P.M. Sun.).

FOOD

Most Killington eateries are about fast food—not junk food, mind you, but rather turning tables over as fast as possible to accommodate the hordes that fill their doorways every night. During ski season, go early or prepare yourself for a long wait for a table. Such is the case at **The Garlic** (1724 Killington Rd., 802/422-5055, 5–10 P.M. Mon.–Fri., 4–10 P.M. Sat.–Sun., $10–30), where you can literally smell the namesake ingredient before you even open the door. Cozy with dim lighting, the dining room is filled with the comforting scent of marinara sauce—not surprising, as freshly made pastas are a specialty. (Also don't miss the osso buco and saltimbocca.)

For hearty après-ski comfort foods, make your way to **Casey's Caboose** (2841 Killington Rd., 802/422-3795, www.killingtonsbest.com, 5–11 P.M. daily, $14–21), where house specialties like salmon with potatoes and spinach in cream sauce and banana chocolate cake fly from kitchen to table.

Billing itself first and foremost a rotisserie, **Choices** (2820 Killington Rd., 802/422-4030, www.choices-restaurant.com, 5–10 P.M. Sun.–Thurs., 5–11 P.M. Fri.–Sat., $17–24) is home to quite a few choices, in fact. There's a daily rotisserie special (meat as well as poultry), plus everything from Cajun fettuccine to chicken *marsala.*

SPORTS AND RECREATION
Hiking and Camping

In addition to the hiking trails at Killington, a popular short trek is the one up to the scenic overlook on Deer Leap Mountain, located in **Gifford Woods State Park** (34 Gifford Woods

AND EVERYTHING NICE...

Breakfast fiends come from all over to dig into the groaning platters of truly excellent pancakes cooked up at **Sugar and Spice** (Rte. 4, Mendon, 802/773-7832, www.vtsugarandspice.com, 7 A.M.-2 P.M. daily, $6-11), a working sugar shack turned restaurant. Feather-light and studded with juicy blueberries, the specialties are a thing worthy of addiction—especially under a pour of the house-made maple syrup. In fact, during sugar season waitstaff will draw off hot syrup right from the evaporation tank and bring it directly to your table upon request. And this may be the only breakfast spot where artificial syrup costs extra.

Rd., 802/775-5354, www.vtstateparks.com). The trail starts behind the Inn at Long Trail on Route 4 and is two miles round-trip to fantastic views of Pico Peak and Killington Mountain. Alternatively, you can hike the four-mile round trip from the state park campground, which also has 4 cabins, 22 tent sites, and 20 lean-tos for overnights (campsites $16–27/night, cabins $46–48/night). The northern tent loop is much more secluded than the southern. Several "prime" lean-tos are especially secluded in a hardwood old-growth forest of giant sugar maple, white ash, and beech trees. The best old-growth stand, however, is across the street from the campground. Between the entrance and the northern tent loop, a short interpretive trail leads hikers among the giants and explains the natural and human history of the area.

ACCOMMODATIONS

Sleeping comfortably without breaking the bank isn't always easy during ski season; in general, the closer you get to Rutland, the better value you get. Killington teems with less-expensive motels tailor-built to keep rowdy skiers happy, as well as larger resorts close to the slopes that can run into the hundreds of dollars per night. As with most ski areas, prices drop considerably in the off-season.

Under $100

Offering an outdoor pool, indoor hot tub, and mountain views, the **Edelweiss Inn** (119 Rte. 4, 802/775-5577, www.killington-lodge.com, $60–100) is close to both Killington and Pico Mountain, and offers an excellent price for its amenities.

$100-150

Several generations of Saint Bernards have greeted guests at the **Summit Lodge** (200 Summit Rd., off Killington Rd., 800/635-6343, www.summitlodgevermont.com, $80–250), which is as famous for its canine companions as it is for its friendly staff. Even though the lodge is only a few minutes away from Killington Resort, its position at the top of a steep hill makes it feel secluded. Rooms are nothing fancy but are quiet and clean, with friendly service. (There's also a pool and reading room for extra relaxation.) One caveat—rates here vary dramatically throughout the season. The same room can be $80 in summer, $150 in foliage season, and $250 in the height of ski season. Study the website carefully to get the best deal.

$150-250

If you're searching for a romantic spot seconds away from the base lodge, **Inn of the Six Mountains** (2617 Killington Rd., 802/422-4302, www.sixmountains.com, $159–239) is a good compromise. Still more convenient, the property offers ski lockers outside to keep all your gear perfectly safe.

Eleven miles north of Killington, **The Mountain Top Inn & Resort** (195 Mountain Top Rd., Chittenden, 802/483-2311 or 800/445-2100, www.mountaintopinn.com,

$170–545) sits in what was once the barn for a historic turnip farm. Since then, it has been renovated many times over as an inn (it played host to President Eisenhower in the 1950s). A year-round destination resort, Mountain Top offers everything from horseback riding and hiking trails to rustic-but-refined rooms with private balconies, vaulted ceilings, and fireplaces. Among the top amenities, however, has to be a meal in the inn's Dining Room, which is dedicated to serving local ingredients and supporting local farms.

INFORMATION AND SERVICES
The **Killington Chamber of Commerce** (2026 Rte. 4, 802/773-4181, www.killingtonchamber.com) operates a visitor information center at the intersection of Route 4 and Killington Road. Near the same intersection is a branch of **Lake Sunapee Bank** (1995 Rte. 4, 802/773-2581). Additional ATM machines are available at **Merchants Bank** (286 Rte. 7 S., Rutland, 802/747-5000, 9 A.M.–5 P.M. Mon.–Thurs., 9 A.M.–6 P.M. Fri.) as well as at Killington Resort's base lodge.

GETTING THERE AND AROUND
Killington is a 20-mile (30-min.) drive down Route 4 from Woodstock. For such a popular destination, public transport options are limited. It's possible to schedule pickup service with **Killington Transportation** (802/770-3977) from Rutland or White River Junction. Within Killington, the resort offers shuttle bus service between the various base lodges and nearby lodging.

Rutland and Vicinity

Vermont's second-largest city is tucked into the valley between the Green Mountains and the Taconic Range, gracing it with a scenic horizon of purple peaks in whichever direction you look. Unfortunately, Rutland's industrial outskirts aren't quite so scenic. The city's brief Golden Age occurred in the mid-19th century with the exploitation of the milky-white marble deposits found along the Taconics from Manchester to Middlebury. The marble, in demand in civic buildings in New York, Washington, and other cities around the world, quickly made Rutland very rich indeed. Since then, it has struggled to reinvent itself as a tourist destination, touting the nearby ski resorts, the grand historic buildings in the downtown area (many of them, not surprisingly, built with native marble), and tourist attractions scattered throughout the valley.

RUTLAND
Rutland's downtown area, known as Merchants Row, was once one of the busiest commercial streets in the country, and Victorian houses of the marble barons sprang up on the hills around town. Rutland also became an early example of multiculturalism, as Italian, Irish, and French-Canadian workers poured into the region to work in the quarries. The city slowly declined after the Civil War, and as other sources of marble became available; the last quarries closed sadly in the mid-1990s, costing the city many jobs. While that heyday is now long gone, the city does provide a budget home base for exploring the surrounding attractions and mountains. The city is also still more of a melting pot than the rest of the state—though it will never be mistaken for Brooklyn.

Sights
For 15 years, pop artist Norman Rockwell lived

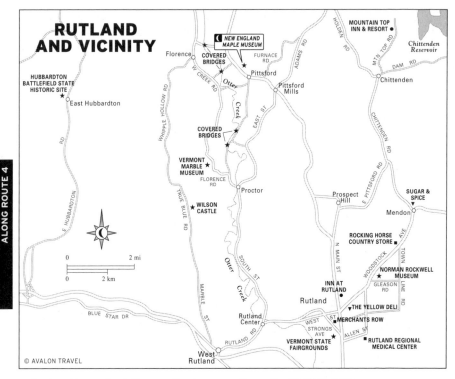

and painted in nearby Arlington. On the eastern outskirts of Rutland, the small **Norman Rockwell Museum** (654 Rte. 4, 802/773-6095, www.normanrockwellvt.com, 9 A.M.–4 P.M. daily, $6.50 adults, $6 seniors, $2.50 8–17, children under 8 free), located just across the Rutland city line on Route 4, doesn't contain any original work by the artist. It does, however, present an impressive overview of his career via several thousand original magazine covers, books, and reproductions—from Rockwell's beginnings in the 1910s as art editor of *Boys' Life* magazine to the illustration of Johnny Carson he made for *TV Guide* shortly before his death in 1978. A sizable gift shop has both original covers and reproduction posters.

Entertainment and Events

Once upon a time, the **Paramount Theatre** (30 Center St., 802/775-0570, www.paramountvt. org) drew top names such as Harry Houdini, Groucho Marx, and Sarah Bernhardt. Restored to its 19th-century splendor, the theater now hosts musical performers from Branford Marsalis to "Weird" Al Yankovic as well as touring musicals and national comics.

For 10 days every September, the **Vermont State Fair** (175 S. Main St., 802/775-5200, www.vermontstatefair.net, $4–10 adults, $4–5 seniors, $3–4 children 6–12, children under 6 free) lights up the Vermont sky with a Ferris wheel and other nausea-inducing midway rides and hosts the state's premier agricultural competitions. One recent fair included the state championship demolition derby, equestrian harness races, and musical performances by country legends Randy Travis and Charlie Daniels. Throughout the

© MARCIO SILVA/DREAMSTIME.COM

Christmastime in downtown Rutland

year, the fairgrounds play host to other agricultural and musical events.

Shopping

Get your country store fix along Route 4 and in Rutland Center, where a number of stores peddling handmade crafts, toys, and memorabilia are clustered. Start at **Rocking Horse Country Store** (Rte. 4 E., 802/773-7882, 9 A.M.–6 P.M. daily), which is chock-full of the state's requisite cheese and maple products, plus T-shirts, postcards, and Vermont cookbooks and other books on Vermont culture. Speaking of rocking horses, Santa's workshop has nothing on **Michael's Toy Company** (64 Merchants Row, 802/773-3765, www.michaelstoys.com, 9 A.M.–5 P.M. Mon.–Fri., 9 A.M.–4 P.M. Sat.), a trip back to the Norman Rockwell era with wooden rocking horses (and rocking cows) and other decidedly non-plastic toys. The proprietor also makes custom-carved signs and even serves ice cream for the kids.

Stock up for all seasons at **Mr. Twitters Garden and Gift Emporium** (24 McKinley Ave., 800/924-8948, www.mrtwitters.com, 9:30 A.M.–5:30 P.M. Mon.–Fri., 9 A.M.–4 P.M. Sat., 9 A.M.–3 P.M. Sun.), a hodgepodge of hand-painted birdhouses, wind chimes, garden statues, homemade potpourri, seeds, bulbs, and garden implements to tend your own plot.

In most states, malls are hardly a rarity you need to seek out. In Vermont, they are. So should you need staples from Kmart or Sears, be aware that both anchor the **Diamond Run Mall Place** (46 Diamond Run Mall Pl., 802/773-1145, www.diamondrunmall.com, 10 A.M.–9 P.M. Mon.–Sat., 11 A.M.–5 P.M. Sun., holiday season hours may vary), alongside other mall standards like American Eagle, Victoria's Secret, and Old Navy.

Food

Hearty fare served with ceremony is what you can expect at **Three Tomatoes Trattoria** (88

Merchants Row, 802/747-7747, www.threetomatoestrattoria.com, 5–9 P.M. Sun.–Thurs., 5–10 P.M. Fri.–Sat., $13–18). The stylish spot's open kitchen churns out gourmet pizzas from a wood-fired oven, alongside pastas and seafood dishes. Diners, meanwhile, can relax at their white-linen tables among miniature topiary.

Simple and organic fare is the lure at **The Yellow Deli** (23 Center St., 802/775-9800, www.yellowdeli.com, open 24 hours 5 P.M. Sun. to 3 P.M. Fri., $5–8). Part cafe and juice bar, part hostel foyer, The Yellow Deli serves homemade soups, great salads, and sandwiches, plus fresh mate drinks. Note that it is closed on weekends.

It's pretty much a party every night at **Little Harry's** (121 West St., 802/747-4848, www.littleharrys.com, 5–10 P.M. daily, $5–8). Customers line up to sup on pork loin with peach chutney and many swear by the duck glazed with sweet-and-sour garlic sauce. The high-energy bar scene, swift-moving staff, and commendable mix of people keep things going until closing.

Taking farm-to-table dining to a new level is **Roots Restaurant** (51 Wales St., 802/747-7414, www.rootsrutland.com, 11 A.M.–9 P.M. Tues.–Thurs., 11 A.M.–10 P.M. Fri.–Sat., 11 A.M.–9 P.M. Sun., $16–20).

Information and Services

Rutland Region Chamber of Commerce (802/773-2747, www.rutlandvermont.com) runs a seasonal visitors center at the junction of Routes 4 and 7.

Emergency services are centered in Rutland—including Vermont's second-largest hospital. **Rutland Regional Medical Center** (160 Allen St., 802/775-7111) offers a full range of services, inpatient and outpatient. Several pharmacies are in the area, though none operate all night. Most central are **Walgreens** (10 Woodstock Ave., 802/773-6980, open 24 hours daily, pharmacy 8 A.M.–10 P.M. Mon.–Fri.,

9 A.M.–6 P.M. Sat.–Sun.) and **CVS** (31 N. Main St., 802/775-6736).

A number of banks with ATM machines line U.S. Route 4, especially on either side of the crossroads with U.S. Route 7. **Rutland Free Library** (10 Court St., 802/773-1860, http://rutlandfree.org, 9 A.M.–9 P.M. Mon., 11:30 A.M.–9 P.M. Tues.–Wed., 9 A.M.–5:30 P.M. Thurs.–Fri., 9 A.M.–5 P.M. Sat.) provides free Wi-Fi to patrons.

State troopers can be found at **Vermont State Police** (124 State Pl., 802/773-9101), and local authorities are at **Rutland Police** (108 Wales St., 802/773-1816).

PROCTOR AND PITTSFORD

North of Rutland, the terrain opens up quickly into the bucolic kind of scenery you'd expect of Vermont—all red barns and Holsteins framed by the majestic silhouettes of the Greens. Marble was first quarried in these parts in the 1830s, but didn't crank into high gear until former Vermont governor Redfield Proctor took control of the Vermont Marble Company in the 1880s and wrested the town that bears his name from parts of Rutland and Pittsford. (Proctor later became Secretary of War under President Benjamin Harrison and is credited with inspiring the Spanish-American War.) The legacy of the valley's agricultural and industrial past lives on in two museums, one dedicated to maple, the other to marble. North of Proctor, get off Route 7 to explore the back roads of Pittsford, a colonial-era village known for its concentration of covered bridges.

◖ New England Maple Museum

Vermont produces an estimated 500 million gallons of maple syrup each year—accounting for more than a third of the production of the entire country. And each one of those gallons of golden goodness takes 40 gallons of sugar sap to produce. If you are beginning to doubt there are enough trees in the state to

THE MAKING OF A CLASSIC: MAPLE SYRUP

Many a pancake lover has silently thanked the state of Vermont for producing what is arguably its most glorious food product (referred to as "liquid gold" by many an addict), and Vermont has always been happy to oblige by producing more. After all, the process of making the stuff—known as "sugaring"—requires weather conditions that Vermont tends to get in spades: repeated alternating freezing and thawing in very early spring, so that the tree sap will start to flow. Once that happens (usually in March, when snow is still on the ground), the sap is then collected from the maple trees by drilling small tapholes into each tree, fixed with either tubing or a bucket. When a freeze hits, it acts as a suction to draw the sap out; the sap is then released during the next thaw. It's collected, then boiled to remove all of its water content, concentrating it into a rich syrup.

make that possible, check out this museum (Rte. 7, just north of Pittsford, 802/483-9414, www.maplemuseum.com, 10 A.M.–4 P.M. daily mid-Mar.–late May, 8:30 A.M.–5:30 P.M. daily late May–Oct., 10 A.M.–4 P.M. daily Nov.–late Dec., closed Jan.–Feb., $2.50 adults, $0.75 children) on the outskirts of Rutland. It takes visitors inside the history and art of sugar maple sap. One hundred feet of murals depict the history of syrup making, from the Native Americans who heated sugar maple logs over the fire to the smokestacks of modern syruping outfits. These are complemented by black-and-white photographs, antique taps and other sugaring artifacts, and an evaporation tank that runs all year long, or as the museum puts it, "even when the sap isn't." And of course, there's the gift shop, which provides free samples of different grades of syrup—though unfortunately no flapjacks to go with them.

The Vermont Marble Museum

Located on the grounds of an abandoned quarry, The Vermont Marble Museum (52 Main St., Proctor, 800/427-1396, www.vermont-marble.com, 9 A.M.–5 P.M. daily mid-May–Oct., $7 adults, $5 seniors, $4 teens, free for children) is filled with exhibits and photographs that tell the story of the Rutland marble industry and the thousands of immigrants who once labored in the quarries. A grand gallery contains marble bas-reliefs of all of the nation's presidents, along with other marble statuary carved over the years. Modern-day marble carver Allen Dwight, the museum's artist-in-residence, gives demonstrations on the craft.

Wilson Castle

Nearby the Vermont Marble Museum is Wilson Castle (2909 W. Proctor Rd., Proctor, 802/773-3284, www.wilsoncastle.com, 9 A.M.–5 P.M. daily late May–mid-Oct., $10 adults, $5.50 children 6–12, children under 6 free), built in the late 19th century by a doctor with a taste for extravagance. The five-story mansion is a mishmash of European styles, with 19 proscenium arches, a turret, parapet, and balcony. Inside, the building is filled with antiques from around the world, including Chinese scrolls, Tiffany chandeliers, and a Louis XVI crown jewel case. Guided tours lasting 45 minutes are given throughout the day. (Last tour leaves at 5 P.M.) If you can, time your visit for a Sunday morning, when an electronic organ fills the art gallery with church music. Combination tickets for the maple museum, marble museum, and castle give a discount on admission.

Covered Bridges

One of the more attractive covered bridges in the state, the 144-foot **Gorham Bridge,** is just north of Proctor center, where Gorham Bridge

Road crosses Otter Creek. Farther down the same road, take a turn onto Elm Street to find the **Cooley Bridge,** a 53-foot bridge over Furnace Creek. North of Pittsford, take Kendall Hill Road to view **Hammond Bridge,** a 139-foot bridge similar in design to Gorham Bridge, though closed to traffic. As you continue to Depot Hill Road, the 121-foot **Depot Bridge** also crosses Otter Creek, with the road continuing on back to Route 7.

Events

The **Proctor Fall Festival** (Main Street Park, 802/770-7223, late Sept.) features fall foliage train rides, a pumpkin pie bake-off, and sales of marble gifts.

Shopping

Tom's Treasures (3295 U.S. Rte. 7, Pittsford, 802/483-2334, 10 A.M.–5 P.M. Mon.–Wed. and Fri.–Sat., noon–5 P.M. Sun.) peddles antiques, silver, vintage toys, and other rarities that are more than enough to complete a collection—or compel a collector to start one.

An almost daily stop for many locals, **Kamuda's Country Store** (Rte. 7 between Rutland and Brandon, Pittsford, 802/483-2361, 7 A.M.–7 P.M. Mon.–Fri., 7 A.M.–6 P.M. Sat., 7 A.M.–1 P.M. Sun.) is where to find tasty made-to-order sandwiches, souvenirs and greeting cards, and a bevy of Vermont-made specialties to take home.

SOUTHWESTERN LAKES REGION

The area along the New York border west of Rutland is a sleepy stretch of villages that time has mostly forgotten. Tourists usually bypass it on their way zipping up and down Route 7, while residents jealously guard the bucolic beauty of a hilly landscape studded with general stores, clapboard churches, and a pretty necklace of deep blue lakes. The downtowns of **Castleton** and **Poultney** are both on the Register of Historic Places for their profusion of Federal-style architecture. Other towns in the area, such as **Benson** and **Hubbardton,** are blink-and-you'll-miss-'em small. Nearby, Lake St. Catherine is one of the prettiest in the state, while Bomoseen Lake is a major recreational center with Revolutionary history to boot.

Hubbardton Battlefield State Historic Site

Early on in the Revolutionary War, the Americans at Fort Ticonderoga and Mount Independence were outflanked by the British and made a hasty retreat south through Vermont. The British, under General "Gentleman Johnnie" Burgoyne, caught up with them near the hamlet of Hubbardton (5696 Monument Rd., 802/273-3901 or 802/273-2242, www.hubbardton.net, 9:30 A.M.–5 P.M. Thurs.–Mon. late May–mid-Oct., $2 adults, children under 15 free). There, a rear guard of more than 1,000 troops led by Green Mountain Boys colonel Seth Warner stayed back to delay the Redcoats, setting up defenses on a hilltop and repulsing repeated attacks. The action, one of the most successful rear-guard actions in history, headed off the British advance as Burgoyne stayed behind for several days to bury dead and rest his troops, allowing American general Arthur St. Clair to escape with his men and eventually return victorious at the Battle of Saratoga.

Today, the site includes a visitors center with relics of the battle, along with a three-dimensional map with fiber-optic lighting that takes visitors inside the heat of the engagement.

Snowflake Farms

Often confused with its South American cousin the llama, the alpaca was specifically bred for its soft fibrous coat, not for the ability to carry packs across the Andes. And among alpacas, the cream of the crop are suri alpacas, who sport a lustrous coat prized for its fineness and softness. At Snowflake Farms (5676 Stage Rd., Benson, 802/537-2971, 3 P.M.–dark, daily), two former computer techies from New York retired to Vermont to breed suri alpacas. In their spare time they give tours with meet-and-greets with their 10 animals. An on-site store sells fiber products as well as raw fiber.

Events

The highlight of the year in these parts is the annual **Frosty Derby** (802/287-9742, www. poultneyvt.com/frosty-derby-2), an ice-fishing contest on Lake St. Catherine that brings residents out for fierce competition for bass, perch, and pike as well as general winter merriment.

Shopping

Find good discounts from cover to cover at **Hermit Hill Books** (95 Main St., Poultney, 802/287-5757, www.hermithillbooks.com, 10 A.M.–5 P.M. Tues.–Sat.), a store specializing in rare and vintage books and blessed with plenty of reading chairs, a knowledgeable staff, and two friendly mascots—Tucker the dog and Harriet the cat.

Stock up on lots of colorful yarns, beads, and a slew of other materials to create your magnum opus at **The Craft Seller** (66 Depot St., Poultney, 802/287-9713). An utterly adorable shop filled with seemingly endless locally made pieces of art, the **Original Vermont Gift Shop** (163 Main St., Poultney, 802/287-9111, www.originalvermontstore.com, 10 A.M.–6 P.M. Mon.–Sat., 11 A.M.–3 P.M. Sun.) is one-stop shopping for holiday presents. Think pineapple motifs on home accessories, slate hangings, old-fashioned homemade jams, children's books, and maple cookies, among plenty of other cute buys.

Or jump back in time with a walk through **East Poultney General Store** (11 On the Green, East Poultney, 802/287-4042, 7 A.M.–7 P.M. Mon.–Sat., 9 A.M.–3 P.M. Sun.). The 1830s country store sells lots of snacks,

candy, toys, and crafts, and even houses its own post office.

Food

A favorite for sandwiches, **Perry's Main Street Eatery** (253 Main St., Poultney, 802/287-5188, 6 A.M.–7 P.M. Mon., 6 A.M.–8 P.M. Tues.–Thurs., 6 A.M.–9 P.M. Fri.–Sat., 6 A.M.–2 P.M. Sun., $9–16) feeds a hungry crowd American standards (including good burgers) for breakfast, lunch, and dinner. Or grab some classic American fare at **Tot's Diner** (25 Main St., Poultney, 802/287-2213, 7 A.M.–9 P.M. daily, $6–12), a great place to mix with locals and fill up on big stacks of pancakes, club sandwiches, and heaping slices of pie. Equally dependable fare is on the menu at **Poultney House of Pizza** (20 Main St., Poultney, 802/287-9439, 11 A.M.–9 P.M. Tues.–Thurs., 11 A.M.–10 P.M. Fri., 11 A.M.–9 P.M. Sat., 11 A.M.–1 P.M. Sun., closed Mon., $8–15)—the likes of chewy-crusted pies filled with tons of toppings, plus overstuffed submarine sandwiches.

Information and Services

For more information on the area, contact the **Poultney Area Chamber of Commerce** (802/287-2010, www.poultneyvt.com). **Drake's Pharmacy** (188 Main St., Poultney, 802/287-5281) is conveniently located downtown.

SPORTS AND RECREATION
Hiking and Camping

There are several scenic hikes in **Bomoseen State Park** (22 Cedar Mountain Rd., Fair Haven, 802/265-4242, www.vtstateparks.com/htm/bomoseen.cfm, campsites $16–27), including the moderate 1.5-mile Bomoseen Hiking Loop, which takes hikers through an overgrown early-20th-century farm. Look out for apple trees, where deer, fox, and other wildlife are wont to congregate for a snack. The more strenuous Glen Lake Trail stretches for more than four miles of beaver ponds, slate cliffs, and meadows; the highlight is a 100-meter-high overlook with spacious views of Glen Lake. The park has 56 tent sites and 10 lean-tos located in a mix of wooded and grassy spots. The most desirable are the five lean-tos located directly on the lakeshore (ask for Deer, Porcupine, Coyote, Squirrel, or Moose). The campground is a busy one, with a snack bar concession stand and boat rentals on the beach.

An alternative is **Half Moon Pond State Park** (1621 Black Pond Rd., Hubbardton, 802/273-2848, www.vtstateparks.com/htm/halfmoon. cfm, campsites $16–27, cabins $46–48), an area located within Bomoseen State Park designated strictly for camping, which means its 52 campsites and assorted cabins and lean-tos are particularly secluded and quiet. Cool off in a small swimming area for campers only.

Also popular is the campground at **Lake St. Catherine State Park** (3034 Rte. 30, Poultney, 802/287-9158, www.vtstateparks.com/htm/ catherine.cfm, campsites $16–27), which has 50 tent/trailer sites and 11 lean-tos located in a mix of grassy and wooded sites. The prime spots are the five tent sites along the lakes and the dozen or so located in a wooded loop by Parker Brook. The park is a great one for kids, with a play area, two sandy beaches, snack bar, and large grassy field to get out their energy. Unlike Bomoseen, Lake St. Catherine doesn't have a lot of hiking trails, but it does have a one-mile nature trail through the famed "Big Trees" of St. Catherine (enormous Red Oak and other species), which includes a stunning view of nearby Birdseye Mountain.

Boating and Fishing

A boat ramp at the southern end of **Lake St. Catherine State Park** (3034 Rte. 30, Poultney, 802/287-9158, www.vtstateparks. com/htm/catherine.cfm) offers access to the lake's crystal-clear water. For those without their own craft, the park rents canoes. Boat rentals including kayaks, canoes, rowboats, and paddleboats are also available at the campground at **Bomoseen State Park** (22 Cedar Mountain Rd., Fair Haven, 802/265-4242, www.vtstateparks.com/htm/bomoseen. cfm, $5–12/hr, $20–32 half-day, $35–50 full day). Bomoseen and St. Catherine are also famed for their fighting population of rainbow trout, pike, and largemouth and smallmouth bass. For chartered expeditions, contact **Foothills Outdoor Expeditions** (802/483-2020, www.foothillsoutdoorexpeditions.com), which leads expeditions on many of the area lakes, with the option of fishing aboard a 16-foot canoe.

Horseback Riding

A 2,000-acre horse ranch outside Castleton, **Pond Hill Ranch** (1373 Rte. 4, East Castleton, 802/468-2449, www.pondhillranch.com, $35/ person for hour-long ride, appointments necessary) leads daily horseback rides on backcountry trails; ponies are available for the kids.

Rock Climbing

An 8,000-square-foot gym with dozens of rope stations on 25-foot climbing walls is just the beginning at the **Green Mountain Rock Climbing Center** (223 Woodstock Ave., Rutland, 802/773-3343, www.vermontclimbing.com). Owner Steve Lulek, who once served as head instructor at the military's Mountaineering School, also leads a full range of mountaineering classes and guided tours of Deer's Leap and other nearby cliff faces through his companion outfit, **Vermont Adventure Tours** (www.vermontadventuretours.com).

ACCOMMODATIONS
Under $100

Close to great downhill and cross-country skiing, **Memory Lane Bed & Breakfast** (Main St., Castleton, 802/468-5394, $55–100) lives up to its name with its well-kept antique collections and traditional decor in 17 rooms. Memory Lane is located a half-mile down Main Street from Castleton College.

Blessed with impressive collections of antiques from all over the world and a dedication to serving organic foods, **Iron Master's Inn** (1661 Furnace Rd., Pittsford, 802/483-9335, $85–135) has decorated its five rooms individually in everything from Balinese crafts to French paintings. Breakfasts and dinners are all-natural and gourmet in nature; the inn even has its own fresh water supply from the mountains.

Three simple rooms (each named after birds, each laid out with quilts and dark woods) are at the heart of **Birdhouse Inn B&B** (1430 E. Main St., Poultney, 802/287-2405, www.birdhouseinnvt.com, $85–110). Breakfasts are large and excellent.

$100-150

Steps away from Green Mountain College, **The Bentley House Bed & Breakfast** (399 Bentley Ave., Poultney, 802/287-4004, www.thebentleyhouse.com, $105–145) pampers with soft comforters and a country aesthetic. The Queen Anne Victorian home is graced with lots of stained-glass windows, period antiques, and a wraparound porch that's perfect for relaxing and reading on.

Once the home of a feed and grain merchant, the 1889 **❮ Inn at Rutland** (70 N. Main St., Rutland, 802/773-0575, $120–230) is a time-warp into the opulence of the city's Victorian era. Common rooms are filled with period details like parquet floors, tooled-leather wainscoting, and a grand oak staircase that takes guests to eight upstairs bedrooms with cable TV and whirlpool tubs. Hosts Leslie and Steven Brenner prepare a three-course breakfast every morning with treats like crème brûlée French toast and gingerbread blueberry pancakes; a wraparound front porch offers views of the Green Mountains and the city below.

GETTING THERE AND AROUND

Rutland is 15 miles (20 min.) west of Killington on Route 4 and 35 miles (45 min.) north of Manchester or 15 miles (20 min.) south of Brandon on Route 7. From Rutland, Castleton is 15 miles (20 min.) west on Route 4, while Poultney is another 8 miles (15 min.) south on Route 30.

In terms of public transportation, Rutland is a major transportation hub. Continental's CommutAir flies routes from Boston to **Rutland Airport** (802/747-9963, www.flyrutlandvt.com) for just $99 each way. **Amtrak** (800/872-7245, www.amtrak.com) runs trains to Rutland with its Ethan Allen service from New York City, stopping at the Rutland Depot behind Wal-Mart. **Vermont Transit Lines** (800/642-3133, www.vermonttransit.com) runs buses to the local bus station (102 West St., 802/773-2774). **Marble Valley Regional Transit** (802/773-3244) runs bus routes throughout the Rutland area.

ALONG ROUTE 4

CHAMPLAIN VALLEY

Lake Champlain is New England's Great Lake, an inland sea of expansive views and rich history. Twenty thousand years ago, the entire valley between Vermont's Green Mountains and New York's Taconic Range was under more than 400 feet of water—the remnants of glacial meltwater called Lake Vermont. After a few millennia, the Atlantic Ocean backed up the St. Lawrence River valley, filling the lake with seawater. Geologists still find whale fossils along the shoreline. As the sea level fell, the lake gradually dried up, leaving a giant sliver 100 miles long and up to 20 miles wide at its widest points.

Driving northward on Route 7 toward Burlington, you can still feel the presence of the ancient lakebed. The sky opens up and the land flattens, giving the area an almost Midwestern appearance, if it weren't for the spruce trees among the farms and mountains on the horizon. Despite the remoteness of this area today, it was actually one of the first areas of New England to be settled. Two hundred years ago, rivers were the equivalent of roads, and the St. Lawrence was a mighty river that gave French fur-trappers access to the interior. Eventually, settlers from New Hampshire and Massachusetts came up to cut down the trees and build farms to take advantage of the moderate temperatures (for Vermont!) and the fertile clay soil left behind by the glacial lake, settling around the thriving city of Burlington. Now with 100,000 people in its

© VERMONTVACATION.COM/JEFF CLARKE

HIGHLIGHTS

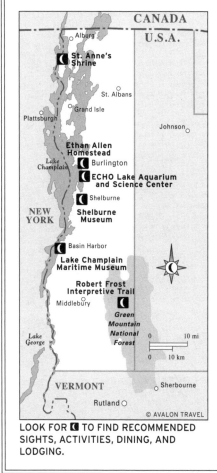

◖ ECHO Lake Aquarium and Science Center: Here the kids will be delighted by interactive exhibits, live animals, and a sea monster named Champ (page 103).

◖ Ethan Allen Homestead: The Robin Hood of Vermont comes alive in all of his complexities (page 103).

◖ St. Anne's Shrine: Contemplation is the order of the day at this Catholic shrine and historic site (page 117).

◖ Shelburne Museum: A miniature city holding art, artifacts, and buildings from all over the country spreads across a former farm in Vermont (page 122).

◖ Lake Champlain Maritime Museum: Benedict Arnold's flagship is the centerpiece of this fascinating lakeside history museum (page 125).

◖ Robert Frost Interpretive Trail: The beloved poet often walked some of the same trails that are now lined with his poetry (page 139).

LOOK FOR ◖ TO FIND RECOMMENDED SIGHTS, ACTIVITIES, DINING, AND LODGING.

CHAMPLAIN VALLEY

metropolitan area, the city is the largest in the state.

Among the early settlers was Vermonter Ethan Allen, who along with the Green Mountain Boys helped foment resistance to encroachment from New York flatlanders. Ironically, today the region looks toward New York more than to Massachusetts or New Hampshire. It's still easier to cross the lake than to cross the Green Mountains, which rise much higher here than they do down south. It's perfectly reasonable to include a jaunt to the historical sites on the lake's western shore or a hike in the Adirondacks along with a tour of Vermont's Champlain Valley. Meanwhile, in terms of demographics, this is not a region of

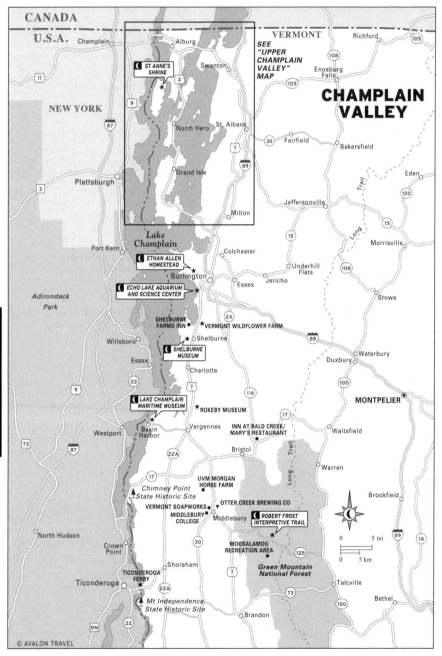

CANADA
U.S.A.

VERMONT

SEE "UPPER CHAMPLAIN VALLEY" MAP

CHAMPLAIN VALLEY

NEW YORK

Champlain

Alburg

Richford

105

108

Swanton

Enosburg Falls

105

St. Albans

36 Fairfield

Bakersfield

North Hero

7

89

Grand Isle

Eden

100

Plattsburgh

Jeffersonville

Milton

15

Morrisville

Lake Champlain

Colchester

15

108

Stowe

Port Kent

ETHAN ALLEN HOMESTEAD

Burlington

Underhill Flats

ECHO LAKE AQUARIUM AND SCIENCE CENTER

Essex

Jericho

2A

89

Waterbury

SHELBURNE FARMS INN

VERMONT WILDFLOWER FARM

Duxbury

Shelburne

100

Willsboro

SHELBURNE MUSEUM

Charlotte

MONTPELIER

Essex

7

116

22

17

LAKE CHAMPLAIN MARITIME MUSEUM

ROKEBY MUSEUM

Waitsfield

Basin Harbor

Vergennes

INN AT BALD CREEK/ MARY'S RESTAURANT

Westport

22A

Bristol

Warren

9

87

17

UVM MORGAN HORSE FARM

Brookfield

73

Chimney Point State Historic Site

VERMONT SOAPWORKS

OTTER CREEK BREWING CO

MIDDLEBURY COLLEGE

Middlebury

ROBERT FROST INTERPRETIVE TRAIL

89

14

North Hudson

30

MOOSALAMOO RECREATION AREA

125

Adirondack Park

3

0   5 mi

0   5 km

Crown Point

Shoreham

7

Green Mountain National Forest

Talcville

TICONDEROGA FERRY

22A

Ticonderoga

Bethel

Mt Independence State Historic Site

73

100

9N

22

Brandon

© AVALON TRAVEL

country bumpkins. Vermont's two elite universities, Middlebury College and the University of Vermont in Burlington, span the valley like intellectual goalposts, giving their respective cities an energetic student atmosphere.

PLANNING YOUR TIME

Plan to spend at least a day or two in Burlington; the city's isolation on Lake Champlain, together with its vibrant student population, has given it a quirky character unlike any other city. Historically, it was home to Vermont's very own reputed Robin Hood; the **Ethan Allen Homestead** is open for tours. Another prime attraction in the city is the **ECHO Lake Aquarium and Science Center,** which details the lake's unique natural history, including the story of the sea monster purported to be plumbing its depths. If you are trained in scuba diving, you can't miss the chance to check out Lake Champlain's collection of well-preserved shipwrecks, managed through the Burlington branch of the **Lake Champlain Maritime Museum.**

If you have another day or two, escape to the windswept Lake Champlain islands, which are filled with small farms and forested campgrounds. While you are there, bask in the quiet tranquility of **St. Anne's Shrine.**

In the lower valley, base yourself in the delightful college town of Middlebury, which in addition to restaurants and museums provides prime access to the hiking trails of the Green Mountains. The **Robert Frost Interpretive Trail** is one of the most moving tributes to the poet, who used to summer in the area. For a different view of the mountains, a hot air balloon ride is unforgettable, especially when foliage lights up the hills in fall.

Between Burlington and Middlebury, Route 7 passes through a schlocky area of family vacationland; one exception is the **Shelburne Museum,** a miniature village filled with fine art and historical artifacts. Another sure bet is the main branch of the **Lake Champlain Maritime Museum** in Vergennes, which gathers together the history of the lake from Native American to modern times.

By and large, restaurants in the cities and the islands stay open with regular hours year-round, but many don't serve all meals. Call ahead when planning.

CHAMPLAIN VALLEY

Burlington

Vermont's largest city is a surprisingly harmonious mixture of cultures: Start with a base of alternative undergrad culture, add plenty of wholesome families vacationing on the lake, and top that with a booming retail industry, and you've got Burlington in a nutshell. This is the kind of place where the average resident stays up late into the night to sip organic beer and hoot at the latest folk band at a local cafe, only to wake up early to don a fleece vest for a kayak trip in the bay.

Not that Burlington is entirely cosmopolitan. After all, the city only has 30,000 residents—10,000 of which are students—and the surrounding area is still relatively depressed economically. The outskirts of town are an unsightly blemish of strip malls, and even the downtown area has more chain stores than independent boutiques. But Burlington has two big things going for it: the university and the lake. The waterfront area has been spruced up in recent years into a park, Waterfront Park, with frequent concerts and events on the grassy area along the water. The waterfront is still a working one, with ships carrying cargo up and down the lake to New York State. But nowadays, most of the boats docked in the marina are pleasure craft dedicated to exploring the lake.

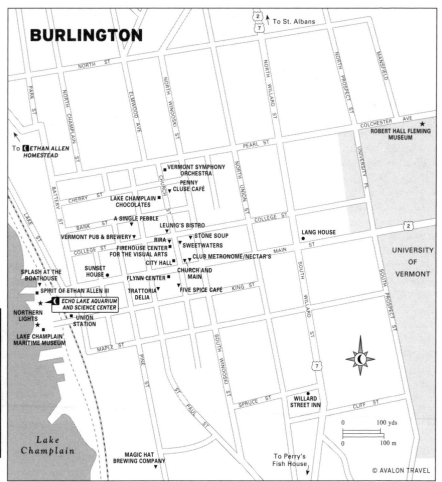

BURLINGTON

To St. Albans

To ETHAN ALLEN HOMESTEAD

ROBERT HALL FLEMING MUSEUM

COLCHESTER AVE

PEARL ST

VERMONT SYMPHONY ORCHESTRA

PENNY CLUSE CAFÉ

CHERRY ST

LAKE CHAMPLAIN CHOCOLATES

A SINGLE PEBBLE

BANK ST

LEUNIG'S BISTRO

VERMONT PUB & BREWERY

COLLEGE ST

RIRA

STONE SOUP

SWEETWATERS

FIREHOUSE CENTER FOR THE VISUAL ARTS

CLUB METRONOME/NECTAR'S

CITY HALL

LANG HOUSE

UNIVERSITY OF VERMONT

SPLASH AT THE BOATHOUSE

SUNSET HOUSE

CHURCH AND MAIN

FLYNN CENTER

SPIRIT OF ETHAN ALLEN III

TRATTORIA DELIA

FIVE SPICE CAFÉ

KING ST

ECHO LAKE AQUARIUM AND SCIENCE CENTER

NORTHERN LIGHTS

UNION STATION

LAKE CHAMPLAIN MARITIME MUSEUM

MAPLE ST

WILLARD STREET INN

SPRUCE ST

CLIFF ST

Lake Champlain

MAGIC HAT BREWING COMPANY

To Perry's Fish House

0   100 yds
0   100 m

© AVALON TRAVEL

Elsewhere in town, it's hard to tell where the University of Vermont, with its reputation for crunchiness and funkiness, ends and the rest of the city begins. The university was founded in 1791 by Ira Allen, the wealthy landowner who, with his brother Ethan, dominates early history in these parts. Later, Burlington established itself as the major mercantile and trading port in the region, exploiting the vast reserves of timber and stone in the area, which could be easily carted down the lake to New York. All over town, monuments to the city's wealth remain, from the imposing Unitarian Church that lords over Church Street to the monumental granite government buildings that ring the city's heart at City Hall Park. The main drag of Church Street combines town and gown into a pedestrian arcade of atmospheric, student-geared eateries that define the term "culinary ghetto," with lovely views of the waterway below.

COURTESY OF ECHO LAKE AQUARIUM AND SCIENCE CENTER

ECHO Lake Aquarium and Science Center

SIGHTS
◖ ECHO Lake Aquarium and Science Center

With ancient coral reefs, whale skeletons, and a supposed sea monster in its depths, Lake Champlain is one of the most distinctive bodies of freshwater in the world. The scientists behind this small aquarium (1 College St., 802/864-1848, www.echovermont.org, 10 A.M.–5 P.M. daily, $12.50 adults, $10.50 seniors and students, $9.50 children 3–17, children under 2 free) have done a bang-up job of making the geology and fauna of the lake accessible and family-friendly. "Hands-on" is the watchword here, with plenty of interactive exhibits to get kids good and wet while they learn about river currents or pull critters out of lake pools. That's not to say there isn't a lot here for adults, too—in the form of a film and exhibit exploring the enduring myth of Champ, the plesiosaur supposedly stranded in the lake millions of years ago, and plenty of aquarium

tanks full of the fish, turtles, snakes, and frogs you may encounter on trips out on the lake. An addition to the aquarium's permanent exhibits is a display that tells the history of the Abenaki Indians who lived around the lake. Another new exhibit allows residents and visitors to share their own stories of the lake in recordings, pictures, photographs, and songs—creating a giant living history archive of the area.

◖ Ethan Allen Homestead

Today, Ethan Allen is better known as the name of a furniture company, but he remains one of the most colorful—and enigmatic—figures of early Vermont history. The modest Cape Cod–style home (1 Ethan Allen Homestead Way, 802/865-4556, www.ethanallenhomestead.org, 10 A.M.–4 P.M. Thurs.–Mon., $7 adults, $5 seniors, $3 children 3–6, children 3 and under free) has been restored to the period, though only his kitchen table and a few other small Allen artifacts survive. The

ETHAN ALLEN

Colonial mountain man Ethan Allen looms large over the history of Vermont. Depending on which account you believe, he was an American Robin Hood, a war hero, a traitor, or a drunk. Born in Litchfield, Connecticut, Allen came to Vermont before the Revolutionary War with his brother Ira to start a farm near Bennington on a land grant received from New Hampshire governor Benning Wentworth. When King George found out that Wentworth was giving out grants under his nose (without paying duties to the Crown), he declared them void and gave the governor of New York rights to the same land. Caught in the middle, Allen and other landowners weren't about to give up without a fight. They defied the courts with a hastily arranged militia called the Green Mountain Boys, which helped enforce the New Hampshire Grants by persuasion, threat, and force, and eventually led to the founding of Vermont as a separate state.

The Boys achieved legitimacy through valiant fighting in the Revolution, where they played key roles in the battles of Hubbardton and Bennington. After leading the capture of Fort Ticonderoga in the beginning days of the war, however, Allen himself took little part. He was captured by the British during an ill-planned raid on Montreal and lived out the war as a prisoner in England and New York.

After the war, he was briefly named the general of the Army of Vermont, and then he became fabulously wealthy through the Onion River Land Company, a holding company that bought up and distributed much of the land in Vermont. Though his brother entered into politics, Ethan Allen preferred to influence government behind the scenes—such as his controversial role in the ill-fated attempt to return Vermont to the British in 1782.

By the time he built the homestead on the Onion River near Burlington in 1787, he was spending most of his time walking his land with surveyor's tools and a hip flask. He lived in the home for only two years before he was killed in a freak sledding accident on Lake Champlain (the hip flask was no doubt involved). Almost as soon as he died, the arguments began about the role he played in early Vermont history. Only one thing is for sure: If it weren't for him, Vermont probably wouldn't exist as a state today.

homestead offers a low-budget film exploring the conflicting accounts of the man himself as well as a guided tour of the property.

While the exhibits relating to Allen may leave a bit to be desired, the tour guides are spirited in their evocation of Vermont's larger-than-life founding father, espousing opinions about his legacy that make him seem like a politician from the 20th century, not the 18th. And Allen aside, the home is an excellently restored lesson in how early Americans lived. (On our tour, we learned the origins of the phrases "Pop goes the weasel" and "Sleep tight, don't let the bedbugs bite." Trust us, you're glad you didn't live in the days of straw mattresses.)

Lake Champlain Maritime Museum

The Burlington branch of Lake Champlain Maritime Museum (The Lyman Building at Perkins Pier, 802/475-2022, www.lcmm. org) was damaged by floods from 2011's Hurricane Irene. At time of publication, it remains closed. The waterfront does, however, still host the museum's flagship *Lois McLure,* an 88-foot, painstakingly reconstructed replica of an 1862-class canal schooner, which is open for free tours when it's in town. (Call ahead to find out whether the craft will be docked in Burlington or at the LCMM's main museum in Basin Harbor.)

LAKE CHAMPLAIN SHIPWRECKS

On a dark night in December 1876, the canal schooner *General Butler* lost its steering and crashed headlong into the Burlington Harbor, sinking just as the crew jumped to safety. The *Butler* is now one of hundreds of ships that line the bottom of the lake, one of the best surviving collections of shipwrecks in the world. Many of them are remnants of the 3,000 schooners built to haul timber, iron ore, and coal across the lake in the active shipping trade of the 19th century. Currently, nine vessels are open to those with scuba gear and the wherewithal to explore this unique state park. In addition to the *Butler,* which rests under 40 feet of water in the harbor, other ships include a canal boat loaded down with granite blocks, a rare horse-powered ferry boat, and two long sidewheel steamboats.

For underwater tours and equipment rentals, visit **Waterfront Diving Center** (214 Battery St., 802/865-2771 or 800/283-7282, www.waterfrontdiving.com). Basic scuba classes are $295, while two- and three-day summer trips are around $300 per person. The shop also works with a local charter company for day trips at $40 a head. All divers are required to register with a dive shop or the **Burlington Community Boat House** (College St., Burlington, 802/865-3777).

You don't have to be a diver to experience the wrecks, however. The **Lake Champlain Maritime Museum** offers dry-foot tours of the deep from their Basin Harbor location (4772 Basin Harbor Rd., Vergennes, 802/475-2022, www.lcmm.org, June–Oct., $22 adults, $18 youth). The tour uses an ROV (remotely operated vehicle) equipped with a camera to view the *Butler* or one of the other wrecks virtually on a video screen mounted onboard. Not only is the experience the next-best thing to viewing them through a diving mask, but the guides tell the stories of the boats as well, bringing alive the final hours of each wreck in lurid detail. If interested, be sure to book well in advance; tours are given only once every two weeks and the boat holds only 42 people.

Lake Tours

To get out on the water, board the ***Spirit of Ethan Allen III*** (Burlington Boathouse, 348 Flynn Ave., 802/862-8300, www.soea.com, 10 A.M., noon, 2 P.M., and 4 P.M. daily May–Oct., $15.49 adults, $7.49 children 3–11), a 141-foot luxury cruise ship that conducts narrated cruises of the lake during the day as well as dinner and sunset cruises in the evenings.

Alternatively, take the slightly smaller and slightly less expensive ***Northern Lights*** (Ferry Dock, 1 King St., 802/864-9669, www.lakechamplaincruises.com, noon, 2 P.M., 4 P.M. and 7 P.M. daily mid-June–early Oct., $16 adults, $6 children ages 3–11), a 115-foot cruise boat recently built to mimic a 19th-century steamboat and sharply appointed with gleaming brass and mahogany finish. It offers a similar line-up of guided tours and meal cruises.

BCA Center

Contemporary art with a Vermont theme is the purview of the BCA Center (135 Church St., 802/865-7166, www.burlingtoncityarts.org, 11 A.M.–5 P.M. Sun. and Tues–Thurs., 11 A.M.–8 P.M. Fri.–Sat. in summer; 9 A.M.–5 P.M. Mon.–Fri., noon–5 P.M. Sun. in winter, free), which pushes the envelope with multimedia and interactive exhibitions in oversized gallery spaces. Some of its shows are more successful than others; all are provocative. A recent exhibit, for example, looked at perspectives from Iraq vets turned artists working in media, including U.S. currency and flags and their own uniforms, to come to grips with their experiences in war.

University of Vermont

On the east side of town, the University of

CHAMPLAIN VALLEY

Vermont (194 S. Prospect St., 802/656-3131, www.uvm.edu) educates some 10,000 students on a campus overlooking the lake. Chartered in 1791 by a group of Vermonters including Ira Allen, it was the fifth college in the country (after Harvard, Yale, Dartmouth, and Brown). For visitors, its prized attraction is the **Robert Hull Fleming Museum** (University of Vermont, 61 Colchester Ave., 802/656-0750, www.uvm.edu, noon–4 P.M. Tues.–Fri., 1–5 P.M. Sat.–Sun. May–early Sept., 9 A.M.–4 P.M. Tues. and Thurs.–Fri., 9 A.M.–8 P.M. Wed., 1–5 P.M. Sat.–Sun. early Sept.–Apr., $5 adults, $3 students and seniors, $10 family, children 6 and under free), an art and archaeology museum with mummies, Buddhas, Mesoamerican pottery, and other artifacts from all the world's great civilizations, presented in an up-to-date style that avoids the paternalism of many archaeology museums. It also has a small collection of American and European paintings.

Lake Champlain Chocolates Factory Store and Cafe

If you've ever dreamed of getting a golden ticket to Willy Wonka's, stop in at Lake Champlain Chocolates Factory Store and Cafe (750 Pine St., 800/465-5909, www.lakechamplainchocolates.com, tours hourly 9 A.M.–2 P.M. Mon.–Fri., free chocolate tasting hourly 9 A.M.–2 P.M. Fri., store/cafe hours 9 A.M.–6 P.M. Mon.–Sat., 11 A.M.–5 P.M. Sun.), where tours of the chocolate-making operation are enough to send any chocoholic into a swoon. The company has been producing gourmet chocolates for more than two decades, incorporating sweet cream from Vermont cows and other local ingredients such as honey and maple syrup. Tours take in huge chocolate-filled melting tanks, a chocolate bar assembly line, and the chocolate waterfall that douses hand-fashioned truffles in velvety goodness. Free samples, of course, are available.

Magic Hat Brewing Company

We've always suspected there's something magical about beer—how else to explain the wicked visions experienced after a few pints? Peddling elixirs with names like Blind Faith, Lucky Kat, and Hex, Magic Hat Brewing Co. (5 Bartlett Bay Rd., South Burlington, 802/658-2739, www.magichat.net, tours hourly 3–4 P.M. Tues.–Wed., 3–5 P.M. Thurs.–Fri., 1–5 P.M. Sat., 1:30 P.M. Sun. in summer; 3–5 P.M. Thurs.–Fri., 1–5 P.M. Sat., 1:30 P.M. Sun. in winter). This brewery outside Burlington has always captured the thaumaturgical potential in a good pint. Group tours are led by brewers quirkier than their brews, and there's an in-house bar with experimental and hard-to-find concoctions (Green Apple beer, anyone?). You can tipple 3-ounce samples of as many beers as you want; or even better, pay to fill a growler. Visions no extra charge.

ENTERTAINMENT AND EVENTS
Nightlife

Grab a homemade beer and some local color at the state's first brewpub, the comfortable **Vermont Pub & Brewery** (144 College St., 802/865-0500, www.vermontbrewery.com, 11:30 A.M.–1 A.M. Sun.–Wed., 11:30 A.M.–2 A.M. Thurs.–Sat.). The pub pours all-natural brews, like its award-winning Burley Irish Ale and Handsome Mike's Smoked Stout, which are unfiltered, unpasteurized, and—many Burlingtonites claim—unparalleled. Their latest experiment: flower beers, such as Blue Nile, a rye beer brewed with Egyptian blue lotus flowers. Occasional live entertainment—usually rock or folk—and pub noshes are also on offer.

Regular live music—everyone from the Black Crowes to Ben Harper—takes the stage at **Club Metronome** (188 Main St., 802/865-4563, www.clubmetronome.com), a hangout loved by local hipsters as much for the big acts it attracts as for its spacious dance floor and high-tech light and sound systems.

One in a small chain of Irish pubs, **RiRa** (123 Church St., 802/860-9401, www.rira.com/burlington, 11:30 A.M.–midnight Mon.–Wed., 11:30 A.M.–1 A.M. Thurs., 11:30 A.M.–2 A.M. Fri.–Sat., 9 A.M.–midnight Sun.) prides itself on authentic atmosphere, and delivers, with a setting—and often a staff—that has been imported from Dublin. Live nightly Irish music, dancing, and a great beer selection make the spot that much more appealing. And speaking of music, **Nectar's** (188 Main St., 802/658-4771, www.liveatnectars.com, 5 P.M.–2 A.M. daily) has made its name on it, primarily as the spot that gave the band Phish its first following. Just as it did back then, the pub-cum-club spotlights nightly live music, weekly pool tournaments, and lots of bar food—and it's earned the love of local regulars for all of it.

The Arts

A former vaudeville house, the **Flynn Center for the Performing Arts** (153 Main St., 802/863-5966, www.flynncenter.org) was restored to its art-deco grandeur in 2000. It now serves as the cultural hub of the city, with musicals, dance performances, and shows by mainstream jazz and country acts from Diana Krall to Pink Martini. Meanwhile, the **Vermont Symphony Orchestra** (2 Church St., Suite 3B, 802/864-5741, www.vso.org) is all about playing the masters, from Tchaikovsky to Strauss. The group plays at numerous venues around the state throughout the season but can be found most frequently at its home base in Burlington.

Events

Omnivores unite every year at the **Green Mountain Chew Chew Food & Music Festival** (Burlington waterfront, June, $2 adults, $1 children 12 and under), along the lakefront. For $5, attendees receive nine tokens that can be exchanged for food items peddled at booths by local restaurants and food producers.

If you notice people stumbling down the streets, it's probably just the weekend of the **Vermont Brewers Festival** (802/760-8535, www.vermontbrewers.com, July, $25–125), a waterfront boozefest featuring Long Trail, Otter Creek, Magic Hat, Harpoon, and two dozen other beermeisters from around New England.

The most exciting day on the lake is the annual **Dragon Boat Festival** (802/999-5478, www.ridethedragon.org, Aug.), a boat race in which teams of 20 paddle 40-foot brightly painted canoes to raise money for local charities. The winner is invariably the team that works the best together, not necessarily the strongest.

Burlington's biggest festival, the **Champlain Valley Fair** (105 Pearl St./Rte. 15, Essex Junction, 802/878-5545, www.champlainvalleyfair.org, $12 adult, $5 children 5–12, children under 5 free, late Aug.–early Sept.) has been bringing amusement rides and agricultural exhibits to the area for more than 80 years.

Every mid-to-late November, South Burlington gears up for the holiday season with the **Vermont Hand Crafters & Art Show** (800/373-5429, www.vermonthandcrafters.com, $7 admission)—a four-day exhibit and shopping event packed to its gills with 150-plus booths of handblown glass, woodworking, paintings, sculpture, and weavings.

SHOPPING

With its deluge of national chain stores, it can be hard to tell Burlington's stores from those of any other mall in America. At least, that is, until you look a little harder. Tucked in among the Banana Republics and the Gaps, the town's outdoor pedestrian promenade does indeed host a handful of distinctive and local shops. Representing Burlington's large lefty element in fine style is **The Peace & Justice Store**

© VERMONTVACATION.COM/DENNIS CURRAN

shopping on Church Street

(21 Church St., 802/863-2345, www.pjcvt.org, 10 A.M.–5 P.M. Mon.–Fri., 11 A.M.–6 P.M. Sat., 11 A.M.–5 P.M. Sun.), a nonprofit shop dedicated to educating on everything from globalization and civil rights to healthy eating.

Looking to stock your kitchen right? Look to the selection of high-end cutlery and cookware at **Kiss the Cook** (72 Church St., 802/863-4226, www.kissthecook.net, 9 A.M.–9 P.M. Mon.–Sat., 10 A.M.–6 P.M. Sun.). The locally owned business stocks Fiestaware, bakeware, and pots and pans by names like Emile Henry, Braun, and Viking.

The staff is as welcoming as the clothing at **Bella Boutique** (96 Church St., 802/865-1754, 10 A.M.–6 P.M. daily), a well-edited collection of organic and fair trade women's apparel that's surprisingly chic.

At **City Market** (82 S. Winooski Ave., 802/861-9700, www.citymarket.coop, 7 A.M.–11 P.M. daily), you'll find every type of beer made in Vermont, plus Vermont-made

foodstuffs including cheeses, honey, and maple syrup.

A mixture of both national outlet stores (read: bargains) and local Vermont specialty stores (read: souvenirs), **Essex Shoppes & Cinema** (21 Essex Way, 802/878-4200, www.essexshoppes.com, 10 A.M.–8 P.M. Mon.–Sat., 11 A.M.–6 P.M. Sun. May–Dec., 10 A.M.–7 P.M. Mon.–Sat., 11 A.M.–5 P.M. Sun. Jan.–May) packs a retail punch, with everything from Ralph Lauren and Brooks Brothers to shops filled with Vermont-made toys and books by Vermont authors.

FOOD
American
Wind up at **Sweetwaters** (120 Church St. 802/864-9800, www.sweetwatersvt.com, 11:30 A.M.–midnight Sun.–Thurs., 11:30 A.M.–1:30 A.M. Fri.–Sat., $16–24) and you won't be disappointed. Part pub, part bistro, with lovely alfresco dining in warm weather, it offers a

slightly trendy but solid menu of dishes like a Kobe beef burger with bacon and cheese.

Hipster vegetarians aren't the only ones crowding **Stone Soup** (211 College St., www.stonesoupvt.com, 802/862-7616, 7 A.M.–9 P.M. Mon.–Fri., 9 A.M.–9 P.M. Sat.). The hearty breads, soups, and sandwiches and incredible chocolate chip cookies have a fan base that reaches far beyond veganism.

The food is as whimsical as the hosts are at **Penny Cluse Cafe** (169 Cherry St., 802/651-8834, www.pennycluse.com, 6:45 A.M.–3 P.M. Mon.–Fri., 8 A.M.–3 P.M. Sat.–Sun., $4–9), named for the hipster owner's childhood dog and decked out with an ever-rotating collection of posters and local art. Dig into gingerbread pancakes at breakfast, or hang out until lunch and order up Baja fish tacos and a Bloody Mary.

From the affable bartenders to the homey but ambitious menu, **Church and Main** (156 Church St., www.churchandmainvt.com, 802/540-3040, 11:30 A.M.–9 P.M. Tues.–Thurs., 11:30 A.M.–9 P.M. Fri.–Sat., $12–29) draws its patrons in with an extensive wine list and keeps them there with the food. Settle into the bustling wine-bar-meets-modern-bistro and dig into watermelon and feta salads, salmon with horseradish aioli, and free-range chicken with peach salsa.

At **Sky Burgers** (161 Church St., www.skyburgersvt.com, 802/881-0642, 11 A.M.–9 P.M. Tues.–Thurs., 11 A.M.–10 P.M. Fri.–Sat., 11 A.M.–8 P.M. Sun., $6–11), the game is stacked in diners' favor. Orders here are meant to be highly customized, from toppings like grilled mushrooms and chili to blue cheese and sundried tomatoes. The kids' menu is equally packed with options.

Asian

Forget Americanized Chinese food. The immensely popular **A Single Pebble** (133-35 Bank St., 802/865-5200, www.asinglepebble. com, 11:30 A.M.–1:45 P.M. Mon.–Fri. and Sun., 11:30 A.M.–3 P.M. Sat., 5–10 P.M. nightly, $9–20) cooks authentic Szechuan fare like "Ants Climbing a Tree" (a traditional pork and cellophane noodle dish) and "Red Chili Shrimp," all served family-style.

Italian

Serious Italian takes center stage at ◖**Trattoria Delia** (152 Saint Paul St., 802/864-5253, www.trattoriadelia.com, 5–10 P.M. daily, $18–24), with an excellent wine list and an emphasis on freshly-made pastas and authentically cooked high-quality meats.

French

Expertly prepared French bistro food like filet mignon and fig-and-blue cheese stuffed pork always makes dining at ◖**Leunig's Bistro** (115 Church St., 802/863-3759, www.leunigsbistro.com, 11 A.M.–3 P.M. and 5–10 P.M. Mon.–Thurs., 11 A.M.–3 P.M. and 5–11 P.M. Fri., 9 A.M.–2 P.M. and 5–11 P.M. Sat., 9 A.M.–2 P.M. and 5–10 P.M. Sun., $18–29) a night to remember. The fin de siècle décor and cast of local characters from gallery owners to University professors (many of whom have standing reservations) are just as much a part of the scene.

Seafood

Seafood lovers shouldn't pass up a chance to eat dinner at **Perry's Fish House** (1080 Shelburne Rd., South Burlington, 802/862-1300, 4–9 P.M. daily, $12–20), which has been voted best seafood in town for 10 years straight. The casual spot steams gargantuan lobsters and also serves straightforward dishes like steamed clams and fried flounder. On any pleasant-weather day, the place to be is **Splash at the Boathouse** (College St., 802/343-5894, www.splashattheboathouse.com, 11 A.M.–10 P.M. daily, $6–12), housed on the floating boathouse at the end of College Street. The ultra-casual setting (looking out to the lake's waters) matches the casual menu—the likes of Asian tuna sandwiches and fish tacos.

SPORTS AND RECREATION
Biking
Lake Champlain Bikeways (1 Steele St. #103, 802/652-2453, www.champlainbikeways.org) runs a clearinghouse in Burlington with trail maps and information on the 1,300 miles of bikeways around the lake. Closer to home, the city has recently constructed the excellent **Burlington Bike Path** (Burlington Parks and Recreation, 802/864-0123, www.enjoyburlington.com), an eight-mile path that runs along the river and connects several parks perfect for picnicking. A spur leads off the Ethan Allen Homestead. Located on the bike path, nonprofit **Local Motion** (1 Steele St., 802/861-2700, www.localmotion.org, 10 A.M.–6 P.M. daily May–Oct.) rents out bikes and provides a map to other bike paths in the city.

Boating
The sheer size of Lake Champlain makes venturing out in a kayak an unforgettable experience. The lake's famous changeability, however, requires paddlers to stay on their toes; be sure not to get too far out from shore lest a sudden squall leaves you stranded. The **Lake Champlain Committee** (802/658-1414, www.lakechamplaincommittee.org) has established the Lake Champlain Paddlers Trail, with suggested routes for paddling. **True North Kayak Tours** (25 Nash Pl., 802/238-7695, www.vermontkayak.com, $125 per person) rents boats and sponsors tours of the lake around Kingsland Bay and Button Bay State Parks south of Burlington, secluded Isle La Motte, and other locations.

If paddling into the lake seems too daunting, sit back on the decks of *Friend Ship,* the flagship of **Whistling Man Schooner Co.** (1 College St., 802/598-6504, www.whistlingman.com, three tours daily noon, midafternoon, and

early evening, hours vary slightly by season, $35 adults, $20 children under 12). Based on the Burlington waterfront, the boat takes intimate three-hour sails around the harbor with a maximum of 12 people on board.

ACCOMMODATIONS
The Far East is the prevailing inspiration for the mustard-yellow cedar-built **Overlook Park Bed and Breakfast** (1560 Spear St., South Burlington, 802/862-2762, www.overlookparkbnb.com, $100–130). Filled with Oriental rugs, Asian decor, and Asian gardens, rooms have views of Lake Champlain and the Adirondack Mountains.

If convenience and simple comfort are your priorities, reserve one of the four guest rooms at **Sunset House** (78 Main St., 802/864-3790, www.sunsethousebb.com, $119–169). Rooms are outfitted with quilts, queen or twin beds, and old photos (the home was built in 1908), and it's a close walk to downtown Burlington.

The Willard Street Inn (349 S. Willard St., 802/651-8710, willardstreetinn.com, $125–255) is as beautiful inside the rooms as it is out; the sprawling Victorian manse lays claim to impeccably decorated rooms. Each is filled with thoughtful details—a hand-carved antique chest here, a gas fireplace with antique mosaic tile there. Terry bathrobes, wireless Internet access, and a full breakfast served in the marble-floored solarium come with every stay. Children under 12 are not welcome. They are, however, welcome at **Lang House** (360 Main St., 877/919-9799, www.langhouse.com, $145–245), where portable cribs are but one of the many perks. The beautifully decorated rooms, meanwhile, are perfectly grown up, appointed with antique beds and rich tapestries, plus complimentary wireless Internet and personal supplies (toothbrushes, hair dryers, and such). Breakfasts are excellent and served on the lovely sun porch.

INFORMATION AND SERVICES

The **Lake Champlain Chamber of Commerce** (877/686-5253, www.vermont.org) runs an information booth on Church Street at the corner of Bank Street. Also look for a copy of the **Blue Map** (www.bluemap.com), a detailed tourist map of downtown and the Greater Burlington Area.

For emergency and hospital services, head to **Fletcher Allen Hospital** (Colchester Ave., 802/847-0000), while **Vermont Children's Hospital** (111 Colchester Ave., 802/847-5437) is equipped to handle younger patients' needs. Fill prescriptions at **Lakeside Pharmacy** (242 Pearl St., 802/862-1491, www.lakerx.org, 8:30 A.M.–7 P.M. Mon.–Fri., 9 A.M.–3 P.M. Sat.) or **Rite Aid** (158 Cherry St., 802/862-1562), which also offers faxing services and has a second location (1024 North Ave., 802/865-7822). A handful of banks are in the downtown blocks of Burlington's retail area along Church Street. In that same area, ATMs seem to be on every block.

Internet access is offered at **Speeder & Earl's Coffee** (412 Pine St., 802/658-6016, www.speederandearls.com, 6:30 A.M.–5:30 P.M. Mon.–Fri., 8 A.M.–5 P.M. Sat.–Sun.) and **FedEx Office Center** (199 Main St., 802/658-2561, 24 hours Mon.–Thurs., noon–11 P.M. Fri., 9 A.M.–9 P.M. Sat., 9 A.M.–midnight Sun.), which also offers fax services and shipping services.

GETTING THERE AND AROUND

The easiest driving route to Burlington is I-89 across Vermont, a two-hour trip (90 mi.) from White River Junction. The more scenic route is to take winding Route 7 up from Rutland along the foothills of the Greens (65 mi., 1.75 hr.).

Flights from many major cities land at **Burlington International Airport** (BTV, 1200 Airport Dr., South Burlington, 802/865-7571, www.btv.aero), which is served by half a dozen airlines. Reservation desks for major rental car companies are available at the airport.

Amtrak (800/872-7245, www.amtrak.com) runs trains to Burlington (29 Railroad Ave., Essex Jct.), and **Greyhound Bus Lines** (800/231-2222, www.greyhound.com) runs buses to **Burlington Bus Station** (345 Pine St., 802/864-6811).

Chittenden County Transit Authority (802/864-2282, www.cctaride.org) has bus routes throughout Burlington and the surrounding area, including buses downtown from the airport and train station. To get to and from the airport, take bus route 1, which takes approximately 25 minutes to travel between BIA and downtown's Cherry Street station. From the train station, take bus route 2, which takes approximately 40 minutes to make the trip between Essex Junction and Cherry Street. Bus fare is $1.25. Taxi stands are also available at the airport and the train station; to call a cab from other locations, contact **Burlington Taxi** (905/333-3333, www.burlingtontaxi.com).

From New York, it's possible to get to Burlington via ferry from Port Kent. Several boats a day are run by **Lake Champlain Transportation** (King Street Dock, 802/864-9804, www.ferries.com, late May–early Oct., $5 adults, $2.20 children, children under 6 free, $17.50 vehicle and driver one-way), which take about an hour to cross the lake. The round-trip threading through the lake's islands is also one of the most economical ways to enjoy Champlain's scenery.

In non-medical emergencies, contact the headquarters for the **Burlington Police Department** (1 North Ave., 802/658-2704).

Upper Champlain Valley

North of Burlington, Lake Champlain sheds any pretensions of being just a large river and expands into a full-blown inland sea, with wide blue vistas across its up-to-12-mile span. After the Great Lakes, Lake Champlain is the sixth-largest body of freshwater in the country. In fact, it was briefly declared to be a Great Lake for all of three months in 1997, thanks to a rider in a bill for lake research inserted by Vermont senator Pat Leahy. After an uproar, the designation (along with funds for research) was rescinded, leaving Champlain a Great Lake in character if not in name. While not nearly as large as the Great Lakes, Champlain is unnaturally deep, reaching 400 feet deep in some areas (twice as deep as Lake Erie). That fact has helped to perpetuate the myth of a giant sea monster named Champ that inhabits the lake's depths and occasionally surfaces for sightings by pleasure-boaters and kayakers. The lake is a popular destination for water-borne recreation, with dozens of state parks scattered around its northern end.

The region contains the former railroad town of **St. Albans,** home every year to the Vermont Maple Festival. The main attractions, however, are the several large islands moored at the northern end of the lake, which offer a quiet getaway or rambling day trip. Banish thoughts of spruce-coated wilderness; these islands have been settled as long as Vermont has and are now mainly residences and farmland—most are connected to the mainland by the highway from Burlington.

NORTH OF BURLINGTON

Heading north on Route 7, the industrial clog of Burlington quickly gives way to a rural tableau of sheep and dairy farms. Residents of the area, which includes the quaint small towns of **Milton, Colchester, Jericho,** and **Georgia**

claim the best of both worlds, with a slow pace of life within striking distance of both the big-city charms of Burlington and the recreational offerings of the mountains.

Sights

If all you've tasted is cheddar and Swiss, you may begin to doubt whether you have *ever* really tasted cheese after sampling the raw sheep's milk varieties at **Willow Hill Farm** (313 Hardscrabble Rd., Milton, 802/893-2963, www.sheepcheese.com, 10 A.M.–5 P.M. daily). Master cheesemakers Willow Smart and David Phinney produce nine varieties from their flock of East Friesian and Suffolk crossbred sheep, and then ripen the result in a naturally humidified cave. Viewing windows look down on the cheese-making process, which uses a special European method.

Entertainment

A professional theater company operating out of Saint Michael's College, **St. Michael's Playhouse** (1 Winooski Park, Colchester, 802/654-2281, www.saintmichaelsplayhouse. org) is where to catch regular productions like *Into the Woods, Educating Rita, Biloxi Blues,* and *The Pirates of Penzance.* The playhouse is very popular locally, so it's wise to call ahead for tickets.

Shopping

Score newly made period pieces at **Randall Henson Handcrafted Furniture** (1276 East Rd., Colchester, 802/878-6149, www.randallhenson.com); the staff uses reproduction hand tools and centuries-old techniques to turn out exquisite Windsor-style wooden chairs. Diverse, locally handmade crafts line the shelves of the **Old Red Mill Craft Shop** (Rte. 15, by the river bridge on your left as

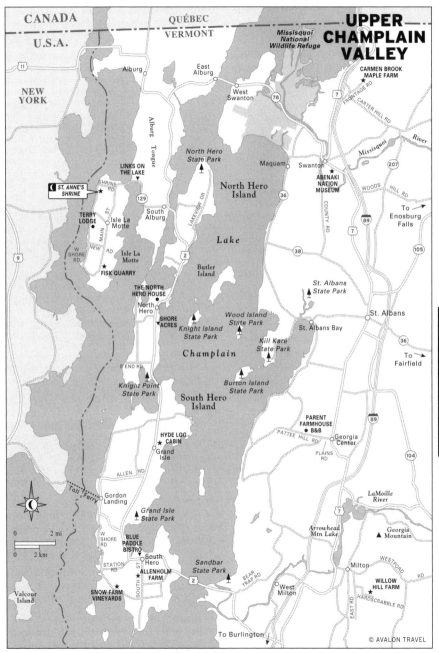

© AVALON TRAVEL

THE ST. ALBANS RAID

Of all the quirky schemes dreamed up in wartime, the raid organized by Lieutenant Bennett Young takes the cake. A Kentucky cavalry officer during the Civil War, Bennett received a commission from the Confederacy to stage raids from Canada to rob Union banks to line the South's coffers. His one and only action was the successful raid of St. Albans, in which he and 20 other cavalrymen galloped the 15 miles from the Canadian border and took over the town on October 19, 1864, herding the panicked townsfolk onto the village green and simultaneously robbing three banks. The soldiers made off with some $256,000, though their celebration was cut short when they were captured in Montreal a few weeks later and forced to give back some $90,000 they still had on them. Despite the best efforts of the United States, however, neutral Canada refused to extradite the soldiers. In the subsequent "celebrity" trial in Canada, Young and his confederates were eventually discharged on the grounds that they were soldiers acting under official orders.

As a postscript, the incident was made into a mildly successful movie, *The Raid,* in 1954, in which the Bennett Young character, played by Van Heflin, comes to St. Albans weeks before the raid and falls in love with a pretty townswoman played by Anne Bancroft. Needless to say, that part is heavily fictionalized.

you enter town, Jericho Village, 802/899-3225, www.jerichohistoricalsociety.org, 10 A.M.–5 P.M. Mon.–Sat., 11:30 A.M.–4 P.M. Sun. Apr.–Dec.; 10 A.M.–5 P.M. Wed. and Sat., 11:30 A.M.–4 P.M. Sun.), which is housed in an old mill and run by volunteers from the community for the Jericho Historical Society. The store has a plethora of snowflake-themed items, as well as artist-drawn greeting cards, jewelry, and pottery.

Food

Burgers, a full roster of fried snacks, and near-legendary shakes populate the menu at **Joe's Snack Bar** (45 Rte. 15, Jericho, 802/899-3934, 11 A.M.–9 P.M. daily, closed in winter, $5–14), a local hangout that is so beloved that it inspired the children's book *Where Does Joe Go?* which ponders where restaurant owner Joe goes when the snack bar shuts down every winter.

ST. ALBANS

Situated north of Burlington on the eastern shore of the lake, St. Albans was one of the first towns to fight and win against the incursion of Wal-Mart in the 1990s. Its main street is still a thriving center of mom-and-pop stores, set down from a town green half the size of a football field. The town's claim to fame is as the unlikely site of a Civil War "battle," the so-called St. Albans Raid, which occurred in 1863. Following the war, St. Albans became a headquarters of the Central Vermont Railroad, which passed through the town on its way to Montreal and Quebec. In its heyday, it was known as "Railroad City," with some 1,500 workers employed in the town and great wealth from the railroad being invested in the Victorian homes that grace the top of the hill.

Sights

Situated on the east side of the green, the three-story **St. Albans Historical Society Museum** (Church St., 802/527-7933, www.uvm.edu, 1–4 P.M. Tues.–Sat. July–early Oct., $3 adults, children 14 and under free) is chock-full of historical artifacts, including relics from the Civil War raid, a 3-D re-creation of Norman Rockwell's painting *A Study for the Doctors Office,* and railroad memorabilia. Its pièce de résistance is a new 18-foot-long LED-festooned diorama of the Lake Champlain region.

Perhaps the most fascinating exhibit, however, is the northwest room, dedicated to two medical curiosities—the skull of a man who had a railroad spike rammed through his head in an accident and was a subject for early brain researchers, and another fellow with a flap of skin over his stomach that allowed daily inspection of his innermost workings. Make sure you go in with a full stomach yourself.

Events

St. Albans's big annual event is the **Vermont Maple Festival** (802/524-5800, www.vtmaplefestival.org, late Apr., free admission for most events and activities), which has grown from a humble celebration of the state's vaunted syrup into a grand festival that draws thousands each year from all over Vermont and beyond. The fair includes carnival rides, a craft show, a fiddling competition, a pancake breakfast (with maple syrup of course!), and the crowning of the Maple King and Queen, who "have the responsibility and FUN of representing the Green Mountain State's signature product during their reigning year."

Shopping

It's no secret what's on sale at **Lenny's Shoe & Apparel** (295 Swanton Rd., 802/527-0532, www.lennyshoe.com, 9:30 A.M.–8 P.M. Mon.–Fri., 9:30 A.M.–6 P.M. Sat., 10 A.M.–4 P.M. Sun.). The popular shop stocks sneakers and dress shoes for men, women, and kids.

There's something for everyone on your gift list at **Moonshadows Gifts** (89 Main St., 802/524-6758, 10 A.M.–5 P.M. Mon.–Sat., 11 A.M.–5 P.M. Sun.). With a hodgepodge of clever items from near and far, this is a great place to stock up on handmade pieces such as sculptures and knit scarves.

Food

Chow! Bella (24 N. Main St., 802/524-1405, www.chowbella.us, 4–9 P.M. Mon.–Tues.,

© VERMONTVACATION.COM/STEPHEN GOODHUE

an array of St. Albans maple products

5–9 P.M. Wed.–Thurs., 5–10 P.M. Fri.–Sat., $12–21) may just be the best choice in town for curious palates. The cozy brick-walled restaurant emphasizes seasonal foods in a rotating menu—the likes of crabmeat-stuffed chicken breast and salmon in cider cream sauce. The list of wines by the glass is refreshingly long and thoughtfully chosen.

Information and Services

For more information about St. Albans contact the office of **St. Albans for the Future** (100 N. Main St., 802/524-1500, www.stalbansvt.com), located at City Hall.

The only hospital north of Burlington is the **Northwestern Medical Center** (133 Fairfield St., 802/524-5911, www.northwesternmedicalcenter.org). For pharmacy needs, there's a **Rite-Aid Pharmacy** (133 N. Main St., 802/524-2141, 8 A.M.–9 P.M. Mon.–Sat., 9 A.M.–6 P.M. Sun., pharmacy 8 A.M.–9 P.M. Mon.–Fri., 9 A.M.–6 P.M. Sat., 9 A.M.–5 P.M. Sun.) downtown, as well as the independent **Jack Rixon's Pharmacy** (40 N. Main St, 802/524-2020).

A cluster of banks sits at the crossroads of U.S. Route 7 and Route 36, including **TD Banknorth** (8 N. Main St., 802/527-5000) and **Citizens Bank** (152 S. Main St., 802/524-9597, 9 A.M.–5 P.M. Mon.–Fri., 9 A.M.–noon Sat.). In non-medical emergencies, contact the **St. Albans Police Department** (32 Lower Welden St., 802/524-2166).

SWANTON TO ENOSBURG FALLS

North of St. Albans, the mountains peter out and the forests take over. The land here was some of the earliest settled territory in the state, home to Native Americans at least 8,000 years ago. When Samuel Champlain arrived in 1609, he claimed the tribal camp for himself. More recently, vast swaths of land on the Canadian border have been turned into a wildlife refuge that is an important stopping-off point to many rare species of migratory wildfowl. The surrounding towns of **Swanton, Highgate, Fairfield,** and **Enosburg Falls** are only slightly more settled.

Sights

The little town of Swanton lives up to its name by sheltering two **swans** descended from a pair sent by England's Queen Elizabeth II on the occasion of the town's bicentennial. The birds inhabit a palatial enclosure on the town common. Swanton is also the tribal headquarters for the **Abenaki Nation** (100 Grand Ave., Swanton, 802/868-2559, www.abenakination.com), the western branch of the "People of the Dawn," the Native Americans who inhabited most of northern Vermont, New Hampshire, and Maine for thousands of years before the coming of European settlers. The Nation runs a museum with exhibits including headdresses, masks, and an authentic birch-bark canoe.

Chester A. Arthur was never *supposed* to be president. The 21st president of the United States was vice president when James Garfield was shot in 1881, just four months into his term of office. Nonetheless, Arthur rose to the occasion to become a decent if not great sovereign, reigning in the worst of the Gilded Age excess with rigorous prosecution of fraud and the establishment of the modern civil service. The **Chester A. Arthur Historical Site** (off Rte. 36 or 108, Fairfield, 802/828-3051, 11 A.M.–5 P.M. Sat.–Sun. July–mid-Oct., donations accepted) displays a pictorial history of the president in a reconstruction of the home where Arthur was purportedly born (though modern research shows he actually moved to the house when he was one year old). Arthur's father used to preach at the nearby 1840 brick Baptist church. To get to the site, head north from the small village of Fairfield and bear right after one mile. Continue for five miles along the road, which eventually turns to gravel.

The family-run **Carman Brook Maple Farm** (1275 Fortin Rd., 802/868-2347, www.cbmaplefarm.com, 8:30 A.M.–4:30 P.M. Tues.–Sat. late May–Oct., $4 adults, $2 children 2–12, children under 2 free) mixes two of Vermont's best flavors with a sugarhouse and dairy barn in one place. A self-guided tour brochure leads you through the sugarhouse, while paths around the farm allow you to stretch your legs among the maples and pastures.

Entertainment and Events

Marching bands from around the state parade in honor of Vermont's favorite animal at the **Vermont Dairy Festival** (802/933-9691, Enosburg Falls, www.vermontdairyfestival.com, first Saturday in June), held each year in the hamlet of Enosburg Falls. The highlight of the festival is the annual "cow plop" contest, in which a grass-fed beast is let loose on a grid of numbered squares.

The renovated **Opera House at Enosburg Falls** (123 Depot St., Enosburg Falls, 802/933-6171) hosts community theater and musical performances.

Food

The straightforward specials at **The Abbey Restaurant** (6212 Rte. 105, Enosburg Falls, 802/933-4747, www.theabbeyrestaurant.net, restaurant 5–9 P.M. Fri.–Sat., 10:30 A.M.–1 P.M. Sun.; pub 11:30 A.M.–close daily) have earned a local following—as has the convivial atmosphere in the establishment's tavern. Depending on what's available daily, you'll sup on the likes of prime rib, fresh scrod, or grilled chicken.

The highlights of dinner at **Jamerson's Place Restaurant** (73 First St., Swanton, 802/868-3190, 7 A.M.–8 P.M. Mon., Wed.–Thurs., and Sun., 7 A.M.–9 P.M. Fri.–Sat., $21–27) are the superb buttermilk and chocolate pancakes and desserts. Getting from one to the other isn't so bad either, thanks to stick-to-your-ribs specialties like cheesy garlic breadsticks and soul-warming French onion soup.

LAKE CHAMPLAIN ISLANDS

With more shoreline than any other part of Vermont, this cluster of five quiet islands feels entirely separate from the rest of the state—if not the world. Water seems to be everywhere, as do farms, humble homes, and friendly residents who all seem to be on a first-name basis with each other. The central island is appropriately named **Grand Isle,** flanked to the south by the attached **South Hero** and to the north by the sinuous **North Hero,** which has as much of a downtown as the islands have to offer. By contrast, the most secluded of the isles is the haunting **Isle La Motte,** home to a Catholic pilgrimage site and former site of the first settlement in the state. La Motte offers tranquil views of the lake all the way to the New York coast.

Discovered approximately 400 years ago by Samuel de Champlain, the islands are good for those seeking history as well as a little R&R. They're home to New England's oldest log cabin (on Grand Isle), and each island's individual historical societies showcase artifacts from the islands' early settlers. All that said, besides a handful of other sights of note there isn't much else to do here—which is precisely how many visitors would have it.

◖ St. Anne's Shrine

Situated at the far northern end of Lake Champlain, the Isle La Motte is a haunting terrain of sparse forest and windswept solitude. It must have seemed all the more desolate in 1666, when the first settlement in Vermont, Fort St. Anne, was built by French explorers under the command of Pierre de St. Paul, Sieur La Motte. They took solace in a shrine built to St. Anne, staffed by Jesuit priests who accompanied the expedition.

© VERMONTVACATION.COM/SKYE CHALMERS

St. Anne's Shrine

Four hundred years later, the shrine (West Shore Rd./Shrine Rd., Isle La Motte, 802/928-3362, www.saintannesshrine.org, 9 A.M.–7 P.M. daily mid-May–mid-Oct., tours every half-hour, $2 adults) still exists as a Catholic pilgrimage site, though the current building dates only from the late 19th century. In addition to the main building, where mass is still said regularly in season, the picturesque lakeshore is dotted by various grottoes filled with religious statues, including a 15-foot gold-leaf statue of the Virgin Mary rescued from a Burlington cathedral. Up the hill, a rectory and cafeteria has a small museum full of relics dating back to the French occupation in the 17th century. The lake itself is fittingly graced by a statue of the man who discovered it in 1609, explorer Samuel de Champlain, sculpted by F. L. Weber for the Montreal Expo in 1967.

Hyde Log Cabin

The "heroes" for which the islands are named lived at the Hyde Log Cabin (228 U.S. 2, Grand Isle, 802/828-3051, http://historicsites. vermont.gov, 11 A.M.–5 P.M. Thurs.–Mon. July–mid-Oct., $2 adults, children 14 and under free), an original 1785 home built by Jedediah Hyde and his father, who were both veterans of the Revolutionary War. The cabin was originally located two miles to the southwest; it was moved to its current location by the Vermont Historical Society and filled with old surveyor maps and other artifacts from the earliest days of the islands.

Allenholm Farm

The best place to get in touch with the agricultural ambience of the islands is Allenholm Farm (150 South St., South Hero, 802/372-5566, www. allenholm.com, 9 A.M.–5 P.M. daily), which has a petting paddock full of animals, including two donkeys, a Scotch Highland cow, and a fat ewe with a taste for peppermints. A farm stand sells apples and farm-made apple pies.

Fisk Quarry

The legacy of Lake Champlain's prehistoric sojourn in the tropics is on view at the Fisk Quarry (The Main Road, Isle La Motte, 802/862-4150, www.lclt.org). Poking out of the quarry walls are the fossilized remains of the 480-million-year-old Chazy Coral Reef, the oldest known coral reef in the world. Its stony sides are visibly embedded with stromatoporoids, ancient ancestors of modern-day sea sponges.

Snow Farm Vineyards

Vermont's oldest winery, Snow Farm Vineyards (190 W. Shore Rd., South Hero, 802/372-9463, www.snowfarm.com, 10 A.M.–5 P.M. daily May–Dec.) has won multiple awards for its delicate pinot noirs and vidal blanc ice wines. Tours of the winery are offered daily at 11 A.M. and 2 P.M. During the summer, the vineyard sponsors a Music in the Vineyard series on

Thursday nights, in which locals bring blankets and corkscrews and sip under the stars.

Entertainment and Events

All of Lake Champlain becomes a stage each summer, when the **Vermont Shakespeare Company** (North Hero, 877/874-1911, www.vermontshakespeare.org) performs outdoors at Knight Point State Park. A celebration as American as you-know-what, **Apple Fest** (South St., South Hero, 802/372-8400, Oct.) celebrates the yearly harvest with cider, auctions, a craft show—and, of course, plenty of pies.

Shopping

Retail is sparse among the islands; most folks here seem more interested in forgetting the rest of the world than buying something from it. There are, however, a few shops, such as **Hero's Welcome** (3537 Rte. 2, North Hero, 802/372-4161, www.heroswelcome.com, 6:30 A.M.–8 P.M. Mon.–Sat., 7 A.M.–7 P.M. Sun. in summer; 6:30 A.M.–6:30 P.M. Mon.–Sat., 7 A.M.–7 P.M. Sun. in winter), a general store stocked with Adirondack chairs, books on and maps of the area, squall jackets, and assorted gadgets.

And if you didn't find what you were looking for at Hero's Welcome, odds are it's on shelves—along with seemingly every other object on the planet—at **New England Via Vermont** (4 Milk St., Alburg, 802/796-3665, 10 A.M.–5 P.M. Mon.–Tues. and Thurs.–Sat.). No one disputes that the place is a souvenir shop, but the question—souvenirs of what?—has not yet been settled. Civil War buffs will find plenty to buy among the antique-bullet selection and book section dedicated to the war. Those hoping to take a piece of Vermont home will do well to pick up any of the maple or cheese products or videos and books on the state; natural-science lovers, meanwhile, thrill to the fossilized shark teeth and rocks.

Food

Eat like the locals do (not that you'll have much of a choice; restaurants are few and far between on most islands), and you won't go wrong. Start at the **Blue Paddle Bistro** (316 Rte. 2, South Hero, 802/372-4814, www.bluepaddlebistro.com, 5–8:30 P.M. daily, $9–16) for friendly service, town gossip, and terrific gorgonzola-stuffed meatloaf. The bar is crowned with a full-sized canoe.

For memorable views of the lake and mountains, grab a table at **Links on the Lake** (230 Rte. 129, Alburg, 802/796-3586, www.alburggolflinks.com, 5–8 P.M. Sat.–Sun., $11–15) in the Alburg Golf Links public golf course. The casual restaurant is open May through October and serves staples like clam chowder and fettucine alfredo, as well as more inventive fare such as cherry balsamic duck breast and prosciutto-wrapped chicken breast.

The view is as delicious as the food at **Shore Acres, The Lake Champlain Room** (237 Shore Acres Dr., North Hero, 802/372-8722, www.shoreacres.com, 5–8 P.M. Mon.–Sat., $21–27), part of an inn set on rolling hills overlooking Lake Champlain. Take it all in while you sup on simple but flavorful dishes like homemade grilled polenta and roasted rack of lamb in port-rosemary sauce.

Information and Services

The **Lake Champlain Islands Chamber** (3501 Rte. 2, North Hero, 802/372-8400, www.champlainislands.com) has information at its office on North Hero Island. There's a **Merchants Bank** (301 U.S. Route 2, Grand Isle, 802/372-4222, 9 A.M.–4 P.M. Mon.–Thurs., 9 A.M.–5:30 P.M. Fri.) right before the bridge to North Hero.

SPORTS AND RECREATION
Missisquoi National Wildlife Refuge

Bird-watchers flock to this refuge (29 Tabor

Rd., Swanton, 802/868-4781, www.fws. gov, dawn–dusk daily) for a glimpse of the ducks, grebes, and mergansers that make this 6,000-plus-acre preserve their temporary home during migrations to and from Canada. Several interpretive trails take in a mile and a half of wooded wetlands, which are also inhabited by beavers and other small mammals. The refuge can attract up to 20,000 waterfowl during the autumn migration. On-site, Shad Island is the state's largest great blue heron rookery. Trails are also open for snowshoeing and cross-country skiing in the winter months.

Biking

Lake Champlain Bikeways (1 Steele St. #103, Burlington, 802/652-2453, www.champlain-bikeways.org) distributes a pamphlet titled *Champlain Island Bikeways,* which details five loops around the islands taking in sand dunes, a log cabin, and the quirky stone castles built by a Swiss gardener. **Bike Vermont** (800/257-2226, www.bikevt.com) offers rentals as well as three-day tours of the area starting from North Hero House Inn.

In the St. Albans area, the **Missisquoi Valley Rail Trail** (802/524-5958, www.mvrailtrail.com) provides some 26 miles of crushed limestone surface that wends its way through quiet farms and woodlands nearly to the Canadian border.

Boating

Given that the islands are home to more shoreline than anywhere else in Vermont, you rarely have to fight for a quiet place to put a canoe in the water, cast about for fish, go for a dip, or simply sit and watch the sunset over the water. And, despite the small populations on each island, there are several places around to lend a hand to your water expeditions. On Grand Isle, **Ladd's Landing** (412 U.S. 2, Grand Isle, 802/372-5320) is a 100-slip marina open all summer that also offers restoration and boat winterization services. **Heritage Kayak Tours** (100 Carry Bay Ln., North Hero, 802/372-4274) runs tours led by a local historian and rents both boats and equipment. And **An Bradon Fishing Charters** (23 Sunrise Dr., South Hero, 802/654-9282, www.anbradon-charters.com, $325/half-day, $525/full-day) specializes in finding and catching salmon.

Hiking and Camping

Runners, beachgoers, birdwatchers, anglers, and hikers find plenty of activity and wildlife at **North Hero State Park** (3803 Lakeview Dr., North Hero, 802/372-8727, www.vtstateparks.com/htm/northhero.cfm, late May–early Sept.), a picturesque playground on a quiet peninsula sticking out onto the lake. The floodplain forest is home to white-tailed deer and migratory waterfowl, as well as several species of turtles that nest along the lakeshore. Unfortunately, overnight camping is not currently permitted.

Several of Lake Champlain's smaller islands, however, offer a unique opportunity to really "get away from it all." Case in point: the former agricultural island that is now **Burton Island State Park** (St. Albans Bay, 802/524-6353, www.vtstateparks.com/htm/burton.cfm, late May–early Sept., campsites $16–37). Take a ferry to enjoy its campground, along with its swimming and recreation area; a resident naturalist gives deer-spotting tours. Ferry service is available several times a day from Kill Kare State Park, southwest of St. Albans center. The island itself has 17 tent sites in a loop near the ferry landing and 26 lean-tos, most directly on the shore, within a relatively comfy campground offering hot showers and Wi-Fi Internet. Canoes and rowboats are also available for rent.

If even that's too much civilization for you, take a rented boat to **Woods Island** (St. Albans Bay, 802/524-6353, www.vtstateparks.com/htm/woodsisland.cfm, late May–early Sept., campsites $16–18), a primitive getaway that lives up to its name. A so-called "remote area" campground, the facilities here are Spartan—consisting of five carry-in/carry-out campsites along the beach, each with only a simple fire-ring and basic latrine. Permits are available through Burton Island State Park. Despite the hassle of arranging a stay here, the experience of a remote wilderness only a few miles from Vermont's largest city is unbeatable. Only the calls of the loons will disturb your sleep.

ACCOMMODATIONS

The friendly and homey **Terry Lodge** (2925 W. Shore Rd., Isle La Motte, 802/928-3264, $79–99) feels a world away from everything, tucked into a shoreside corner of sleepy Isle La Motte. Rooms are humbly decorated, but all have private baths, and the inn has a private beach.

Beautiful winding flower gardens surround **Parent Farmhouse B&B** (854 Pattee Hill Rd., Georgia, 802/524-4201, www.parentfarmhouse.com, $99–175) outside, while antiques and elegant country furnishings fill it within. Breakfasts are large and delicious (the apple-rhubarb crumble squares are alone worth a visit), and the Green Mountains are a quick drive away.

No less than 400 acres of quiet countryside crisscrossed with country roads surround **The Inn at Buck Hollow Farm** (2150 Buck Hollow Rd., St. Albans, 800/849-7985, www.buckhollow.com, $100–140). Inside, there always seems to be a fire going in one of the sitting rooms or wine being served in the sunroom. Private chambers are anchored with queen-sized canopy beds and quilts. Breakfasts and pizza nights draw regular raves.

Arguably the most gentrified spot in the Lake Champlain Islands, ◖ **The North Hero House** (3643 Rte. 2, North Hero, 802/372-4732, www.northherohouse.com, $125–350) is poised on the banks of the lake in one of the islands' more central areas. The colonial-style inn houses 26 lovely individually decorated rooms, most with antique beds (four-poster to wrought-iron), floral linens, and some with a private balcony. The semiformal on-site restaurant overlooks the water and serves an excellent menu of ambitious dishes (the shrimp and scallop tian is a favorite).

GETTING THERE AND AROUND

From Burlington, most of the Champlain Islands are accessible by highway. Take I-89 to exit 7, then U.S. 2 north to North Hero (30 mi., 45 min.). To get to St. Albans from Burlington, take I-89 north to exit 18, then Route 7 north (25 mi., 40 min.), or connect from the islands to St. Albans via Route 78 east to U.S. 7 south (30 mi., 45 min.). The entire round-trip loop from Burlington around the islands and St. Albans takes approximately 2 hours (90 mi.) without stops.

Amtrak (800/872-7245, www.amtrak.com) also runs trains to St. Albans (40 Federal St.) on its Vermonter line. **Green Mountain Transit Agency** (802/223-7487, www.gmtaride.org) runs scheduled shuttle bus service throughout the Champlain Islands and northwestern Vermont.

Lower Champlain Valley

Is it just your imagination, or does every bit of this area seem (and smell) like cow country? Actually, you're right on the nose: The Champlain Valley is currently home to most of the state's dairy farms, though a good number of fruit farms are also mixed in here. This means plenty of places to stop and sample ice cream, cheese, or apples as you drive along the wooded stretches of Lake Champlain's banks—and plenty of scenic vistas of working farmhouses framed by mountains and calm waters.

SHELBURNE

Blessed with plenty of scenic roads and pastoral mountain views, Shelburne has always been a community based primarily on farming, and it shows, with farmland seemingly everywhere you look. Lacking the active downtown center that anchors so many other country towns, Shelburne is more a spread-out collection of various tourist magnets—the most impressive

of which is the Shelburne Museum, one of Vermont's premier attractions.

◖ Shelburne Museum

If your jaw doesn't drop when you step onto the grounds of this 45-acre museum campus (5555 Shelburne Rd., 802/985-3346, www.shelburnemuseum.org, 10 A.M.–5 P.M. Mon.–Sat., noon–5 P.M. Sun. May–Oct., $20 adults, $10 children 5–18, children under 5 free, $50 family day pass), you might want to check your pulse. "Museum" might be too small a word for 38 buildings displaying hundreds of thousands of items, including a full-size Lake Champlain steamship, a 1920s carousel, a fine horse-drawn vehicle collection, and galleries of American folk art and French Impressionist paintings. The museum is the work of art collector Electra Havemeyer Webb, who relocated buildings from across the country to display her collection, opening the museum in 1947.

THE LEGEND OF CHAMP

Hang around Lake Champlain long enough and you are bound to hear about Champ. Like the Loch Ness in Scotland, the lake is supposed to be the abode of a modern-day sea monster that has been "sighted" many times over the past 400 years. In fact, Samuel de Champlain himself supposedly spotted a "20 foot serpent thick as a barrel and [with] a head like a horse" when he discovered the lake in 1609. Since then, the legend has only grown over the last four centuries. In 1873, circus impresario P. T. Barnum offered $50,000 as a reward for its skin; subsequently both Vermont and New York have passed laws against harming the (supposed) creature. The most conclusive evidence of the monster is a photo taken in 1977 by vacationer Sandra Mansi that clearly shows a curved neck and head poking out of the lake.

When Champ fans try to explain what the "monster" is, however, they begin running into problems. Most theories hold that the creature is related to a dinosaur called a plesiosaur that got trapped in the lake back when Champlain used to be an arm of the ocean. However, the lake is only 10,000 years old, whereas plesiosaurs are thought to have been extinct for 65 million years. So in order to have a dinosaur in the lake, you'd need to have one plesiosaur who had been alive 65 million years—or 500 plesiosaurs to make a viable breeding population over the last 10,000 years. Whatever the truth, Champ has been embraced as a symbol by locals who have put his moniker on everything from Champ's Potato Chips to Burlington's Lake Monsters, a minor league baseball team.

the *Ticonderoga*, a restored 220-foot Lake Champlain steamship at the Shelburne Museum

After her death, Webb's children brought her own home to the museum, and it is still set up with the art and furniture in the exact locations Webb intended them, providing an intimate window into the private life of a wealthy collector. Hanging in the rooms of the Greek Revival mansion are many first-rate paintings by Cassatt, Degas, Monet, Corot, and Manet, including the first Impressionist painting brought to America, a Monet painting of a drawbridge, which was purchased by Webb in Paris for $20. Webb and her parents were also important contributors to the Metropolitan Museum of Art in New York; because of that association, the Shelburne Museum is able to snag world-class traveling exhibitions. Recent shows featured a retrospective of Georgia O'Keeffe's paintings, including some of her best-known flower canvases, and an exhibit of never-before-seen furniture and glasswork by art-nouveau master craftsman Louis Comfort Tiffany.

Shelburne Farms

The Webb family certainly thinks big. In addition to the Shelburne Museum, they are the benefactors behind Shelburne Farms (1611 Harbor Rd., 802/985-8686, www.shelburnefarms.org, 9 A.M.–5:30 P.M. daily mid-May–Oct., $8 adults, $6 seniors, $5 children 3–17, children under 3 free), a sprawling agricultural estate perched literally on the shores of the lake. Attractions include a petting barn where kids can milk a cow or brush a donkey, a cheese-making operation, and eight miles of walking trails through achingly bucolic meadows and woodland. The farm also lets out rooms in its baronial estate.

Vermont Teddy Bear Company

Everyone knows the teddy bear was named after American president Theodore Roosevelt. But in 1981, John Sortino was shocked to find out that the singularly American invention was made exclusively overseas. He started

© MICHAEL BLANDING

CHAMPLAIN VALLEY

the Vermont Teddy Bear Company

making his own teddy bears, selling them from a pushcart in Burlington in 1983. From those humble beginnings, the cotton-stuffed empire of the Vermont Teddy Bear Company (6655 Shelburne Rd./Rte. 7, 802/985-3001, www. vermontteddybear.com, 9:30 A.M.–5 P.M. daily early July–Oct.; 10 A.M.–4 P.M. daily Oct.–June, $3 adults, children 12 and under free) was born. Now the company's flagship store is always packed with groups touring the operation and picking out fabric and stuffing to make their own creations. The factory and gift shop (if anything, bigger than the factory) retain enough homegrown charm to avoid seeming like a complete tourist trap.

Vermont Wildflower Farm

Butterflies and flower-lovers alike make a bee-line to the Vermont Wildflower Farm (3488 Rte. 7, Charlotte, 802/425-3641, www.ver-montwildflowerfarm.com, 10 A.M.–5 P.M. daily Apr.–Oct.) a gargantuan flower seed shop with

six acres worth of gardens in the back. A free 20-minute self-guided tour includes information on all of the different blooms, which are grouped by category along the quarter-mile path. Depending on the season, you might see dame's rocket, penstemons, coreopsis, cosmos, or asters.

Events

Past performers at the **Concerts on the Green** (5555 Shelburne Rd., 802/985-3346, www. shelburnemuseum.org) music series include Willie Nelson, Emmylou Harris, and Crosby, Stills, and Nash. Musicians play on select summer weekends on the grounds of the Shelburne Museum.

Shopping

The best bargains in town can be found among the crowded shelves at **Champlain Valley Antique Center** (4067 Shelburne Rd., 802/985-8116, www.vermontantiquecenter. com, 10 A.M.–5 P.M. Mon.–Sat., 11 A.M.–4 P.M. Sun.), a conglomeration of collectibles and furnishings from more than 25 local antiques dealers. Pick through the offerings to find fine china, vintage posters, folk art, and handmade armoires.

Food

A little slice of French country resides at **Cafe Shelburne** (5573 Shelburne Rd., 802/985-3939, www.cafeshelburne.com, 5:30–9 P.M. Tues.–Sat., $19–26), a lovely but low-key eatery with soft lighting, a well-chosen wine list, and an affable staff. Settle in for dinner and dig in to the Gallic menu, with specials such as delicately flavored quail salad and escargot with prosciutto and almonds. Also French-leaning and subtly romantic is the **(Bearded Frog** (5247 Shelburne Rd., 802/985-9877, www.the-beardedfrog.com, 5–9 P.M. daily, $6–25), a restaurant named for owner Michel Mahe's facial hair and French heritage. The spot has been a hit since it opened in spring of 2006, mostly thanks to Mahe's eclectic menu. A pastiche of international flavors, such as mussels with chipotle, is served to an enthusiastic crowd in the large, polished room against oversized windows and elegant palms.

Information and Services

The **Shelburne Museum** (5555 Shelburne Rd., 802/985-3346, www.shelburnemuseum.org, 10 A.M.–5 P.M. Mon.–Sat., noon–5 P.M. Sun., May–Oct.) has a visitor information center stocked with maps and brochures; no admission required.

A **Rite-Aid Pharmacy** (30 Shelburne Shopping Park, 802/985-2610, 9 A.M.–6 P.M. Mon.–Sat. for both store and pharmacy) is located in the center of downtown. Free Wi-Fi is available at **Bruegger's Bagel Bakery** (2989 Shelburne Rd., 802/985-3183, 5:30 A.M.–5 P.M. Mon.–Fri., 6 A.M.–5 P.M. Sat.–Sun.). In an emergency, contact the **Shelburne Police** (5420 Shelburne Rd., 802/985-8051).

VERGENNES AND FERRISBURGH

The little settlement on the banks of Otter Creek was the first city in Vermont, and one of the first in America. No, that's not a typo—though it may be a bit of an exaggeration. Until the late 1700s, most settlements in New England were known as "towns." When the mill center of Vergennes was formed out of bits of land from neighboring towns, it was so bully on its prospects that it took the grandiose name of "city." Now with a population of 2,800, Vergennes is dwarfish, even by Vermont standards, but it has risen up to its name with a citified atmosphere of fine restaurants and upscale shops. During the War of 1812, it was the home base for a shipyard along Otter Creek that heroically built a fleet to defeat the British on the lake—one of the few bright spots in a disastrous war.

A few miles east of town, on the part of Lake Champlain known as "the Narrows," the port of Basin Harbor makes a good base from which to venture out onto the water. Nearby Ferrisburgh is the most northern town in the county, and with its lively, picturesque town center and handful of shops and sights, it's certainly worth an afternoon or day trip.

Lake Champlain Maritime Museum

It's tempting to forget about Lake Champlain when contemplating New England's maritime history—focusing instead on the clipper ships and schooners that plied the Atlantic. But the lake was once the lifeblood of the country's interior, before the cutting of the Erie Canal and settlement of Ohio territory moved the frontier farther to the west. Champlain's history dates back even before the Pilgrims landed at Plymouth Rock, when Native Americans traversed its shores in birch-bark canoes and French trappers established camps on its islands.

This museum (4472 Basin Harbor Rd., 802/475-2022, www.lcmm.org, 10 A.M.–5 P.M. daily late May–mid-Oct., $10 adults, $9 seniors, $6 students 5–17, children under 5 free, admission good for two consecutive days), just a few miles from the lakeshore, does an exceptional job of bringing alive the scope of the lake's domestic and military history, with a hands-on boat-building workshop, an exhibit on the more than 200 shipwrecks that line the lake bottom, and an interactive display on the lake's importance in the Revolutionary War.

Perhaps the biggest surprise is the story of patriot-turned-traitor Benedict Arnold, who led a heroic defense of the lake in the early years of the war. Arnold commissioned a fleet of gunships to be built at the lake's southern end in Skenesborough and fought a hopeless battle with the British off the shore of Valcour Island, a few miles up from Basin Harbor. The engagement scuttled British plans for invasion in 1776, leaving another year for the Americans to plan their defenses. In 1997, the museum undertook the mammoth task of rebuilding one of Arnold's gunboats, the *Philadelphia II,* which now floats in the harbor.

Bixby Memorial Library

The imposing Greek Revival facade of Bixby Memorial Library (258 Main St., 802/877-2211, www.bixbylibrary.org, 12:30–8 P.M. Mon., 12:30–5 P.M. Tues. and Fri., 10 A.M.–5 P.M. Wed.–Thurs., 10 A.M.–2 P.M. Sat., free) is only the beginning of its charms. Inside, the library has one of the largest collections of artifacts in the state, with exhibits of Indian arrowheads, antique maps, stamps, and documents relating to the early history of the region, including the Revolutionary and Civil Wars.

Rokeby Museum

By the time escaped slaves arrived in Ferrisburgh, just north of Vergennes, they must have been able to taste the freedom of Canada on their tongue. The Rokeby Museum (4334 Rte. 7, Ferrisburgh, 802/877-3406, www.rokeby.org, tours 11 A.M., 12:30 P.M., and 2 P.M. Thurs.–Sun., $6 adults, $4 seniors and students, $2 children under 12) preserves the time when Quakers Rowland Thomas and Rachel Gilpin helped countless slaves escape on the Underground Railroad, hiding them and providing them employment on their sheep farm. In addition to being one of the best-documented Underground Railroad sites in the country, the museum contains artifacts relating to 200 years of Vermont history.

Round Barn Merinos

Across from the Rokeby Museum, learn why merino sheep are the most coveted in the flock at Round Barn Merinos (4263 Rte. 7, Ferrisburgh, 802/877-6544, www.

roundbarnmerinos.com, noon–5 P.M. Thurs.–Sat.), which sells knitware including hats, scarves, and blankets, as well as hand-dyed yarn and other items crafted out of the impeccably soft wool of their on-site flock. Visitors can meet and greet their sheep, as well as other animals, including an alpaca and a camel (which produces its own incredibly soft down). True to the farm's name, there is a historic Shaker round barn.

Entertainment and Events

In its 100-year history, the **Vergennes Opera House** (120 Main St., 802/877-6737, www.vergennesoperahouse.org) has seen many permutations, from a grand classical music hall to a moving-picture theater to a condemned old building. In 1997, the town raised money to restore the hall to its Victorian splendor, and it now serves as a cultural hub with an impressive array of entertainment offerings. Recent shows ranged from a 12-part a cappella jazz group to "Metal Fest," featuring bands with names like Blinded by Rage, Seething, and Black Out Frenzy.

The entire *city* comes out to celebrate **Vergennes Day** (802/388-7951, www.midvermont.com/events/vergennesday) every year at the end of the summer. Amusement rides, historical tours, and a 5K-road race add to the fun.

Shopping

It just doesn't make sense to leave Vergennes without stocking up on the area's delicacies. Start at the craft- and treat-lover's jackpot that is the **Kennedy Bros. Factory Marketplace** (10 Main St., 802/877-2975, www.kennedybrothers.com, 9:30 A.M.–5:30 P.M. daily), which features a huge selection of antiques, artisanal maple sugars and fudges, and woodware.

An unusual find that's full of unusual finds is **Sweet Charity** (141A Main St., Vergennes, 802/877-6200, http://sweetcharityvt.com, 10 A.M.–5 P.M. daily), a gift shop run by a charity for underprivileged women and children, and selling handmade crafts and art for their cause.

Everything at the retail store of **Dakin Farm** (5797 Rte. 7, Ferrisburgh, 800/993-2546, www.dakinfarm.com, 8 A.M.–5 P.M. daily) comes directly from the family farm's bounty—from cob-smoked bacon and maple frozen yogurt to kettle corn and cheddar cheese.

Food

Small-town sophistication is exemplified in a handful of eateries, primarily centered along Main Street. For a solid dose, settle in at a table at the modern country deli **(Three Squares** (221 Main St., 802/877-2772, www.3squarescafe.com, 8 A.M.–9 P.M. Mon.–Sat., 8 A.M.–8 P.M. Sun., $5–8), and tuck into one of the house's panini of teriyaki flank steak with red onion and garlic mayonnaise.

One of the most happening joints in Vergennes is **(Bar Antidote** (35 Green St., 802/877-2555, www.barantidote.com, 3–11 P.M. Tues.–Sat., $8–18). It's a mishmash of stylish yet relaxed ambience and a bar scene that hops with young friends and families. Specials like braised pork belly burgers and spicy chicken tacos fill the dining room tables.

Originally a cider press, the setting for **Starry Night Cafe** (5371 Rte. 7, Ferrisburgh, 802/877-6316 www.starrynightcafe.com, 5:30–9 P.M. Wed.–Sun., $17–26) is a historic complex that includes a covered bridge. The dining room itself is blessed with an antique bar, chairs custom-made by local artists, and handblown glassware. And the menu certainly isn't lacking in creativity; it's found in plates of steak tartare with chipotle aioli, tagine with tilapia and fennel, and duck with sour cherry-wine sauce.

There's a little slice of Paris to be found at a great price at **(Black Sheep Bistro** (253 Main St., 802/877-9991, www.blacksheepbistrovt.

com, 5–8:30 P.M. daily, $14–19), where high-quality dishes like black sesame–crusted salmon with ginger beurre blanc make up the specials.

Information and Services

For more information on Vergennes, contact or visit the **Addison County Chamber of Commerce** (2 Court St., Middlebury, 802/388-7951, www.addisoncounty.com). Pharmacy needs can be taken care of downtown at **Marble Works Pharmacy** (187 Main St., 802/877-1190, 8:30 A.M.–6 P.M. Mon.–Fri., 8:30 A.M.–5 P.M. Sat., 9 A.M.–2 P.M. Sun.). In an emergency, contact the **Vergennes Police** (120 Main St., 802/877-2201).

BRISTOL

While little Bristol has few bona fide sights, it makes up for that with a kind of "frozen in time" atmosphere that many towns boast and few deliver on. Cradled in the crook of Dearleap Mountain, the village is a welcoming sight for drivers who have just braved the pass over the Green Mountains from the Mad River Valley; it's also a last chance to fuel up for those venturing up into the peaks. The town's all-American downtown recalls the one Marty McFly stumbled upon in *Back to the Future,* with solid brick rows of storefronts strung with red, white, and blue bunting and filled with neighbors chatting at the bakery or launderette. If you are looking for a place to turn off your cell phone for a while, this might be just the ticket.

Sights

Don't get the wrong idea when you come into town and see **Lord's Prayer Rock,** a giant boulder with the "Our Father" carved into its face. No, you haven't entered a religious enclave. The rock dates back to the 19th century, when a local boy was tasked with bringing logs down the roller-coaster road from the mountaintop;

he breathed a prayer whenever he made it down to see the boulder at the end of the road. A few decades later, after the boy had become a wealthy physician in New York, he returned to Bristol and had the prayer carved into the rock, hoping it would bring similar comfort to other travelers over the mountain.

Events

The biggest event of the year is Bristol's annual **Fourth of July** (802/453-2486, www.bristol4th.com), a 150-year-old celebration of national pride that features a footrace, parade, live band music, and of course fireworks. In past years, Miss Vermont National Teenager has put in an appearance. Bristol also holds a **Harvest Festival** (802/453-5885, www.bristolrec.org) each year at the end of September. In addition to the usual craft vendors and agricultural competitions, the event includes an antique car rally, with trophies given in more than 20 different categories.

Shopping

Pick up local artwork at **Art on Main** (25 Main St., 802/453-4032, www.artonmain.net, 10 A.M.–6 P.M. Tues.–Sat., 11 A.M.–3 P.M. Sun. May–Dec.), a cooperative community art center brimming with watercolors, oils, and acrylics, plus hand-carved walking sticks, quilts, and stained-glass kaleidoscopes. Potter Robert Compton and wife Christine are the forces behind **Robert Compton Pottery** (2662 N. Rte. 116, 802/453-3778, www.robertcomptonpottery.com, 10 A.M.–5 P.M. Mon.–Tues. and Thurs.–Sun., mid-May–mid-Oct.), a showroom and studio filled with pieces the artist has created with a salt glaze—a special process that introduces salt into the kiln at extremely high temperatures.

Food

The best of local fare tends to be tied to the area's farms—like the fresh produce and goods at **Almost Home Market** (28 North St., 802/453-5775, www.almosthomemarket.net, 7 A.M.–7 P.M. Mon.–Fri., 8 A.M.–5 P.M. Sat., 9 A.M.–3 P.M. Sun., $6–15). Half-country store, half-cafe, it whips up fresh-baked breads and pastries, plus sandwiches and snazzy meals like lavender-roasted chicken with lemon and garlic or salmon teriyaki.

Even closer to the source is ◖ **Mary's Restaurant** (1868 N. Rte. 116, 888/424-2432, www.innatbaldwincreek.com/marys, 5:30–9 P.M. Wed.–Sat., 9:30 A.M.–1:30 P.M. and 5:30–9 P.M. Sun., $18–28), located at the Inn at Bald Creek, where much of the menu comes straight from the property's farm and other area farms. (Don't miss the cream of garlic soup.) And don't forget to make a reservation for the English-style **Bobcat Cafe** (5 Main St., 802/453-3311, www.bobcatcafe.com, 5–9 P.M. Sun.–Thurs., 5–9:30 P.M. Fri.–Sat., $9–16), which gets packed with regulars for the burgers made from locally raised beef and sweet-potato fries.

For dessert, stop in at **Village Creeme Stand** (41 West St., 802/453-6034, 10 A.M.–10 P.M. daily), an ice-cream stand whose yellow-and-white awning has spelled summer refreshment for generations of Vermonters. Everywhere else in the country, "creemees" are known as soft-serve ice cream, but in Vermont they've taken on the air of religion. Try the chocolate-vanilla twisted with butterscotch dip.

Information and Services

The **Bristol Parks Arts & Recreation Department** (1 South St., 802/453-5885, www.bristolrec.org) runs an information center during the summer at the Howden Hall Community Center (19 West St.). You can also visit the **Island Pond Welcome Center** (11 Birch, 802/723-9889, 10 A.M.–2 P.M. Tues., 9 A.M.–2 P.M. Wed.–Sat.). For more information on Bristol, contact or visit the **Addison County Chamber of Commerce** (2 Court St.,

Middlebury, 802/388-7951, www.addison-county.com).

SPORTS AND RECREATION
Hiking and Camping
A favorite place for a stroll along Lake Champlain is **Button Bay State Park** (5 Button Bay Rd., Ferrisburgh, 802/475-2377, www.vtstateparks.com/htm/buttonbay.cfm, $3 adults, $2 children 4–13, free for children under 3), about four miles west of Vergennes. Located on the site of a tropical coral reef that remains from the time when Lake Champlain was attached to the ocean, the 1.5-mile walk passes by limestone deposits embedded with sea snail fossils. The bay gets its name from the "buttons" or smooth clay deposits strewn around the beaches. The park also has a campground, with more than 70 tent and lean-to sites ($16–27/night) on a grassy area overlooking the lake.

One of the best views of the lake is the sweeping panorama from **Mount Philo State Park** (5425 Mt. Philo Rd., Charlotte, 802/425-2390, www.vtstateparks.com/htm/philo.cfm, $3 adults, $2 children 4–13, children under 3 free). The 968-foot mountain sits all by itself on the shore, affording drop-dead views west to the Adirondacks. The heights are capped by a picnic area and small campground with just 10 sites ($14–21 nightly base rate).

Biking
The Lake Champlain area is a cyclist's dream, with miles of flat terrain studded with farm stands, country stores, and stunning views of the lake and Adirondack Mountains on the western shore. The **Lake Champlain Bikeways** (802/652-2453, www.champlainbikeways.org) trail system stretches for 1,300 miles on both sides of the lake. Wind from the wider sections of the lake can make for tough going at points, but the ride is worth it for the sparkling views of the water. The Rebel's Retreat Trail is a 42-mile loop through the rolling farmlands around Vergennes. Parking is available at the trail's start downtown. Another trail starting from the same point, called Otter Creek Wandering, follows the river along mostly flat terrain for the 30 miles between Vergennes and Middlebury.

ACCOMMODATIONS
If none of the recommended lodging choices are available, Shelburne is a safe bet for moderately priced inns and B&Bs, the vast majority of which are in historic homes.

Under $100
It may have just three rooms, but **Crystal Palace Victorian Bed & Breakfast** (48 North St., Bristol, 802/453-7609, www.crystalpalacebb.com, $90–140) welcomes guests with the fanfare of a major resort. Rooms are replete with stained-glass windows, poster beds, fireplaces, and whirlpool or claw-foot tubs. Meanwhile, the Victorian home's common spaces are refinished with white and red cherry, butternut, ash, and quarter oak. At breakfast, don't pass up the graham-cracker French toast.

$100-150
Simple and romantic, the **Inn at Baldwin Creek** (1868 N. Rte. 116, Bristol, 888/424-2432, www.innatbaldwincreek.com, $110–245) appoints its spacious rooms with four-poster queen beds, gas-fired woodstoves, and TVs with VCRs or DVD players. Most overlook the property's gardens, and all come with free wireless Internet access, CD players, and fluffy bathrobes—not to mention a three-course breakfast and afternoon snacks (think chocolate chip cookies, blackberry scones, or apple and cheddar cheese fondue). One suite has trundle beds, ideal for families, and there's an outdoor heated swimming pool. The on-site restaurant, Mary's, is renowned for its dinners of local farm specialties.

$150-250

An old-fashioned family resort set on a 700-acre wooded cove of Lake Champlain, **Basin Harbor Club** (4800 Basin Harbor Rd., Vergennes, 802/475-2311, www.basinharbor. com, May–Oct., $195–580) has been owned and hosted by the same family for four generations. From May through October, it swarms with families (who can stay in either individual rooms or cabins) who thrill to the property's long roster of activities—from water skiing and tennis to hiking, Pilates, bonfires, and fishing. Children's programs are available with a similar richness of offerings, including capture-the-flag games, digital scrapbooking, a ropes course, and more (the teen program even has its own Facebook page). There are also a number of restaurants—the tavern-style Red Mill, the more formal Main Dining Room (with a classic menu and deep wine list), and alfresco buffets on the North Dock. Pets are welcome for a $10 surcharge.

C **Shelburne Farms Inn** (1611 Harbor Rd., Shelburne, 802/985-8498, www.shelburnefarms.org, $155–475) sits on a 1,400-acre working farm dedicated to conservation. (Regular classes and tours are offered, and you can buy any of the products made here—all humanely—at the retail store.) The inn, meanwhile, offers 24 tidy and sunny rooms (some with shared bath, some with private) and cottages decked out with country decor—soft handmade quilts, antique beds (many original to the home), and lake or garden views.

GETTING THERE AND AROUND

Shelburne is a short drive south down Route 7 from Burlington (7 mi., 15 min.). From Shelburne, Vergennes is another 15 miles down the road (25 min.). Alternatively, you can reach Shelburne by driving north on Route 7 from Middlebury (10 mi., 15 min.). From Vergennes, drive east on Route 17 to reach Bristol (15 mi., 20 min.). Or, to drive to Bristol from the highway, leave I-89 at exit 9, take Route 100B and then Route 100 south through Waitsfield, then head west along Route 17 through the breathtaking Appalachian Gap (95 mi., 2 hr. 30 min. from White River Junction).

Addison County Transit Resources (802/388-1946, www.actr-vt.org) runs buses between Middlebury (Exchange St. or Merchants Row), Bristol (Shaw's Plaza), and Vergennes (Main St. and Green St.). The **Chittenden County Transit Authority** (802/864-2282, www.cctaride.org) runs buses from Vergennes (Main St. and Green St.) to Burlington. From New York, **Lake Champlain Transportation Company** (802/864-9804, www.ferries.com) runs car ferries from Essex, New York, to Charlotte, halfway between Vergennes and Shelburne.

Middlebury

Competing theories exist about how the college town of Middlebury got its name. Some theorize that it was named for its location halfway between the Massachusetts and Canadian borders; others surmise it was named as the midpoint between two neighboring towns that were settled the same day in 1761. Whatever the origin, Middlebury has grown over the years into the cultural hub of the Champlain Valley, due in large part to its eponymous liberal arts school, Middlebury College.

The college was founded in 1800 by Gamaliel Painter, one of the town's first settlers and a profoundly religious man who wanted to safeguard the spiritual education of local farmers' sons against the savage secularism of the

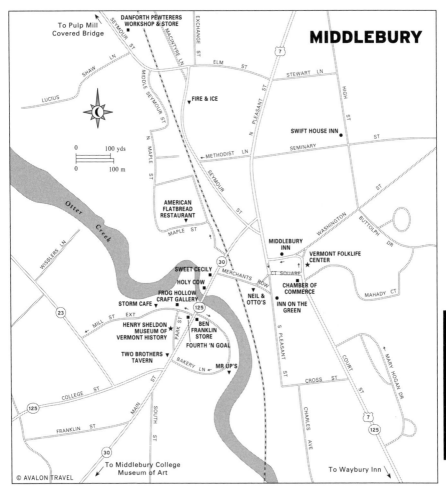

MIDDLEBURY

To Pulp Mill Covered Bridge

DANFORTH PEWTERERS WORKSHOP & STORE

FIRE & ICE

SWIFT HOUSE INN

SEMINARY

AMERICAN FLATBREAD RESTAURANT

MIDDLEBURY INN

VERMONT FOLKLIFE CENTER

SWEET CECILY

HOLY COW

FROG HOLLOW CRAFT GALLERY

STORM CAFE

CHAMBER OF COMMERCE

NEIL & OTTO'S

INN ON THE GREEN

HENRY SHELDON MUSEUM OF VERMONT HISTORY

BEN FRANKLIN STORE

FOURTH 'N GOAL

TWO BROTHERS TAVERN

MR UP'S

To Middlebury College Museum of Art

To Waybury Inn

© AVALON TRAVEL

CHAMPLAIN VALLEY

nascent University of Vermont in Burlington. Buoyed by the college and a variety of industries, including grist and woolen mills and marble quarrying, Middlebury became the largest community west of the Green Mountains by the mid-19th century, surpassing Bennington, Manchester, Rutland, and even Burlington. Since then, its population has leveled off at a modest 8,000 souls, who enjoy an energetic downtown full of upscale shops and restaurants. In town are several high-quality museums associated with the college; many students come here equally for the college's enviable access to the outdoors in the form of the Green Mountain National Forest, just a few miles east.

SIGHTS
Middlebury College

Few college campuses are as visually harmonious as Middlebury's (802/443-5770, www.middlebury.edu), which consists of a collection of granite and marble academic halls capped with white spires and cupolas arranged around a wide central quad. For a stroll around campus, park in the visitors' lot behind the admissions office on South Main Street. Better yet, sign up for a student-led tour (10:30 A.M. and 2:30 P.M. Mon.–Fri. year-round; 10 A.M. Sat. Aug.–mid-Nov.). A campus highlight, the **Middlebury College Museum of Art** (S. Main St./Rte. 30, 802/443-5007, www.middlebury.edu/arts/museum, 10 A.M.–5 P.M. Tues.–Fri., noon–5 P.M. Sat.–Sun., free) is a Met in miniature, with terra-cotta Greek urns, Roman marble reliefs, Chinese ceramics, Japanese woodcuts, and European paintings—many of which are used in the college's various art classes. Upstairs, a large open gallery displays changing exhibits of modern art and photography.

Community Museums

The culture and history of all of Vermont is on display at the **Henry Sheldon Museum of Vermont History** (1 Park St., 802/388-2117, www.henrysheldonmuseum.org, 10 A.M.–5 P.M. Tues.–Sat., 1–5 P.M. Sun. June–Aug., 10 A.M.–5 P.M. Tues.–Sat. Sept.–May, $5 adult, $4.50 senior, $3 youth 6–18, children under 6 free, $12 family), which has a rich collection of furniture and portraits stretching back more than 100 years. Rather than concern itself with battles and politicians, the museum sets out to demonstrate how the common people lived; one of its most affecting exhibits, "A Glimpse of Christmas Past," displays antique decorations and toys every year during the holiday season.

The common people also get their fanfare at the **Vermont Folklife Center** (88 Main St., 802/388-4964, www.vermontfolklifecenter. org, 10 A.M.–5 P.M. Mon.–Sat., free), whose mission is to preserve the voices and cultural traditions of Vermont's people. The centerpiece is a collection of 4,000 living-history recordings, preserved by field anthropologists who have scoured the state for local characters. The small museum also stages changing exhibits on the traditions of Native Americans, farmers, woodsmen, and quarrymen from all corners of the state.

Otter Creek Brewing Company

If all the history is making you thirsty, recoup at Otter Creek Brewing Company (793 Exchange St., 802/388-0727, www.ottercreek-brewing.com, 11 A.M.–6 P.M. daily), which makes one of the better craft beers in New England. Tours of the brewing process include samples of its signature Copper Ale and other varieties. (And if you want to skip the tour, free samples are given out all day to visitors.)

Vermont Soapworks

Vermont Soapworks (616 Exchange St., 866/762-7482, www.vermontsoap.com, 9 A.M.–5 P.M. Mon.–Fri.) gives explanations of its product-making process, which uses all-natural ingredients to make the world's first truly organic soaps. A small "soap museum" has antique bars from over the ages.

UVM Morgan Horse Farm

When George Custer was defeated at the Battle of Little Bighorn, the only survivor was a Morgan horse named Comanche. Praised for their strength, versatility, and athleticism, the Morgan breed has long been associated with Vermont, where it has been bred since the late 1700s. That tradition continues at the UVM Morgan Horse Farm (74 Battell Dr., Weybridge, 802/388-2011, www.uvm.edu/morgan, 9 A.M.–4 P.M. daily May–Oct., $5 adults, $4 youth 12–18, $2 children 5–12, free under 5), which is recognized as having one of the best bloodlines for breeding and competition. A video about the breed and tours of the barn are given every hour.

© VERMONTVACATION.COM/ANDRE JENNY

UVM Morgan Horse Farm

Covered Bridge

Otter Creek is crossed by just one covered bridge, but it's a unique one. On the northwest side of town, Seymour Street's **Pulp Mill Covered Bridge** is not only the oldest in Vermont, dating from 1820, but it is also one of six in the country that have two lanes, each with its own separate covered arcade. In 2012, the bridge was rehabilitated with new siding, roof, and other repairs, ensuring that it remain operative well into the future.

ENTERTAINMENT AND EVENTS
Nightlife

Most of the nighttime action in Middlebury takes place on campus, leaving scant choices for the unmatriculated. There are, however, a few attractive bar options, including the casual watering hole **Two Brothers Tavern** (86 Main St., 802/388-0002, www.twobrotherstavern. com, 11:30 A.M.–2 A.M. daily). It's the kind of place every college town should have. Students pour into its pub area to down tapas and cold beers within its brick walls, under photos of the historic town.

The Arts

The college's various musical and theater groups perform at the **Middlebury College Center for the Arts** (S. Main St./Rte. 30, 802/443-3168, www.middlebury.edu/arts), a 100,000-square-foot facility housing an intimate black-box theater, a dance studio, and large recital hall.

Events

Some towns have a day-long festival, others party for a weekend. Middlebury goes for a whole week's worth of musical and family events in its summertime **Festival on the Green** (802/462-3555, www.festivalonthegreen. com, mid-July). Each day of the event features several free musical performers in "brown bag" lunchtime shows and evening performances. The festival culminates with a Saturday jazz block party.

North of Middlebury, in New Haven, the

ARTISAN TRADITIONS

Vermont is justifiably proud–and notably supportive–of its artistic community. The state has the highest concentration of writers and visual artists in the country, plus upwards of 1,500 professional craftspeople, including quilters, printmakers, potters, metalworkers, weavers, painters, glassblowers, and any other kind of artisan you can dream up.

One of the state's biggest artistic resources (and one of the largest in the country, in fact) is the **Vermont Studio Center** (80 Pearl St., Johnson, 802/635-2727, www.vermontstudiocenter.org), which offers residency programs to artists and writers from around the globe on its campus outside of Stowe. Meanwhile, the **Vermont Crafts Council** (Montpelier, 802/223-3380, www.vermontcrafts.com), with more than 300 members, helps organize open studios and craft fairs for artists around the state, and helps visitors find the artists and galleries closest to them. The council publishes a map of artisan studios in the state to coincide with the annual statewide Open Studio Weekend in October. Or for one-stop shopping, try **Frog Hollow Vermont State Craft Center** (85 Church St., Burlington, 802/863-6458, www.froghollow.org), an organization that sells work from more than 200 artisans in its juried gallery in Burlington, as well as through an online gallery on its website.

Addison County Fair and Field Days (1790 Field Days Rd., New Haven, 802/545-2557, www.addisoncountyfielddays.com, early Aug.) is one of the largest county fairs in Vermont. In addition to the usual lineup of midway rides and tractor pulls, it features a milking barn and "dairy bar" that dispenses fresh local ice cream.

SHOPPING

Housed in a stylishly converted old mill building and perched over the waters of Otter Creek Falls, **Frog Hollow Craft Gallery** (1 Mill St., 802/388-3177, www.froghollow.org, 10 A.M.–6 P.M. Mon.–Wed., 10 A.M.–8 P.M. Thurs.–Sat., noon–5 P.M. Sun., mid-Apr.–Nov.) has made a profitable business of gathering arts and fine crafts from all over the region. Pick up delicate gourds turned holiday decorations, earthenware, hooked rugs, wood carvings, semiprecious jewelry, hand-carved furniture, and Vermont-made bath oils and hand creams.

If paying homage to the state's favorite animal seems in order, do so at **Holy Cow** (44 Main St., 802/388-6737, www.woodyjacksonart.com, hours vary, call for appt.), an art gallery dedicated entirely to said bovines. There, artist Woody Jackson sells his creative odes to livestock—in the form of cow glassware, mugs, notecards, and limited-reproduction prints of iconographic Holsteins swimming in fields of fluorescent grass.

Whether you're an alum, proud parent, or simply an avid fan, you can score plenty of Middlebury College athletic gear at **Forth 'N Goal** (68 Main St., 800/540-3447, www.middleburyshop.com, 9:30 A.M.–5:30 P.M. Mon.–Fri., 9:30 A.M.–5 P.M. Sat., 11 A.M.–4 P.M. Sun.). The space is packed to its brim with logo-bearing sweatshirts, shot glasses, and baby onesies (downstairs everything comes in blue and white).

Martha Stewart herself would feel right at home at **Sweet Cecily** (42 Main St., 802/388-3353, www.sweetcecily.com, 10 A.M.–5:30 P.M. Mon.–Sat., 11 A.M.–4 P.M. Sun.), a collection of country knickknacks, bright hand-woven socks, Provencal decor, and ceramics. No less quaint is the **Ben Franklin Store** (63 Main St., 802/388-2101, www.benfranklinstores.com, 9:30 A.M.–5:30 P.M. Mon.–Sat., 11 A.M.–3 P.M. Sun.), a retro variety and toy store stashed with penny candy and aisles of educational play-things and crafts for kiddies.

Original and gleaming gifts fill the studio of **Danforth Pewterers Workshop & Store** (52 Seymour St., 802/388-0098, www.danforth-pewter.com/workshop, 10 A.M.–6 P.M. Mon.–Sat., 11 A.M.–4 P.M. Sun.), which makes vases, holiday ornaments, and baby gifts worth investing in. (The owner is also extremely helpful at placing special orders and otherwise helping with selections.)

Grooviness reigns at the hippie emporium that is **Wild Mountain Thyme** (48 Main St., 802/388-2580, 9:30 A.M.–6 P.M. Mon.–Sat., 11 A.M.–5 P.M. Sun.), where patchouli fills the nostrils and rack after rack of tie-dyed, flowing garments greets you.

Pick up hiking gear plus whatever footwear you need for hiking the nearby trails, at **Green Mountain Shoe & Apparel** (20 Main St., 802/388-4399, 9:30 A.M.–8 P.M. Mon. and Sat., 11 A.M.–5 P.M. Sun.). The shop stocks reasonably priced designs for men, women, and kids.

FOOD
American

As much a museum as it is a restaurant, every inch of the upscale (but family-friendly) ◖ **Fire and Ice** (26 Seymour St., 802/388-7166, www.fireandicerestaurant.com, 5–9 P.M. Mon.–Thurs., noon–9 P.M. Fri.–Sat., 1–9 P.M. Sun., $12–28) is covered with old photographs, books, Victorian lamps, and map covers. A warren of interlocking rooms, the friendly, dimly lighted establishment focuses on classic American dishes—the likes of hand-cut steaks, boiled lobster, and broiled salmon. The home-made carrot cake is a local legend.

The undisputed best spot in town for a burger is **A&W Drive-In** (Rte. 7, across from Middlebury transit, 802/388-2876, 11:30 A.M.–8 P.M. daily, $3–6), a classic bit of Americana that's been around for more than

40 years. Park your car near the window, and carhops on rollerblades will fetch you old-fashioned root beer floats in real glass A&W mugs, plus cooked-to-order sandwiches and falafel.

On its relaxing, bucolic perch above Otter Creek, **Mr. Up's** (25 Bakery Ln., 802/388-6724, www.misterupsvt.com, 11:30 A.M.–11 P.M. Mon.–Thurs., 11:30 A.M.–midnight Fri.–Sat., 11 A.M.–11 P.M. Sun., $12–21) is an easygoing place to chill out over good seafood dishes and hearty salads. In good weather, the outdoor patio dining is particularly inviting. Or head into **Neil & Otto's Pizza** (52 Merchants Row, 802/388-6774, 4–10 P.M. daily, $9–15), located in a church cellar, for terrific crisp-crust pizza and creative pastas.

You may feel like you're eating in a barn when supping at **Rosie's** (Route 7 South., 802/388-7052, www.rosiesrestaurantvt.com, 6 A.M.–9 P.M. daily, $5–23), largely because the exposed post-and-beam structure is as homey as the food. Homemade hot-turkey sandwiches are a favorite at lunch, as are the no-fuss prime rib and apple crumb pie.

Italian

Gourmets and bohemians alike flock to ◖ **American Flatbread Restaurant** (137 Maple St., 802/388-3300, www.american-flatbread.com, 5–9 P.M. Tues.–Sat., $16–19), a funky and artsy wholesale bakery by weekday and an informal restaurant on Friday and Saturday nights. Hand-formed, wood-fired pizzas using all-organic ingredients are the mainstay of the menu; the locally made maple-fennel-sausage pizza with caramelized onions and Vermont mozzarella is alone worth the trip.

Vegetarian

Its name notwithstanding, the in fact quite peaceful enclave of **Storm Cafe** (3 Mill St., 802/388-1063, www.thestormcafe.com, 11:30 A.M.–2:30 P.M. and 5–8 P.M. Mon.–Sat., 5–8 P.M. Sun., $13–19) does a swift business in excellent vegetarian specials and sandwiches, all of them from local purveyors.

SPORTS AND RECREATION
Hiking and Biking

There's no better way to explore Middlebury than the Trail Around Middlebury (TAM), a 16-mile path that connects the town's various conservation areas, taking in bridges, cow pastures, wooded trails, and the impressive Otter Creek Gorge. Several of the trails in the network are bike and stroller accessible. Look for a map and guide produced by the **Middlebury Area Land Trust** (802/388-1007, www.maltvt. org), or print out a copy from the group's website.

ACCOMMODATIONS

If you're looking for the Vermont of entertainment-world dreams, look no further than the **Waybury Inn** (457 E. Main St., East Middlebury, 800/348-1810, www.wayburyinn. com, $130–285). The exterior was used at the beginning of the Bob Newhart show, *Newhart,* which ran from 1982 to 1990. The interior is just as picturesque; guests lounge in suites enjoying views of the lush lawns and mountains. Some rooms have four-poster beds and whirlpool tubs. Several rooms are located in private cabins. A quiet, elegant restaurant is on-site, as are beautifully kept gardens.

Name any creature comfort, and odds are you'll find it in spades at the **Middlebury Inn** (14 Court Sq., 802/388-4961, www.middleburyinn.com, $149–179). From free access to the fitness center and extra-deep tubs with original fixtures to elegant breakfasts and afternoon tea, the 180-year-old spacious inn leaves guests wanting for very little indeed. Suites are also available.

An 1814 home turned inn (once belonging to Vermont judge and governor John Stewart), **Swift House Inn** (25 Stewart Ln., Middlebury, 866/388-9925, www.

swifthouseinn.com, $149–259) is actually three buildings, each renovated and appointed with ornate stained glass and luxury furnishings. Pristine and individually decorated rooms, many outfitted in subtle florals, come with claw-foot tubs, quilt-covered wood or iron-wrought beds, or working fireplaces.

The Federal-style **Inn on the Green** (71 S. Pleasant St., Middlebury, 802/388-7512, www. innonthegreen.com, $179–299) overlooks the Middlebury town green. With a handful of suites, plus rooms with twin and queen beds, it's perfect for families (or couples looking to relax—the kitchen serves breakfast in bed). Rooms are cheerfully decorated with bright color, bay windows, and high-quality country wooden furniture—some antiques.

INFORMATION AND SERVICES

For more information on Middlebury and the surrounding area, contact the regional tourism office, **Addison County Chamber of Commerce** (2 Court St., 802/388-7951, www. addisoncounty.com), which runs a visitors center across from the Vermont Folklife Center. For Middlebury proper, you can also contact the **Middlebury Business Association** (802/377-3557, www.bettermiddleburypartnership.org), which produces a helpful map of the town.

Middlebury is a regional hub, with hospital services at **Porter Medical Center** (115 Porter Dr., 802/388-4701, www.portermedical.org). Several pharmacies are located along Route 7, including **Kinney's Drugs** (38 Court St., 802/388-0973) in the center of town and **Rite-Aid Pharmacy** (263 Court St., 802/388-9573, 8 A.M.–8 P.M. Mon.–Sat., 9 A.M.–5 P.M. Sun., pharmacy 8 A.M.–8 P.M. Mon.–Fri., 9 A.M.–6 P.M. Sat., 9 A.M.–5 P.M. Sun.).

Your best bet for a cash machine is the intersection of U.S. Route 7 and Route 30, where there are a half-dozen banks, including an ATM at **Chittenden Bank** (1 Court

St., 802/388-6316) and **Citizens Bank** (36 Middle Rd., 802/388-6791, 9 A.M.–5 P.M. Mon.–Fri., 9 A.M.–noon Sat.). Free Wi-Fi can be found at **Ilsley Public Library** (75 Main St., 802/388-4095, www.ilsleypubliclibrary.org, 10 A.M.–6 P.M. Mon., Wed., and Fri., 10 A.M.–8 P.M. Tues. and Thurs., 10 A.M.–4 P.M. Sat., 1–4 P.M. Sun.) and **Two Brothers Tavern** (86 Main St., 802/388-0002, www.twobrotherstavern.com). In an emergency, contact **Middlebury Police** (1 Lucius Shaw Ln., 802/388-3191).

GETTING THERE AND AROUND

There's no easy way to get to Middlebury from the highway—whatever route you take involves a long (though beautiful) drive across the Green Mountains. Probably the best option from I-89 is to take exit 3 south to Route 107, then head west on Route 125 and cross the mountains at Middlebury Gap (70 mi., 2 hr. from White River Junction). To drive to Middlebury from Rutland, take Route 7 north (35 mi., 1 hr.).

Run by the Chittenden County Transportation Authority, the **Middlebury LINK** (802/864-2282, www.cctaride.org) provides regular bus service every day but Sunday between Middlebury (Exchange St. or Merchants Row) and Burlington.

Addison County Transit Resources (802/388-1946, www.actr-vt.org) runs bus routes throughout the town of Middlebury.

Around Middlebury

Middlebury stands at the crossroads of several routes. To the east, Route 125 climbs into the mountains to the so-called Middlebury Gap, a dizzying pass through the mountains on roller-coaster slopes. Southward, Route 7 plays leapfrog with Otter Creek, Vermont's longest river, which tumbles down from the Green Mountain foothills into the southern end of Lake Champlain. To the west, meanwhile, the lake narrows at this point to a distance of only a few miles across. That made it prime defensive ground for generations of French, British, and American soldiers who protected the waterway from attack at **Fort Ticonderoga, Chimney Point,** and **Mount Independence,** just some of the many historic sites still present in the area.

CHIMNEY POINT TO MOUNT INDEPENDENCE

In the early days of the Revolutionary War, Lake Champlain was recognized as a prime strategic directive by both the colonial defenders and British attackers. If the Brits were able to sail down the lake from their home base in Canada, they could effectively cut the Americans' territory in half, isolating New England and forcing an early surrender of the troops there. To make sure that didn't happen, the Americans moved quickly to secure the lake's southern narrows on both the New York and Vermont side. Many of the fortifications they put in place still exist as some of the best-preserved Revolutionary War sites anywhere. History is still very much alive in the area, with tours and events that take advantage of their proximity.

Chimney Point State Historic Site

On the Vermont side of the lake are the remains of an earlier French settlement at the Chimney Point State Historic Site (7305 Rte. 125, Addison, 802/759-2412, http://historicsites.vermont.gov/chimneypoint, 9:30 A.M.–5 P.M. Wed.–Sun. late May–mid-Oct., $3 adults, children 14 and under free). In fact, the strategic area had seen waves of settlement by Native American tribes for more than 12,000 years. An 18th-century tavern on-site now has an exhibit of prehistoric Native American artifacts as well as interpretive maps that detail the history of the area.

Crown Point State Historic Site

At the time of the Revolutionary War, Lake Champlain was defended by two forts on the New York side of the lake, Crown Point and Fort Ticonderoga, both built several years before during the time of the French and Indian War. They were lightly defended in the early days of the war, allowing American troops under Benedict Arnold and Ethan Allen to capture them without bloodshed. Two years later, however, it was the Americans' turn to abandon Crown Point when they didn't have enough men to staff both forts in the face of a new British advance. The well-preserved ruins of the fort still stand at Crown Point State Historic Site (739 Bridge Rd., Crown Point, NY, 518/597-4666, www.nysparks.com, 9:30 A.M.–5 P.M. Thurs.–Mon. May–Oct., $4 adults, $3 students and seniors, children under 12 free), accessible by a bridge across the lake. A visitors site on the premises details the various chapters of French, British, and American occupation.

Mount Independence State Historic Site

Farther south down the lake, the Americans made their stand against the British at Fort Ticonderoga, also on the New York side of the lake. Because that fort faced south, however, the Americans also constructed a huge new fort on the Vermont side of the lake named Mount Independence. They survive today as the Mount Independence State Historic Site (497 Mount Independence Rd., Orwell, 802/759-2412 or 802/948-2000, http://historicsites.vermont.gov/MountIndependence,

9:30 A.M.–5 P.M. daily late May–mid-Oct., $5 adults, children 14 and under free), a virtual city where some 12,000 defenders once lived, making it the largest military city in the New World at the time. Today, a visitors center has exceptional exhibits of the life of the average colonial soldier during the Revolution, made up in part of artifacts found in archaeological digs on the site. Remains of some of the cannon batteries, blockhouses, barracks, and hospital have also survived and can be viewed on several trails that run around the mountain. The longest route, the orange trail, takes about an hour round-trip.

In the end, all of the colonists' preparations were for naught, when they woke up on the morning of July 4, 1777, to find that the British had scaled the heights of Mount Defiance, which overlooked Fort Ticonderoga, and placed their cannons there. The Americans staged a daring midnight retreat across a floating bridge to Mount Independence, living to fight another day. Though that bridge is long gone, you can still take the nearby **Ticonderoga Ferry** (4675 Rte. 74 W., Shoreham, 802/897-7999, www.forttiferry.com, 7 A.M.–6 P.M. late Apr.–June and Sept.–Oct.; 7 A.M.–7 P.M. July–Aug., $9 cars, $1 pedestrians one-way) across to New York to view the **Fort Ticonderoga National Historic Site** (Ticonderoga, NY, 518/585-2821, www.fortticonderoga.org, 9:30 A.M.–5 P.M. late May–late Oct., $17.50 adults, $14 seniors, $8 youth 5–12, children under 5 free), which has been meticulously reconstructed to its Revolutionary-era glory and populated with costumed historical re-enactors.

Events

One of the more unusual sporting competitions you'll see is the **Atlatl Championship** (Addison, 802/759-2412, http://historicsites.vermont.gov/chimneypoint, Sept.), an exhibition of the spear-throwing stick used to hunt woolly mammoths in prehistoric times. The competition is part of Chimney Point's Festival of Nations, which also features demonstrations of Native American crafts.

MIDDLEBURY GAP

The only pass across the Green Mountains for 25 miles, Middlebury Gap was designated as a scenic byway by the state of Vermont as early as 1897. Route 125, which climbs steeply up from **Middlebury** to its peak at the village of **Ripton** before plunging just as precipitously down the other side, is lined with a dense forest of maple and birch mixed in with boreal spruce and fir. The route is best driven during the fall, when the foliage puts a lie to the mountains' name with a brilliant symphony of red and yellow leaves.

◖ Robert Frost Interpretive Trail

One thing is for sure—New England's preeminent 20th-century poet got around. Sites where he lived in New Hampshire, Massachusetts, and Vermont can all lay claim to significant chunks of his life. But perhaps none of them quite capture the spirit of his poetry more than this 1.2-mile walking trail located just past Ripton, near where Frost spent each of his last 22 summers. The trail begins by a parking lot at the Robert Frost Wayside Area, on the south side of Route 125, two miles east of Ripton, four miles west of Middlebury Gap.

As the path wends its way through a gentle terrain of forest and meadow, it is studded with plaques containing some of his poems set at contemplative spots along the way. The placement of the poems, which include "The Last Mowing" and "Stopping by Woods on a Snowy Evening," has an uncanny way of teasing out more meaning from the lines with the smell of pine boughs or the chirping of a lonely bird above. In fact, the trail was developed by Middlebury professor Reginald Cook, a friend

of Frost's who used to hike with him in these very woods. The only poem that falls a bit flat is the "Road Not Taken," situated at an intersection in the path with an arrow pointing out the right direction—which is clearly the road far more often taken.

Events

When Frost summered in Middlebury, he was here for the **Breadloaf Writers' Conference** (1192 Rte. 125, Ripton, 802/443-5000, www. middlebury.edu/blwc, Aug.), one of the first retreats to bring working and aspiring writers together each summer for inspiration. The conference has grown in stature for more than 80 years; in addition to Frost, guests have included John Irving, Toni Morrison, and Norman Mailer. Now it lasts for 10 days in August, taking place in the little town of Ripton in the mountains 10 miles east of Middlebury; many of the readings by distinguished writers are open to the public.

BRANDON

Situated about halfway between Rutland and Middlebury, the delightful little village of Brandon makes a good lunch stop or home base for exploring the northern branch of Green Mountain National Forest. The town was founded in 1761 and quickly became an important mill town, with both sawmills and gristmills situated at strategic points on Otter Creek. Supplies of iron ore nearby later led the town to become an important manufacturing center constructing iron stoves and railroad cars in the 19th century. More recently, Brandon has been reborn as a center for art galleries, which inhabit the brick storefronts of its downtown mill area and attract teary-eyed parents on their way up from New York to drop their kids off at college in Middlebury.

Take a time-out to saunter around Brandon's quaint brick downtown, which is listed on the National Register of Historic

Places. At the eastern end of town, where Routes 7 and 73 first intersect, **Lower Falls** is an impressive urban waterfall that once powered the town's mills.

Brandon Museum

On the western side of town, the Brandon Museum (Grove St. at Champlain and Pearl Sts., 802/247-6401, www.brandon. org, 11 A.M.–4 A.M. daily, mid-May–mid-Oct.) is located in the birthplace of Stephen A. Douglas, the politician who challenged Abraham Lincoln in a famous series of debates on slavery to decide the 1860 presidential race. The small museum contains exhibits relating to Douglas's life, including the famous cross-country debates, an examination of the Civil War and Vermont's active role in the abolition movement, and lots of historic old photographs and other memorabilia.

Thelma's Maple Sugarhouse

One of the most coveted tastes of spring in these parts is the maple-flavored fried dough on sale at Thelma's Maple Sugarhouse (1851 Arnold District Rd., 802/247-6430, 11 A.M.–5 P.M. Mon.–Fri., 10 A.M.–5 P.M. Sat., noon–5 P.M. Sun.). During boiling season, proprietor Thelma Miner gives tours of the sugaring process as well as tastings of the different grades.

Entertainment

Upstairs from Briggs Carriage Bookstore, the **Ball and Chain Cafe** (16 Park St., 802/247-0050, www.briggscarriage.com, 10 A.M.–6 P.M. Mon.–Wed., 10 A.M.–9 P.M. Thurs.–Fri., 9 A.M.–9 P.M. Sat., 11 A.M.–5 P.M. Sun.) is Brandon's one-stop cultural hub. Regular events include author readings; folk, jazz, and classical music performances; and a weekly knitting circle. During the day, the cafe serves up espresso drinks, pastries, and free wireless Internet.

Shopping

More than 35 artists have banded together to form the **Brandon Artists Guild** (7 Center St., 802/247-4956, www.brandonartistsguild. org, 10 A.M.–5 P.M. daily), a gallery showcasing modern and whimsical takes on typical Vermont scenes. Works for sale include jewelry, hooked rugs, and modern folk art paintings. Brandon's most famous folk artist, Warren Kimble, sells his distressed wood paintings at **Liza Myers Gallery & Studio** (22 Center St., www.lizamyers.com, by appointment only,), which also features Myers's arresting acrylics of birds and other animals from around the world.

Food

Owned and run by a French couple, **Cafe Provence** (11 Center St., 802/247-9997, www. cafeprovencevt.com, 11:30 A.M.–4:30 P.M. and 5–9 P.M. Mon.–Sat., 9 A.M.–4:30 P.M. and 5–9 P.M. Sun., $17–21) successfully evokes south-of-France charm with both its yellow walls and its flavor-rich seafood stew. The bustling open kitchen adds to the energy of the handsome room at dinnertime; if you can work it into your weekend itinerary, the brunch is terrific and filling.

Information and Services

Located in the Brandon Museum is a well-stocked information center, run by the **Brandon Area Chamber of Commerce** (4 Grove St., Rte. 7, Brandon, 802/247-6401, www.brandon.org, open year-round), with gobs of brochures and a map for walking tours of town.

Brandon has a downtown **Rite-Aid Pharmacy** (1 Carver St., 802/247-8050, 8 A.M.–8 P.M. Mon.–Sat., 8 A.M.–5 P.M. Sun., pharmacy 8 A.M.–8 P.M. Mon.–Fri., 9 A.M.–6 P.M. Sat., 9 A.M.–5 P.M. Sun.).

A 24-hour ATM is available at **First Brandon Bank** (2 Park St.) at the intersection of U.S. Route 7 and Route 73, as well as at the

National Bank of Middlebury (5 Carver St., 877/508-8455, 8:30 A.M.–5 P.M. Mon.–Thurs., 8:30 A.M.–5:30 P.M. Fri., 9 A.M.–noon Sat.).

Wi-Fi is available with ice cream at **The Inside Scoop** (22 Park St., 802/257-6600, www.brandon.org, 10 A.M.–9 P.M. daily mid-May to Labor Day; 10 A.M.–6 P.M. Wed.–Mon. Labor Day to mid-May). In an emergency, contact the **Brandon Police** (1 W. Seminary St., 802/247-0222).

SPORTS AND RECREATION
Moosalamoo Recreation Area

Those who have discovered this 20,000-acre wilderness reserve in the heart of the Green Mountain National Forest are not eager to let the word out. For now at least, Moosalamoo is a pristine area with more than 70 miles of quiet hiking trails leading to waterfalls, lakes, and striking views of Lake Champlain and the Adirondacks. From Route 125, a popular hike is to take the Oak Ridge and Moosalamoo Trails eight miles into the forest to end up at **Moosalamoo Campground** (tent sites $10/person). For those planning an overnight stay, the campground has 19 wooded sites, along with toilets, trash facilities, a grassy field, and self-guided nature trail. It's accessible by car from Goshen-Ripton Road, off Route 125 a little south of Ripton center.

A shorter but equally amazing hike begins at the roaring Falls of Lana, from whence you can hike up the Rattlesnake Cliff Trail for amazing views of the mountains and Lake Dummore below. The best time to climb is just before sunset; bring a flashlight for the descent. Another trail, popular with bird-watchers, is the Bluebird Trail, which takes hikers through meadows stocked with 40 houses that serve as habitats for cavity-nesting birds. In the winter, many of the trails are groomed for snowshoeing and cross-country skiing. And if you don't feel like getting your boots muddy, the area also advertises a loop trail that's a sure bet

for seeing moose in the spring. For more information, contact the nonprofit **Moosalamoo Association** (802/747-7900, www.moosalamoo.org).

Hiking

In addition to Moosalamoo, a popular hike is the nature trail at **Texas Falls Recreation Area,** which overlooks a series of waterfalls through a gorge formed by glacial meltwater. For more information on this and other hikes in the Green Mountain National Forest, contact the **Middlebury Ranger Station** (1007 Rte. 7, Middlebury, 802/388-4362).

Just after the Robert Frost Interpretive Trail, a set of "interfaith nature paths" offers another meditative walking experience. Managed by the Middlebury-based **Spirit in Nature** (Rte. 125/Goshen Rd., Brandon, 802/388-3694, www.spiritinnature.com), the network consists of 11 different paths studded with inspirational texts from the world's great religious thinkers.

Skiing

Middlebury has a long history of fielding champion ski teams in the Northeast College Athletic Conference. The team practices at the **Middlebury College Snow Bowl** (6886 Rte. 125, Middlebury, 802/388-4356, www.middleburysnowbowl.com, $22–42 adults, $20–30 students and seniors, $10 children under 6), which dates back to 1934, making it the third-oldest ski area in Vermont. While the dozen or so trails won't win any awards for difficulty, they are no cakewalk either, with several expert trails careening down from the 2,650-foot main peak. More to the point, in an area full of ski resorts, the Snow Bowl is often deserted on weekdays, allowing skiers to take a half-dozen runs in the time it takes to get up and down Killington once. Throw in cheap prices and an atmospheric base lodge, and the bowl is a good bet for an afternoon of fun.

A mile and a half away at the Breadloaf

campus, the **Rikert Ski Touring Center** (Rte. 125, 12 mi. west of Middlebury, Ripton, 802/443-2744, www.middlebury.edu, 8:30 A.M.–4:30 P.M. daily, $17 adults, $10 Middlebury students, $5 children under 5, seniors free) has more than 25 miles of trails open to the public, skirting through the wilderness of the Green Mountain National Forest. The base lodge has rentals ($18 adults, $16 students, $8 children under 5) and a warm wood stove in winter.

ACCOMMODATIONS

Plunked right between Rutland and Middlebury sits the modest, affordable **Brandon Motor Lodge** (2095 Franklin St., Rte. 7, Brandon, 800/675-7614, www.brandonmotorlodge.com, $69–199). Rooms have standard motel decor but are well kept, and all have access to a communal hot tub and pool. Well-behaved pets are welcome (with a $15 surcharge), and continental breakfast is included May through October.

A favorite for couples, **Lilac Inn** (53 Park St., Brandon, 800/221-0720, www.lilacinn. com, $120–290) walks the fine line between bed-and-breakfast and luxury inn. Perks like in-room fireplaces and whirlpool tubs are available, while a location convenient to local activities (from shopping to skiing and hiking) and an on-site brewpub lure guests out of their rooms.

GETTING THERE AND AROUND

From Middlebury, take Route 125 west to Chimney Point (20 mi., 30 min.) or Route 30 south and Route 73 west to Mount Independence (30 mi., 45 min.). Take Route 125 east to Bread Loaf and Middlebury Gap (10 mi., 20 min.). Take Route 7 south to Brandon (15 mi., 25 min.). You can also reach Brandon by taking Route 7 north from Rutland (15 mi., 25 min.).

Run by the Chittenden County Transportation Authority, the **Middlebury LINK** (802/864-0211, www.ccta.org) provides regular bus service every day but Sunday between Middlebury (Exchange St. or Merchants Row) and Burlington.

Addison County Transit Resources (802/388-1946, www.actr-vt.org) runs bus routes between Middlebury and Brandon on its Rutland Connector route, as well as a Snow Bowl Shuttle Bus to Bread Loaf and the Robert Frost trail.

NORTHERN GREEN MOUNTAINS

As the mountains climb northward, they get higher and wilder than their southern cousins. At the same time, the largely unspoiled northern parts of Vermont get far less traffic than the southern parts of the state. What does that mean for the visitor? For starters, stunning views nearly every way you turn: dramatic mountain sunrises, pristine church steeples rising from verdant valleys, cute-as-can-be hilltop farms, and serene lakes.

Meanwhile, plenty of visitors come to this region just for the food: maple syrup harvested fresh from the trees; cheesemakers tucked into little valley farms; and of course, the sweet enticements of the Ben & Jerry's Factory, the number one tourist destination in Vermont. Another big draw is Stowe Mountain, which has resisted the overdevelopment of other ski resorts to give visitors both a lovely little New England village and killer ski trails. Stowe is rightfully bustling with tourists three seasons out of the year (only during the "mud season" of spring do the chalets close up shop).

Tucked between the Green Mountains and a spur called the Worcester Range, the Mad River Valley is Vermont's own Shangri-La, a magical valley of white steeples and red barns against a backdrop of omnipresent peaks. The sobriquet extends to the character of the surrounding community, a quirky mix of farmers, artists, and ex-urbanites that calls to mind

HIGHLIGHTS

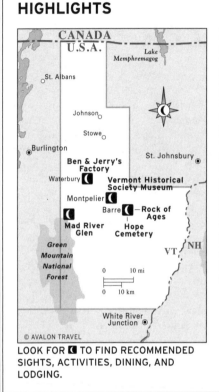

◖ Rock of Ages: Stare deep into the heart of Vermont's granite-quarrying past from the vantage of a 600-foot-high viewing platform (page 155).

◖ Hope Cemetery: The final resting place of granite stonecutters is as much sculpture garden as graveyard (page 156).

◖ Vermont Historical Society Museum: This historical museum is thoroughly modern in its unvarnished depiction of Vermont's historical contradictions (page 160).

◖ Ben & Jerry's Factory: This is the birthplace of Chunky Monkey, Cherry Garcia, and Chocolate Chip Cookie Dough. Two words: free samples (page 163).

◖ Mad River Glen: Leave your designer sunglasses and spa packages at home, and come tackle a righteous ski mountain on its own terms (page 166).

LOOK FOR ◖ TO FIND RECOMMENDED SIGHTS, ACTIVITIES, DINING, AND LODGING.

the live-and-let-live attitude of an episode of *Northern Exposure*.

Not all of the northern part of the state feels like the boondocks, however. The capital city of Montpelier may be the smallest state capital in the nation, but it still provides enough big-city culture and (with the New England Culinary Institute within its borders) culinary sophistication to satisfy urban travelers. Vermont's independent streak is on full display here—with dozens of locally owned businesses and nary a McDonald's in sight. The city's natural beauty and educated populace have led to a creative renaissance, with art galleries and artsy cafes moving into the downtown historical area.

Despite such "urban sophistication," however, ski runs and sugarhouses are still just a few minutes away.

PLANNING YOUR TIME

Many visitors to Vermont make a beeline straight to the **Ben & Jerry's Factory** in Waterbury before discovering what other charms the region has on offer. A trip to the ice cream factory can be combined with a stay of several days in the mock-Tyrolean **Stowe** village, with its eponymous ski resort and village full of restaurants and outdoor activities. (As in other towns in the area, some Stowe restaurants serve only dinner in the less-touristed summer

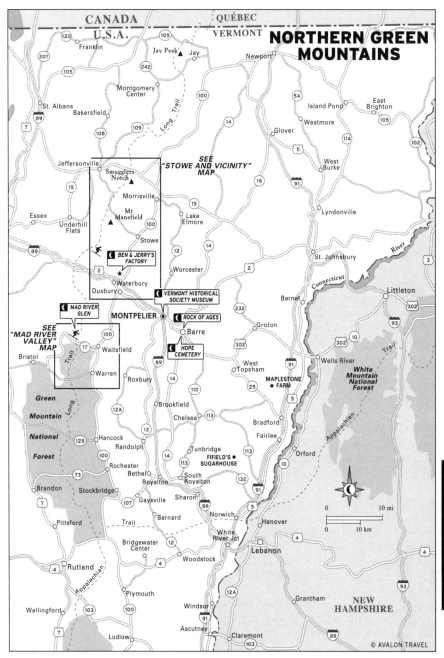

NORTHERN GREEN
MOUNTAINS

NORTHERN MOUNTAINS

season. In all cases, it pays to call ahead in planning.) Alternatively, stay in the magical Mad River Valley, which boasts its own ski area, **Mad River Glen**, which has righteously earned a fanatic following for its challenging trails and uncompromising attitude. The capital city of Montpelier has grown into a delightful city full of art galleries and museums, including the underrated **Vermont Historical Society Museum;** next door the city of Barre is a living legacy to the granite industry, with working quarries at the **Rock of Ages** company and the work of the master carvers on display in **Hope Cemetery.**

White River Valley

Inhabiting a bit of a no-man's land of the Vermont Piedmont along the eastern fringe of the mountains, the stretch of I-89 between White River Junction and Montpelier is often passed over by tourists taking the express route to the mountains. It's worth taking the time to slow down and take a few exits off the highway, however, to lose yourself in the quiet pace of rural life here, not to mention to check out a pair of unusual attractions in the **Joseph Smith memorial** and **Randolph Music Box museum.**

BETHEL AND SOUTH ROYALTON

The first town founded after Vermont became an independent state in 1779, the little town of Bethel has proudly held onto its historical roots, boasting a quaint historic downtown complete with old-time soda fountain. The town was put on the map in the 19th century with the discovery of a superior strain of "white granite," which was used to build many Washington monuments and buildings, including Union Station and the Smithsonian's Museum of Natural History.

Next door, the agrarian town of South Royalton looks like it was cut straight from a Grandma Moses folk-art painting, with a picturesque town green that hosts summer concerts and winter ice-skating. The rural beauty is deceptive, however, as the presence of the Vermont Law School, the state's only accredited law school, lends the area a hidden air of sophistication (though the town's nickname, SoRo, is said with tongue firmly in cheek).

Sights

One of the most singular characters in U.S. history, Joseph Smith started a movement that grew into a religion when he unburied a set of golden plates in the woods of upstate New York that he claimed were left there thousands of years earlier by the angel Moroni. The revelations he transcribed from them became the basis of the Church of Jesus Christ of Latter-day Saints, or Mormonism, an incredibly successful (and because of its historical embrace of polygamy, controversial) religion that now counts millions of adherents around the world.

Smith's saga starts in South Royalton, where he received his first visits from God, and where a 40-foot-tall granite shaft comprises the **Joseph Smith Birthplace Memorial** (357 LDS Ln., South Royalton, 802/763-7742, www.lds.org/placestovisit, 9 A.M.–5 P.M. Mon.–Sat., 1:30–5 P.M. Sun. Nov.–Apr.; 9 A.M.–7 P.M. Mon.–Sat., 1:30–7 P.M. Sun. May–Oct., free). Now an important pilgrimage site for Mormons, the site has a visitors center that tells the story of the prophet and his Latter-day Saints through a combination of paintings, films, and artifacts.

South Royalton's other white granite memorial, an arch on the town green, memorializes

THE ROYALTON RAID

© MICHAEL BLANDING

Royalton Raid Memorial

After the early years of the Revolutionary War, most of the fighting moved south out of New England. One exception was the infamous Royalton Raid, which occurred in 1780 toward the end of the war. Some 300 Mohawk fighters under British command descended upon Royalton as well as several other towns along the White River, burning homes, destroying livestock, and killing four men. The raid seems to have been an attempt to terrorize the frontier settlements and burn anything of value that might have aided the Americans in another attempt at attacking Montreal or Quebec. It's still remembered in Royalton as a savage act of terrorism on a mostly civilian population; an arch on the town green is dedicated to a woman who lost her child in the attack, then successfully negotiated for the release of several other children taken captive as the raiders retreated back to Canada.

the infamous **Royalton Raid,** an incident during the Revolutionary War in which 300 Native Americans, commanded by the British, raided several settlements in the area, killing 4 and taking another 25 captive.

Events

For a true taste of rural Vermont, South Royalton's **Old Home Day** (802/234-6400, mid-July) celebration is the real deal. The annual summer fair includes a parade, animal exhibits, antique trucks and tractors, and a big chicken dinner featuring bean-hole beans: beans baked for 48 hours in an underground hole in special pots that have been passed down for generations since the 1950s.

An even bigger production is the modestly named **Tunbridge World's Fair** (802/889-5555, www.tunbridgeworldsfair.com, mid-Sept.), the state's premier dairy cow festival, which takes over the Tunbridge Fairgrounds for four days

of hot competition for "Best of Moo," as well as midway rides, games, and entertainment.

Shopping

In the crafts studio of **Jeanne V. Robacker** (2826 Allen Hill Rd., South Royalton, 802/763-7862, 10 A.M.–5 P.M. Mon.–Fri., noon–5 P.M. Sat.–Sun.), you'll find walls full of colorful woodblock prints and luminescent paintings of landscapes, portraits, and floral still lifes.

Those with an aching sweet tooth won't want to bypass **Eaton's Sugar House** (RR 1 Box 112, South Royalton, 802/763-8809, www.eatonssugarhouse.com, 7 A.M.–3 P.M. daily), where shelves groan under the weight of stacked maple candy, maple lollipops, and maple-centric gifts—all made on-site every day.

Food

Gaze out to the picturesque town green as

NORTHERN MOUNTAINS

A Morgan horse pulls a carriage at the Tunbridge World's Fair.

you munch inexpensive sandwiches and burgers at **Chelsea Station** (108 Chelsea St., South Royalton, 802/763-8685, 8 A.M.–9 P.M. Mon.–Fri., 11 A.M.–9 P.M. Sat.–Sun., $6–8), where both booth and counter service are swift and friendly.

The vibe at **Crossroads Bar and Grill** (108 Rainbow St., South Royalton, 802/763-2002, www.xroadsbar.com, 3–9 P.M. daily, $6–13) is as local as it gets. As the only watering hole in the area, it's the place everyone gathers to play pool between bites of dependably good burgers and beers.

Known for its extra-crispy, addictive onion rings, the casual and fun **Onion Flats** (2659 Pleasant St., Bethel, 802/234-5169, 4–8 P.M. Mon.–Tues., 11:30 A.M.–8 P.M. Wed.–Sun., $5–9) also serves excellent burgers to a local following.

The popular pies at **Village Pizza** (1 S. Main St., South Royalton, 802/763-2800, 11 A.M.–9 P.M. Sun.–Thurs., 11:30 A.M.–10 P.M.

Fri.–Sat., $5–9) are crispy, hot, and topped with everything from peppers to pepperoni.

Information and Services

For info on the area, pop into the **Royalton Memorial Library** (23 Alexander Pl., South Royalton, 802/763-7094, www.royaltonlibrary. org, noon–6 P.M. Tues.–Fri., 9 A.M.–1 P.M. Sat.), which also offers wireless Internet.

There are branches of **Randolph National Bank** in Bethel (1583 Rte. 107, Bethel, 802/234-5549, 8 A.M.–4 P.M. Mon.–Thurs., 8 A.M.–5:30 P.M. Fri., 9 A.M.–noon Sat., 24-hour ATM) and in South Royalton (85 N. Main St., South Royalton, 802/767-4222, 8 A.M.–4 P.M. Mon.–Thurs., 8 A.M.–5:30 P.M. Fri., 9 A.M.–noon Sat.). A **Rite-Aid Pharmacy** (1823 Rte. 107, Bethel, 802/234-5289, 9 A.M.–6 P.M. Mon.–Thurs., 9 A.M.–5 P.M. Fri.) can be found in Bethel. In an emergency, contact the regional **State Police** (2011 Rte. 107, Bethel, 802/234-9933).

ROCHESTER

Once declared the "model town of the United States," the tiny village of Rochester often induces double-takes in visitors who stumble upon its wide town green, which could serve as a set-piece for a production of *Our Town* or *It's a Wonderful Life*. The four-acre park is surrounded by stately 19th-century homes and an eclectic collection of shops and galleries. They combine to make the village a pleasant home base for exploring the mountains or a convenient stopover on your way across the peaks.

Events

Rochester Park hosts an annual **Harvest Fair** (www.rochestervermont.org/harvest-fair, early Sept.), with a chicken barbecue, flower show, and children's activities.

Shopping

Pottery fiends will delight in the one-of-a-kind pieces created and sold at **Judy Jensen Clay Studio** (61 N. Main St., 802/767-3271, www.judyjensen.com, 9 A.M.–4 P.M. Mon.–Sat., occasionally open Sun.)—from vases and bowls to rustic teapots and outdoor lanterns. Stroll through exhibits by local artists (and pick up a few of their pieces while you're at it) at **Bigtown Gallery** (99 N. Main St., 802/767-9670, www.bigtowngallery.com, 10 A.M.–5 P.M. Wed.–Sat., 11 A.M.–4 P.M. Sun., and by appt.). Thought-provoking collages, watercolors, sculpture, and paintings abound, mostly of a contemporary ilk.

One of Vermont's last remaining soda fountains still bubbles at **Rochester Cafe & Country Store** (Rte. 100, 802/767-4302, www.rochestercafe.com, 7 A.M.–5 P.M. daily), where you'll also find everything from handmade toys and candy, bottles of maple syrup, and mittens knit by locals.

Read up on a little bit of everything at **Seasoned Booksellers** (30 N. Main St., 802/767-4258, www.seasonedbooks.com, 7:30 A.M.–6 P.M. Mon.–Sat., 7:30 A.M.–2 P.M.

Sun.), a hodgepodge of new, used, and rare collectible titles. Throughout, the focus is on environmental topics, from building homes with renewable resources to animal husbandry.

Food

In an antiques-filled, candlelit room, **The Huntington House** (19 Huntington Pl., 802/767-9140, www.huntingtonhouseinn.com, 5–8 P.M. Wed.–Sun., $20–27) serves dishes both local (locally raised tenderloin with mushroom butter) and international (New Zealand mussels with pesto and Sambuca) in persuasion. The wine list is exceptionally chosen. The restaurant is part of an inn that also houses Doc's Tavern, a relaxed option serving lots of fresh salad, sandwiches, and pastas.

Information and Services

Info on the area, along with a wireless hotspot, can be found at **Rochester Public Library** (22 S. Main St., 802/767-3927, www.rochestervtpubliclibrary.com, 12:30–7 P.M. Tues. and Thurs., 9 A.M.–1 P.M. Sat.). There's an ATM downtown at **Randolph National Bank** (85 N. Main St., 802/767-4222, 8 A.M.–4 P.M. Mon.–Thurs., 8 A.M.–5:30 P.M. Fri., 9 A.M.–noon Sat.).

RANDOLPH

What passes for a population center in these parts, Randolph is a collection of brick storefronts and mill buildings ranged over the rushing torrents of the White River, home to all of 5,000 souls. The town packs a lot into such a small package, however, with several museums and cultural attractions and an aesthetically appealing downtown that evokes a 1950s vision of Main Street.

Sights

In the age of iPods and MP3s, it may be difficult to conceive of a time when the only home entertainment system a family had was a music box as big as a mini-fridge. **Porter Music Box Museum** (424 Rte. 66, 800/811-7087, www.portermusicboxmuseum.com, 9:30 A.M.–4 P.M. Mon.–Fri., June–Oct., $6.50 adults, $4.50 children 3–12, children under 3 free) takes visitors back to those days, with dozens of inlaid cherry-wood automata and spool-fed music boxes. Tours include songs played on some of the models on display. The museum is on the site of the Porter Music Box Company, which is still making them today.

Randolph is heaven to covered-bridge hunters, claiming three all built in the same year, 1904. The pick of the bunch is the **Braley Bridge** in East Randolph. No fewer than five more covered bridges span the river in the nearby town of Northfield. Three of them are lined up on **Cox Brook Road,** including two that can be seen at once (the only place that's true in the whole state).

The **Randolph Historical Museum** (9 Pleasant St., 802/728-6677, 2–4 P.M. third Sun. of the month May–Oct., admission by donation) is one of the better small historical museums in the state. It exhibits the tombstone of Justin Morgan, owner of the colt that started the bloodline of the famous Morgan horse, one of the first breeds developed in America. (The tombstone for the horse, meanwhile, is in a graveyard in nearby Tunbridge.) Other exhibits include a reconstructed early barbershop and drugstore.

Most dairy farmers are too busy milking and feeding the cows to have much time for entertaining guests. The family farmers at the all-organic **Neighborly Farms of Vermont** (1362 Curtis Rd., 802/728-4700, www.neighborlyfarms.com, 9 A.M.–5 P.M. Mon.–Sat. year-round) are an exception, happy to show off their 50 Holsteins and demonstrate milking and cheese-making (10 different varieties) to visitors. Be sure to try the farm's clothbound cheddar, which took the Gold medal in the Eastern States Exhibition—in Vermont that's

worth bragging rights for life. In the spring, the farm runs a maple sugar operation as well.

A little bit farther down the road is another great farm worth a visit. Vermont's farmers are increasingly turning from cows to goats to supply the milk for their cheeses. **Fat Toad Farm** (787 Kibbee Rd., Brookfield, 802/279-0098, www.fattoadfarm.com, 10 A.M.–5 P.M. daily) has fast become a favorite for its farmstead chevre, available in regular or flavored varieties (maple, olive, ginger-cilantro). What's really put this farm on the map, however, is its delectable goat's milk caramel, a variation on the Mexican version of dulce de leche called *cajeta*. Inspiration for the concoction was brought back by one of the farmer's daughters after a study abroad in Mexico, and the combination of tangy sweetness has fast become a local favorite. The farm runs a small self-serve store with varieties including vanilla, cinnamon, and coffee; farmworkers are always happy to take visitors on tours to meet the goats. The farm can be tricky to find; check online for directions, or stop at Floyd's Store in downtown Randolph to ask for a map.

Entertainment and Events

The pride of Randolph is the **Chandler Center for the Arts** (71–73 Main St., 802/728-9878, www.chandler-arts.org), a turn-of-the-20th-century music hall restored to its former glory in the 1970s. The hall plays host during the year to a schedule of plays and musicals, as well as annual events: the Central Vermont Chamber Music Festival offers string quartet performances by some of the state's best music performers on two Saturdays in August (www.centralvtchambermusicfest.org); and the hotly anticipated Mud Season Variety Show each March showcases the talents of local community members, who perform everything from Broadway numbers to clogging.

More than 100 dancers and musicians from as far away as Canada descend on Randolph each Labor Day weekend for the **New World Festival** (802/728-9878, www.newworldfestival.com), a celebration of Celtic and French music at the Chandler Center and other venues around town.

Shopping

Grab a few crafty gifts at **Belmain's** (15 N. Main St., 802/728-3781, 8:30 A.M.–6 P.M. Mon.–Fri., 8:30 A.M.–5 P.M. Sat., 10 A.M.–3 P.M. Sun.), as well as some Vermont souvenirs (cow-print pot-holders, anyone?). Around since 1845 (the original hitching rail for horses is still in front), **Floyd's General Store** (3 Main St., Randolph Center, 802/728-5333, 7:30 A.M.–6 P.M. Mon.–Fri., 7:30 A.M.–5 P.M. Sat., 9 A.M.–noon Sun.) is both grocery store to locals and tourist shop for visitors. Step inside and grab a few pieces of penny candy or locally made cheddar for the road.

In the craft studio of **White River Craft Center** (50 Randolph Ave., 802/728-8912, www.whiterivercraftcenter.org, 9 A.M.–5 P.M. Mon.–Sat.), housed in a well-kept Victorian mansion, artisans share work space with retail shelves. On the latter, find their handmade Shaker baskets, pottery, blankets and throws, and furniture. And there's enough nicely restored American period furniture at **Page Jackson Antique Gallery** (1529 Ridge Rd., 802/728-5303, by appt. only) to fill a few homes. The pottery selection is worth a gander, too.

Food

There are plenty of home-style specials to choose from at **Patrick's Place** (2 Merchants Row, 802/728-4405, www.patricksplacerestaurant.comcastbiz.net, 11 A.M.–2 P.M. Tues.–Wed., 11 A.M.–9 P.M. Thurs.–Sat., $5–13). Standouts at breakfast include the ultra-fluffy pancakes and enormous omelets.

Grab a quick bite at centrally located **Randolph Village Pizza** (1 S. Main St.,

802/728-9677, www.villagepizza.net/Randolph, 11 A.M.–9 P.M. Sat.–Thurs., 11 A.M.–10 P.M. Fri., $7–16), where all of Randolph seems to convene.

The owners of **Ariel's Restaurant** (29 Stone Rd., 802/7276-3939, www.arielsrestaurant.com, 5:30–10 P.M. Wed.–Sun., $7–16) have built an eatery in their own home, and they welcome guests accordingly. The hospitable staff brings out course after course of dishes such as sweet corn bisque with cilantro and shellfish paella, always encouraging everyone to come back.

Information and Services

For more information about Randolph and the entire White River Valley, contact the **Randolph Area Chamber of Commerce** (66 Central St., 802/728-9027, www.randolphvt.com), which stocks the usual assortment of maps and brochures in its downtown office. The state also runs a Welcome Center along I-89 in Randolph.

Randolph is the area's regional hub, with routine and emergency medical services available at **Gifford Medical Center** (44 S. Main St., 802/728-7000, www.giffordmed.org). Pharmacy needs can be taken care of at **Rite-Aid Pharmacy** (12 N. Main St., 802/728-3722, 8 A.M.–8 P.M. Mon.–Fri., 8 A.M.–6 P.M. Sat., 8 A.M.–3 P.M. Sun., pharmacy 8 A.M.–7 P.M. Mon.–Fri., 9 A.M.–6 P.M. Sat., 9 A.M.–3 P.M. Sun.). Get cash at any of a cluster of banks downtown, including **Randolph National Bank** (21 Main St., 802/728-9611, 8 A.M.–5 P.M. Mon.–Thurs., 8 A.M.–5:30 P.M. Fri.). The local arm of the law is the **Randolph Police Department** (6 S. Bay St., 802/728-3737).

FAIRLEE AREA

Back in the days of the Revolutionary War, General George Washington commissioned a road along the Connecticut River to help troops march into Canada. Never finished, the

Bayley-Hazen Road north from Newbury was dubbed the "road from nowhere to nowhere." That's an apt description for most of the winding country roads along the northern stretch of the Upper Valley—in a good way. The area around such towns as **Fairlee, Strafford, Corinth,** and **Bradford** is a forgotten swath of rolling farmland, historic town centers, and community suppers insulated from the temptations of civilization.

Sights

If you attended a state college in the United States, you may have Senator Justin Morrill to thank. A lion of the legislature in the 19th century, Morrill spearheaded passage of the Land Grant Act, which changed the face of American education by establishing land-grant colleges, extending education for the first time beyond the rich elite. You can educate yourself about Morrill at the **Justin Smith Morrill Homestead** (214 Justin Morrill Hwy., Strafford, 802/765-4288, www.morrill-homestead.org, 11 A.M.–5 P.M. Sat.–Sun. late May–mid-Oct., $5 adults, children under 14 free). The homestead is also a fine example of a Gothic Revival cottage, a rare form of architecture that was all the rage for a brief period in the late 19th century.

As a bonus, less than a mile north of the homestead on the Justin Morrill Highway is scenic **Old City Falls,** a pretty double waterfall that tumbles a combined 50 feet down over a ledge of the Waits River. A trail from the parking area on Old City Falls Road takes you along the top of a ravine, then down a long flight of stairs to the pool in the middle.

Sugarhouses

During sugar season, the proprietor of **Fifield's Sugarhouse** (51 Maple Hill Rd., Thetford Center, 802/333-4467 or 802/333-9576, by appt.) will give tours of the sugaring process with the purchase of a pint. The folks at

Maplestone Farm (4146 Tucker Mountain Rd., East Corinth, 802/439-5241, www.maplestonefarm.com, 9 A.M.–5 P.M. daily) churn out specialties including maple cream, granulated maple sugar, and maple candies, as well as ordinary maple syrup. As with all sugarhouses in Vermont, the best time to visit is late winter or early spring when the sap is flowing. Even at those times, however, call ahead, if possible, as hours can be mercurial at best.

Events

For a true taste of Vermont life, bring your appetite to the town of Bradford's annual **Wild Game Supper** (Nov.), an old Vermont tradition in which residents hunt and cook game animals and then serve them up family-style in a big potluck. If it sounds a bit "bumpkin," it isn't—local amateur chefs have perfected recipes for rabbit, pheasant, venison—and even bear—that would seem at home in the finest gourmet restaurants. The event takes place at Bradford's **Congregational Church** (245 N. Main St., 802/222-4034).

The valley comes out every weekend to trade and barter antiques and other wares at the **Fairlee Flea Market** (Rte. 5, Fairlee, 802/333-9653, 7:30 A.M.–3 P.M. Sat.–Sun., June–Aug.), a swap meet in an outdoor market next door to an old train station.

Shopping

There's plenty to chew on at **Bread and Chocolate Factory** (1538 Industrial Park Rd., Wells River, 802/429-2920, www.burnhamandmills.com, 4–6 P.M. Mon., 6–8 P.M. Wed., 2:30–5:30 P.M. Fri., 9 A.M.–7 P.M. Sat., closed Sun., Tues., and Thurs.)—namely oversized lollies, good-quality hot chocolate mixes, and a selection of barbecue and pasta sauces, mustards, and other specialty condiments. You'll find similarly tasty stock at the **Farmer Hodges Roadside Stand** (2112 U.S. 5 N., Fairlee, 802/333-4483, 9 A.M.–5 P.M.), purveyor of maple syrup, jams, jellies, cider, and honey—all locally made.

Outfit your kitchen in custom-made and truly unique mugs found at **South Road Pottery** (3458 South Rd., Bradford, 802/222-5798, www.brucemurraypotter.com, 10 A.M.–5 P.M. daily). Here potter Bruce Murray creates lovely stoneware works in an 18th-century timber-frame barn, all by hand. Stock up on outdoorsy gear and clothing for men, women, and kids at **Farm Way** (286 Waits River Rd., Bradford, 802/222-9316, www.vermontgear.com, 8:30 A.M.–5:30 P.M. Mon.–Sat., 8:30 A.M.–8 P.M. Fri.). Don't be fooled by the name, however; Farm Way carries goods that go far beyond the farm, from luggage and handmade swings to kayaks and hunting gear.

Food

You'd expect to find quaint wares in the historic building that houses **Newbury Village General Store** (4991 Main St., Newbury, 802/866-5861, 6 A.M.–8 P.M. Mon.–Fri., 7 A.M.–8 P.M. Sat., 8 A.M.–6 P.M. Sun., $6–13), and you'd be correct. But you'll also find a deli to write home about; bread is baked fresh daily and the soups and salads are all made from scratch.

Simple pizzas fly out of the oven at **Leda's Pizza** (Rte. 5, Fairlee, 802/333-4773, 11:30 A.M.–8:30 P.M. Wed.–Sun., $9–15). More-formal dining can be found shore-side in the dining room of **Lake Morey Resort** (1 Clubhouse Ln., Fairlee, 800/423-1211, www.lakemoreyresort.com, 6–8:30 P.M. daily mid-May–Dec., $18–31). Take a seat in the airy restaurant, gaze at the shimmering lake view, and sup on the likes of duck confit with port wine reduction, seared yellowfin tuna with spiced miso, and creamy almond cheesecake.

Information and Services

The state of Vermont runs a Welcome Center along I-91 between Bradford and Newbury. For more information, contact the **Upper Valley Chamber of Commerce** (White River Junction, 802/295-6200, www.uppervalleychamber.com). Several area libraries offer free wireless Internet, including **Blake Memorial Library** (676 Village Rd., East Corinth, 802/439-5338) and **Fairlee Public Library** (221 Rte. 5 N., 802/333-4716, 9 A.M.–5 P.M. Tues., 1–7 P.M. Wed., 1–5 P.M. Thurs.–Fri., 9 A.M.–noon Sat.).

SPORTS AND RECREATION
Green Mountain Sports Center

One-stop shopping for all your exercise whims, this sprawling recreational complex (665 Stock Farm Rd., Randolph, 800/424-5575, www.3stallioninn.com) at the Three Stallion Inn manages 1,300 acres with some 30 miles of trails for hiking, biking, and cross-country skiing. The complex also sports volleyball and tennis courts and can arrange fly-fishing trips on the White River with Orvis-certified guides.

Hiking and Biking

Rochester is the jumping-off point for numerous hikes into a wild portion of the **Green Mountain National Forest** (Rochester Ranger Station, 99 Ranger Rd., Rochester, 802/747-6700, www.fs.usda.gov/greenmountain), which has been proposed as a national wilderness area. One of the most popular is the climb to the top of Philadelphia Peak, a 3,200-footer that looms over Rochester Village. The peak is in the center of a cluster of tall mountains with evocative names, including Romance Mountain, Monastery Mountain, and Mount Horrid (the last of which features a steep 0.75-mile hike up to the Great Cliff, a 600-foot vertical overlook of Brandon Gap). A trail map for the area is available at the ranger station.

If you'd rather tackle the forest on two wheels, you can rent a suitable steed at **Green Mountain Bicycle Service** (105 N. Main St., Rochester, 802/767-4464, www.greenmountainbikes.com, 10 A.M.–6 P.M. daily, $25–50/day), which also specializes in arranging personalized mountain biking tours that circumvent the sometimes Draconian policies of the National Forest Service.

Camping

The state parks in this area are for the most part day-use only. One exception is **Silver Lake State Park** (214 North Rd., Bethel, 802/234-9451, www.vtstateparks.com/htm/silver.cfm, campsites $16–27), a small campground on the shores of a lake popular for swimming, boating, and fishing in summer. The 40 tent sites and 7 lean-tos are well spread out, and the camping area is equipped with restrooms, running water, hot showers, and a sanitary station (but no hookups). During the day, however, the campground can get quite crowded with families and tourists up from Woodstock and Quechee. The grassy beach has canoe and rowboat rentals, as well as a shaded picnic shelter.

Boating and Fishing

While it won't win any awards for rapids, the White River is an extremely pleasant one for canoeing, with clear, fast-moving water that takes paddlers past unspoiled family farms and dairy pastures as it meanders through Randolph and Royalton. **BattenKill Canoe** (802/362-2800 or 800/421-5268, www.battenkill.com) offers a two-day "Safari on the White" ($497) based at the Three Stallions Inn in Randolph.

The river also has some of the best fly-fishing in the Northeast. Contact **Stream and Brook Fly Fishing** (802/989-0398, www.streamandbrook.com) for guided trips along the river as well as float-tube trips to remote mountain ponds where the fish have never seen a hook.

ACCOMMODATIONS
Under $100

Simple and pretty, if smallish, rooms beckon at **Sweetserenity B&B** (40 Randolph Ave., Randolph, 888/491-9590, www.sweetserenitybb.com, $95–105), as does the house's hearty

breakfast. Suites for four guests are available, as are rooms with both twin and double beds—all outfitted with quilts and country floral prints.

$100-150

Don't feel like relaxing on your trip? **Liberty Hill Farm** (1 Clubhouse Ln., Fairlee, 802/767-3926, www.libertyhillfarm.com, $105 adults, $75 youth, $58 children under 12) will put you and your kin to work—gathering eggs, milking cows, and bailing hay. The working farm teaches visitors the daily routine of taking care of the animals and gardens. The per-person rate gets you a comfortable country room, plus breakfast and dinner.

A bit more upscale is the **Three Stallion Inn** (665 Stock Farm Rd., Randolph, 802/728-5575, www.3stallioninn.com, $125–200). With 15 traditional country rooms, a full-service restaurant and a pub, and sauna and fitness center all sitting on no less than 1,300 acres, the place is more mini-resort than inn. Rooms are pure country elegance, with plenty of marble and antique touches, including four-poster beds.

In a restored 19th-century home (and next door, in what used to be a country store), **Huntington House Inn** (19 Huntington Pl., Rochester, 802/767-9140, www.huntingtonhouseinn.com, $100–295) offers handsomely furnished rooms decorated with pencil-post beds, beautiful quilts, and old writing desks.

$150-250

The enormous **Lake Morey Resort** (1 Clubhouse Ln., Fairlee, 800/423-1211, www.lakemoreyresort.com, $150–250) offers upwards of 100 guest rooms, many of which connect to create family suites. All have satellite TV, iron and ironing boards, and wireless Internet. Golf lovers can tee off on the 18-hole course; stressed-out vacationers can get massaged at the spa; and water babies can dive into the abutting lake.

GETTING THERE AND AROUND

The White River Valley area is located in the "V" formed by the intersection of I-89 and I-91. To drive to South Royalton from White River Junction, take I-89 to exit 2, then Route 14 east (20 mi., 25 min.). For Bethel, take exit 3 to Route 107 west (25 mi., 30 min.). For Rochester, continue along Route 107 west to Route 100 north (12 mi., 20 min.). For Randolph, take I-89 north from White River Junction to exit 4, then Route 66 west (32 mi., 40 min.). For the northern Upper Valley area, take exit 2 from I-89 to Route 132 east to Strafford (22 mi., 30 min.). Alternatively, take I-91 north from White River Junction to exit 15 for Fairlee (22 mi., 25 min.) or exit 16 for Bradford (28 mi., 30 min.).

Amtrak's Vermonter service stops in Randolph at Depot Square (800/872-7245, www.amtrak.com). Elsewhere in the area, public transportation is by shuttle bus offered through **Stagecoach Transportation Services** (802/728-3773, www.stagecoach-rides.org), which runs regular service to Randolph (Depot Sq.), Bethel (Mascoma Bank parking lot, 264 Main St.), Rochester (Village Green), and Connecticut river towns including Thetford, Fairlee, Bradford, Newbury, and Wells River.

Capital Region

With only 15,000 people between them, it's probably a bit overstated to call the sister cities of Barre and Montpelier a metropolitan area. This will just have to do for Vermont, however, with the majority of the businesses between Brattleboro and Burlington clustered in the area. As you'll no doubt hear countless times, Montpelier takes pride in being the smallest state capital in the country. With a charming downtown honeycombed with art galleries, it feels more like a quaint county seat than headquarters for an entire state. Just a few miles down the road, Barre has a grittier, more working-class feel, accentuated by the still-active granite quarries that give the town its claim to fame.

BARRE

You may not have seen Barre, but you've definitely seen Barre Gray, the most highly prized grade of granite for government buildings and monuments. Local residents of Barre (pronounced "berry") first discovered the predominance of stone in their hills shortly after the War of 1812, but the industry didn't take off until Montpelier wanted to build a new State House in 1836 and ordered up a load of granite from its sister city for the task. The high quality of the stone's texture led to orders by other cities down the Eastern Seaboard, and almost overnight, the town mushroomed into a city.

Many of the workers who performed the arduous task of cutting the stone blocks out of the quarries were immigrants, first from Scotland, then, after the turn of the 20th century, from Italy. The city still has one of the most ethnically diverse populations in Vermont. While the granite trade is still a flourishing industry (mostly for cemetery headstones), the city has gone through hard times in the 20th and 21st centuries as other industries have dried up. The downtown now has a depressed feel that stands in contrast to the glory of the granite monuments that grace its parks and street corners.

⟨ Rock of Ages

The granite industry isn't just a thing of Barre's past. Rock of Ages Corporation (560 Graniteville Rd., Graniteville, 802/476-3119, www.rockofages.com) still cuts stone out of the

NORTHERN MOUNTAINS

headstones at Hope Cemetery

same deep holes it has mined for more than 100 years. The company now gives narrated tours (9 A.M.–5 P.M. Mon.–Sat. late May–mid-Oct., $5 adults, $4.50 seniors, $2.50 children 6–12) of its main quarry, where a platform looks out on massive machines cutting blocks of granite more than 600 feet below. Guides explain the meticulous methods for cutting the ginormous blocks, which include boring dozens of small holes beneath the blocks and then blasting them free with dynamite. (Fun fact: The quarry was used in the opening shot of the 2009 *Star Trek* film, in which a young Captain Kirk drives a Corvette off the cliff.)

The site also features a visitors center (9 A.M.–5 P.M. Mon.–Sat. May–Oct., free) that includes historical memorabilia about the granite trade as well as a "cut stone activity center" where you can try your hand at sandblasting and other activities. And if you are *really* thinking ahead, you can order your own headstone from a showroom on the premise.

Hope Cemetery

The immigrants who worked in the quarries were given one unusual perk: each of them received one block of granite for their very own. Many chose to work on their own tombstones, creating a lasting tribute to the handiwork of men who mostly toiled and died for monuments to others. The enormous Hope Cemetery (224 E. Montpelier Rd., 802/229-4619, www. central-vt.com, dawn–dusk, tours available upon request, $5 adults, $3 seniors) is now a giant open-air sculpture gallery, with more than 10,000 gray granite headstones carved with art deco lettering and intricate representations of flowers, ships, and religious symbols. The town still administers burials here—with the only stipulation being that the headstones must be made of Barre Gray.

In modern times, residents have pre-ordered more and more fanciful markers, such as a granite soccer ball, a granite armchair, and an actual-size granite race car. Some stones even

© MICHAEL BLANDING

contain life-sized figures, such as the touching carving of a man and woman in adjoining beds reaching out to clasp hands for eternity. It's impossible to walk among them without contemplating a sculpture for your own plot.

Monuments and Museums

Evidence of the granite trade remains all over town in the form of monuments erected by master carvers who worked in the quarries. At the turn of the 20th century, Scottish immigrant stonecutters banded together to produce a statue of **Robert Burns** on an enormous base on Washington Street. The memorial, considered one of the best granite sculptures in the world, was unveiled in 1899 on the occasion of the 100th anniversary of Burns's death. (As a point of national pride, the actual carving was done by Italian sculptors working on models by the Scots.)

The massive art deco warrior depicted in the 1924 **Soldiers and Sailors Memorial** on North Main Street is reminiscent of the figures at Rockefeller Center in New York. The statue, also known as *Young Triumphant,* was adopted as Barre's city seal.

A more recent memorial at last gives the generations of Italian stonecutters their due; erected in 1985, the **Italian-American Monument** on North Main Street depicts a 23-foot-high apron-clad figure heroically grasping a hammer and chisel. The monument is dedicated to Italian sculptor Carlo Abate, who established the first school for stone carving in Barre in the early 20th century.

Separately, a volunteer group is working on transforming a former 30,000-square-foot granite shed right off Route 302 into an even more elaborate **Vermont Granite Museum** (7 Jones Bros. Way, 802/476-4605, www.granitemuseum.org). The site has been under construction for what seems like ages; it's now open for tours by appointment, but does not yet have regular hours for visitors. For now, the

volunteers run a more modest **visitors center** (Pinsly Depot, 9 A.M.–2 P.M. Wed.–Fri.) with historical memorabilia.

The excellent Vermont Historical Society Museum in nearby Montpelier opened its own exhibit paying due to Barre's past. The **Vermont History Center** (60 Washington St., 802/479-8500, www.vermonthistory.org, 9 A.M.–4 P.M. Mon.–Fri., open year-round) features two exhibits. "The Emergence of the Granite City" showcases old photographs and memorabilia that especially focus on the stories of Barre's ethnic granite workers, including regalia worn by Scottish clans, a still for making grappa owned by an Italian family, and artifacts from a violent strike in the 1930s. "Icons, Oddities and Wonders" is full of things that make you go "Hmmmm," including rare stamps, a child's cape made out of milkweed, and (no joke) Lord Byron's sword.

Vermont Butter and Cheese

One of the country's biggest names in artisan cheese, Vermont Butter and Cheese (40 Pitman Rd., Websterville, 800/884-6287, www.vermontcreamery.com) offers tours of its picturesque farm, where you can watch them make everything from crème fraîche to aged beauties like the much-lauded "Bijou" goat cheese.

Entertainment and Events

The 1899 **Barre Opera House** (6 N. Main St., 802/476-0292, www.barreoperahouse.org) is a community theater space that hosts local and national musical performances.

You knew it was coming. The **Granite Festival of Barre** (7 Jones Bros. Way, 802/476-4605, www.granitemuseum.org, early Sept.) celebrates all things gray and stony, with stonecutting and etching demonstrations on the grounds of the granite museum, hands-on activities, and Irish music and a bocce tournament to pay homage to Barre's ethnic heritage.

Shopping

A bit like Vermont itself, the wares at **Linda B. Pottery** (576 Higuera Rd., 802/476-4143, www.lindabpottery.com, by appt.) are equal parts rustic and pretty. The potter specializes in boldly glazed cappuccino mugs, oil lamps, bowls, and vases—each of which is individually handcrafted and unique in its color and design.

Ogle three floors—a total of 12,000 square feet—of restored furnishings in **East Barre Antique Mall** (133 Mill St., East Barre, 802/479-5190, 10 A.M.–5 P.M. Tues.–Sun.), which has noteworthy china and Americana collections. Or stock up on Vermont-made crafts, snacks, and gifts at **Dente's Market** (406 N. Main St., 802/476-3764, 6 A.M.–10:30 P.M.), part traditional Vermont country store, part treasure trove of locally made goodies.

Food

Call ahead for breakfasts and lunches on the go at **Bag Ladies Express Cafe** (47 Patterson St., 802/479-2233, 11 A.M.–2 P.M. Mon.–Fri., $3–11). The creative wraps and overstuffed panini fly out the door, while others choose to sit and read the paper over the soups and salads. The grilled panini, homemade tarts, and hand-stuffed ravioli are prepared in the wood-fired oven. A separate room offers a cluster of pool tables.

The centrally located **Uncle Joe's NY Style Pizza & Pasta** (136 N. Main St., 802/479-9299, 11:30 A.M.–8:30 P.M. daily, $7–12) does a brisk takeout pizza business, but also attracts a dedicated following of regulars for easygoing, flavorful dishes like rigatoni with chicken, smoky sausage pizzas, and grilled steaks.

Information and Services

For more info on the area, contact the **Central Vermont Chamber of Commerce** (802/229-4619, www.central-vt.com/chamber), or stop by the **Barre Welcome Center** (60 Depot Sq., 802/476-4605, 9 A.M.–2 P.M. Wed.–Fri.)

in the old Pinsly Depot. Free Wi-Fi is available at **Espresso Bueno** (136 N. Main St., 802/479-0896, 6 A.M.–5 P.M. Mon.–Thurs., 6 A.M.–9 P.M. Fri., 7 A.M.–9 P.M. Sat., 8 A.M.–2 P.M. Sun.), a coffee shop downtown.

There is a string of banks along North Main Street, including **Key Bank** (315 N. Main St, 802/476-4135) and **Merchants Bank** (105 N. Main St., 802/476-4107, 8:30 A.M.–4:30 P.M. Mon.–Thurs., 8:30 A.M.–5:30 P.M. Fri.). You can fill prescriptions and fulfill other medical needs at **Rite-Aid Pharmacy** (335 N. Main St., 802/476-4311, 8 A.M.–8 P.M. Mon.–Fri., 8 A.M.–6 P.M. Sat., 9 A.M.–5 P.M. Sun., pharmacy 8 A.M.–8 P.M. Mon.–Fri., 9 A.M.–6 P.M. Sat., 9 A.M.–5 P.M. Sun.). For more serious medical care, the area's foremost hospital is **Central Vermont Medical Center** (130 Fisher Rd., 802/371-4100, www.cvmc.org). For non-medical emergencies, contact **City of Barre Police Department** (15 4th St., 802/476-6613).

MONTPELIER

Vermont's state capital was founded in the last days of the Revolutionary War, at a time when the intercession of the French Navy in the war effort was creating a rage for all things French. (Neighboring Calais, founded the same day, was similarly given a Francophone name.) The fact that it became the capital of the state in 1804 was probably more an accident of geography than anything else. The big cities of Bennington, Burlington, Rutland, and the like were all vying for the brass ring themselves; each eventually agreed it was better to give the government to a town in the center of the state than let any of its rivals get it.

From such tenuous beginnings, Montpelier thrived during the 19th century, mostly on the strength of the granite trade. Its downtown today is a uniform district of brick Federal-style mansions and gingerbread Victorians clustered around the shining gold dome of the Vermont State House.

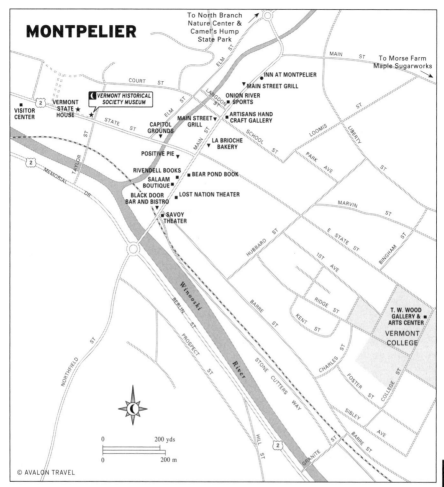

Sights

For such a small capital, Montpelier has an impressive **State House** (115 State St., 802/828-2228, www.leg.state.vt.us, tours every half-hour 10 A.M.–3:30 P.M. Mon.–Fri., 11 A.M.–2:30 P.M. Sat. July–mid-Oct.; 9 A.M.–3 P.M. Mon.–Fri. mid-Oct.–June), with a 57-foot golden dome capping a columned Renaissance Revival building. (Try for a moment to imagine the dome painted dark red, as it was between 1857 and 1907.)

Fittingly for the state, the dome is topped by a wooden statue of Ceres, the goddess of agriculture. Facing the building, look for a **statue of Ethan Allen** in the Greek Revival front portico, a remnant of an earlier state house on the site. Tours of the building's interior take in statues and paintings of Vermont politicians who figured in state and national history, including Presidents Calvin Coolidge and Chester A. Arthur.

To take a walk on the wild side, visit the

NORTHERN MOUNTAINS

© KATHRYN OSGOOD

the state's capitol, Montpelier

North Branch Nature Center (713 Elm St., 802/229-6206, www.northbranchnaturecenter.org, 9 A.M.–4 P.M. Mon.–Fri., donations welcome), which boasts a "critter room" and butterfly garden in a converted barn two miles from the center of town. Its grounds include walking trails to wooded beaver ponds and a replica of an Abenaki wigwam.

In Vermont, you are never far from a sugarhouse. On the edge of the city, seventh-generation mapler Burr Morse has turned his farm into one of the premier maple syrup producers in the state. **Morse Farm Maple Sugarworks** (1168 County Rd., 800/242-2740, www.morsefarm.com, 8 A.M.–8 P.M. daily, donations accepted) is a virtual museum of the industry, with old photographs and a "split-log" movie theater that shows a film of the sugaring process. A cavernous gift shop sells maple kettle corn and that most Vermont of treats, maple creemees (a.k.a. soft-serve maple ice cream cones).

◖ Vermont Historical Society Museum

From the beginning of Vermont's history as an independent republic, its residents have struggled with the tension between "Freedom and Unity," the state's oxymoronic state motto. A few years ago, the state took that paradox as a starting point for a complete renovation of its history museum (109 State St., 802/828-2291, www.vermonthistory.org, 10 A.M.–4 P.M. Tues.–Sat., May–mid-Oct.; 10 A.M.–4 P.M. Tues.–Fri. mid-Oct.–Apr., $5 adults, $3 students and seniors, children under 6 free, $12 families), a surprisingly sophisticated journey back into the story of the state. Exhibits start with full-scale reconstructions of an Abenaki dwelling and the Revolutionary-era Catamount Tavern, and continue on to include Civil War artifacts, a room dedicated to Vermont-born president Calvin Coolidge, and even a collection on the early history of skiing. The museum continues to evolve and expand; a new building in Barre features its own collection of exhibits and artifacts. The gift shop has an extensive selection of books on Vermont history and culture.

Galleries

One of the best of Montpelier's galleries is also the oldest. The **T.W. Wood Gallery & Arts Center** (36 College St., 802/828-8743, www.twwoodgallery.org, noon–4 P.M. Tues.–Sun.) has been showcasing the work of Vermont artists for more than 100 years, with a permanent collection of modern art and rotating shows by local contemporary artists.

Mary Stone's hand-sculpted clay animal whistles are just one of the unique crafts on display at the **Artisans Hand Craft Gallery** (89 Main St., 802/229-9446, www.artisanshand. com, 10 A.M.–6 P.M. Mon.–Sat., noon–4 P.M. Sun.), a hub for jewelry, pottery, woodwork, and metalwork from Vermont artisans.

Entertainment and Events

Montpelier's professional theater company, **Lost Nation Theater** (39 Main St., 802/229-0492, www.lostnationtheater.org) performs an eclectic mix of musicals, contemporary drama, and an annual fall Shakespeare production. The **Savoy Theater** (26 Main St., 802/229-0509, www.savoytheater.com) screens first-run and classic art films.

Upscale pizzeria **Positive Pie** (22 State St., Montpelier, 802/229-0453, www.positivepie.com, 11:30 A.M.–9 P.M. Sun.–Thurs., 11:30 A.M.–9:30 P.M. Fri.–Sat.) might have anything from reggae to belly dancing in its music lounge Thursday through Saturday. The entire third floor of the **Black Door Bar and Bistro** (44 Main St., 802/225-6479, www.blackdoorvermont.com, 5 P.M.–midnight Wed.–Thurs., 5 P.M.–2 A.M. Fri.–Sat.) is given over to live music on the weekends. Offerings might include funk, bluegrass, or old-school soul.

A raging bonfire takes off some of the winter chill at **Ice on Fire** (802/223-0577, Jan.), Montpelier's annual winter carnival. Activities include storytelling, games, and old-fashioned sled pulls.

Seems like every city of consequence has a film festival these days, and Montpelier is no exception. The **Green Mountain Film Festival** (26 Main St., 802/229-0598, www.savoytheater.com, Mar.) focuses on international films in two-dozen screenings at the Savoy Theater.

Shopping

Get the pick of the local crops (for a hiking picnic, an edible souvenir, or just as a snack) at **Hunger Mountain Co-op** (623 Stone Cutters Way, 802/223-8000, www.hungermountain. com, 8 A.M.–8 P.M. daily), a bounty of locally grown organic produce, gourmet cheeses, and vitamins.

Readers searching beyond the bestseller lists can rely on the shelves of **Rivendell Books** (100 Main St., 802/223-3928, www.rivendellbooksvt.com, 9 A.M.–7 P.M. Mon.–Fri., 9 A.M.–8 P.M. Sat., 10 A.M.–8 P.M. Sun. in summer; 9 A.M.–6 P.M. Mon.–Thurs., 9 A.M.–7 P.M. Fri.–Sat., 11 A.M.–5 P.M. Sun. in winter) for rare, antique, and otherwise collectible books. Or read what all the state's local authors have to say at **Bear Pond Books** (77 Main St., 802/229-0774, www.bearpondbooks.com, 9 A.M.–7 P.M. Mon.–Thurs., 9 A.M.–9 P.M. Fri., 9 A.M.–6:30 P.M. Sat., 10 A.M.–5 P.M. Sun.), which sells a roster of Vermont's best fiction and nonfiction—plus sponsors regular readings.

Fetch urban clothing in a country setting at the chic **Salaam Boutique** (40 State St., 802/223-4300, www.central-vt.com/web/salaam, 10 A.M.–6 P.M. Mon.–Wed. and Sat., 10 A.M.–8 P.M. Fri., noon–4 P.M. Sun.), the walls of which are neatly hung with jackets by An Ren, Twill 22, Tulle, and Velvet.

For the most expansive stock of outdoor gear around, step into **Onion River Sports** (20

NORTHERN MOUNTAINS

THEY'RE NOT LOVIN' IT

An old trivia question asks, "What is the only U.S. state capital without a McDonald's?" The answer: Montpelier. The fast-food chain has tried many times to make inroads into the little city; the latest attempt was in 1996, when the company planned to occupy a historic building in Montpelier's downtown. That effort was bitterly fought by residents, who packed zoning hearings and made impassioned arguments against the restaurant, citing everything from the chain's destruction of local businesses to its destruction of rainforest in South America. The zoning commission voted 4-3 to turn it down, retaining Montpelier's Ronald-less status. If you just have to have a Big Mac, however, don't fret: There are two McDonald's just down the road in Barre.

Langdon St., 802/229-9409, www.onionriver.com, 9 A.M.–6 P.M. Mon.–Thurs., 9 A.M.–8 P.M. Fri., 9 A.M.–5 P.M. Sat., 11 A.M.–4 P.M. Sun.). The selection of bicycles, cross-country skis, snowshoes, and camping and hiking gear (plus the footwear and clothing appropriate for all of it) is indeed impressive—as is the knowledgeable staff selling it.

Food

As much a local gathering spot as a place to find something to eat, **Capitol Grounds** (27 State St., 802/223-7800, www.capitolgrounds.com, 6:15 A.M.–6 P.M. Mon.–Thurs., 6:15 A.M.–8 P.M. Fri., 7 A.M.–8 P.M. Sat., 8 A.M.–5 P.M. Sun., closes daily at 5 P.M. in winter, $6–10) whips up made-to-order sandwiches, offers free wireless Internet service, and froths fair-trade cappuccinos all day long.

The New England Culinary Institute runs a small handful of esteemed restaurants in the area, all of which are worth a visit—particularly ◖**La Brioche Bakery** (89 Main St., 802/229-0443, www.necidining.com, 6:30 A.M.–5 P.M. Mon.–Fri., 7 A.M.–5 P.M. Sat., $9–16), a European-style cafe that bakes up scrumptious pastries and beautiful rustic breads and churns out a daily spread of creative sandwiches on them all. Another don't-miss is the school's **Main Street Grill** (118 Main St., 802/223-3188, www.necidining.com, 11:30 A.M.–9 P.M. Tues.–Sat., 10 A.M.–2 P.M. Sun., $12–19), a

swanky and professionally run place that's as likely to feed you a pulled-pork sandwich as it is a plate of carrot, hazelnut, and tofu sausage.

One part music lounge to two parts hipster pizza joint, **Positive Pie** (22 State St., 802/229-0453, www.positivepie.com, 11:30 A.M.–9 P.M. Sun.–Thurs., 11:30 A.M.–9:30 P.M. Fri.–Sat.) is a great place to hang out for the night over homemade pastas (like the fettuccine with broccoli and ricotta) and a beer.

Information and Services

The **State of Vermont** (134 State St., 802/828-3236, www.vtliving.com) runs a comprehensive information center across from the State House. A small, unstaffed information booth is located at 64 State Street. Free Wi-Fi is available at many spots downtown, including **Capitol Grounds** (45 State St., 802/223-7800) and **Langdon Street Cafe** (4 Langdon St., 802/223-8667).

ATMs are available at many downtown locations, including at **Citizens Bank** (7 Main St., 802/223-9545, 9 A.M.–5 P.M. Mon.–Fri.). Pharmacy needs can be taken care of at several locations as well, including **Rite-Aid Pharmacy** (29–31 Main St., 802/223-4787, 8 A.M.–9 P.M. Mon.–Sat., 9 A.M.–9 P.M. Sun., pharmacy 9 A.M.–9 P.M. Mon.–Fri., 9 A.M.–6 P.M. Sat., 9 A.M.–5 P.M. Sun.) and the independent **Montpelier Pharmacy** (69 Main St., 802/223-4633). In emergency, contact

Vermont State and Montpelier City police (1 Pitkin Ct., 802/223-3445).

WATERBURY

For all the hype surrounding Ben & Jerry's operation, the rest of the small city of Waterbury could only be something of a disappointment. North of the highway, Route 100 is a long touristy stretch of gift shops and inns. South of I-89, a small downtown area has a few shops and historic buildings without much character. But does that really matter? Everyone knows why you came here—so grab a cone of cookie dough and indulge.

🄲 Ben & Jerry's Factory

After a five-dollar correspondence course in ice cream making from Penn State, Ben Cohen and Jerry Greenfield opened their first shop in Burlington in 1978. From that small seed grew a company that revolutionized the American ice cream market, proving that Häagen-Dazs didn't have a lock on thick and creamy. Though most of it is made in a second factory in St. Albans, the company still makes ice cream in its flagship Waterbury factory (1401 Rte. 100, 866/258-6877, www. benjerrys.com, 10 A.M.–6 P.M. daily mid-Oct.–June; 9 A.M.–9 P.M. daily July–mid-Aug.; 9 A.M.–7 P.M. daily mid-Aug.–mid-Oct., $3 adults, $2 seniors, children 13 and under free). A cowbell signals the start of tours, which take in a self-congratulating biopic about the duo, as well as a look from the mezzanine onto the factory floor—where ice cream is mixed, flavored, frozen, and packed into pints.

The secret to the ice cream's richness, as tour guides will tell you, isn't more butter or heavier cream—it's less air stirred into the mix. Of course the best part of the tour is saved for the end: the Flavoroom, where guests can taste free samples of whatever is coming off the floor, oftentimes a new or experimental flavor. While you are downing the cold stuff, you can

---

FLAVA GRAVE

On your way out of the Ben & Jerry's Factory, take a short walk up to the hill by the playground, where you can find the "Flavor Graveyard," with 30 tombstones marked with flavors that didn't make it. Among them, you'll find Honey, I'm Home, a honey-vanilla ice cream with chocolate-covered honeycomb pieces; Lemon Peppermint Carob Chip, which just speaks for itself; and the ill-fated Sugar Plum, a plum ice cream with caramel swirl that was the worst-selling flavor in B&J history. In three weeks on the market, it sold exactly one pint.

---

fantasize about the fact that B&J employees are each allowed to take home 15 pints a week of factory seconds. Pack a picnic to take advantage of the playground and picnic tables on site.

Cold Hollow Cider Mill

Forget the cider; those in the know really come to Cold Hollow Cider Mill (3600 Waterbury-Stowe Rd., Rte. 100, Waterbury Center, 800/327-7537, www.coldhollow.com, 8 A.M.–6 P.M. daily) for the donuts, homemade gooey O's that blow Krispy Kreme out of the water. Of course, you'll need something to wash them down with, and that's where the cider comes in. Cold Hollow is one of the leading producers of apple cider, which submits apples to a souring process to make a drink much tarter than just ordinary juice. Cold Hollow gives free samples of its cider, which is still made on an old-fashioned hydraulic cider press from the 1920s.

Shopping

Need proof that tea isn't just for drinking? Get it at **Vermont Liberty Tea Company** (1 Derby Ln., 802/244-6102, www.vermontlibertytea. com, 10 A.M.–5 P.M. Mon.–Sat.), a panoply of exotic herbal infusions all under one roof. Find catnip toys, accessories like tea strainers and caddies, plus teas you actually do drink—rare black tea blends and chamomiles, and fruit teas from apple to blackberry.

Nestled among patches of wildflowers, **Cabot Annex** (2657 Rte. 100, 802/244-6334, www.cabotcheese.com/annex.html, 9 A.M.–6 P.M. daily) is as cute as cheddar houses come. Stop in to sample Cabot cheeses and pick up a hunk of cheddar for the road. The shop also sells local crafts, microbrews, and wines.

Watch the goods get made right before your eyes at **Ziemke Glassblowing Studio** (3033 Waterbury-Stowe Rd., 802/244-6126, www.zglassblowing.com, 10 A.M.–6 P.M. daily), then buy the cups, vases, and jewelry that result.

Food

Named for the rare mushroom that grows wild in the forests, **Hen of the Wood** (92 Stowe St., 802/244-7300, www.henofthewood.com, 5–9 P.M. Tues.–Sat., $16–28) is dedicated to seasonal cuisine fresh from local farms. The 19th-century mill building-turned-dining room features an ample North American wine list and an ever-changing artisan-cheese list.

Hearty and piled-up flatbreads are the draw at the aptly named **Zachary's Pizza House** (2 Butler St., Waterbury, 802/244-5650, 3–9 P.M. daily, $10–19), although the chicken parmesan and pastas also come highly recommended.

When you need a hit of lemongrass, head to **Ocha Thai Restaurant** (6 North Main St., Waterbury, 802/244-7642, www.ochathairestaurant.com, 12:30–9:30 P.M. daily, $6–24). The traditional menu spotlights noodle and curry dishes, served in an unusually pretty dining room.

Information and Services

The **Waterbury Tourism Council** (www.waterbury.org) runs an information booth on Route 100 just north of the highway exit. Wireless Internet is available at the **Waterbury Public**

Library (28 N. Main St., 802/244-7036, www.waterburypubliclibrary.com, 10 A.M.–8 P.M. Mon.–Wed., 10 A.M.–5 P.M. Thurs.–Fri., 9 A.M.–noon Sat.).

Pharmacy services are available at **Vincent's Drug and Variety** (59 S. Main St., 802/244-8458) as well as **Shaw's** (820 Waterbury-Stowe Rd., 802/241-4113, 7 A.M.–11 P.M. Mon.–Sat., 7 A.M.–9 P.M. Sun., pharmacy 8 A.M.–8 P.M. Mon.–Fri., 8 A.M.–5 P.M. Sat.–Sun.). Find an ATM at **Chittenden Bank** (80 S. Main St., 802/244-5108) or **Merchants Bank** (994 Waterbury-Stowe Rd., 802/244-1587, 8:30 A.M.–5 P.M. Mon.–Fri.).

SPORTS AND RECREATION
Camping

Justly one of Vermont's most popular campgrounds, **Little River State Park** (3444 Little River Rd., Waterbury, 802/244-7103, www.vt-stateparks.com, campsites $16–27) has some 100 campsites nestled into state forest land on the Waterbury Reservoir. With 81 tent/trailer sites and 20 lean-tos tightly packed into two loops overlooking the water, the campground doesn't afford a lot of privacy—but it is centrally located amidst some of Vermont's most popular tourist destinations (Waterbury, Stowe, Montpelier, and the Mad River Valley), and the campground itself offers lots of amenities, including two beaches, several playgrounds, a nature center, and boat rentals. The campsites include several restrooms with hot showers and a dumping station, but no hookups. Trails leave the area to hike up to the river's massive flood-control dam.

Skiing

In Montpelier, maple syrup producer Burr Morse also runs a cross-country ski touring center in the winter. **Morse Farm Ski Touring Center** (1168 County Rd., Montpelier, 802/223-2740 or 800/242-2740, www.skimorsefarm.com, 8 A.M.–6 P.M. daily, $12 adults,

$8 youth 6–18, children under 6 free) has 25 kilometers of trails through light woods and meadows, designed by two-time Olympian skier John Morton. After skiing the trails, you can warm up by the fire with a cup of cider or chill out with a maple syrup snow cone.

ACCOMMODATIONS

Looking for cheap but clean? The **Pierre Motel** (362 N. Main St., Barre, 802/476-3188, www.vtpierremotel.com, $55–99), with 20 rooms with cable and fridges, is your answer. If that and the conveniently close location to downtown Barre don't convince you, the complimentary continental breakfasts and the outdoor pool will.

Handmade quilts and snowshoes decorate the compact but tidy rooms at the Austrian-style chalet **Grunberg Haus** (94 Pine St., Waterbury, 800/800-7760, www.grunberghaus.com, $120–160), tucked into a maple forest. Each room comes with large en suite bathrooms, private balconies, gas-fired wood stoves, fridges, and microwaves. Cabins are also available, and all rooms come with a full, home-cooked breakfast.

Two gracious Federal-style buildings (filled with no fewer than 10 fireplaces) comprise the ◖ **Inn at Montpelier** (147 Main St., Montpelier, 802/223-2727, www.innatmontpelier.com, $165–250). The antiques-filled common areas lead into 19 neat rooms, with canopy beds, colonial-style bureaus, and walls ranging from tomato-red to bold floral.

GETTING THERE AND AROUND

Montpelier is located directly off I-89 at exit 8, a 55-mile (1-hr.) trip from White River Junction. To travel to Barre, from I-89 north take exit 6 and drive 10 miles east along Route 63, or from I-89 south take exit 7 and drive 10 miles east along Route 62. Waterbury is on I-89 at exit 10, 65 miles (1 hr. 10 min.) from White River Junction.

Amtrak (800/872-7245, www.amtrak.com) runs trains to stations on Route 2 and Park Row in Waterbury, and Junction Road in Montpelier. **Wheels Transportation** (802/223-2882) provides shuttle service to the Montpelier area from Burlington airport. Buses from **Vermont Transit** (802/223-7112) stop at the Montpelier Bus Station (1 Taylor St.), while the **Green Mountain Transit Agency** (802/223-7287, www.gmtaride.org) operates bus routes around Montpelier, Barre, and Waterbury.

Mad River Valley

The Mad River is named for the fact that, unlike most rivers in North America, it flows south to north and is therefore crazy or "mad." The valley is anchored by two villages, Waitsfield and Warren, which both date back to Revolutionary times and together boast a formidable collection of historic buildings. But the area isn't a set piece. Its two world-class ski resorts, Mad River Glen and Sugarbush, are only the beginning of an absurd number of outdoor activities pursued with vigor by the townsfolk all year round.

WAITSFIELD

Eleven of the 13 original settlers of this historic village were veterans of the Battle of Lexington, the kickoff to the Revolutionary War. Remnants of architecture from the Colonial period are still sprinkled throughout the hamlet of 2,000 people. These days, however, the farms and forests are honeycombed with a dozen startup technology companies and artists' studios that significantly up the sophistication level of the populace (to say nothing of the continually burgeoning number of second

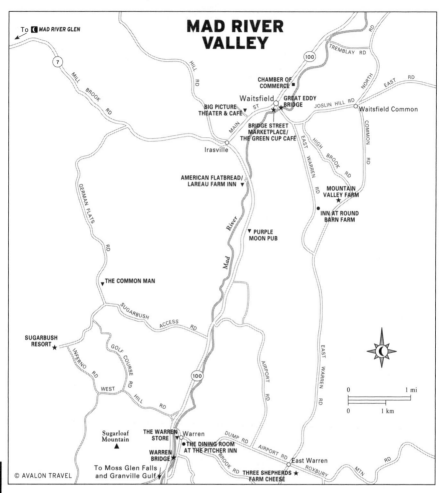

homes owned by rich New Yorkers). If there is something that all residents share in common, it's an emphasis on local preservation. The simple act of moving a driveway can turn into an epic zoning battle; on a more positive note, the weekly farmers market draws half the town's population for organic produce and locally produced crafts.

C Mad River Glen

In an era of ski-resort consolidation, rising lift-ticket prices, and runaway base-lodge development, Mad River Glen (Rte. 17, 5 mi. west of Waitsfield, 802/496-3551, www.madriverglen. com, $49–70 adults, $43–60 seniors and youth ages 6–18) stands alone in stubbornly resisting the winds of "progress." Its trails are ungroomed, teeth-grittingly narrow, and chock-full of trees, moguls, and any other impediment the mountain can throw in your way. In fact, almost half of the trails on the mountain are for experts—an unheard-of marketing suicide for which the resort is unapologetic. Its motto, "Ski It If You Can," is more than just hype; the mountain has earned a stiff allegiance from diamond dogs who come to ski, not to boast or model the latest sunglasses.

In fact, the mountain was sold in 1995 to a cooperative of skiers who pledged to keep the spirit of the resort alive. They've remained true to the promise, continuing to run one of the few ski resorts in the country that ban snowboarding (the boards have a tendency to derail the 1950s-era single chairlifts anyway) and leaving the trails in their natural, unadulterated state. You can get a little bit of an idea of the mentality from the run named Paradise, a precipitous tumble down exposed ledges, rocky moguls, and a frozen waterfall to get to the bottom. If that doesn't seem like paradise to you, don't even bother.

Covered Bridge

The historic downtown of Waitsfield is anchored by the 1833 **Great Eddy Bridge,** the second-oldest operating covered bridge in the state, which crosses the Mad River at the intersection of Route 100 and Bridge Street. (Only the Pulp Mill Bridge in Middlebury is older.) During the flooding following Hurricane Irene in 2011, the water line came up all the way to the base of the bridge, but the span stood, a testament to the nearly 200 year-old construction.

Mountain Valley Farm

Lest you think "Jingle Bells" made up all that "one-horse open sleigh" stuff, climb aboard one at Mountain Valley Farm (1719 Common Rd., 802/496-9255, www.mountainvalleyfarm.com) for an impossibly quaint horse-and-carriage ride through the mountain landscape. The farm has a range of carriages, sleighs, and hay wagons to fit the season. During other times of the year, sleighs are replaced with hay rides and carriages. Kids will love seeing the animals and

participating in farm activities, like collecting goose eggs, as well.

Entertainment and Events

The **Purple Moon Pub** (Rte. 100 and Rte. 17, 802/496-3422, www.purplemoonpub.com, 4 P.M.–midnight Tues.–Sun.) is a big part of the reason for the area's nickname, the "Bad Liver Valley." It has plenty of comfy couches for resting sore muscles après ski or canoe—to say nothing of the specialty list of martinis and a host of other potent libations. It also offers live jazz and folk music throughout the week.

The sophisticated, artsy vibe at **Big Picture Theater and Cafe** (48 Carroll Rd., off Rte. 100, 802/496-8994, www.bigpicturetheater. info, 7 A.M.–10 P.M. daily) makes for one-stop evening fun—cutting-edge movies, film series, and a dinner that happens one hour before your show. (Reservations are recommended.)

To call the weekly music festival/craft fair/gossip session the **Waitsfield Farmers' Market on the Mad River Green** (802/472-8027, www. waitsfieldfarmersmarket.com, 9 A.M.–1 P.M. Sat. May–Oct.) is giving it short shrift indeed. For many residents, it's an event to look forward to all week; for visitors, there is perhaps no better way to clue into the communal spirit of the valley than the boisterous event full of craft booths, organic produce from local farms, and stages full of folk, Latin, and Celtic musical performers.

All of that goes double for the month of August, when the whole valley comes alive for the month-long **Festival of the Arts** (802/496-6682, www.vermontartfest.com), in which the area's many artisans hold art shows and classes, and local restaurants and lodging offer special rates and events.

Shopping

Step into the **Artisans' Gallery** (20 Bridge St., 802/496-6256, www.vtartisansgallery.com,

NORTHERN MOUNTAINS

FARMER FOR A DAY

Chalk it up to the increasingly popular interest in sustainable and organic foods, or to small family farms' need to find additional sources of income—both have been driving forces behind the blossoming of agritourism in New England. And few states have embraced the trend more wholeheartedly than Vermont, where the majority of farms are eager to not only host visitors (often overnight), but to educate them about where their food comes from and how it's harvested. Farm stays are widespread across the Green Mountain State; many are in quaint, traditional, and rustic farm homes, and most offer visitors a room rented by the night, with meals, and the opportunity to pick produce, ride horses, help tend the animals, and buy from the farmstands. If the farm is one with a sugarhouse, you can watch maple syrup being made. If it's a dairy farm, you'll watch cows being milked and cheese being made. While farm stays are obviously a great experience for families with kids, many farms are catering more and more to the "foodie" crowd who are interested not only in eating local and organic foods, but also in finding out where it comes from and exactly how it all gets made.

Liberty Hill Farm (511 Liberty Hill Rd., Rochester, 802/767-3926, www.libertyhillfarm. com, $105 adults, $75 teens, $58 children), for example, supplies local restaurants with hormone- and antibiotic-free beef and pork, but they also use fresh local produce and delectable house-made maple pork sausage in meals prepared at the farm. **Four Springs Farm** (776 Gee Hill Rd., Royalton, 802/763-7296, www.fourspringsfarm.com, $25-65 per campsite) runs an organic Community Supported Agriculture (CSA) program for 50 area families, as well as a campground where families can help with chores and tag along with the farmer to pick their own vegetables for cooking or to purchase. And **Allenholm Farm Orchards B&B** (150 South St., South Hero, 802/372-5566, www.allenholm.com, $98-135), serves fresh-made apple pie for breakfast, along with beefalo, pork, chicken, and eggs all produced on the farm.

For more information, the **Vermont Farms Association** (P.O. Box 828, Montpelier, 866/348-3276, www.vtfarms.org) provides detailed and current information on the farm stays in its membership.

---

11 A.M.–6 P.M. daily) in the Old Village area of Waitsfield, and prepare to feel bewildered by the enormous selection. Upwards of 175 local craftspeople sell their goods here, which means you'll have no problem finding jewelry, woodblock prints, hand-painted wooden bowls, jewelry, and stoneware.

The most respected outdoors outfitter in the area, **Clearwater Sports** (4147 Main St., 802/496-2708, www.clearwatersports.com, 10 A.M.–6 P.M. Mon.–Fri., 9 A.M.–6 P.M. Sat., 10 A.M.–5 P.M. Sun.), offers scads of gear and all the equipment rentals and guided tours you need to put it to proper use.

On the corner of Route 100 and Bridge Street (the same intersection as the Great Eddy Bridge), the **Bridge Street Marketplace** was once an inn and tavern for wayfarers; damaged in an earlier devastating flood in 1998, it was restored into a country version of Covent Garden, with craft shops and eateries spread out between five different buildings.

Food

Looking for lively food and a livelier atmosphere? The **Purple Moon Pub** (Rte. 100 and Rte. 17, 802/496-3422, www.purplemoonpub.com, 5:30–9:30 P.M. Tues.–Sun., $6–15) also serves a tasty pub menu of crispy fish wraps, Vermont-goat-cheese fondues, and maple flan.

Arguably the Ben & Jerry's of the pizza world, ◖ **American Flatbread** (48 Lareau Rd., 802/496-8856, www.americanflatbread.

© MEGAN DUNI

A pizza pie cooks at American Flatbread.

com, 5–9:30 P.M. Thurs.–Sun., $7–16) just about has its own cult, and deservedly so. Thursday through Saturday nights, the unassuming farmhouse setting turns into a party, swarmed by lovers of the organic menu of wholesome and gourmet pies, salads, and desserts made entirely of sustainable, farm-fresh Vermont ingredients. Reservations aren't accepted, but do as the locals do and show up at 5 to put your name on the waitlist. You can request a specific time to come back, or just wait by the bonfire with a pint until your name is called.

A culinary star in the Mad River Valley is **The Green Cup Cafe** (40 Bridge St., 802/496-4963, 7 A.M.–2 P.M. Fri.–Tues. and 6–9 P.M. Sat.–Mon., $4–30), an unassuming bakery by the covered bridge. By day it serves up fresh homemade sandwiches and soups, but at night, it's transformed into a speakeasy cafe serving artful, but not precious, dishes prepared by CIA-trained chef Jason Gulisano. The flavors, mostly drawn from fresh, local ingredients, fairly burst off the plate.

Information and Services

The **Mad River Valley Chamber of Commerce** (800/828-4748, www.madrivervalley.com) runs a visitors center in the historic General Wait House on Route 100 in Waitsfield. Log onto the Internet through Wi-Fi hotspots at **Three Mountain Café** (107 Mad River Green, 802/496-5470, www.threemountaincafe.com) or **Big Picture Cafe** (48 Carroll Rd., 802/496-8994, www.bigpicturetheater.info).

An ATM is located at **Chittenden Bank** (Mad River Shopping Center, 802/496-2585, 9 A.M.–4:30 P.M. Mon.–Wed., 9 A.M.–5:30 P.M. Fri.), right on the Mad River Green. Pharmacy goods can be found at the aptly-named **The Drug Store** (5091 Main St., 802/496-2345) in the Village Square Shopping Center, as well as at **Northfield Pharmacy** (9 A.M.–6 P.M. Mon.–Fri., 9 A.M.–2 P.M. Sat., 8 A.M.–noon Sun.).

NORTHERN MOUNTAINS

© PAINETWORKS.COM

the Warren Bridge and waterfall

WARREN

If Waitsfield is the commercial and cultural heart of the valley, Warren is its quainter and quieter cousin. Not a shingle is out of place in its achingly cute town center, which looks as if it hasn't changed in the past 200 years. (Though in fact its centerpiece, the Pitcher Inn, is a re-creation of the original that has been around for less than 20 years.) Befitting its colonial past, the town was named after General Joseph Warren, the tragic hero of the Battle of Bunker Hill, who died in battle. Now the village may be the ultimate place to get away, with a slow pace of life and easy access into the surrounding mountains.

Sights

Warren has its own covered bridge, the 55-foot-long **Warren Bridge,** which sports an unusual asymmetrical design. (The angles on the eastern and western sides are slightly different.) The bridge is off Route 100, just below downtown.

On the outskirts of the village, **Three Shepherds Farm Cheese** (42108 Roxbury Mountain Rd., 802/496-3998, www.three-shepherdscheese.com, 11:30 A.M.–6:30 P.M. Mon., Tues., and Thurs., 8 A.M.–8 P.M. Fri.–Sat., 8 A.M.–6:30 P.M. Sun.) is a father-daughter cheese-making operation that goes beyond cheddar to craft its own artisanal raw-milk sheep cheese varieties. The farm runs an organic food shop in an 1897 old schoolhouse. Out back you can see the cheeses being shaped through a small viewing window. Currently there aren't any sheep on the farm, as the family's flock was slaughtered by the U.S. government over the mad cow disease scare a few years back—an incident dramatically recounted by scientist-turned-shepherdess Linda Faillace in her book *Mad Sheep*. If you feel inspired (or outraged) you can sign up for one- or three-day cheese-making classes offered by the family to get started on your own varieties.

A few miles south down Route 100 in

Granville (population 309), **Moss Glen Falls** has few equals in the state. A multi-pitched cataract that drops 125 feet through a narrow gorge, the waterfall is just as beautiful frozen in winter as it is gushing in summer. A viewing platform is accessible from the highway; the falls themselves are part of the **Granville Gulf State Reservation,** a seven-mile-stretch of pathless wilderness that is among the most scenic drives in the Greens. From the road keep an eye out for moose, who are wont to frequent the area's streams and beaver ponds.

Events

Three sports weren't enough for the outdoor-crazy Mad River residents, so the **Sugarbush Triathlon** (800/537-8427, www.sugarbush. com, mid-Apr.) has four—running, kayaking, cycling, and cross-country skiing. The race starts on foot at Warren School and ends on skis at Sugarbush base lodge; its layout makes it easy for spectators to catch the action.

Shopping

Some places are more hangout than store, and **The Warren Store** (284 Main St., 802/496-3864, www.warrenstore.com, 8 A.M.–7 P.M. Mon.–Sat., 8 A.M.–6 P.M. Sun.) counts itself among them. Everyone seems to be on a first-name basis at this eclectic provisions shop, full of Vermont-made odds and ends (from pillows to salad bowls). They churn out excellent creative sandwiches from the deli—all on bread baked on-site—and have a nice selection of unusual wines for sale.

A definite do-not-miss is the **Granville Bowl Mill** (45 Mill Rd., Granville, 800/828-1005, www.bowlmill.com, 9 A.M.–5 P.M. Mon.–Sat, 11 A.M.–4 P.M. Sun.), a venerable factory and showroom originally founded in 1857 that makes wooden bowls and cutting boards from Vermont wood the old-fashioned way—on 19th-century equipment, then perfected with 20th-century sanding techniques. While not

cheap, the one-of-a-kind bowls come in a multiplicity of shapes, sizes, and woods, including cherry, yellow birch, and sugar maple (some with the hole from the sugar tap still in the wood).

Food

Upscale and meticulously run, the restaurant at ◖ **The Dining Room at The Pitcher Inn** (275 Main St., 802/496-6350, www.pitcherinn.com, 6–9 P.M. Wed.–Mon., $28–35) boasts a superlative and hefty international wine list and an impressive menu to match. Global in its influences but local in most of its ingredients, the kitchen emphasizes organic seasonal produce and fresh game such as grilled Vermont-raised lamb. Want to raise the romance bar even further? Reserve a private dinner for two in the restaurant's wine cellar.

Find everything from cornmeal-crusted salmon with braised leeks to simple crab cakes on the menu at the relaxed and comfy **The Common Man** (3209 German Flats Rd., 802/583-2800, www.commonmanrestaurant. com, 6–9 P.M. Tues.–Sat., $16–29). The restaurant's airy building is 150 years old and outfitted with crystal chandeliers, candlelight, and a gargantuan fireplace.

SPORTS AND RECREATION

The Mad River Valley abounds with recreational activities. In addition to the suggestions below, the Mad River Glen ski area runs the **Mad River Glen Naturalist Program** (802/496-3551, www.madriverglen.com/naturalist) with guided tours that range from moonlit snowshoeing expeditions to wildlife-tracking trips to rock climbing.

Hiking and Biking

Three out of five of the peaks in Vermont above 4,000 feet rise from the Mad River Valley. While not the highest mountain in Vermont, the distinctly shaped **Camel's Hump** might be the best loved by state residents. Its shape is identifiable for miles around, and its summit remains completely undeveloped and pristine. The most popular ascent is up the 7-mile Monroe Trail, a rock-hopping ascent from a birch-and-beech forest up to the unique alpine vegetation zone of its undeveloped summit. The parking area for the trail is at the end of Camel's Hump Road in Duxbury. There is a trail map available on the website for **Camel's Hump State Park** (www.vtstateparks.com/htm/camelshump.htm). The state park itself doesn't have a visitors center or services, much less a campground. However, camping is allowed within the park in lower elevations away from trails. In addition, several shelters and tent sites are operated around the summit.

Two more demanding peaks, **Mount Ellen** and **Mount Abraham,** can be hiked singly or together, taking in the 4,000-foot ridge between them. For information on all of these hikes, contact the **Green Mountain Club** (802/244-7037, www.greenmountainclub.org), or pick up a copy of the club's indispensible *Long Trail Guide,* available at most bookstores and outdoors stores in Vermont.

If the mountains seem too daunting, the **Mad River Path Association** (802/496-7284, www.madriverpath.com) manages several walking and biking trails that weave in and out of the villages of the valley, taking in farms, woodland, and bridges along the way. Bicycles can be rented from **Clearwater Sports** (4147 Main St., Rte. 100, Waitsfield, 802/496-2708, www.clearwatersports.com).

Boating

With a quick flow and a few spots of good white water, the Mad River is ideal for canoeing and kayaking. **Clearwater Sports** (4147 Main St., Rte. 100, Waitsfield, 802/496-2708, www.clearwatersports.com) leads affordable all-day tours on the Mad and Winooski Rivers ($80 per person), as well as moonlight paddles.

They also offer canoe and kayak rentals ($40–90), either drive-away or with a return shuttle included.

Skiing

Once known as "Mascara Mountain" for its tendency to draw a jet-setting, zinc oxide-sporting population of skiers more into modeling their latest parka than tackling the slopes, **Sugarbush** (1840 Sugarbush Access Rd., Warren, 802/583-6300 or 800/537-8427, www.sugarbush.com, $49 adults, $39 seniors and youth 7–18) has come a long way to rightly earn its place as Vermont's Second Slope, often favorably described as a more welcoming "alternative" to Killington. It's second to the Beast in the number and difficulty of the slopes it offers, with 111 trails descending from two peaks, Lincoln Peak and Mount Ellen. But it may have the most difficult trail in the East: the rock-and-glade ride known as the Rumble. Sugarbush is also prized for the high amount of natural snow it gets each year, as storms from Lake Champlain unload their cargo after passing over the mountains. Not that it needs it—the Bush has one of the most sophisticated snow-making systems in the East. As a bonus, Sugarbush and Mad River Glen have worked out lift packages that include both mountains—so you can experience big-mountain skiing on the Bush and still not lose out on the intimacy of the smaller mountain down the valley.

In the shadow of Sugarbush and the surrounding mountains, **Ole's Cross Country Center** (Airport Rd., Warren, 802/496-3430, www.olesxc.com) has 45 kilometers of trails through deep woods and farm country.

Ice Skating

Waitsfield's outdoor skating rink, the **Skatium** (Village Sq., Waitsfield, 802/496-8909) is a community gathering place in winter. The rink has skate rentals during public skating hours,

© KARE TRABANT

the Sugarbush ski resort

generally all day on Saturday and Sunday from early December as long as the ice lasts, as well as other hours during the week that vary by season. During the winter, call the rink directly for a full schedule.

Horseback Riding

Icelandic horses are genetically programmed to traverse the snowy landscape. The **Vermont Icelandic Horse Farm** (3061 N. Fayston Rd., Waitsfield, 802/496-7141, www.icelandichorses.com) breeds well-mannered purebreds for half- and full-day trips ($80/$190) and longer overnight trail rides all year-round.

ACCOMMODATIONS
Under $100

Under the same ownership as the lovably bohemian American Flatbread, the hub of which is based on the property, **Lareau Farm Inn** (48 Lareau Rd., Waitsfield, 802/496-4949, www.lareaufarminn.com, $90–135)

names its rooms after principles its management holds dear—love, patience, and respect among them. A copy of Dr. Seuss's *The Lorax* is found in every room, and of course, children are welcome. In fact, guests of every age are made to feel like part of the family. With delicious breakfasts and free wireless Internet included—not to mention the attention of a genuinely warm staff—Lareau couldn't offer better value.

$150-250

Get a little R&R with your maple syrup fix when you bunk down at **Sweet Retreat Guesthouse and Sugarworks** (329 Frost Rd., Northfield, 802/485-8525 or 800/707-8427, www.sweetretreat-vermont.com, $220). Visitors can use the unit's kitchen to sample the breakfast fixings for morning meals and help themselves to fresh veggies from the garden and to maple syrup from the sugarhouse.

Romance, thy name is **Round Barn Farm**

COURTESY OF ROUND BARN FARM

Round Barn Farm

(1661 E. Warren Rd., Waitsfield, 802/496-2276, www.theroundbarn.com, $165–285). Most rooms in the 19th-century farmhouse have skylights, king-size canopy beds, whirlpool tubs, gas fireplaces, wireless Internet access, and jaw-dropping mountain views.

Over $250

Exquisitely decorated, the Relais & Chateaux–designated **Pitcher Inn** (275 Main St., Warren, 802/496-6350, www.pitcherinn.com, $425–800) houses 11 rooms and suites—each individually decorated in a Vermont theme and with Wi-Fi, CD players, TVs, whirlpool tubs, and radiant floor heating; a few have wood-burning fireplaces. There's also a stand-alone spa on the property, offering everything from hair care and pedicures to facials.

GETTING THERE AND AROUND

For the Mad River Valley, take exit 9 to Route 100B and then Route 100 south to Waitsfield. The distance from Montpelier is 20 miles (30 min.) The **Mad Bus** (802/496-7433, www.madrivervalley.com) shuttle stops at various locations in Waitsfield and Warren, along with routes to Sugarbush, Mad River Glen, and Montpelier.

Stowe

The Green Mountains begin to taper off as they climb northward into Canada, but not before one last peak performance with Mount Mansfield, the highest in the state. Along its southern slopes, the ski village of Stowe is the main attraction in this area. Look up "cute" in the dictionary, and it wouldn't be too surprising to see a photo of Stowe—not, at least, after you've visited the adorable resort village. A bit like Aspen without the attitude, this is mountain living gone upscale: world-class shopping, eating, and resorts with lots of crisp, fresh air; views of lush green Mount Mansfield in the summer, mind-blowing foliage in the fall, and excellent skiing in the winter.

Founded in 1763, Stowe earned its early living from sawmills and gristmills. But its beautiful setting and alpine climate started drawing tourists during the summer after the Civil War.

Three Swedish families first aroused interest in skiing in 1913. A year later, a librarian from Dartmouth College was the first to ski down the sides of Mount Mansfield, and tourists began coming during the winter as well. By 1937, pioneer Charlie Lord had installed the first ski lift on the mountain, and the modern ski resort was born. Despite Stowe's popularity, however, the resort has eschewed the modern trend of building up the base lodge with condos and restaurants, preferring to work with independent businesses in the community instead. For that reason, Stowe still feels like a real community that happens to have a ski resort, rather than the other way around.

SIGHTS
Trapp Family Lodge
What happens after "happily ever after?"

COURTESY OF THE TRAPP FAMILY LODGE

NORTHERN MOUNTAINS

cross-country skiing at the Trapp Family Lodge

Well, you start a ski lodge in Vermont. At least, that's the trajectory of Baron and Maria von Trapp, whose story as depicted in the musical *The Sound of Music* has made generations swoon. After escaping the Nazis, the von Trapps came to Stowe to re-create the quintessential ski chalet as the Trapp Family Lodge (700 Trapp Hill Rd., 802/253-8511 or 800/826-7000, www.trappfamily.com), which has grown over the years into a skiers' resort complex complete with spa and slope-side villas. The family is still actively involved, and each generation, it seems, adds its own unique stamp. Recent additions include a brewery specializing in authentic Austrian styles of beer, and a cheese-making operation which churns out award-winning alpine-style cheeses, including the popular "Oma" variety (German for grandmother).

Visiting for a linzer torte at the over-the-top Austrian Tea Room and a family sing-a-long around the bonfire at night is a requirement for any serious Rodgers and Hammerstein fan. The lodge also shows a documentary about the family three times a day (10 A.M., 4:30 P.M., and 7 P.M.) in St. George's Hall. And of course there's the obligatory showing of *The Sound of Music* every Thursday night at 8 P.M.

Gondola Skyride

The Abenaki called the highest peak in Vermont *Moze-o-de-be-Wadso* or "Mountain with a Head Like a Moose." The 4,393-foot mountain has come down to us as the more prosaic Mount Mansfield. In the summer, Stowe Mountain Resort operates an eight-person high-speed gondola skyride (Mountain Rd./Rte. 108, 800/253-4754, www.stowe.com, 10 A.M.–4:30 P.M. late June–mid-Oct., $20–25 adults, $20–25 seniors, $16–17 youth 6–12, $76 families) up to the summit that takes in views of the village and surrounding mountains on the way up.

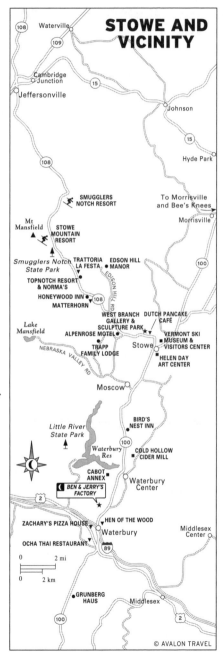

Museums and Galleries

After going up the mountain you may wonder what made those first alpine pioneers decide it was a good idea to strap two boards to their feet and hurl themselves down a mountainside. Well, you might not find the answer to that question at the **Vermont Ski Museum** (1 S. Main St., 802/253-9911, www.vtssm.com, noon–5 P.M. Wed.–Mon., donations accepted), but you will gain a greater appreciation for the lunacy of the early practitioners of the sport, as well as an appreciation for modern equipment, lifts, and clothing. Located in Stowe's former town hall, the museum has several rooms of exhibits, a plasma screen with ski videos, and a Hall of Fame of great names in Vermont skiing history.

The community-supported **Helen Day Art Center** (5 School St. at Pond St., 802/253-8358, www.helenday.com, noon–5 P.M. Wed.–Sun. year-round, $3–5 adults, $13 students and seniors, $0.50 youth 12–18, children under 12 free) has been dedicated to showcasing local art for more than 25 years. It inhabits the second floor of a Greek Revival building in the center of town, with a sculpture garden out back.

A more extensive sculpture garden fills the grounds of the **West Branch Gallery and Sculpture Park** (17 Towne Farm Ln., 802/253-8943, www.westbranchgallery.com, 11 A.M.–6 P.M. Wed.–Sun. year-round, free), a fantasia of random metal and stone objects strewn about a bucolic landscape a mile north of town.

ENTERTAINMENT AND EVENTS

The **Stowe Theatre Guild** (67 Main St., 802/253-3961, www.stowetheatre.com) presents crowd-pleasing musicals throughout the year at the Stowe Town Hall Theatre.

The village abounds with bars for après-ski libations. The **Rusty Nail** (1190 Mountain Rd., 802/253-6245, www.rustynailbar.com, noon–9 P.M. Mon.–Thurs., noon–10 P.M. Fri.–Sat., noon–8 P.M. Sun.) is classier than its name might imply, with a martini menu and DJ dancing on weekends. The **Matterhorn** (4969 Mountain Rd., 802/253-8198, www.matterhornbar.com, call for reservations) has comedy nights and cover-band performances, along with pool tables and sushi.

The Von Trapp Family continues its musical legacy with **Music in our Meadow** (802/253-8511, www.trappfamily.com), a summer concert series of classical and popular music held in the meadow behind the lodge.

For more than 20 years, the Stoweflake Resort has literally been full of hot air. The annual **Stoweflake Hot Air Balloon Festival** (802/253-7355 or 800/253-2232, www.stoweflake.com, mid-July) offers opportunities for $10 tethered balloon rides, along with longer flights for those paying $500 for a package stay at the resort.

Stowe becomes the Austrian village it has always wanted to be each fall for **Stowe Oktoberfest** (802/253-3928, www.stoweoktoberfest.com, late Sept.), a two-day crush of oompah bands, schnitzel, beer, and more beer. Miss Vermont even makes a showing. Ski-jumping and ice-sculpture carving shake Stowe out of the winter doldrums during the **Stowe Winter Carnival** (www.stowecarnival.com, late Jan.). A highlight is the Village Night Block Party, which fills the streets with bulky parkas and merriment.

SHOPPING

Designer and furniture maker John Lomas makes all of the high-quality furniture at **John Lomas Custom Furniture Shop** (2778 Shelburne Falls Rd., 802/747-8564, 8 A.M.–6 P.M. Mon.–Fri.). By turns contemporary and traditional, the pieces are paired in the showroom with lighting, pottery, and glassware by other Vermont artists. Meanwhile, artist Susan Bayer Fishman owns and runs **Stowe**

Craft Gallery (55 Mountain Rd., 802/253-4693, www.stowecraft.com, 10 A.M.–6 P.M. daily, holiday season 10 A.M.–7 P.M. daily, summer 10 A.M.–6 P.M. daily), an epic collection of many other artists' works—knickknacks like pewter measuring cups, glazed vases, and hand-carved backgammon sets.

FOOD
American

It's tough to beat the setting at 【 **Norma's** (4000 Mountain Rd., 800/451-8686, www.topnotchresort.com, 7 A.M.–9:30 P.M. daily, $14–49), the glass-enclosed dining room at Topnotch Resort. Looking out to a poster-worthy view of the mountains and a wide stretch of sky, the spot highlights chef Brian Tomlinson's organic ingredients in classic dishes like grilled tenderloin and creative turns like coffee-cured duck breast. There's also a well-edited wine list and a gorgeous outdoor terrace—the better to take in sunsets in warm weather.

The decor at the **Blue Moon Cafe** (35 School St., 802/253-7006, bluemoonstowe.com, 6–9 P.M. Tues.–Sun., $18–33) house charms diners with an honest, warm interior of exposed beams, white table cloths, and wooden chairs. The menu is equally comforting, with a weekly-changing menu of locally grown creations such as free-range chicken enchiladas and pear and parsnip soup.

Dutch

The hearty, stick-to-your ribs breakfasts at **Dutch Pancake Cafe** (Grey Fox Inn, 990 Mountain Rd., 802/253-8921, www.greyfoxinn.com, 8–11 A.M. daily in winter; 8 A.M.–12:30 P.M. daily in summer, $6–13) are just the (lift) ticket for carbo-loading before outdoor activities. Start with any of the 80 kinds of Dutch pancakes (which are thinner and more crepe-like than regular pancakes). The casual, noisy spot does an admirable job keeping big groups and kids happy.

Italian

The bustling low-ceilinged 【 **Trattoria La Festa** (4080 Upper Mountain Rd., 802/253-8480, www.stowetrattorialafesta.com, 5:30–9:30 P.M. Mon.–Sat., $16–22) is owned by Italian brothers Antonio and Giancarlo DeVito, who greet everyone at the bar by the door. The place is a paragon of the trattoria genre: casual and family-style, but serving sophisticated dishes—solidly prepared pastas like spaghetti with tender baby shrimp in garlic white-wine sauce, or yellowfin tuna with white puttanesca sauce. The tiramisu is to die for.

SPORTS AND RECREATION
Hiking

Vermont's highest peak, **Mount Mansfield,** is a tough slog, but the panoramic view of three states is well worth it. The trailhead starts north of Stowe on Route 108 and climbs four miles up steep terrain to the peak. Save some energy for the last third of a mile, "the Chin." (The parts of the mountain are named for the parts of a reclining person's profile, which it resembles.) The near-vertical slope is the toughest part of the climb—and is even more treacherous on the descent.

A longer but slightly easier climb to the summit approaches from the west along the six-mile Sunset Ridge Trail. To get a bird's-eye view of Mount Mansfield itself, take the trail up **The Pinnacle,** the 2,740-foot peak on the east side of town. The trail rises gradually from Stowe Hollow for about a mile and a half, with a short rocky scramble at the top. For more information on these and other climbs, contact the **Green Mountain Club** (802/244-7037, www.greenmountainclub.org) or pick up a copy of the *Long Trail Guide.*

Biking

Tracing lazy loops around Mountain Road and the West Branch River, the five-mile **Stowe Recreation Path** is perfect for a

Stowe Mountain Resort

relaxed afternoon ride through the village. **AJ's Ski & Sports** (350 Mountain Rd., 802/253-4593 or 800/226-6257, www.stowe-sports.com) rents hybrid and mountain bikes ($16–38 half-day, $24–45 full day) at the foot of the path near the intersection with Main Street in Stowe.

Downhill Skiing
Stowe Mountain Resort (5781 Mountain Rd./Rte. 108, 800/253-4754, www.stowe.com, $92 adults, $81 seniors, $72 children 6–12, children under 6 free) is about half the size of neighboring Sugarbush and Killington, but the challenges posed by its famous "Front Four" trails are as heady as any on the East Coast. Most difficult of all is the Goat trail, a 36-degree ice chute through moguls, ledges, and boulders that will test the skill of any snow dog. Not all of Stowe's terrain is so difficult; the mountain presents some of the best skiing around for intermediate skiers, with two separate peaks devoted almost entirely to blue-square and single-diamond trails.

Cross-Country Skiing
Behind the Trapp Family Lodge, the **Trapp Family Lodge Touring Center** (700 Trapp Hill Rd., 802/253-8511 or 800/826-7000, www.trappfamily.com, $22 adults, $18 seniors, $14 youth 12–18, $5 children 6–11, children 5 and under free) has some 100 kilometers of cross-country ski trails, through both groomed and ungroomed forest and meadowland.

Across town, **Edson Hill Manor** (1500 Edson Hill Rd., 802/253-7371 or 800/621-0284, www.edsonhillmanor.com) offers 25 kilometers of groomed trails for cross-country skiing and snowshoeing, along with lessons and guided midnight snowshoeing tours. For the long-distance skier, the trails connect to the Catamount Trail, which runs 300 kilometers down the length of Vermont.

NORTHERN MOUNTAINS

Horseback Riding and Sleigh Rides

A quiet country resort on the edge of Stowe, **Edson Hill Manor** (1500 Edson Hill Rd., 802/253-7371 or 800/621-0284, www.edsonhillmanor.com, $40 per person) has riding stables with horses and ponies available for backcountry trots. The resort also offers sleigh rides through the surrounding woodland—including romantic sleigh-and-dine packages.

Snowmobiles and Sledding

Take a ride with **Stowe Snowmobile Tours** (802/253-6221, www.stowesnowmobiletours.com) allow you to explore the woods in comfort, with fast-paced tours on top-of-the-line Polaris machines with heated handlebars.

For gravity-powered entertainment, rent a toboggan from **Shaw's General Store** (54 Main St., 802/253-4040, www.heshaw.com, 9 A.M.–6 P.M. Mon.–Fri., 9 A.M.–5 P.M. Sun.) or a more extreme sled from **Umiak Outdoor Outfitters** (849 S. Main St., 802/253-2317, www.umiak.com, 9 A.M.–6 P.M. daily), which features the latest from Mad River Rockets and Hammersmith, and which will point you to the vertiginous heights on which to test them. Umiak also sponsors special events like a wine & cheese snowshoe tour to a hidden sugarhouse.

Camping

On the flanks of Mount Mansfield just before the Stowe Mountain Resort, the small **Smuggler's Notch State Park** (6443 Mountain Rd., 802/253-4014, www.vtstateparks.com/htm/smugglers.htm) offers some 20 tent sites ($16–20) and 14 lean-tos ($23–27) for overnight camping. The sites are quite close together, though several "prime sites" offer more privacy and nice views from the cliffs flanking Mountain Road. The campsite has a restroom employing alternative energy, as well as a hot showers and a trash station.

the solarium at Stoweflake Mountain Resort and Spa

© STOWEFLAKE MOUNTAIN RESORT AND SPA

Across the street, a moderately strenuous trail leads just under a mile downhill to the cascading Bingham Falls.

Spas

Consistently voted one of the Top 10 Spas in the country, **Topnotch Resort and Spa** (4000 Mountain Rd., 800/451-8686, www.topnotchresort.com, 7 A.M.–7 P.M. daily) is tucked into a picturesque corner of Mount Mansfield. Glorious vistas result, best admired while undergoing one of the spa's quirky services—the likes of tarot reading, life coaching, and a slew of acupuncture. Of course, the requisite facials, massages, and herbal body treatments are also on offer.

The ultra-professional, expert staff at **Stoweflake Mountain Resort and Spa** (1746 Mountain Rd., 800/253-2232, www.stoweflake.com, 9:30 A.M.–7 P.M. Mon.–Thurs., 9:30 A.M.–8 P.M. Fri., 8 A.M.–8 P.M. Sat., 8 A.M.–7 P.M. Sun.) doles out a long list of

Vermont-themed treatments in its serene, plush rooms. (Don't pass up the Vermont Maple Sugar Body Polish.) Ayurvedic treatments are also a specialty—each based on the ancient Indian science of life and wellness.

At the family-friendly **Golden Eagle Resort and Spa** (511 Mountain Rd., 802/253-4811, www.goldeneagleresort.com, 8 A.M.–9 P.M. Sun.–Thurs., 8 A.M.–10 P.M. Fri.–Sat.), the mountain views are as soothing as the spa itself—enhanced by amenities like the indoor heated pool and cedar sauna.

ACCOMMODATIONS
Under $100

Easy access to the Stowe Recreation Path isn't the only reason to stay at **Alpenrose Motel** (2619 Mountain Rd., 802/253-7277, www.gostowe.com/saa/alpenrose, $70). The rooms are moderately priced and come with private baths, coffeemakers, and kitchenettes. The property also has a swimming pool, pleasant gardens, and a patio for outdoor lounging.

$100-150

An Austrian-style inn with slightly cutesy rooms (lots of pink and blue pastels), **Honeywood Inn** (4527 Mountain Rd., 800/821-7891, www.honeywoodinn.com, $100–289) offers significant perks and convenient services: babysitting and child care, business services, fireplaces, kitchenettes in some suites, and a pool. Pets are welcome.

$150-250

Uniquely appointed rooms—many with working fireplaces, canopy four-poster beds, and mountain views—make **Edson Hill Manor** (1500 Edson Hill Rd., 802/621-0284, www.edsonhillmanor.com, $179–289) a worthy spot to rest your head. There's also complimentary afternoon tea, a library for relaxed reading, and a country breakfast served in the lovely dining room every morning.

Over $250

With loads of pampering and fantastic recreation for adults and kids, ◖ **Topnotch Resort** (4000 Mountain Rd., 800/451-8686, www.topnotchresort.com, $385–535) wins the luxury-for-families award, hands-down. Grownups can chill out on the slopes, at either of the beautifully-kept mountainside pools (one indoor, one outdoors), or in the glorious new spa's treatment rooms. Meanwhile, the children's activity program is extensive and extremely well-organized, so both they and mom and dad feel entertained by the day's end. Not for families only, the resort also manages to make couples feel catered to, with romantic dining at Norma's, sumptuously decorated suites with oversized tubs, and couples' massages.

Even better than visiting the **Trapp Family Lodge** (700 Trapp Hill Rd., 802/253-8511 or 800/826-7000, www.trappfamily.com, $245–375) for serious *Sound of Music* fans is staying there overnight. The lodge definitely stresses the "family" part of the name, with comfortable accommodations and staff who are especially patient with children. Once a bit worse for wear, the lodge has slowly renovated over the past few years into a more modern, up-to-date style.

INFORMATION AND SERVICES

The **Stowe Area Association** (51 Main St., 877/467-8693, www.gostowe.com) runs a welcome center at the crossroads of Main Street and Mountain Road. Wi-Fi Internet can be accessed around the corner at **Stowe Free Library** (90 Pond St., 802/253-6145). Also at Main and Mountain is a branch of **People's United Bank** (1069 Mountain Rd., 802/253-8525, 8:30 A.M.–4:30 P.M. Mon.–Fri.).

Medical needs can be filled at **Heritage Drugs** (1878 Mountain Rd., 802/253-2544) as well as **Kinney Drugs** (155 S. Main St., Cambridge, 802/644-8811, 8:30 A.M.–8 P.M. Mon.–Fri., 8:30 A.M.–7 P.M. Sat., 9 A.M.–5 P.M.

Sun., pharmacy 8:30 A.M.–7 P.M. Mon.–Fri., 8:30 A.M.–4 P.M. Sat.). In an emergency, contact the **Stowe Police Department** (350 S. Main St., 802/253-7126).

GETTING THERE AND AROUND

To get to Stowe take I-89 north from White River Junction to exit 10, then Route 100 north to Stowe (75 mi., 1 hr. 20 min.). The **Green Mountain Transit Agency** (802/223-7287, www.gmtaride.org) operates bus routes to Stowe, stopping at Town Hall and other locations downtown. In the winter, it also operates the free **Stowe Shuttle** (www.gostowe.com) between the town and the mountain.

Lamoille Valley

North of Stowe, small-town relaxation meets big-time outdoor adventure in the sleepy little Lamoille Valley, with the towns of Jeffersonville and Morrisville as the highlights. It's as pretty a drive as any along Route 100, which cuts through villages full of clean, white church steeples, neat-as-a-pin farmhouses, brick-sidewalk main streets, and covered bridges. Along the way, you'll find plenty of arts and crafts to pore over, as well as kid-friendly eateries and hotels.

SMUGGLERS' NOTCH AND JEFFERSONVILLE

On the other side of Mount Mansfield from Stowe, Smugglers' Notch was named for its reputation as a favorite passage for bootleggers smuggling whiskey from Canada during the 1920s to evade the law during Prohibition. Now the mountain pass is home to a family-friendly ski resort that is anything but shady. Steep walls descend into the valley from Mount Mansfield to the west and the Sterling Mountain ridgeline to the east, making the drive along Route 108 especially scenic and the village of Jeffersonville seem especially snug. The town is a favorite for art mavens and antique-seekers taking a break from the slopes.

Sights

Jeffersonville is home to several fine galleries worth taking a peek at. The **Bryan Memorial Gallery** (180 Main St., Jeffersonville, 802/644-5100, www.bryangallery.org, 11 A.M.–4 P.M. Thurs.–Sun. spring–fall; 11 A.M.–4 P.M. daily in summer) is known as one of Vermont's premier showcases for local landscape artists, many of whom have drawn their inspiration from the countryside but a scant few miles away.

More local talent is on display at the aptly named **Visions of Vermont** (94 Main St., Jeffersonville, 802/644-8183, www.visionsofvermont.com, 10 A.M.–4 P.M. Tues.–Sun.). The gallery started out featuring the artwork of impressionistic landscape painter Eric Tobin, but has since grown to three buildings showcasing landscapes, still-life, and figure painting.

Entertainment and Events

Relax with a pint of microbrew at the convivial **Village Tavern** (55 Church St., Jeffersonville, 802/644-6607, www.smuggsinn.com, 4–10 P.M. daily) at Smugglers Notch Inn. The handsome-but-casual pub is a favorite for locals and visitors looking for a place to kick back and unwind at the end of a day.

Old-time pleasures abound at **Smugglers' Notch Heritage Winterfest** (Jeffersonville, 802/644-2239, www.smugnotch.com, late Jan.), which dials the clock back a century or two to fill downtown with sleigh rides, marionette shows, and a community bonfire. The highlight of the weekend is a traditional biathlon, where participants don wood-framed snowshoes and hoist muzzle-loaded muskets to test their endurance and shooting ability. Many participants get into the spirit with period dress as well.

Shopping

If you haven't sated your sweet tooth by now, stop in at the **Vermont Maple Outlet** (3929 Rte. 15, Jeffersonville, 800/858-3121, www.vermontmapleoutlet.com, 9 A.M.–5 P.M. daily), which produces maple candy and maple cream in addition to all grades of syrup. Or, if you'd rather buy specialized containers for that syrup instead of the syrup itself, step into **Green Apple Antique Center** (60 Main St., Jeffersonville, 802/644-2989, www.tggweb.com/posies, 9 A.M.–5 P.M. Mon.–Sat., 11 A.M.–4 P.M. Sun.). Here shelves are loaded with retro glass jars and bottles, plus antique plates and other home accessories. There's also a selection of cards and jewelry made by local artists.

Food

Reasonably priced barbecue and burgers keep a crowd of regulars coming back to **Brewster River Pub** (4087 Rte. 108, Jeffersonville, 800/644-6366, www.vermontmapleoutlet.com, 5–10 P.M. daily, $7–19). It's particularly popular as an après-ski hangout. The menu features a large list of (mostly organic) salads and locally grown veggies served by an affable staff.

It's breakfast most of the day at **The Mix** (55 Church St., Jeffersonville, 800/644-6371, www.themixcafevt.com, 7 A.M.–2 P.M. daily, $4–9), where the specialty is *huevos rancheros* made with local farm eggs. Pancakes (blueberry, chocolate chip, or banana) are also a hit.

Information and Services

The **Smugglers' Notch Area Chamber of Commerce** (802/644-8232, www.smugnotch.com) stocks an unstaffed information booth at the corner of Routes 15 and 108 in Jeffersonville.

You can find an ATM at **Union Bank** (44 Main St., 802/644-6600, 8 A.M.–4 P.M. Mon.–Thurs., 8 A.M.–6 P.M. Fri.) and a pharmacy at **Kinney Drugs** (155 S. Main St., Cambridge, 802/644-8811, 8:30 A.M.–8 P.M. Mon.–Fri., 8:30 A.M.–7 P.M. Sat., 9 A.M.–5 P.M. Sun., pharmacy 8:30 A.M.–7 P.M. Mon.–Fri., 8:30 A.M.–4 P.M. Sat.).

MORRISTOWN

Funky little Morristown is quintessential Vermont—sleepy and fiercely rural, yet with a distinct counterculture edge in the many independent businesses and eateries in the town center, which belies its sleepy veneer. Oddly enough, though officially Morristown, the town is more often referred to as Morrisville (and as Mo'Vegas to certain area youth). Whatever you call it, the village serves as a perfect lunch stop or quiet home base away from the bustle of Stowe and Smugglers' Notch from which to explore the recreational offerings of the area.

Sights

On the east side of Morrisville is a rare covered railroad bridge. The 109-foot **Fisher Bridge** (Rte. 15, 11 miles south of Rte. 100) once served to carry the St. Johnsbury and Lamoille Country Railroad trains over the Lamoille River. It was built double-high to let the trains through, with a vented cupola (which now serves as a giant birdhouse for local tweeters) to allow the steam to escape.

Just outside town, the family-run **Applecheek Farm** (567 McFarlane Rd., Hyde Park, 802/888-4482, www.applecheekfarm.com, by appt. only) is on the leading edge of Vermont's agritourism boom. The sustainable, organic farm has thrown open its fields to visitors wanting to get closer to the land with horse-drawn cart and sleigh rides, hiking paths amid the fields, and of course, a full paddock of animals to meet and pet. In addition to the

NORTHERN MOUNTAINS

usual cows and chickens, the farm is home to llamas, emus, dwarf goats, and miniature horses. (Ask about llama picnic treks.) A gift shop sells therapeutic emu oil and pasture-raised veal.

To wash down your organic meal, stop by **Rock Art Brewery** (254 Wilkins St., 802/888-9400, www.rockartbrewery.com, 9 A.M.–6 P.M. Mon.–Sat.), one of Vermont's highest quality craft brewers. (Its symbol is the flute-playing rascal Kokopelli, who shows up in Native American petroglyphs in the American Southwest.) On informal tours, friendly brewmaster Matthew Nadeau and his associates offer samples of its signature brew—a "barley wine" called Ridge Runner whose smoothness masks 7.2 percent alcohol content. Or if you are lucky, you can try one of the "real ales"—unfiltered, naturally carbonated English-style brews.

Events
Genuine country fun for one and all can be found at **Lamoille County Field Days** (Johnson, 802/635-7113, www.lamoillefielddays.com, July), a weekend fair featuring the usual animals, rides, lumberjack competitions, and the like. The most-anticipated event is the "gymkhana," a fast-paced equestrian competition in which contestants contend on horseback in games such as barrel racing and pole bending.

Shopping
Midway between Jefferson and Morristown sits **Johnson Woolen Mills Outlet Store** (Box 612, Johnson, 802/635-9665, www.johnsonwoolenmills.com, 9 A.M.–5 P.M. Mon.–Sat., 10 A.M.–4 P.M. Sun.), which has been weaving clothing for hardy Vermonters since the mid-19th century. Nowadays the company produces and peddles quality jackets, overalls, shirts, nighties, and kids' clothing.

Food
The cafe-cum-playroom that is **The Bee's Knees** (82 Lower Main St., 802/888-7889, www.thebeesknees-vt.com, 7:30 A.M.–10 P.M. Tues.–Sun., $7–12) might just be the perfect place to take kids. Lovably crunchy in decor and attitude (nearly everything on the menu is organic, vegetarian options loom large, and live music plays regularly), it offers a wall of toys to borrow and healthy plates like mac 'n' cheese (with locally made cheddar).

Information and Services
The **Lamoille Valley Chamber of Commerce** (34 Pleasant St., 802/888-7607, www.lamoillevalleychamber.com) has information on Morristown and the surrounding area. Regional hospital services are available at **Copley Hospital** (Washington Hwy., 802/888-8888). Find Wi-Fi along with your tofu burrito at **The Bee's Knees** (82 Lower Main St., 802/888-7889, 7:30 A.M.–10 P.M. Tues.–Sun.).

The Bee's Knees

Fill prescriptions at **Rite-Aid Pharmacy** (48 Congress St., 802/888-2226, 8 A.M.–8 P.M. Mon.–Sat., 9 A.M.–5 P.M. Sun., pharmacy 8 A.M.–7 P.M. Mon.–Fri., 9 A.M.–6 P.M. Sat., 9 A.M.–5 P.M. Sun.), and take out cash at **Union Bank** (20 Lower Main St., 802/888-6600, 8 A.M.–4 P.M. Mon.–Thurs., 8 A.M.–6 P.M. Fri.).

SPORTS AND RECREATION
Hiking and Biking
Good for families, the moderate hike up to **Prospect Rock** is a 90-minute round-trip jaunt that affords a good view of the notch's dramatic cliff face. The trailhead is in Johnson, seven miles east of Jeffersonville, on Hogback Road. A more strenuous hike is the climb up to **Sterling Pond,** a four-mile hike with a 900-foot vertical rise up the precipitous Sterling Mountain. At the top is the highest trout pond in the state.

The impossibly quaint scenery of the Lamoille Valley makes it a favorite for cyclists. You can rent your steed at **AJ's Ski and Sports** (350 Mountain Rd., Stowe, 800/226-6257, www.stowesports.com, $16–38 half-day, $24–45 full day) and pedal up to Morristown yourself. Or leave the arrangements to the reassuringly named **Peace of Mind Guaranteed Bike Tours** (888/635-2453, www.pomgbike.com), which offers two-day bike tours starting from the Smugglers Notch Inn in Jeffersonville.

Camping
One of the most unique state parks in Vermont, **Green River Reservoir** (Green River Reservoir Dam Rd., Morrisville, 802/888-1349, www.vtstateparks.com/htm/grriver.htm, $15–18) is a strictly "paddle-in" campground, with 28 campsites scattered along the undeveloped shoreline of the reservoir, accessible only by canoe or other car top boat. Motorboats are prohibited on the lake, and some of the campsites require a paddle of a mile or more, offering a new definition for the term "getting away from it all." Each of the sites has a maximum

number of people allowed—from 3 to 12—and some are so remote that at night you won't see another light, unless you count the millions of stars above you. The reservoir is surrounded by a hardwood forest of beech, birch, and maple, which is home to animal species including white-tailed deer, moose, black bears, bobcats, and coyote. The waterway itself is home to a loon nesting site as well as other avian species including mergansers, great blue heron, and occasionally, bald eagles. Campers are asked to "leave no trace" behind them—that includes cooking on a portable stove rather than a campfire. The experience is not for everyone, but for those hankering to commune with natural Vermont, there may be no better place to do it.

Boating and Fishing
It doesn't get much better than a paddle down the Lamoille River, which meanders gracefully through a country landscape of mountain-framed farms. **Umiak Outdoor Outfitters** (849 S. Main St., Stowe, 802/253-2317, www.umiak.com) rents kayaks and canoes by the hour or the day. The outfitter also leads guided trips down the Lamoille and Winooski Rivers.

The fast-running rivers of Northern Vermont are literally swimming with trout—not to mention other fish such as northern pike and bass. **Green Mountain Troutfitters** (233 Mill St., Jeffersonville, 802/644-2214, www.gmtrout.com) rents fishing equipment and leads two-day fly-fishing clinics to nearby trout streams with "Orvis-endorsed" guides. In the spring, it offers special trips to meet the runs of steelhead and Atlantic salmon.

Skiing
On the other side of the mountain pass from Stowe, **Smugglers' Notch** (4323 Rte. 108, Smugglers' Notch, 800/419-4615, www.smuggs.com, $66 adults, $52 seniors and youth 6–18, children under 6 and seniors over 69 free) has positioned itself as the ideal family resort.

In addition to three peaks (roughly broken down into beginner, intermediate, and expert), the resort has a half-pipe for snowboarders and an indoor FunZone complete with inflatable slides and mini-golf.

ACCOMMODATIONS

A working farm converted to a B&B, **Nye's Green Valley Bed & Breakfast** (8976 Rte. 15 W., Jeffersonville, 802/644-1984, www.nyes-greenvalleyfarm.com, $75–95) still has the vestiges of its past—namely, extensive gardens and fields full of sheep, goats, and horses.

The renovated rooms at **Smugglers Notch Inn** (55 Church St., Jeffersonville, 802/644-6607, www.smuggsinn.com, $89–129) include Jacuzzi tubs, fireplaces, and fantastic views, plus they are completely kid-friendly. The on-site restaurant and bakery are worth checking out, too—particularly the latter's fresh-baked scones.

The four guest rooms and two one-room suites at ◖ **Fitch Hill Inn** (258 Fitch Hill Rd., Hyde Park, 802/888-3834, www.fitchhillinn. com, $99–189) all have prime views of the inn's surrounding gardens and mountains. Inside, they sport simple but well-kept antiques, beds laid with handmade quilts, private baths (some with whirlpool tubs); the suites have miniature kitchens and fireplaces.

GETTING THERE AND AROUND

From Stowe, head up Route 100 for 8 miles (15 min.) to Morristown. For Jeffersonville and Smugglers' Notch, take Route 108 north from Stowe up and down the precipitous sides of Mount Mansfield for 10 miles (20 min.). Note, however, that the road is often closed because of snow from November to April. During those months, you'll need to take the long way around to Jeffersonville from Morristown along Routes 100 and 15 West (16 mi., 30 min.). The **Green Mountain Transit Agency** (802/223-7287, www.gmta-ride.org) also operates routes to Morristown from Waterbury and Stowe, with transfers from Montpelier. There is no public transportation to Smugglers' Notch; however, the resort offers van service from Burlington's airport and train station (802/644-8851 or 800/419-4615, ext. 1389) for a $45 charge each way (one child free per paying adult, additional children are $35 each).

NORTHEAST KINGDOM

A triangular chunk carved out of the upper-right part of the state, the so-called "Northeast Kingdom" is a world unto itself. Its name stems from a memorable utterance of U.S. Senator George Aiken, who said in 1949 that the area "is such beautiful country up here—it should be called the Northeast Kingdom." Something about the name stuck, and residents began proudly thinking of themselves as belonging to a somewhat mythical principality, with brilliant red foliage for raiment and golden maple syrup stored up for treasure. Those who live here love it for its sense of isolation from the madding crowds, its independent spirit, and its quirky population—which can include anyone from political artists and dropout lawyers to fourth-generation farmers. Indeed, while Vermont as a whole has drawn its fair share of writers, the Northeast Kingdom (or NEK for short) is legendary for its creative ilk—including Vermont's favorite author, Howard Frank Mosher, who has spun the personalities of the area into a unique form of countrified magical realism.

As for the visitors, they similarly come to experience Vermont the way it used to be, but they also come to get out into nature. Unlike the mountainous majority of the state, the Northeast Kingdom more closely resembles the wild scenery of Ireland or Nova Scotia, with rolling green hills cradling working dairy farms and unspoiled lakes and ponds, and cell phone signals wavering in the face of vast

HIGHLIGHTS

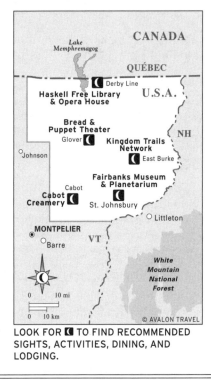

◖ Fairbanks Museum & Planetarium: A trip around the world, a trip to the stars, and a trip back in time all in one place (page 190).

◖ Cabot Creamery: Cheddar cheese from this famous farmers co-op has single-handedly kept Vermont dairy farming alive and mooing (page 195).

◖ Kingdom Trails Network: Bike the Kingdom on more than 100 miles of trails, ranging from scenic railway paths to grueling mountain pitches (page 202).

◖ Bread & Puppet Theater: The legendary abode of papier-mâché giants and goddesses is a dairy barn in the Northeast Kingdom (page 203).

◖ Haskell Free Library & Opera House: The black line on the floor of this beautifully resurrected international performance hall demarcates the U.S.-Canada border (page 208).

LOOK FOR ◖ TO FIND RECOMMENDED SIGHTS, ACTIVITIES, DINING, AND LODGING.

unbroken stretches of trees. The NEK is not without its comforts, however, many of which come in culinary form—home-baked pastries, fresh dairy products, wild game suppers, and of course, plenty of maple syrup farms. The most stunning thing about the Kingdom, however, is what it doesn't offer: namely traffic of any kind, or any hurried pace whatsoever. While many places are described as "frozen in time," the NEK is very much alive, with cantankerous residents well aware of the charms of the modern world—and choosing to live without them, much the way they did six decades ago when their kingdom was first named.

PLANNING YOUR TIME

They don't call it a kingdom for nothing! This part of Vermont is impressively vast—or perhaps just feels that way from the long stretches of road between population centers. While you can easily spend a week here settling into the rhythms of Kingdom life, it's best to pick one area to base yourself and explore the rest of the area with rambling day trips.

On the way into the Kingdom, stop off at Cabot to see the world-renowned cheese-making operation at **Cabot Creamery.** Or if you're coming from the west, make a pit stop in St. Johnsbury to tour the smorgasbord of natural

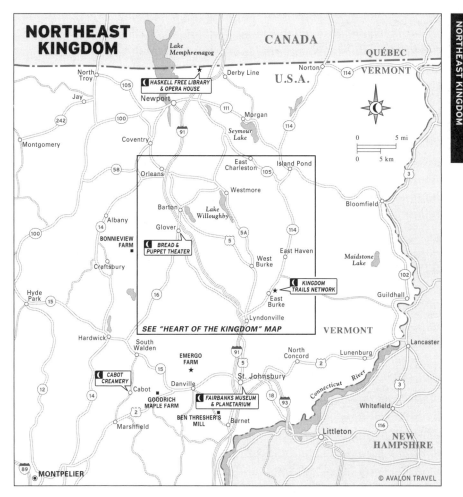

NORTHEAST KINGDOM

Lake Memphremagog

CANADA
QUÉBEC
VERMONT

North Troy

HASKELL FREE LIBRARY & OPERA HOUSE

Derby Line
Norton
U.S.A.

Jay

Newport

Morgan

Montgomery

Coventry

Seymour Lake

East Charleston
Island Pond

Orleans

Westmore

Bloomfield

Albany
BONNIEVIEW FARM

Barton
Lake Willoughby

Glover

BREAD & PUPPET THEATER

Craftsbury

West Burke

East Haven

Maidstone Lake

Hyde Park

KINGDOM TRAILS NETWORK

Guildhall

East Burke

Lyndonville

SEE "HEART OF THE KINGDOM" MAP

VERMONT

Hardwick

South Walden

EMERGO FARM

North Concord

Lunenburg

Lancaster

St. Johnsbury

CABOT CREAMERY

Cabot

Danville

FAIRBANKS MUSEUM & PLANETARIUM

Connecticut River

Whitefield

GOODRICH MAPLE FARM

BEN THRESHER'S MILL

Barnet

Marshfield

Littleton

NEW HAMPSHIRE

MONTPELIER

0   5 mi
0   5 km

© AVALON TRAVEL

history exhibits at the **Fairbanks Museum & Planetarium.** A good choice for a home base within the Kingdom is Craftsbury, with its picturesque town common and proximity to several attractions, including the Stone House Museum and the one-of-a-kind **Bread & Puppet Theater.**

Alternatively, stay in the East Burke–Lyndonville area, with its many covered bridges and white-powdered skiing on underrated Burke Mountain—or white-knuckle mountain

biking on the **Kingdom Trails Network.** If even those areas are too much civilization for you, head north to the Canadian border for the ultimate getaway, where a trio of towns await— Newport, situated on international waterway of Lake Memphremagog; Derby, which includes the international cultural attraction of **Haskell Free Library & Opera House** (which draws crowds of tourists to straddle the line between the United States and Canada that runs through its reading room); or ultra-remote Jay, known for its big-mountain skiing in Jay Peak. Any time of year, bring a jacket, as unseasonable cold fronts are always a possibility; in the winter, bring two jackets, since the wind can whip up some chilly speed on the highlands to add some bite to already refrigerated air.

Gateway to the Kingdom

The southwest stretch of the Northeast Kingdom is a transitional zone, wherein visitors drop the pretensions of the modern world and sink into the rhythm of Kingdom life. It includes both the largest (and let's face it, only) city in the region, the unexpectedly delightful St. Johnsbury, as well as the area's one can't-miss tourist attraction, Cabot Creamery, the best-known cheesemaker in the state.

ST. JOHNSBURY

The capital of the Kingdom, St. Johnsbury (or "St. J" to residents) is the largest town in the area, with a whopping 7,500 people. Its entire downtown is a monument to the Victorian era,

© MICHAEL BLANDING

Fairbanks Museum & Planetarium

during which St. Johnsbury saw its fortunes made thanks to the ingenuity of Thaddeus Fairbanks and his family. Since ancient times, weight had been measured by the cumbersome balance scale. Fairbanks invented the modern platform scale, with sliding weights on an arm above a spring-loaded platform. Construction of the scales instantly made Fairbanks—and the town—rich. His brother Erastus was later responsible for bringing the railroad to town in 1850, and later he twice became the governor of Vermont.

The Fairbanks family never forgot where they came from, and generations of the family invested heavily in the town, building an academy, natural history museum, and art gallery, all of which they hoped would educate their fellow citizens. Today, St. J's train station has been turned into a visitors center, and the town has turned into more of a country backwater than sophisticated center of industry. But it's worth a stop for the Fairbanks legacy and access to the recreational offerings of the Kingdom.

◖ Fairbanks Museum & Planetarium

Back in the days before Google and Wikipedia, if you wanted to find out something about your world, you went to the local natural history museum, where explorers from around the world displayed random oddities in glass cases. This museum (1302 Main St., 802/748-2372, www.fairbanksmuseum.org, 9 A.M.–5 P.M. Mon.–Sat., 1–5 P.M. Sun. Apr.–Oct., closed Mon. Nov.–Mar.; planetarium shows 11 A.M. Mon.–Fri. and 1:30 P.M. daily July–Aug., 1:30 P.M. Sat.–Sun. Sept.–June) is

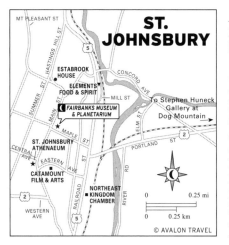

a delicious throwback to that era, with a menagerie of colorful stuffed parrots, menacing polar bears, Egyptian mummies, and Japanese fans displayed in crowded glass cases in a turreted Victorian exhibition hall.

The museum was founded in 1891 by Franklin Fairbanks, a philanthropist who himself made careful daily observations of weather and atmospheric conditions. The museum now carries on his work with a weather gallery, home to the public radio program "Eye on the Sky," which broadcasts weather information and lore to over 10 million listeners daily. Then there is the planetarium, one of only a few in New England, whose regular tours of the heavens have been eliciting gasps from crane-necked visitors for decades.

The St. Johnsbury Athenaeum

St. J's library, The St. Johnsbury Athenaeum (1171 Main St., 802/748-8291, www.stjathenaeum.org, 10 A.M.–5:30 P.M. Mon.–Fri., 10 A.M.–4 P.M. Sat.) is just as much an art museum, with dozens of fine canvases by American landscape and portrait painters. Highlights include the overpowering *Domes of the Yosemite,* by Albert Bierstadt, and the enigmatic *Raspberry Girl,* by Victorian-era realist

Adolphe William Bouguereau. The museum has been left in its original Victorian state, with black-walnut floors and walls.

Stephen Huneck Gallery at Dog Mountain

D-O-G and G-O-D are so close in spelling, it was only a matter of time before someone combined the two. Enter the artist and children's-book author and illustrator Stephen Huneck, whose Stephen Huneck Gallery at Dog Mountain (143 Parks Rd., 800/449-2580, www.dogmt.com, 10 A.M.–5 P.M. Mon.–Sat., 11 A.M.–4 P.M. Sun) was truly a labor of love. After emerging from a life-threatening coma, Huneck was inspired to create a church celebrating the spiritual bonds we have with man's best friend. The so-called **Dog Chapel** he built is a typical New England meetinghouse set high on a hill above St. Johnsbury. Only instead of saints, the stained-glass windows depict canines; instead of holy water, the church offers actual water and treats for four-legged visitors. Huneck encourages guests to bring their dogs for a walk through the hiking paths around the chapel. A gift shop sells the artist's trademark wood-block prints of retrievers. Sadly, Huneck himself committed suicide in 2010; the chapel is as much a memorial to the man as it is a testament to his lifelong work.

Maple Grove Farms

Calling itself the "maple center of the world," Maple Grove Farms (1052 Portland St., 800/525-2540 x5547, www.maplegrove.com, 8 A.M.–5 P.M. Mon.–Fri. Apr.–May; 8 A.M.–5 P.M. Mon.–Fri., 9 A.M.–5 P.M. Sat.–Sun. June–Dec.) expanded beyond syrup to produce its own line of salad dressings and marinades. But the heart of the factory is still the sugarhouse, which has been producing maple syrup for more than 80 years. The farm boasts the world's largest maple candy factory

THE SWEETEST THINGS

The largest producer of pure maple syrup in the country, Vermont creates maple syrup that sets the standards for all others. But syrup isn't the only treasure that maple trees can yield; behold the following sweet rewards.

· **Granulated maple sugar:** Made by heating maple syrup and stirring it until it granulates, the sugar is then sifted to create smooth crumbs.

· **Maple candy:** Syrup that's cooked to a boil, stirred, and poured into molds results in these creamy, often cutely shaped treats.

· **Maple cream:** Boil maple syrup and stir it while it cools to room temperature, and you've got this smooth spread.

· **Maple fudge:** Boiled maple syrup, unstirred, gets spread in a pan to cool. Once hardened, it's cut into squares.

as well; tours include demonstrations of how syrup is set in tanks to crystallize.

Entertainment and Events

A little bit of almost every kind of artistic recreation—from jazz performances to movie revivals and gallery shows to dance and acting lessons—is offered at **Catamount Film & Arts** (115 Eastern Ave., 802/748-2600, www.catamountarts.org). The community center's diverse roster attracts an energetic, enthusiastic segment of the town.

Whether you plan on buying anything or not, the **Caledonia Farmers' Market** (Cherry Valley Plaza, 9944 Cherry Valley Ave., 802/592-3088, 9 A.M.–1 P.M. Sat. May–Oct.) is a sight to behold, bursting with riotous floral bouquets and perfect vegetable specimens that bring out the whole town to gawk.

If you've ever wondered how soap was made, rugs braided, or tools forged, your questions will be answered at the **Fairbanks Festival of Traditional Crafts** (Fairbanks Museum, Sept.), a 30-year tradition that honors those keeping alive the ingenuity we now take for granted; displays are very much hands-on, with modern artisans encouraging participation by visitors.

Shopping

Indulge your parental instincts at **Frogs &**

Lily Pads (443 Railroad St., 802/748-2975, 9:30 A.M.–5:30 P.M. Mon.–Fri., 9:30–5 P.M. Sat.), dedicated to creative and educational toys, impeccable children's clothing, and stylish maternity clothes. Another must-stop for families (not to mention bookworms) is **Boxcar & Caboose Bookstore** (394 Railroad St., 802/748-3551, www.boxcarandcaboose. com, 7 A.M.–7 P.M. Mon.–Fri., 9 A.M.–7 P.M. Sat., 9 A.M.–5 P.M. Sun.), a combination bookstore, cafe, and kids playroom complete with comfy leather chairs, espresso drinks, and a train table.

Score heirloom-quality carved wooden chairs, luminous glass bowls, and hand-woven scarves at **Northeast Kingdom Artisans Guild** (430 Railroad St., 802/748-0158, www.nekartisansguild.com, 10:30 A.M.–5:30 P.M. Mon.–Sat.), a collective of more than 100 craftspeople.

For snacks that are as good for the community as they are for you, choose one of the many organic products off the shelves at **St. Johnsbury Food Co-op** (490 Portland St., 802/748-9498, www.stjfoodcoop. com, 9 A.M.–6 P.M. Mon.–Wed. and Sat., 9 A.M.–7 P.M. Thurs.–Fri., 11 A.M.–4 P.M. Sun.). Stock here is all about natural foods: local produce, cage-free eggs, wild fish, and Vermont farm-made cheeses.

Mystery buffs and poetry fans alike will have

plenty to pore over at **Kingdom Books** (283 E. Village Rd., Waterford, 802/751-8374, www. kingdombks.com, open by appt. only), which also serves as a setting for poetry events and as a base for mystery tours.

Food

Some of Vermont's freshest takes on classic comfort food come off the stoves at **Elements Food & Spirit** (98 Mill St., 802/748-8400, www.elementsfood.com, 5–9 P.M. Tues.–Thurs., 5–9:30 P.M. Fri.–Sat, $15–21). The blue-plate specials are always a hit (most diners just order those), but the kitchen also takes pride in dishes like smoked trout and apple cakes. There's a lengthy list of reasonably priced wines and Vermont-brewed beers.

Standard burgers, sandwiches, and nightly specials are the all-American fare at family-friendly **Mooselook Restaurant** (1058 Main St., Concord, 802/695-2950, 6 A.M.–7:30 P.M. Mon.–Thurs. and Sun., 6 A.M.–8 P.M. Fri., $7–14).

Information and Services

The **Northeast Kingdom Chamber** (2000 Memorial Dr., 802/748-3678 or 800/639-6379, www.nekchamber.com) runs a well-staffed welcome center inside the Green Mountain Mall.

State authorities in the area can be found at the **Vermont State Police** (1068 U.S. Route 5, Ste. #1., 802/748-3111). Two full-service hospitals serve the area: **Northeastern Vermont Regional Hospital** (1315 Hospital Dr., 802/748-7457) and **North Country Hospital** (189 Prouty Dr., Newport, 802/334-3222). Get prescriptions filled at **Rite-Aid Pharmacy** (502 Railroad St., 802/748-5210, 8 A.M.–9 P.M. Mon.–Fri., 8 A.M.–8 P.M. Sat., 8 A.M.–6 P.M. Sun., pharmacy 8 A.M.–8 P.M. Mon.–Fri., 9 A.M.–6 P.M. Sat., 9 A.M.–5 P.M. Sun.). Free public Wi-Fi is available at the **St. Johnsbury Athenaeum** (1171 Main St., 802/748-8291), **Boxcar & Caboose Bookstore** (394 Railroad St., 802/748-3551), and **Elements Food & Spirit** (98 Mill St., 802/748-8400).

SOUTHWEST OF ST. JOHNSBURY

An air of quietude blankets the landscape south and west of St. Johnsbury. The little town of **Barnet** is so tranquil, in fact, that it was chosen as a site for a Tibetan monastery associated with best-selling author American Buddhist Pema Chödrön. By contrast, neighboring **Peacham** has gone Hollywood (sort of), starring in films including *Ethan Frome* and *The Spitfire Grill* as the quintessential small-town New England village. One glance at its town green and white church spire, and you'll see why. Farther west on Route 2, lovely **Danville** is situated around two ponds, Joe's Pond and Molly's Pond, supposedly named after a Native American and his wife who befriended early settlers. Its ordinariness belies the fact that it is home to two of the area's stranger attractions, a giant corn maze and a center for the medieval practice of water-witching.

Sights

If you've ever wondered what it's like to be a lab rat, venture into the rows at the **Great Vermont Corn Maze** (1404 Wheelock Rd., Danville, 802/748-1399, www.vermontcornmaze.com, 10 A.M.–4 P.M. daily Aug.–Sept., 10 A.M.–3 P.M. daily Oct., $12 adults, $9 seniors and children 4–14, children under 4 free), more than two miles of twisting confusion carved each year amidst 12-foot-tall corn stalks. Owners Mike and Dayna Boudreau have been constructing the maze for better than five years, getting progressively trickier with each course. Participants quest for the elusive "bell of success" in the center of the maze, which can take anywhere from one to four hours. If that sounds too tough, the complex has a smaller corn maze for kids, along with a barnyard mini-golf course among the animal paddocks. To relive the '80s horror

© VERMONTVACATION.COM

a barn in Barnet

film *Children of the Corn,* come in October when the farm is transformed into "Dead North: Farmland of Terror" just in time for Halloween.

White-and-black spotted Holsteins dot the pasture at **Emergo Farm** (261 Webster Hill, Danville, 888/383-1185, www.emergofarm. com, 8 A.M.–7 P.M. daily, by appt.) like they were paid to be a Ben & Jerry's advertisement. Sixth-generation family farm owners Bebo and Lori Webster somehow find time in between milking 90 head of Holsteins to lead farm heritage tours explaining farming techniques going back to the 19th century. Visitors wanting to put education into practice can stay the night in the farm's stately white farmhouse B&B and help out with chores in the morning.

An instant trip back to the Vermont of yesteryear, **Ben Thresher's Mill** (2236 W. Barnet Rd., Barnet, 802/748-8180, www.bensmill. com, 11 A.M.–3 P.M. Sat.–Sun. late May–early Oct.) was a major center of industry in the late 19th century—operating first as a dye and print shop, then a woodworking shop, and finally as a machine shop churning out tools for local farmers. Incredibly, all of its machinery is still in working order—one of the last, if not *the* last, buildings of its kind in the country. Much of that is the result of yeoman's work by local residents who have kept the machinery active and literally shored up the foundation of the building. They'll give tours on request, but be prepared to have your ear bent with decades of local yore.

Events

It says something about the Northeast Kingdom that one of its most exciting seasonal rituals is the annual **Joe's Pond Ice Out** (www.joespond.com), a West Danville tradition wherein residents pay $1 each to guess the exact moment that the ice will crack on a local pond. In past years, the winner has claimed more than $4,000, while the same amount goes

ALL WET?

Called dowsing or "water-witching," the practice of using a brass rod or Y-shaped twig to find metals, gems, or water buried in the ground goes back to the Middle Ages. Those who still swear by the ancient art come together at the **American Society of Dowsers Bookstore** (184 Brainerd St., Danville, 802/684-3874, www.dowsers. org, 8:30 A.M.–5 P.M. Wed.–Fri., 9 A.M.–4 P.M. Sat.), which has a full selection of books and divining rods for purchase. While you are there, walk the labyrinth, a magical maze purported to bring wholeness and healing to those who walk it (to say nothing of dizziness). Undaunted by countless scientific studies that have declared the art so much bunk, a hundred-some dowsers come together each June to share stories and techniques at the **American Society of Dowsers Conference** (802/684-3417, www.dowsers.org).

to upkeep of a recreational area. If nothing else, the anticipation helps pass the time during long NEK winters.

Danville is also home to the large **Autumn on the Green** (www.autumnonthegreen.com, Oct.) festival, which brings more than 100 artisans, craft vendors, and live music performers to share in the pleasures of the fall foliage.

Shopping

A jumble of specialty cheeses, quality chocolates, old-fashioned candy, and locally made snacks, **Diamond Hill Store** (Rte. 2 11 E., Danville, 802/684-9797, www.diamond-hillstore.com, 10 A.M.–6 P.M. Mon.–Sat., noon–4 P.M. Sun.) is also both a wine and liquor store and an antiques shop. More edible souvenirs await at **West Barnet General Store** (376 W. Main St., West Barnet, 802/633-9392, 6 A.M.–9 P.M. Mon.–Fri., 7 A.M.–9 P.M. Sat., 8 A.M.–9 P.M. Sun.), which brings together handmade fudge, locally made jellies in flavors

like jalapeno-peach and wild mint, and scads of maple syrup.

Food

The crowd at **Goodfella's Restaurant and Tavern** keeps it real with a casual, unstuffy, and classic pub atmosphere (59 Parker Rd., Danville, 802/748-4249, 4–9 P.M. Wed.–Sat., 11:30 A.M.–8 P.M. Sun., $8–17), along with nightly specials that arrive heaped on plates. On weekends, it gets particularly crowded.

Information and Services

For more info on the area, contact the **Danville Chamber of Commerce** (802/684-2528, www. danvillevtchamber.org). Free Wi-Fi is available at the **Barnet Public Library** (147 Church St., 802/633-4436, www.barnetvt.org/library, 6:30–8:30 P.M. Mon., 10 A.M.–4 P.M. Tues., 12:30–4 P.M. Wed.–Thurs., 10 A.M.–2 P.M.).

CABOT AND HARDWICK

There's not much to see in Cabot—just a collection of modest white clapboard houses arranged around a general store, library, and a couple of gas pumps. If it wasn't for the presence of Vermont's most famous cheesemaker, this is the kind of town you might drive right through without giving a second glance. But the fact that Cabot is home to Cabot Creamery makes it an instant stop on the tourist itinerary. Once a center of the granite industry, the larger Hardwick is the center of population in these parts, with a small downtown area of shops and restaurants set near the shores of a long blue lake.

◖ Cabot Creamery

To quote Monty Python, "Blessed are the Cheesemakers." Vermont might be a different place today had it not been for the industry spawned by some ambitious dairy farmers a century or so ago. From a simple farmer's cooperative started in a farmhouse 100 years ago,

Cabot Creamery

Cabot Cheese has grown to become Vermont's best-known (if not best) producer of cheddar cheese. Though the company now makes 15 million pounds of cheese annually, it is still run as a farmers cooperative (with now more than 2,000 farm families) and still operates on the same land where it began.

Enormous white silos loom over the factory campus of Cabot Creamery (2878 Main St./ Rte. 15, Cabot Village, 800/837-4261, www. cabotcheese.coop, 9 A.M.–5 P.M. daily June–Oct.; 9 A.M.–4 P.M. Mon.–Sat. Nov.–Dec. and Feb.–May; 10 A.M.–4 P.M. Mon.–Sat. Jan., $2 adults and youth 12 and older, children under 12 free). Arrive early for a tour, given every half-hour down the Cheddar Hall, to see the cheese-making process. Giant steel machines looking like something out of *War of the Worlds* have taken the place of hand churning, but in some ways, the cheese is still made the old-fashioned way, without the introduction of enzymes to speed the process. Along the way, tour guides

present the opportunity to try different types of cheddar. Lately, the company has been experimenting with all kinds of additions to the cheese, including horseradish, jalapenos, and chipotle peppers. For our money, the three-year Private Reserve is still the best bet. A gift shop sells wax-wrapped blocks at a steep discount, along with other made-in-Vermont foodstuffs and gifts.

Goodrich's Maple Farm

Nestled among the hills, Goodrich's Maple Farm (2427 Rte. 2, Cabot, 800/639-1854, www.goodrichmaplefarm.com, 9 A.M.–5 P.M. Mon.–Sat.) is one of Vermont's largest maple syrup producers. Proprietors Glenn and Ruth Goodrich are always happy to take time out of evaporating sap to explain the syrup-making process. But they really shine during the farm's semiannual maple seminars, where they explain how to install and repair the plastic tubes for the sap, as well as how to boil it down efficiently. For $20 a person, the Goodriches teach custom seminars on topics such as cooking with maple.

Events

The Northeast Kingdom's annual **Fall Foliage Festival** (802/748-3678, www.nekchamber.com/foliage, early Oct.) is a sort of "progressive dinner" of barbecues, bazaars, and kids' games that starts in Walden (near Cabot) and then moves through different area towns before ending with a fair in St. Johnsbury a week later.

Shopping

Particular to (though not exclusively about) the loon, **Gallery at Loon Cove** (239 Sandy Beach Rd., Cabot, 802/563-3083, www.photosbyrayricher.com, 10 A.M.–6 P.M. Mon–Sat., 10 A.M.–5 P.M. Sun.) showcases pieces by artist duo Evelyn and Ray Richer. Ray photographs everything from birds and mammals to flowers and landscapes, which then inspire Evelyn, who renders separate pieces in pastels and pencils by hand.

Made-by-hand creations of an altogether different sort can be found at **Caspian Glass** (421 Breezy Ave., Greensboro, 802/533-7129, 10 A.M.–5 P.M. daily May 28–Oct. 1). Using a technique known as incalmo, developed by Venetian master glassblowers approximately 500 years ago, artist Lucas Lonegren fuses cups of colored glass together to make the beautiful lighting sconces and bowls in the studio and retail shop.

Food

Talk about communal tables: The citizens of Hardwick all pitched in to open **C Claire's Restaurant and Bar** (41 S. Main St., Hardwick, 802/472-7053, www.clairesvt.com, 5–9 P.M. Mon.–Sat., 11 A.M.–2 P.M. and 5–8 P.M. Sun., $12–22). Neighbors invested $1,000 each initially, and now receive discounts on dinners—and what dinners they are. The kitchen primarily uses local, sustainable foods in simple but flavor-rich dishes. It's always packed, always fun, and needless to say, there's no better place in town to mix with locals.

Information and Services

For the 411 on the area, contact the **Hardwick Area Chamber of Commerce** (802/472-6120, www.heartofvt.com/hardwick). You can find ATMs in downtown Hardwick at **Merchants Bank** (84 Rte. 15 W., Hardwick, 802/472-6556, 8:15 A.M.–4:30 P.M. Mon.–Thurs., 8:15 A.M.–6 P.M. Fri.) and **Union Bank** (103 Rte. 15, 802/472-810). Fill prescriptions at **Rite-Aid Pharmacy** (82 Rte. 15 W., Hardwick, 802/472-6961, 8 A.M.–8 P.M. Mon.–Fri., 8 A.M.–6 P.M. Sat., 9 A.M.–5 P.M. Sun., pharmacy 8 A.M.–6 P.M. Mon.–Fri., 9 A.M.–6 P.M. Sat., 9 A.M.–5 P.M. Sun.). In an emergency, contact the local **police department** (20 Church St., Hardwick, 802/472-5475).

CRAFTSBURY

Immaculate white buildings surround the wide and attractive green in the center of Craftsbury, among them one of the oldest public school academies in the state. The common is just the beginning of its charms, however. The village sits in the middle of the miles of cross-country skiing and biking trails through the surrounding countryside, making it the perfect combination of country cute and outdoor rec.

Sights

Located right on Craftsbury Common, cheese producer **Bonnieview Farm** (2228 S. Albany Rd., Craftsbury Common, 802/755-6878, www.bonnieview.org, noon–7 P.M. Mon.–Fri., 5–7 P.M. June–Nov.) goes far beyond your average cheddar. Varieties include Ewe's Feta, a creamy raw milk sheep cheese, Mossend Blue, a natural rind blue cheese, and Coomersdale, a semi-hard cheese with a natural rind and nutty flavor. Call ahead for tours of the cheese-making process.

Entertainment and Events

The renowned **Craftsbury Chamber Players** (800/639-3443, www.craftsburychamberplayers.org) perform classical music throughout the region in July and August.

The governor picks a different town each year to tap a maple tree inaugurating the **Maple Open House Weekend** (www.vermontmaple.org, Mar.), a syrupy celebration that includes tours, demonstrations, and kids' activities at local sugarhouses. Many of the participating sugarhouses are located in and around the Northeast Kingdom. Call or check the website for locations.

Shopping

With a motto like, "If you can't find it here, you probably don't need it," **Willey's Store** (7 Breezy Ave., Greensboro, 802/533-2554, www.willeysvt.com, 7 A.M.–5:30 P.M. daily) had better deliver the goods—and it does, with vast shelf space holding everything from cast-iron bakeware and nifty tools to flypaper and organic produce. Operating under the same family for 100 years, Willey's is as fun a place to peruse as to shop.

Food

The dining room at **The Craftsbury Inn** (107 S. Craftsbury Rd., 802/586-2848, www.craftsburyinn.com, 5–9 P.M. Tues.–Sun., $16–18) is open only to guests until evening, but at dinner it opens up to the public. In its Greek Revival mansion setting, it serves a French-inspired but wholly international menu of dishes like curried shrimp with ginger or quail with figs and green cabbage, as well as Gallic classics like omelets dressed with caviar.

SPORTS AND RECREATION
Cross-Country Skiing

A favorite among cross-country skiers in New England, the **Craftsbury Nordic Center** (535 Lost Nation Rd., Craftsbury Common, 802/586-7767, www.craftsbury.com) spans more than 300 acres of quiet farmland, lakes, and village centers with groomed cross-country trails. Centered on Craftsbury Common, the outdoor center offers rentals ($15 adults, $10 students and seniors) as well as day passes ($10 adults, $5 students and seniors, children under 7 free) for use of the trails.

Snowshoeing

In the winter months when maple production is slow, Ruth and Glenn Goodrich lead guided snowshoeing tours on their 900 acres of property at **Goodrich Maple Farm** (2427 Rte. 2, Cabot, 800/639-1854, www.goodrichmaplefarm.com). Trips include bird-watching and a warm fireside lunch beneath the trees.

ACCOMMODATIONS

Located in the heart of St. Johnsbury, **Estabrook House** (1596 Main St., St. Johnsbury, 802/751-8261, www.estabrookhouse.com, $95–150) is an 1896 Victorian home that has been lovingly renovated by a Massachusetts transplant who moved to St. J after falling in love with the area more than a decade ago. Listed on the National Register of Historic Places, the home features four individually decorated rooms crawling with antiques, and a shared bathroom with a claw-foot soaker tub. The park-side location is almost as attractive as the reasonable price tag.

Seemingly tailormade for families, **Fairbanks Inn** (401 Western Ave., St. Johnsbury, 802/748-5666, www.stjay.com, $122–145) is an affordable, comfortable, and convenient spot to bunk down. The motel-style operation offers a heated pool, free high-speed wireless Internet, rooms and mini-suites with private balconies or poolside patios, and microwaves and refrigerators. Oh, and it's dog-friendly as well, so no member of the family need get left at home.

Lavishly decorated and tranquil to its core,

⟨⟨ Rabbit Hill Inn (48 Lower Waterford Rd., Lower Waterford, 802/748-5168, www.rabbithillinn.com, $169–359) fills rooms with such amenities as fluffy robes, private porches, and fireplaces, just for starters. But you may be tempted to leave your room once you hear about the perks in the rest of the property—afternoon tea and pastries, apple cheddar crepes at breakfast, and candlelight dinners prepared by Matthew Secich.

GETTING THERE AND AROUND

The remoteness of the Northeast Kingdom virtually demands you bring your own transportation. To drive to St. Johnsbury from the south, take I-91 north (60 mi., 1 hr.) from White River Junction. From Montpelier, you are better off leaving the interstate highways and cutting across the Kingdom on U.S. 2 to Cabot (20 mi., 40 min.) or St. Johnsbury (40 mi., 1 hr.). From St. J, drive west on U.S. 2 to Danville (8 mi., 15 min.) and Cabot (20 mi., 25 min.). From Cabot, drive north on Routes 215 and 15 to Hardwick (12 mi., 25 min.). From Hardwick, it's another 10 miles (20 min.) up Route 14 to Craftsbury.

Vermont Transit (800/642-3133, www.vermonttransit.com) runs buses to the railway station in St. Johnsbury (125 Railroad Ave.).

Heart of the Kingdom

Beautiful rolling meadows surrounded by hills treasured by cross-country skiers, the central area of the Northeast Kingdom runs along I-91 from **Lyndonville** to **Glover.** Of course, you'll want to get off the highway as quickly as possible—the spur of Route 114 that leads to **East Burke** and underrated Burke Mountain might be just the ticket.

LYNDONVILLE

Lyndonville is the self-dubbed "Covered Bridge Capital of the Northeast Kingdom," having no fewer than five examples scattered around town. While the town is imbued with student energy from Lyndon State College, in truth this is quiet living at its most content, with backcountry roads that just cry out for a long, relaxed road trip to the middle of nowhere, summer concerts on the common, and an annual county fair that is one of the oldest in the state.

Sights

The **Miller's Run Bridge** on Route 114 was rebuilt in 1995 using the original 19th-century trusses. The 117-foot-long **Sanborn Bridge** uses the distinctive X-shaped Paddleford trusses. It was moved several years ago onto dry land behind the LynBurke Motel at the intersection of Routes 5 and 114.

Erik Waring is a maple syrup purist. His farm, **Erik's Sugar Bush** (273 Back of the Moon Rd., Kirby, 802/626-3538, www.erikssugarbush.com, hours vary, call for availability) eschews the "reverse osmosis" equipment employed by most syrup producers, as well as any artificial ingredients or preservatives, to produce maple syrup the natural way from his 2,000 trees on Kirby Mountain. He claims you can taste the difference in the final product—and with numerous awards behind him, he may just be right. Tours of the process and meet-and-greets with the farm's oxen are offered during sugaring season.

Events

Tractor pulls, pig races, and alpaca shearing all delight the masses at the **Caledonia County Fair** (802/626-5538, www.vtfair.com, late Aug.), which has taken place in Lyndonville

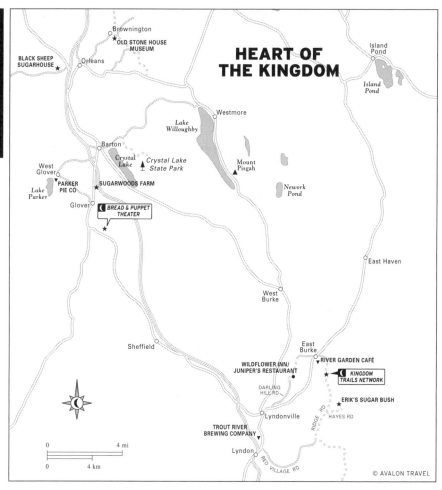

HEART OF THE KINGDOM

© AVALON TRAVEL

for more than 150 years. Just in time for Christmas, the **Burklyn Arts Festival** (early Dec.) brings out the creativity of the Kingdom for a juried craft competition and gift sale.

Shopping

Invented in 1899 for use on farm animals, the now-famous **Bag Balm** (91 Williams St., 800/232-3610, www.bagbalm.com, by appt.) product is these days used by people—to soothe cuts, scratches, skin irritations, and abrasions.

It's made right in Lyndonville at the Dairy Association Co., where you can swing by for a visit and pick up a canister for the winter.

Browsing is encouraged at **Green Mountain Books & Prints** (1055 Broad St., 802/626-5051, 9 A.M.–5 P.M. Mon.–Sat.), a quiet shop stocked to its gills with used and rare books and old maps and prints.

Food

Housed in the Wildflower Inn, the casual,

THE BRIDGES OF LYNDONVILLE

Known as the covered bridge capital of the Northeast Kingdom, Lyndonville is home to an impressive total of five such specimens, two of which are still working. And while modern-day admirers may view the structures as quaint relics, they were an absolute necessity when most of them were constructed in the 19th century; uncovered wooden bridges deteriorate quickly from the elements, and a covering protects them—and thus extends their lifetime. Lyndonville's bridges are well-kept, and even those that aren't operational are still excellent examples of their kind. They are:

· **Chamberlain Mill Bridge,** South Wheelock Road: This Queenpost bridge has unusual gables.

· **Miller's Run Bridge,** off Route 22: Miller's Run Bridge is a reconstruction from the mid-1990s.

· **Randall Bridge,** off Route 114: Built in 1867, the 68-foot-long bridge sports very open construction, so taking a gander at the internal structure is easy.

· **Sanborn Bridge,** at the junction of Routes 5, 122, and 114: This bridge dates back to 1867.

· **Schoolhouse Bridge,** South Wheelock Road: Built in 1879, the 42-foot-long structure replaced another bridge original to the spot.

crimson-walled **Juniper's Restaurant** (2059 Darling Hill Rd., 800/627-8310, www.wild-flowerinn.com, 5:30–9 P.M. Mon.–Sat., seasonal hours may vary, $9–24) uses all-natural ingredients (many from nearby farms and purveyors), including everything from hormone-free dairy products and free-range turkey to organic wines. There's a full roster of Vermont-brewed beers, too.

The conversation's as good as the eating and drinking at **Trout River Brewing Company** (Rte. 5, 1 mi. north of I-91, 802/626-9396, www.troutriverbrewing.com, 4–9 P.M. Fri.–Sat., $6–14). During the week, the microbrewery churns out ales and stouts, but on Friday and Saturday nights it opens its pub, where seemingly the entire town gathers to eat hand-tossed gourmet pizzas, drink good ales, and gossip.

Information

Located on I-91 South, the state of Vermont's **Lyndonville Information Center** (I-91 S. between exits 24 and 25, 802/626-9669) has information on the entire Northeast Kingdom.

The **Lyndon Area Chamber of Commerce** (802/626-9696, www.lyndonvermont.com) runs an information booth on Memorial Drive right off exit 24 in downtown Lyndonville.

Several banks are located in Lyndon town center, including **Union Bank** (183 Depot St., 802/626-3100, 8 A.M.–5 P.M. Mon.–Thurs., 8 A.M.–6 P.M. Fri., 8:30 A.M.–noon Sat.) and **Community National Bank** (1033 Broad St., 802/626-1111).

Pharmacy needs can be taken care of at **Lyndonville Pharmacy** (101 Depot St., 802/626-6966) as well as **Rite-Aid Pharmacy** (412 Broad St., 802/626-4366, 8 A.M.–8:30 P.M. Mon.–Sat., 9 A.M.–6 P.M. Sun., pharmacy 8 A.M.–8 P.M. Mon.–Fri., 9 A.M.–6 P.M. Sat., 9 A.M.–5 P.M. Sun.). Wi-Fi is available at the **Lyndon Freight House** (1000 Broad St., 802/626-1400, 7 A.M.–2:30 P.M. Sun.–Wed., 7 A.M.–8 P.M. Thurs.–Sat.), along with coffee and a model train set.

EAST BURKE

With its excellent slopes and welcoming town, Burke Mountain is one of the best-kept semi-secrets in Vermont—meaning that while it may be a known destination, those who go there aren't in any hurry to see it become a popular hot spot. It attracts a quieter crowd than many ski areas, and its visitors tend to come back year after year for generations. But Burke is more than just a wintertime destination; it is also headquarters to the Kingdom Trails, a biking network that may be one of the state's best-kept recreational secrets.

◖ Kingdom Trails Network

Biking in the country doesn't get any better than this 100-plus-mile network (Kingdom Trail Association, P.O. Box 204, 802/626-0737, www.kingdomtrails.org) of old carriage paths, railroad right-of-ways, and forest trails that have been stitched together for two-wheeled pleasure. There may be no better way to really gain an appreciation for the size and beauty of the Northeast Kingdom. The Trails have something for every difficulty, from the precipitous Freeride Trail that carves its way down the side of Burke Mountain to the gentler curves of Darling Hill, where you'll have plenty of farmhouses and cows for company. The best part: no cars in sight. The trails leave from the village area in East Burke, just behind Burke General Store.

Events

Burke's own zany version of waterskiing occurs each March during the **Burke Mountain Pond Skimming** (www.skiburke.com). Contestants zoom down the mountain and then attempt to "skim" on skis across a 90-foot freezing cold pond. The crazy costumes worn by participants are almost as crucial to their success as the tricks they use to wax their skis to cross the water.

Shopping

Need to gear up before hitting the slopes? Do it at **East Burke Sports** (Rte. 114 at the

Explore the Northeast Kingdom by biking the Kingdom Trails Network.

village center, 802/626-3215, www.eastburke-sports.com, 8:30 A.M.–5:30 P.M. Mon.–Sat., 8:30 A.M.–5 P.M. Sun. in winter; 9 A.M.–6 P.M. daily in summer). The shop sells whatever you need for cycling, skiing, hiking, camping, or snowboarding, and has a well-trained staff happy to help with the selection process.

Bailey's and Burke Country Store (466 Rte. 114, 802/626-9250, 8 A.M.–7 P.M. Mon.–Thurs., 7 A.M.–8 P.M. Fri.–Sat., 7 A.M.–6 P.M. Sun.) is the kind of place you might just want to hang out at all day. The quaint historic shop sells nicely made country linens, clothing, homemade jams, crafts, and Christmas decorations. And when you need more sustenance to keep shopping, the bakery is full of terrific breads, pastries, and freshly made pizzas.

Food

Tuck into wholesome dishes at the **River Garden Cafe** (Rte. 114, 802/626-3514, www.rivergardencafe.com, 11:30 A.M.–2 P.M. and 5–9 P.M. Wed.–Sun., 11 A.M.–2 P.M. Sun., $6–14 lunch, $18–25 dinner) and look out to the restaurant's lovingly tended gardens. Owners Bobby Baker and David Thomas started this relaxing spot in the early '90s, and since then it's become locally loved for specials like pepper-crusted lamb loin, fried ravioli, and warm artichoke dip.

Still heartier fare graces the menu at **The Pub Outback** (114 Main St., 802/626-1188, www.puboutback.net, 4:30–9 P.M. Mon.–Thurs., 4–10 P.M. Fri., noon–10 P.M. Sat., noon–9 P.M. Sun., $7–19)—groaning plates of homemade meatloaf, pot roast, and vegetarian lasagna. The lively spot particularly caters to families with kids and large groups.

Information and Services

The **Burke Area Chamber of Commerce** (802/626-4124, www.burkevermont.com) runs an information kiosk at corner of Route 5 and Route 5A. Wi-Fi is available at **Bailey's**

and Burke Country Store (466 Rte. 114, 802/626-9250).

BARTON AND VICINITY

Once a mill town producing everything from doors to bowling pins, the central NEK town of Barton is now better known for its easy access to waterborne recreation. Within its borders, glacier-carved Lake Willoughby is often described as the most beautiful lake in the state, inviting comparisons to Lake Lucerne in Switzerland. At the lake's southern tip, the twin peaks of Mt. Pisgah and Mt. Hor are as dramatic as they are amusingly named—confronting each other like battleships about to collide. Between them, fjord-like cliffs plummet to the water, serving as launching pads for endangered peregrine falcons as well as a death-defying ascent for winter ice climbers. While Lake Willoughby and neighboring Crystal Lake were once popular resort destinations during the steamship age, they are now virtually deserted even in the height of summer, making a trip to either lake the ultimate aquatic getaway. Nearby is tiny **Glover,** home to the one-of-a-kind Bread & Puppet Theater troupe, and **Brownington,** which features a better-than-usual historical museum.

◖ Bread & Puppet Theater

"Art is for Kitchens!" proudly trumpets one poster for sale at the barn-cum-museum of Bread & Puppet Theater performing puppet troupe (753 Heights Rd., Glover, 802/525-3031, www.breadandpuppet.org, 10 A.M.–6 P.M. daily June–Oct., free). With its mission that art should be accessible to the masses, B&P began more than 40 years ago with counterculture hand- and rod-puppet performances on New York's Lower East Side. Founder Peter Schumann moved back to the land in the 1970s, taking over an old farm in the middle of the Kingdom and presenting bigger and more elaborate political puppet festivals every summer. Along the way, the troupe virtually invented a new art form, pioneering the construction of larger-than-life papier-mâché puppets of gods and goddesses and other figures that now regularly spice up the atmosphere at left-of-center political protests around the world.

The troupe still performs on its original farm stage in Glover throughout the summer, before taking performances on tour in the fall. On the grounds, the old barn has been transformed into a "museum" filled with 10-foot-tall characters from past plays, along with photographs and descriptions of the political context of the times. A smaller school bus has been converted into a "cheap art" museum, where you can buy original works for $5 or less—and even hang them in your kitchen.

Old Stone House Museum

Literally constructed of heavy stone granite blocks, the Old Stone House Museum (109 Old Stone House Rd., Brownington, 802/754-2022, www.oldstonehousemuseum. org, 11 A.M.–5 P.M. Wed.–Sun. mid-May–mid-Oct., $8 adults, $5 students) once served as a boys' dormitory and school. It now houses the collection of the Orleans Historical Society, including Victorian-era furniture and cooking implements and some of the original schoolbooks from the academy library. Behind the museum is a wooden observation platform on Prospect Hill that commands the surrounding farm country.

Sugarhouses

In addition to the expected syrup, **D&D Sugarwoods Farm** (2287 Glover St., Glover, 802/525-3718, www.ddsugarwoodsfarm.com, 8 A.M.–5 P.M. Mon.–Fri.) is famed for its delectable maple candy, made from the highest-grade syrup without added preservatives.

The **Black Sheep Sugarhouse** (99 Ingalls Rd., Orleans, 802/754-6693, www.blacksheep-sugarhouse.com, 5–10 P.M. daily) was part of the homestead of Vermont founding father Ira

Allen. The black sheep that used to graze in nearby pastures are gone, but visitors are still greeted by two Scottish terriers along with tours of the mapling process.

Events

A "grand cavalcade" of livestock and farm machinery kicks off the annual **Orleans County Fair** (Barton, 802/525-3555, www.orleans-countyfair.net, mid-Aug.), which features a demolition derby and country music performances among its attractions.

Shopping

The artisans who own and run **Silver Crafts** (20 Park Ave., Irasburg, 802/754-6012, 10 A.M.–3 P.M. Mon.–Wed., 10 A.M.–4 P.M. Thurs.–Sat.) fill the place with fine jewelry (some with gems, some without), as well as a high-quality selection of plates, charms, and other gifts. The **Barton Village Corner Store** (155 Main St., Barton, 802/525-1243, 8 A.M.–6 P.M. Mon.–Thurs., 8 A.M.–8 P.M. Fri.–Sat., 9 A.M.–1 P.M. Sun.) is both a godsend for visitors in need of rentals (particularly electronics) and a treasure trove of things to own permanently—handmade jewelry, candles, and wool sweaters.

Food

Locals will tell you the best dinner in the area is found at **The Parker Pie Co.** (161 Country Rd., West Glover, 802/525-3366, www.parkerpie. com, 11 A.M.–10 P.M. daily, $8–16). And while the place does live up to its name with a menu of good pizzas (the Buffalo Chicken version is a favorite), it also turns out very good homemade soups and sandwiches, and decent nachos. Lots of nightly pasta specials, free wireless Internet access, and an excellent bakery on the premises have made regulars out of many.

Information and Services

The local **Barton Chamber of Commerce**

(802/239-4147, www.centerofthekingdom. com) runs three information kiosks in Barton: across from the post office, at the gas station, and at Lake Willoughby's North Beach.

Find medicines and other goods at **Barton Pharmacy** (16 Church St., 802/525-4098, 5 A.M.–8 P.M. Mon.–Fri., 6 A.M.–8 P.M. Sat., 6 A.M.–3 P.M. Sun.), along with an authentic old-time soda fountain in back. There's also a branch of **Community National Bank** (103 Church St., 802/525-3524, 7:30 A.M.–5 P.M. Mon.–Thurs., 7:30 A.M.–6 P.M. Fri., 8 A.M.– noon Sat.) in town.

Free Wi-Fi is available in Westmore at **Northern Exposure Country Store** (1266 Rte. 5A, 802/525-3789, 6 A.M.–7 P.M. Mon.–Thurs., 6 A.M.–8 P.M. Fri.–Sat., 8 A.M.–6 P.M. Sun.).

ISLAND POND

The remote township of Brighton has some eight ponds—the largest of which, Island Pond, has given the town its more common name. The pond surrounds a 22-acre island, which is just the beginning of the surfeit of outdoor offerings of the area, including the seven *million-acre* Silvio O. Conte National Wildlife Refuge. The town's other major claim-to-fame is as the junction of the first international railroad, the Grand Trunk railway, which was completed between Montreal and Maine in the mid-1800s. It gave the area a brief industrial boom, which was tragically cut short when railway entrepreneur Charles M. Hayes died in the sinking of the *Titanic* in 1912, starting the slow decline of the area's economic might.

Sights

Island Pond (or IP as it's known) is prime territory for spotting moose, who regularly feed among the streams and meadows along the Nulhegan Basin (better known as Route 105). The local chamber of commerce produces a "moose map" with locales of back roads and nature refuges where the big quadrupeds are

known to lurk. Your best bets for a sighting are early morning and late evening. It goes without saying that drivers should use caution at night.

Though IP's railroad days are long behind it, the **Island Pond Historical Society** (Canadian National Railway Station, 2nd Fl., Main St., 802/723-4345, 10 A.M.–2 P.M. Sat. July–Sept., or by appt., free) displays photos, tools, old newspapers, and other train-related memorabilia on the second floor of the old international rail station.

Events

Every Friday night in summer, residents gather to dance the night away under the stars at the **Friday Night Live** (802/723-6300, www.islandpondchamber.org). The weekly event features live music and sometimes karaoke at the bandstand on the town green, overlooking the lake.

Shopping

Get your fishing licenses along with a tasty overstuffed sandwich or two at **Northern Exposure Country Store** (1266 Rte. 5A, Orleans, 802/525-3789). The deli-cum-country store sells good lunch fixings, rents videos, and stocks gifts like handmade pillows and candles.

Food

Friendly Pizza Parlor (31 Derby St., 802/723-4616, 11 A.M.–9 P.M. daily, $9–13) lives up to its name with an affable staff that cooks up big, thin-crusted pies with classic toppings like sausage, pepper, and onions. Service is fast, but patrons tend to linger at tables and chat.

Information and Services

For info on Island Pond and around, stop by the downtown **Island Pond Welcome Center** (11 Birch, 802/723-9889, 10 A.M.–2 P.M. Tues., 9 A.M.–2 P.M. Wed.–Sat.), or check out the website of the **Island Pond Chamber of Commerce** (www.islandpondchamber.org).

© VERMONTVACATION.COM

Island Pond

For info on the recreational offerings of this corner of Vermont, check the website or office of the **Nulhegan Gateway Association** (23 Rte. 105, www.nulhegan.com), a nonprofit environmental and tourism organization. Wi-Fi is available at **Island Pond Public Library** (49 Mill St., 802/723-6134, 10 A.M.–7 P.M. Tues. and Thurs., 2–6 P.M. Wed., 10 A.M.–5 P.M. Fri., 10 A.M.–2 P.M. Sat.).

SPORTS AND RECREATION
Hiking

Several trails take hikers to the top of the 3,267-foot Burke Mountain. The best bet is the Red Trail, which leaves from Burke Mountain Base Lodge and climbs moderately up to the peak, a two-hour trip one way. From the summit, a fire tower offers great views of New Hampshire's White Mountains and Vermont as far as Jay.

"Breathtaking" and "spectacular" are just a couple of the words used to describe the views of the fjord-like cliffs of Lake Willoughby, as seen from the top of Mount Pigsah. The 3.9-mile South Trail leaves from Route 5A at the southern end of the lake and passes a peregrine falcon nest on the Pulpit Rock formation on the way up.

Camping

In the remote eastern section of the Kingdom, **Brighton State Park** (102 State Park Rd., Island Pond, 802/723-4360, campsites $16–27, cabins $46–48) has 5 cabins, 23 lean-tos and some 60 tent sites tucked into a stand of white birch on the pristine shores of Spectacle Pond. It's not uncommon to see moose on the park's nature trails. Just a short walk from the campground, campers have use of a sandy beach with boat rentals, play area, and a small nature museum. The beach has a bathhouse with restrooms, while the campground has three restrooms, hot showers, and dumping station (but no hookups).

Swimming and Boating

The shores of **Crystal Lake State Park** (96 Bellwater Ave., Barton, 802/525-6205, www.vtstateparks.com/htm/crystal.cfm, late May–early Sept.) have nearly a mile of sandy beach, marked by a historic art-deco bathhouse, concession area, and several dozen charcoal grills and picnic tables. Rowboats and canoes are also available for rent.

Along Route 5A south of Westmore, **Lake Willoughby** has two naturally sandy beaches and boat ramps at both its north and south ends. The north beach has a bathhouse for changing. The south beach has a rope swing, as well as a clothing-optional area for true "naturelovers." Halfway down the east side of the lake, so-called Devil's Rock is another popular place to take a dive (look for cars parked along Route 5A). To head out onto the lake, rent a canoe or kayak from **East Burke Sports** (802/626-3215, 9 A.M.–6 P.M. Mon.–Sat., 9 A.M.–5 P.M. Sun., $30/day kayak, $40/day canoe), or stay at the Willoughvale Inn, which has complimentary boats for use of guests.

You're virtually assured a moose sighting from the vantage of canoe or kayak along the Clyde and Nulhegan Rivers. The former is surrounded by dairy farms, while the latter cuts its way through dense forest and wetland. For custom-designed trips down these rivers or any other running or flat bodies of water in the area, contact the **NorthWoods Stewardship Center** (154 Leadership Dr., 802/723-6551, www.northwoodscenter.org).

Fishing

Gouged by glaciers, some of the Northeast Kingdom's lakes are more than 100 feet deep. Willoughby is particularly well-known for its trophy-sized rainbow and lake trout, as well as landlocked salmon, yellow perch, and rainbow smelt. For guided expeditions on lakes and rivers fishing for these species as well as large- and smallmouth bass, contact the **Village Inn**

of East Burke (802/626-3161, www.villageinnofeastburke.com).

Skiing

As a ski area, **Burke Mountain** (223 Sherburne Lodge Rd., East Burke, 802/626-7300, www.skiburke.com, $68 adults, $51 youth 12–17, $44 children 6–11) has achieved a cult following, prized as much for its laid-back vibe and lack of crowds as for its range of challenging terrain that serves as training ground to U.S. Olympic hopefuls.

Ice Climbing

For an unforgettable winter experience, **Vermont Adventure Tours** (802/773-3343, www.vermontadventuretours.com, $150–220 per person) offers ice-climbing instruction on frozen waterfalls along the cliffs of Lake Willoughby. Instruction ranges from basic to advanced classes, scaling stretches with names like Glass Menagerie, Reign of Terror, and Frankenstein.

ACCOMMODATIONS

Open year-round, **Labour of Love** (9 Sargent Ln., Glover, 802/525-6695, $99–110) offers one of the state's more unusual "farmstays" with a few rooms in a restored 1800s Greek Revival farmhouse with an adjoining flower nursery. The surrounding gardens displaying local and exotic perennials are spectacular, while guestrooms are filled with antiques and botanical garden–sized tropical plants selected by cheerful proprietress Kate Butler. As a bonus, all of the plants on display are available for sale from bulb or seed.

Comfortable and well-priced, **Village Inn of East Burke** (606 Rte. 114, East Burke, 802/626-3161, www.villageinnofeastburke.com, $99) offers big, relaxing rooms with private baths. An outdoor Jacuzzi, beautifully kept gardens, and the common areas (complete with games and books) make for an even more relaxing stay.

Rooms at **Inn at Mountain View Farm** (Darling Hill Rd., 800/572-4509, East Burke, www.innmtnview.com, $175–275) run from doubles to luxury suites, but all have an air of elegance about them. Filled with armoires, antique poster beds, floral wallpaper, and tasteful down comforters, they're a cosseting place to rest after a day on the slopes. Rates include country breakfast and afternoon tea. Right on the shores of Lake Willoughby, the **WilloughVale Inn** (793 Rte. 5A S., Westmore, 800/594-9102, www.willoughvale.com, $99–239) is a laid-back B&B with gas fireplaces, Jacuzzis, and lake views. Innkeeper Roy Clark is happy to recommend secret swimming spots and hook guests up with other activities around the lake. The inn also offers complimentary kayaks and canoes as well as pub fare and continental cuisine in its dining room. For those planning a longer drop out of society, it has cottages on the lake for rent ($279–289 per night, $1,789–1,999 per week).

GETTING THERE AND AROUND

From St. Johnsbury, much of the heart of the Kingdom is accessible from I-91. For Lyndonville, take exit 23 (8 mi., 10 min.); for Glover and Barton, exit 25 (30 mi., 30 min.); and for Brownington, exit. 26. From Lyndonville, take Route 114 north to Burke (12 mi., 20 min.) or Island Pond (25 mi., 35 min.).

If you must rely on public transportation, **Rural Community Transportation** (802/748-8170, www.riderct.org) runs limited shuttle bus service between St. Johnsbury (leaving from the Vermont Welcome Center) and Lyndonville.

Border Country

The farthest northern corner of Vermont is arguably the most quiet. Along the Canadian border, the towns of **Derby, Newport,** and **Jay** look more toward Montreal than to Boston or Burlington. Don't be surprised to hear French spoken in the streets, or even to see it on street signs. Truth be told, however, this area is far from *any* urban center. Not that there isn't plenty to do: Cyclists, hikers, and skiers alike find thrills galore on the trails of Jay Peak, windsurfers and swimmers swear by the serene waters of the bi-national Lake Memphremagog, and leaf peepers come to, well, just kick back and watch everything turn red and gold.

DERBY LINE

Astride the Canadian border, the town of Derby was founded in 1788 by one Timothy Andrews, who chartered a dozen other towns in the area. It actually contains two villages—Derby Center and Derby Line. The latter was mistakenly extended into Canadian territory by poor surveying that placed it above the 45th parallel. Rather than causing an international incident, however, the erroneous borders were ratified by a treaty between the United States and Canada. Since then, Derby Line has always had a spirit of international cooperation, signified by the town library and opera house that was intentionally built athwart the line.

◖ Haskell Free Library & Opera House

You can find a book in Vermont and check it out in Quebec at this Victorian library and performance center (93 Caswell Ave., Derby Line, 802/873-3022, www.haskellopera.com, 10 A.M.–5 P.M. Tues.–Wed., 10 A.M.–6 P.M. Thurs., 10 A.M.–5 P.M. Fri., 10 A.M.–2 P.M. Sat., $2 suggested donation), the only cultural institution in the world that sits astride an international border. (Look for the thin, black line that runs down the middle of the reading room, separating the United States from Canada.) It also happens to be the answer to the trivia question: "What's the only theater in the United States without a stage?" since the opera house's stage is actually in Canada, while the audience sits in the good ol' U.S. of A.

The building was constructed in 1901 by a local lumber mill owner who had married a Canadian woman—the couple intentionally built it for the use and enjoyment of citizens of both countries. The striking turreted neoclassical building is unique in having a first floor of granite capped with a second story of yellow brick. More than 100 years later, the building was recently gut-rehabbed to revive musical performances in the Opera House upstairs. In addition to the novelty of standing astride the border, staff are often available to give tours of the renovated theater. Call ahead to check availability.

Cowtown Elk Ranch

Once native to Vermont, the mighty American elk was extinct for decades before it was reintroduced at the Cowtown Elk Ranch (Main St., Derby, 802/766-4724, www.derbycowpalace.com) in 1992. The herd of more than 350 animals is cultivated for big-game hunting in a preserve down the road in Irasburg. During daylight hours, the elk are available for viewing in the pasture; the best time to see them is in the late afternoon when they are brought into the front pasture for feeding. Speaking of which, the ranch also serves lean venison steaks at its adjoining restaurant, the **Cow Palace** (11 A.M.–10 P.M. Tues.–Sun., 4 P.M.–10 P.M. Mon.).

Entertainment and Events

The **Haskell Opera House** (802/873-3022, www.haskellopera.com) presents old-time entertainment, including fiddlers, blues, and classical concerts.

One of the most active Native American tribes in the Northeast, the Clan of the Hawk, Northeast Wind Council of the Abenaki Nation of Vermont, holds its **Clan of the Hawk Pow Wow** (123 Evansville Rd., Rte. 58, Brownington, 802/754-2817) the first weekend in August, featuring tribal drumming, dancing, and sales of traditional crafts.

Shopping

Picture the quintessential country store, and you've got **Derby Village Store** (483 Main St., Derby, 802/766-2215, 7 A.M.–9 P.M. daily), a hodgepodge of natural foods and gourmet provisions (including locally made yogurts and butters).

Food

It may not be straight-from-the-Great-Wall authentic, but **Lee Wah Chinese Restaurant** (3032 U.S. 5, Derby, 802/766-2092, 5–10 P.M. daily, $10–16) serves fresh, good Chinese-American dishes in a comfy dining room, and at good prices.

Simple Italian-inspired dishes using locally grown ingredients are the mainstay at **Lake Salem Inn** (1273 Rte. 105, Derby, 802/766-5560, www.lakesaleminn.com, 5–9 P.M. daily, $25–35). The farm-raised venison, vegetarian specials, and desserts are particularly popular options.

Services

There's a branch of **Community National Bank** (69 Main St., 802/334-7915, 8:30 A.M.–5 P.M. Mon.–Thurs., 8:30 A.M.–6 P.M. Fri.) in Derby Center, and a **Rite-Aid Pharmacy** (4408 Rte. 5, 802/334-2313, 8 A.M.–9 P.M. daily, pharmacy 8 A.M.–8 P.M. Mon.–Fri., 9 A.M.–6 P.M. Sat., 9 A.M.–5 P.M. Sun.) on the way to Newport.

NEWPORT

There is poetry in the Abenaki language—nowhere more evident than in the name of Vermont's northernmost large lake, Memphremagog, a name meaning "beautiful waters." The name still fits today, with the 40-mile lake ringed by spruce-covered mountains—none more impressive than the 3,400-foot Owl's Head—and often splashed pink and orange by brilliant sunsets.

At the southern end of the lake, the more prosaically named Newport was a resort center in the late 1800s, with some of the grand hotels of the area still around today. It now serves as the center for summertime boating, swimming, and fishing, as well as the commercial hub of the border region. While there, however, be careful not to disturb Memphre, a sea monster that reputedly lives in the depths of the lake.

Sights

On the second floor of a state office building is the quaint **Memphremagog Historical Society Museum** (100 Main St., 802/334-6195, 9 A.M.–5 P.M. Mon.–Fri., free), with exhibits on the history of the Abenaki, who used the lake as a major trade route, as well as photographs of the early resort history of the area. Along the lake, the society has created a self-guided walking tour with 10 markers in French and English pointing out natural features and historic buildings.

Events

On Friday nights during the summer, Newport residents gather by the lake for **Gateway Center Concerts** (802/334-6345, www.newportvt.org) to listen to jazz, country, or rock music while the sun sets over Memphremagog's lapping waters. The lakeside community center regularly hosts other events over the course of the year, including a fish fry, a craft show, and art exhibition.

Shopping

Kids' books, toys, puzzles, and games populate the shelves at **Wider than the Sky** (158 Main St., 802/334-2322, www.widerthanthesky.com, 10 A.M.–5 P.M. Mon.–Fri., seasonal hours may vary). The shop also stages regular activities for children—from story readings to craft workshops and puppet shows.

Food

The lake views at **The East Side Restaurant & Pub** (47 Landing St. #3, 802/334-2340, www.eastsiderestaurant.net, 8 A.M.–2 P.M. daily, $10–20) are almost as comforting as the food—everything from homemade biscuits and gravy to freshly baked cinnamon-apple pie and corned beef hash. The enormous all-you-can-eat Sunday brunch is hugely popular, and at dinner, the heaping portions of baked ziti are a favorite. There's plenty more pasta where that came from at **Lago Trattoria** (95 Main St., 802/334-8222, www.lagotrattoria.com, 5–9 P.M. daily, $15–24), which serves carb-centric Italian specials (with several meat dishes thrown in for good measure) in a casual dining room.

Services

There are several branches of **Community National Bank** in the area, including one in Newport (100 Main St., 802/334-7915) and one in Troy (4245 Rte. 101, 802/744-2287), at the intersections of Routes 100 and 101 on the way to Jay. There is also a **Chittenden Bank** (15 Main St., 802/334-6511, 8:30 A.M.–5 P.M. Mon.–Thurs., 8:30 A.M.–6 P.M. Fri., 8:30 A.M.–noon Sat.).

Brooks Pharmacy (59 Waterfront Plaza, 802/334-2313) is located in downtown Newport, as is **Rite-Aid Pharmacy** (95 Waterfront Plaza, 802/334-6785, 8 A.M.–9 P.M. Mon.–Fri., 8 A.M.–8 P.M. Sat., 9 A.M.–6 P.M. Sun., pharmacy 8 A.M.–8 P.M. Mon.–Fri., 9 A.M.–6 P.M. Sat., 9 A.M.–5 P.M. Sun.).

JAY AND MONTGOMERY

Situated along the Appalachian Trail in the very center of Vermont's northern border, the town of Jay is best known for its eponymous mountain, Jay Peak, the second highest in Vermont. The mountain is known for getting the most snow of any in Vermont; that and its relative inaccessibility make it a favorite for powder skiers who flock to Jay Peak Resort as soon as the season begins. The resort is in the midst of a $140 million makeover, adding a new hotel, a Nordic Center with direct access to 20km of cross-country trails, and an NHL-size hockey arena, among other improvements. Locals are split on whether or not this constitutes "progress," but few can grumble about the influx of jobs and economic vitality into the area.

Nearby, the location of **Montgomery**—all nestled in a mountain valley—would make it an uncommonly pretty little town even without its claim to fame as the "covered bridge town," owing to its possession of more covered bridges than any other town in the country.

Sights

Jacques and Pauline Couture raised six children in their 1890s farmhouse on the Canadian border. Now they continue to milk 100 head of cattle and produce maple syrup from 6,000 taps. **Couture's Maple Shop and B&B** (560 Rte. 100, Westfield, 800/845-2733, www.maplesyrupvermont.com, 10 A.M.–5 P.M. Mon.–Fri.) sells products ranging from maple French dressing to maple cotton candy, and it also puts up guests in a three-room B&B.

The little town of Montgomery has no fewer than six **covered bridges,** all built with the same design between 1863 and 1890 by brothers Sheldon and Savannah Jewett. You can obtain a map of bridge locations from the website of the **Montgomery Historical Society** (www.montgomeryvt.us/mhs.htm).

Events

While it will never be mistaken for New Orleans, **Jay Peak Mardi Gras** (www.jaypeakresort.com, late Feb./early Mar.) heats up the slopes with a traditional masked parade and food booths, and not-so-traditional snow sculptures and snowball-throwing contests.

Shopping

Trout River Traders (91 Main St., Montgomery Center, 802/326-3058, 8 A.M.–10 P.M. Wed.–Sun.) is part store, part cafe (with wireless Internet access, comfy chairs, and a vintage soda fountain). Close to Jay Peak, it's a natural stop for a bite (fresh-roasted turkey sandwiches and chili—or brunch on Sunday). Or simply run in for souvenirs—various antiques, local art and photography, candles, and pottery.

Food

It may look like your average red barn from the outside, but inside, **The Belfry Restaurant and Pub** (Rte. 242 at Amidon Rd., Montgomery, 802/326-4400, 4–9 P.M. Sun.–Thurs., 4–10 P.M. Fri.–Sat., $7–13) is more like a town meeting hall. The joint teems with families and pasta dishes on Italian night every Wednesday, and with the scent of fresh cod at the fish fries that take place every Friday. And on every other night, the menu (from burgers to homemade pie) still pulls in plenty of regulars.

Located in the Jay Peak Resort, the very family-friendly **Alpine Restaurant** (4850 Rte. 242, 802/988-2611, 7:30 A.M.–10 A.M. and 5:30–9 P.M. daily in winter, $7–24) is where to relax off the slopes and enjoy burgers, big sandwiches, and brownie sundaes.

Information

The **Jay Peak Area Chamber of Commerce** (802/988-2259, www.jaypeakvermont.org) staffs an information center at the intersection of Routes 100 and 242 in Jay.

SPORTS AND RECREATION

Hiking

The **Hazen's Notch Association** (Montgomery Center, 802/326-4799, www.hazensnotch.org,) maintains 15 miles of hiking trails in forested conservation land. High Ponds Farm is a restored organic farm at the base of Burnt Mountain with walking trails among the orchards and woodland speckled with beaver ponds. More rigorous trails lead up to the summit of Burnt Mountain, a 3,100-foot peak with views of the notch below. All of these trails leave from the High Ponds Farm parking area, some two miles east of Montgomery Center. Directions and a trail map are available on the association's website. Trails are open during daylight hours, from mid-May to mid-December. During the winter months, some are groomed for cross-country skiing, when a trail access fee is charged ($12 adults, $5 children).

Swimming and Boating

Split between Canada and the United States, **Lake Memphremagog** is more than just a mouthful—it also has a nice sandy beach for swimming (though be careful not to disturb Memphre, a sea serpent who reputedly lives in the lake). Run by the city, the beach is located at the 36-acre **Prouty Beach Campground** (386 Prouty Beach Rd., Newport, 802/334-7951, www.newportrecreation.org, May–Oct., tent sites $29/night, $7 each additional person, $2–8 day use per person or vehicle). The campground also offers paddle boat and canoe rentals, tennis courts, picnic tables, horseshoe pits, and changing facilities. The lake is also a good place for an afternoon of flatwater canoeing. **Up the Creek Paddle Sports** (802/334-7350) leads tours of the lake's bays and inlets.

Skiing

Situated almost on the border with Canada, **Jay Peak Resort** (4850 Rte. 242, Jay, 802/988-2611, www.jaypeakresort.com, $75 adults, $35 seniors, $55 youth 6–18, $16 children 5 and under) is known for two things: lots of snow and no crowds. The mountain gets hands-down more natural snow than any other peak in the Northeast—yet it takes a determined skier to drive the five hours up from Boston to take advantage of it (especially when there are so many other enticing mountains along the way). Skiers who make the trek are rewarded with 60 runs of mixed difficulty spread out on two peaks. Unique among area mountains, Jay also offers wide swaths of backcountry glade skiing, leaving skiers the freedom to carve their own paths among the trees.

Dog Sledding

The 26 Alaskan huskies that Lori and Keith Sampietro use for dog sledding at **Montgomery Adventures** (262 Deep Gibou Rd., Montgomery Center, 802/370-2103, www.montgomeryadventures.com, $125–175) are friendlier and more eager to please than their imperious Siberian cousins. A sled ride through the northern Vermont wilderness is as much about meeting and greeting the canines as it is taking in the breathtaking mountain scenery. A few years ago, the Sampietros expanded their operation to include dog cart rides in fall as a more extreme way to take in fall foliage. While dog sledding is noiseless and serene, dog carting is the opposite—a bumpy thrill-ride through fall color. Both experiences end with a short hike to a hidden waterfall. Montgomery Adventures also offers canoe and kayak trips in the summer and snowshoe tours and winter camping in the winter.

ACCOMMODATIONS

Simple decor marks the guest rooms at **Jay Village Inn** (1078 Rte. 242, Jay, 802/988-2306, www.thejayvillageinn.com, $85–150). Visitors sleep easy under colorful quilts in sleigh or canopied beds. Located on the outskirts of Montgomery, the **Black Lantern Inn**

(2057 N. Main St., Rte. 118, Montgomery, 802/326-3269, www.theblacklanterninn.com, $95–155) offers the beautiful mountain scenery of Hazen's Notch to go with its friendly hospitality. Rooms are basic, but the inn comes with plenty of perks to help guests relax, including an outdoor hot tub and Adirondack chairs facing the view. A pub room downstairs offers nightly dinners including specialty nights (Italian, prime rib, etc.).

Two big contenders have joined the ranks of the mountain's most promising hotels at **Jay Peak Resorts** (830 Jay Peak Village Rd., Jay, 802/988-2611, www.jaypeakresort.com, $140–300). The first is Hotel Jay, where the 176 suites cater to conference travelers. Rooms include duvet comforters, flat-screen HD TVs, iPod docking stations, and free Wi-Fi. There's also plenty to engage in the downtime, too—an indoor waterpark, arcade, fitness center, and of course, direct access to the slopes. The second lodging is the homier Tram Haus Lodge. Designed as studios and multi-bedroom suites, guest chambers sport kitchenettes, locally made wool blankets, and spot-on views of the mountain's aerial trams.

GETTING THERE AND AROUND

From St. Johnsbury, head up I-91 and take exit 27 for Newport (45 mi., 40 min.) or exit 29 for Derby Line (50 mi., 1 hr.). To travel to Jay, take I-89 to exit 26, then north along U.S. 5, and Routes 14, 100, 101, and 242 (55 mi., 1 hr. 10 min.). From central Vermont, Jay is also accessible along Route 100 north (40 mi., 1 hr. 15 min.) from Stowe. **Rural Community Transportation** (802/748-8170, www.riderct. org) runs shuttle buses between Derby Line and Newport.

BACKGROUND

The Land

Vermont's most prominent feature is right there in its name. The Green Mountains aren't the biggest mountains in the world, but they are incredibly photogenic, whether rolling along forested glens, lit up red and gold in fall, or serving as the hazy backdrop to a cow or cornfield. While you are never far from their comforting bulk, the mountains are not the only landscape the state has to offer. The long flat water of Lake Champlain, the flat fields along the Connecticut River, and the dramatic highlands of the Northeast Kingdom are all part of the state's physical tapestry.

In fact, Vermont is the most rural state in the nation, with more than two-thirds of its territory fitting that description. Geologists categorize six distinct landforms in the state. First, of course, there are the Green Mountains, which stretch in a band averaging 30 miles wide, all the way from Canada to the Massachusetts border, some 160 miles in all. Some of the oldest mountains in America, they date at their youngest from 380 million years ago. All that time, of course, means that they had plenty of time to erode, producing the characteristic rounded tops that make driving along them so pleasing.

© KATHRYN OSGOOD

The highest peak, Mount Mansfield, is a proud 4,395 feet, while five more peaks are 4,000 feet or higher, and several more top 3,000 feet.

In the southwest corner of the state, the Taconic Mountains are even older than the Greens. Stretching along the New York border from Bennington to Lake Bomoseen, the mountains produce an abundance of rain from clouds moving across them from the west—creating the lakes that characterize the area as well as several rivers, including Otter Creek, the longest in the state. Between the two mountain ranges, the Valley of Vermont is a sliver running some 85 miles from Brandon to Stamford, roughly corresponding to Route 7. Formed of limestone sediments, the valley has rich soil for farming and the marble deposits that made Rutland rich.

Farther north, the sky opens up in a broad, flat plain known as the Champlain Lowlands. Stretched some 20 miles wide between the Green Mountains and Lake Champlain, the valley was scooped out by a glacial lake, which deposited soil rich in organic matter that has made this area prime farmland. The agricultural base is further enhanced by the fact that this area is warmer and has a longer growing season than anywhere else in the state. On the other side of the mountains, in the eastern part of the state, the Vermont Piedmont is an area of rolling foothills that descend to the Connecticut River. Stretching from Brattleboro all the way up to Lake Memphremagog, it's a transitional area that also gets the brunt of rain coming off the mountains. Lastly, way up in the northeast corner of the state, the Northeastern Highlands are actually an extension of the White Mountains of New Hampshire. This gives the high country here a totally different look and feel than the rest of the state, with exposed granite cliffs, hardscrabble soil, and numbingly cold temperatures in winter. The harshness and isolation of the area, however, has left a dramatically unspoiled landscape that is often referred to as the most purely Vermont in Vermont.

GEOLOGY

In an eschatological mood, New England poet Robert Frost once mused about whether the world would end in fire or ice. Without taking sides on that question, it's fair to say that fire and ice played equally dramatic roles in the *beginnings* of his adopted state. Fire came first, in the form of molten hot lava that bubbled up violently from the earth's core starting more than a billion years ago. At that time, Vermont's eastern border was waterfront property, leading the edge of a proto-continent known as Laurentia. As the tectonic plate that held Laurentia moved slowly eastward 500 million years ago, it folded under its neighbor and melted, causing an upwelling of magma beneath the surface of the ocean. That upwelling formed a chain of island peaks off the coast of the continent. Eventually, the landmass of Laurentia crashed into these islands during the Ordovician period around 440 million years ago, pushing them up into what is now the Taconic Mountains of southwestern Vermont.

About a hundred million years later, in the Devonian period, Laurentia rammed into another subcontinent to the south called Avalonia, rolling over the smaller landmass to create more upwelling of magma. At the same time, geologically speaking, the continent collided with its neighboring continent, Baltica—the precursor to Europe—causing the ocean floor between them to buckle and fold back over the continent. The combination created the Green Mountains, which at that point were Himalayan-size peaks 15,000 feet high and must have been an awesome sight. A bit later, during the Triassic period, a great fault opened up in the middle of the region, creating a 100-mile-long rift valley that would later become the Connecticut River.

At this time, all of the world's continents

briefly joined together in a giant landmass called Pangaea. The commingling didn't last long, however. By the Jurassic period, 200 million years ago, the continents were again on the move, and North America and Europe split up to create the Atlantic Ocean. (Concurrently, a field of volcanoes opened up in the area of New Hampshire, creating the massive granite peaks of the White Mountains, younger than the Greens by several hundred million years.) New England's fiery birth was followed by a long period of erosion and settling before fire handed off its job to ice—and the last great ice age began.

Temperatures began to cool gradually about a million years ago. By the Pleistocene epoch, some 80,000 years ago (a mere hiccup in geologic time), a massive ice sheet began to build up over Canada, more than a mile thick in places. As it did, the sheer weight of the ice caused it to flow southward in a huge glacier, leveling the earth, gouging out valleys, and breaking off mountaintops as it flowed. Rolling and ebbing across the mountains for several thousand years, the glaciers acted like a giant steamroller, grinding the Greens down to their current more modest heights and carving out long, deep trenches that would eventually fill with water to create the Northeast Kingdom's glacial lakes.

When the last of the glaciers retreated 15,000 years ago, it closed off the Connecticut River Valley and filled it with meltwater to create a huge inland lake named Lake Hitchcock. For more than 2,000 years, the lake stretched 200 miles from Connecticut to Vermont's Northeast Kingdom. (It was probably quite a sight, colored the striking azure blue of the glacial lakes that now grace Canada and Patagonia.) Another glacial lake, Lake Vermont, formed to the west of New England and drained into modern-day Lake Champlain. When the ice dams finally broke, all of the accumulated water drained down the Connecticut and St.

Lawrence Rivers, creating the Vermont we know today.

Global warming notwithstanding, some geologists surmise that our present period is just a brief interlude between ice ages—and Frost might get his answer when the glaciers roll down from Canada again.

CLIMATE

Welcome to New England, where the saying goes, "If you don't like the weather, wait a minute!" With such extremes of wet, hot, cold, and windy, sometimes deciding what coat to wear can take the better part of a morning. The changeability in Vermont's weather comes courtesy of its location on the dividing line between the cold polar air mass to the north and warm tropical air currents from the south. Sometimes one wins out, sometimes the other; but neither goes without a fight. Add a constant supply of moisture from the ocean on one side and a great lake on the other, and you are guaranteed an unpredictable mix. Of all six New England states, Vermont's weather is arguably the most capricious—with the long, flat Canadian plains blasting it with cold air out of the north and the line of mountains dumping moisture from the west.

Despite the regular precipitation, however, Vermont sees more than its fair share of clear days, when the sky is blue and you can see for hundreds of miles from the peak of Mount Mansfield. Moreover, the moderating effect of the warm Gulf Stream ocean currents ensures that for the most part the region doesn't see the same extremes of temperature that affect the middle part of the country. Both summers and winters are comparatively mild—though it might not seem that way in the middle of a frigid January cold snap or the sweltering dog days of August.

The coldest part of the year often occurs between Christmas and New Year's, when the thermometer can drop far below zero in the

Northeast Kingdom and sweaters are piled two or three on top of each other to combat the chill. That snap of extreme cold is often followed by a period of milder weather known as the "January thaw." But that only sets the stage for February, when the region sees the bulk of its snowfall—which can be measured in feet, not inches, in the northern part of the state and the mountains.

After such lashings, you'd think Vermonters would deserve a nice spring, but sadly, they rarely get it. Rather, winter tapers off into a prolonged cold season known as "mud season." Despite the melting snow and thawing topsoil, the deeper subsoil often remains frozen, leaving the resulting water nowhere to go but into soupy puddles and shoe-linings. This is the weather that the famous L. L. Bean made his boots for. Just when Vermonters think they can't take it anymore (somewhere around mid-May), summer finally bursts gloriously upon the scene, bypassing spring entirely and instilling a collective amnesia in residents, who promptly forget the cold ever existed. Summer can be a wonderful time in Vermont, with strings of clear, sunny days and the temperature rarely topping 80 degrees (though humidity from the ocean can make a sticky time of it).

Quickly after Labor Day comes many Vermonters' favorite season—fall. There's a reason so many Hollywood movies have been filmed against a backdrop of a New England autumn. The days are crisp but not yet cold, and the air is often dry and pleasantly breezy. As the green chlorophyll leaches out of the tree leaves, it leaves the spectacular reds, oranges, and yellows of Vermont's star attraction—its famed fall foliage. As October approaches, the days quickly get colder and darker. Before they surrender to winter, however, the state is virtually guaranteed at least one week of politically-incorrectly-named "Indian summer," when the mercury climbs back into the 70s and 80s for one last spectacular respite from the cold. For many, this combines the best of New England weather—sun, dry air, and fiery foliage.

ENVIRONMENTAL ISSUES

Due to a low population density and generally enlightened populace, Vermont has few environmental issues to speak of. Tight zoning regulations and strong historic preservation laws have kept development in check in all but a few communities; if problems exist, it's usually from disgruntled landowners who are stymied by bureaucracy that prevents them from getting the variance they need. Vermont is also one of only two states in the country that has banned billboards and other forms of outdoor advertising on the highway—a fact almost immediately noticeable in the broad mountain vistas that suddenly materialize when crossing into the state from New Hampshire, Massachusetts, or New York. Vermont's regulatory economy has ensured that nearly all of the state enjoys clean air and water, even as efforts have been made to clean up the pollution of the mills and factories that boosted the economy in the 20th century.

That's not to say that Vermont doesn't have its problems. Isolated chemical factories and power plants continue to cause pollution in some specific areas. Elsewhere, the same kind of big-box blight that has caused sprawl in other parts of the country has infected some parts of Vermont—most noticeably in Rutland, Barre, and the southern fringes of Burlington. Another challenge confronting modern Vermont is forest management—that is, how to ensure lumbering jobs and keep the timber industry sustainable while preserving forest for recreational uses and animal habitat. While cutting had decimated up to 80 percent of the state's forests before World War II, an aggressive campaign of replanting, coupled with tax incentives to farmers and foresters to retain their land rather than sell it for development, led to a return of forest land across the state—and with it, a rebound in

VERMONT'S GREEN REPORT CARD

When *National Geographic Traveler* magazine rated the world's destinations (via a survey of 200 specialists in sustainable tourism) on how they have dealt with development pressures, environmental problems, and mass tourism, Vermont came out at the top of the heap. Specific criteria for the rankings included environmental and ecological quality, social and cultural integrity, conditions of historic buildings and archaeological sites, aesthetic appeal, quality of tourism management, and outlook for the future. In all of these, Vermont came in at number five—on the entire planet. Moreover, the report calls out the state's dedication to conservation and environmental concerns, as well as its outlawing of billboards. Apparently they don't call it the Green Mountain State for nothing.

population of many animal species. In addition, the Vermont Land Trust has acquired many new state lands for preservation, including a 130,000-acre tract up in the Northeast Kingdom purchased from the Champion International Paper Company in 1999, ensuring that open space will always be a part of Vermont's unique landscape.

Finally, Vermont remains a hotbed of opposition to nuclear power, directed against the Vermont Yankee nuclear power plant outside Brattleboro. Several years ago, when Vermont denied plant owner Entergy a permit to renew its license, the company sued the state. After several years of back and forth, Entergy won in federal court in 2012 on the grounds that only the federal government could decide the issue. While that decision allowed the plant to remain open 20 years, however, it hardly quelled the opposition among local activists—or the efforts to stop it. Currently, the decision is under appeal in a case that is expected to eventually go to the Supreme Court. At the same time the state, led by governor Peter Shumlin, continues to seek procedural grounds to close the plant. But for now, at least, nuclear power is alive and well in Vermont.

Flora and Fauna

FLORA

There's a reason they call them the Green Mountains. Vermont's landscape is predominantly forested, covered in a green shag carpet of growth in every direction you look (often including up). While centuries of lumbering and land-clearing have taken their toll on the woods of the region, recent decades have seen an active forest preservation movement, as well as reclaiming of abandoned farms by trees, ensuring that the landscape continues to be a wooded one.

Trees

Traditionally, the forests of Vermont have been divided into three zones: an oak-chestnut forest in the south; a hemlock–white pine–transition hardwood forest across much of the state below 2,400 feet; and a spruce–northern hardwood forest in higher altitudes and in the Northeast Kingdom. Of course, this greatly simplifies a landscape in which dozens of different species of trees each have their own range and habitat—but it does provide a good working framework for understanding local fauna.

Chestnuts roasting on an open fire may have been part of the holidays for early New Englanders, but those days are sadly gone. After surviving in New England for millions of years, the mighty chestnut was wiped out by a blight imported from Japan in the early part of the 20th century. The forests of southern Vermont, however, are still abundant with red oak, scarlet oak, hickory, maple, birch, and beech.

By far the majority of the state is covered by a mix of broadleaf trees and evergreens. The forest is dominated by oak and maple—including the famous sugar maple that yields the region's annual crop of maple syrup every spring. The most common tree is the white oak, named for the color of its bark and prized for both its straight timber and wide-spreading canopy. Arguably, this is the best region for leaf peeping, since maples produce some of the brightest colors, while oaks are slower to turn, extending the season and providing a range of colors at any one time.

The phenomenon of leaves changing color is less about beauty than science. Leaves begin to change from bright green to red, orange, and yellow as a way of getting ready for winter, when there is not enough light or water for photosynthesis. Trees use winter as a time to rest, living off the food they have stored up during summertime rather than on the energy created by their leaves. As the green chlorophyll disappears from their leaves, the green fades into yellow, red, purple, brown, and orange hues—many of which are amplified by the leftover glucose trapped in the leaves after the tree has stopped photosynthesizing.

White pine becomes more common as you travel north, where it can frequently be found growing on reclaimed agricultural land. That tree has smoother bark than its cousin, the red or Norway pine; to tell them apart, count the needles: White pine needles grow in clusters of five (W-H-I-T-E), while red needles grow in clusters of three (R-E-D). Other trees growing in this region include hemlock and ash.

As you climb up into the mountains and Northeastern Highlands, the deciduous trees eventually give way to a boreal forest of spruce and fir. Unlike pines, whose needles grow in clusters, on spruces and firs the needles are directly attached to the stem. These coniferous trees are better suited to the harsh climates of higher altitudes. Mixed in with the evergreens is an understory of hardy broadleaf trees, including aspen, beech, and birch. Few New England scenes are more iconic than a stand of white-and-black-striped birch trees in winter, or festooned with canary-yellow leaves in fall.

Flowers

The jewel of the New England woodlands is the delicate lady slipper, a member of the orchid family that grows in wetland areas and gets its name from down-curving flowers that resemble women's shoes. The translucent flower, found in pink, white, and yellow varieties, is notoriously difficult to transplant or grow, since it relies on companionable fungi in the soil for its nutrients. If you are lucky enough to see one in the wild, take care not to disturb it, since some species are endangered.

Much more common, if no less beloved by naturalists, is trillium, so called because of its distinctive three-petal flowers. The flower grows in many colors throughout the Vermont woods, including bright white, deep red, and the particularly beautiful painted trillium, which sports a magenta center tapering off to white edges. One of the first flowers to bloom in April is the bloodroot, which carpets the ground with clusters of white flowers. As the season progresses, other wildflowers visible in the fields and meadows include the fuchsia-colored, anemone-like New England aster; orange clusters of wood poppy; wild bleeding heart; bright-red wild columbine with its

WILDLIFE PHOTOGRAPHY TIPS

You know the feeling—you finally get that moose, black bear, or loon in your viewfinder and snap what you think is the perfect shot, only to get a picture back later of a far-off indistinct blob. Wildlife can be notoriously difficult to photograph well. Here are a few tips for your jaunts in the woods of Vermont.

- A good zoom lens is essential for getting close to your subject. You'll need at least 300 millimeters, if not 400 millimeters. Alternatively, get a digital camera with at least 4.0 or 5.0 megapixels (6.0 or 7.0 would be better). That way, you can "zoom" in on the computer later and the image will hold its resolution.

- Pay attention to the background. Animals with dark bodies will look better against a light background, such as an overcast sky. Those with light bodies will look better against a dark background like water or a blue sky. Avoid backgrounds that are too busy, like a tree-filled forest or green field.

- Bright light isn't always the best for photography, since direct sun can wash out details or create too harsh a contrast. Take photos in the early morning or late afternoon, when soft, indirect light will flatter your subjects. Luckily, that's the time when most animals are most active anyway.

- Good hunters know to let their prey come to them, and photography is no different. Find a hidden spot upwind from a water source, assume a comfortable position, and wait. Once the animals feel the coast is clear, they will come out of hiding to give you a good shot.

distinctive tube-like flowers; and the ghostly sharp-lobed hepatica, which grows in deep woods and swamps and features eight blue-purple petals arranged around an explosion of fine white stamens.

FAUNA

The best opportunities for seeing wildlife in Vermont occur along the water. Many state parks have wetland areas that are prime viewing territory for wading birds, and even with mammals, you are much more apt to stumble upon a moose or black bear from the vantage of a kayak than while hiking along a trail. Most of New England's fauna is harmless—the charismatic mega-fauna of the western states has been mostly hunted to extinction, despite dubious reports of mountain lion sightings that crop up periodically. Even so, use caution when approaching a moose or black bear—especially if its young are in the area. You don't want to get on the receiving end of antlers or claws.

Land Mammals

The lord of the forest is a gentle giant—and that's a good thing, too, since coming face-to-face with a moose is a humbling experience. Up to six feet tall, nine feet long, and with an antler span of five-and-a-half feet, a bull moose often startles those unprepared for just how *big* it is. Because of that, the herbivore has few enemies—natural or otherwise. In recent years, the moose population in Vermont has been growing, now numbering around 3,000 animals. The best places for spotting them are in the Northeast Kingdom, especially in the Island Pond area, and in Granville Gulf in the Mad River Valley. Even in the far southern corners of the state, however, it's possible run into a moose at night. Of course that presents problems as well. Numerous times each season a car is totaled after hitting one of the 2,000-pound beasts, which then serenely walks away from the accident. Take care when driving at night, especially in the Northeast Kingdom, and especially during the spring and summer

© KARE TRABANT

White-tailed deer are common in the backwoods of Vermont.

months, when the giant animals range widely in search of food. In the autumn, moose retreat to the deep forest, where they are much harder to encounter.

Not quite as imposing, but majestic in their own way, are the white-tailed deer that are common in the backwoods. At one point in Vermont's history, deer were hunted almost to extinction; thanks to more stringent hunting and forest protection laws since the 1930s, the population has made a comeback and now numbers more than 150,000 animals.

The last documented specimen of mountain lion—also called catamount—was taken in Maine in 1938, and despite wishful thinking among biologists, the giant cat is generally accepted to be extinct from the region. The smaller bobcat, however, is quite commonly sighted, often mistaken for a small dog. And in the upper Northeast Kingdom a few years ago, officials confirmed for the first time in 40 years a sighting of a Canada lynx, a larger cat identifiable by the pointed tufts on its ears.

Not to be confused with the more aggressive grizzlies of western states, the timid black bear is a reclusive tree-dwelling animal. It can sometimes be seen exploring garbage dumps at night. In recent years, its numbers have been increasing (to as many as 6,000 at last count), which has caused run-ins with campers as the bears search for food. If you encounter one, stay at a safe distance and bellow loudly—that is usually enough to scare one away. Red foxes inhabit both open fields and mixed forest, while the larger gray fox prefers the deep woods. Coyotes are more apt to be heard than seen. Gray wolves, however, were eradicated by farmers in the 19th century. Periodically, efforts emerge to try and reintroduce a breeding population to the state, but so far, they have not succeeded in garnering political support.

The most common mammals, by far, are rodents, which exist in multitudes. Gray and red squirrels, chipmunks, and raccoons are familiar sights in both suburban and rural areas. Wilderness locales are home to skunks, martens, minks, ermines, opossums, six types of shrew, two types of mole, mice, rabbits (including cottontail, jackrabbit, and snowshoe hare), flying squirrels, beavers, voles, otters, and porcupines. One of the lesser-known rodents is the fisher, a large mink-like animal known for its vicious temperament that has become more common in past years. In addition to smaller rodents, the fisher has been known to prey on raccoons, porcupines, and even small deer. Finally, Vermont is home to nine species of bats, which roost in abandoned barns and trees and can often be heard screeching at night in search of insects to eat.

Reptiles and Amphibians

The streams and ponds of Vermont teem with frogs, toads, turtles, and other amphibians. Anyone who has camped near standing water in New England is familiar with the deep-throated sounds of bullfrogs, which can seem like competing bullhorns at night as the eight-inch-long males puff up their resonant throat sacks in competition for mates. An even more cherished sound in spring is the high-pitched chirping of the spring peeper frogs, which heralds the beginning of warm weather. A half-dozen different types of turtle inhabit the area, mostly concentrated around Lake Champlain; most common is the painted turtle, which sports colorful mosaics of yellow stripes on its neck and shell. More rare is the common snapping turtle, which can live up to its name if provoked. Wetland areas and swamps are also home to many species of salamander, which outdo each other with arresting shades of red, blue, and yellow spots and stripes. The most striking of all is the Day-Glo orange body of the eastern newt.

The most commonly encountered snake is the common garter snake, a black-and-green striped snake that is ubiquitous throughout the state. Aquatic habitats around Lake Champlain are inhabited by the large northern water snake, which is harmless despite its aggressive demeanor. Woodland habitats are home to the ringneck, red-bellied, and milk snakes, among other species. Only one type of snake in Vermont is venomous: the timber rattler, which is identifiable by its dark W-shaped crossbands on a tan body. The snake is exceedingly rare, however, and is only sighted with any frequency in the lakes area around Castleton and Fair Haven. Thankfully, rattlers tend to shun areas inhabited by humans—and hibernate a full eight months out of the year, from September to April. If hiking in the backcountry, however, be wary of their distinctive dry rattling sound.

Insects and Arachnids

Ask any Vermonter about native insects, and he or she is apt to immediately identify two: the mosquito and the black fly. The former find ample breeding ground in the wetlands of the region and feast annually on the blood of hikers and beachgoers. The black fly is, if anything, even more vicious. Thankfully it is more limited in both range and time period, thriving only in the late spring and early summer (or as the saying goes, from Mother's Day to Father's Day). The other regional scourge is the gypsy moth, which every 10 years or so appears in the form of thousands of tiny caterpillars that decimate the foliage. Many attempts have been made to curtail the menace, including introduction of a parasitic fly that eats gypsy moth larvae. Unfortunately, the fly also eats larvae of the luna moth, a delicate greenish moth with a wingspan of up to five inches that is Vermont's most beautiful insect. In recent years, the luna moth has made a comeback, and it is a more common nighttime visitor in the region.

Vermont is also rich breeding ground for spiders, most of which are absolutely harmless. The only poisonous variety, however, is

© KARE TRABANT

Chickadees are everywhere.

the black widow, which is recognizable by its jet-black body with a broken red hourglass on its abdomen. These spiders are extremely rare; while their venom is a neurotoxin, only about 1 percent of bites end in death.

Birds

New England's location on the Atlantic Flyway from Canada makes the region prime bird-watching country. The region is home to some 200 species of birds that breed, winter, or live year-round in the region. Some common species like the black-and-white chickadee, blue jay, and cardinal are spotted commonly in both rural and urban areas. Others, like the elusive wood thrush, inhabit only the deep forest, where its liquid warblings reward hikers with a mellifluous serenade. Likewise, the ghostly "laughing" of the common loon is a common sound on northern lakes.

History

EARLY HISTORY
Native Inhabitants

Hard on the heels of the last glaciers retreating northward, humans began to move into the area now known as Vermont about 11,000 years ago. The first to arrive were a people called Paleoindians, who lived mainly in the area of Lake Champlain. For a time when water levels were higher, the lake backed up the St. Lawrence waterway to become an arm of the ocean, and the Paleoindians lived off its rich marine life. When the ocean disappeared, so did the people, who dispersed into other regions or became assimilated into new cultures. For the next few thousand years, Vermont was home to two distinct cultures, the Archaic

A statue of Samuel de Champlain stands near where he landed on Isle La Motte in 1609.

Early Settlement

The first recorded entry of European settlers into Vermont came years before the Pilgrims touched down at Plymouth Rock. In 1609, French explorer Samuel de Champlain sailed with an Algonquin war party down the St. Lawrence River in a raiding party against their enemies, the Iroquois. He discovered the lake that now bears his name, sailing for several months around its rivers before leaving, never to return again. (He also left record of a mythical sea creature that is still said to live in the lake, which later generations would resurrect as "Champ.") As New France continued to expand in Canada and New England began to be populated in Massachusetts Bay and Virginia Colonies, the region that would become Vermont was largely ignored except for occasional forays by the French to trade furs with the Abenaki. In 1666, Fort St. Anne was briefly established on the Isle La Motte by New France's governor, Sieur de Courcelles, for protection against the incursions of the Dutch and their Mohawk allies from New Netherland to the West, but it was abandoned after only a few years.

As population increased, however, it was inevitable that Vermont would become attractive to those on all three sides of its borders. Between 1680 and 1763, the waterways of Vermont saw increasingly bloody clashes between the French and British, along with their Native American allies, who were seeking to control the fur trade and later the farmland along the Champlain and Connecticut River Valleys. The first permanent settlement in Vermont, Fort Dummer, was built in 1724 in modern-day Brattleboro as a defense against increasingly hostile Native American raids in that area. In the decades that followed, the British expanded their hold rapidly up the Connecticut River, at the same time that the French established settlements down along the shores of Lake Champlain.

culture from 7000 B.C. to 1500 B.C., a hunting and fishing people, and the Woodland culture from 1500 B.C. to 700 B.C., a more sedentary people who cultivated vegetables and hunted with bow and arrow. Finally, around A.D. 700, the latter people had developed into a distinct Native American tribe—the Abenaki, the "People of the Dawn."

Unlike the Iroquois Confederacy in upstate New York or the mighty Algonquin tribes of Quebec, the Abenaki were a small and unaffiliated tribe. Even at their height, the Abenaki consisted of bands of just a few hundred each, unlike the much larger populations of Native Americans in neighboring states. In spring and summer they lived in large villages along river floodplains including the Connecticut, Winooski, and Missisquoi, planting corn, beans, and squash; then, in the fall, they migrated to inland hunting grounds in search of moose, deer, and beaver for food and pelts.

It was the British who eventually won out. The French and Indian War, which broke out in the New World in 1754, was but a small theater in the larger Seven Years' War that was fought between European nations from India to the Caribbean. It had the result, however, of permanently wiping the French—as well as the Abenaki—out in the territory. By this time, the French had fortified Lake Champlain with two forts, one named Carillon (which would later be renamed Fort Ticonderoga) and the other Crown Point. Neither was any match for Lord Jeffrey Amherst, the British general who brought his troops up the valley in 1759 and sacked both of them. At the same time, the British raided villages of the Abenaki, who had allied with the French. The next year, the British under General James Wolfe pushed on all the way to Montreal, taking the city and forcing the French to sue for peace. The treaty of Paris in 1763 ended French occupation of the American colonies and set the boundary between Vermont and Canada at the 45th parallel. No sooner did the conflict between France and England end, however, than a new conflict began.

Flatlanders and Mountain Boys

Now that Vermont was rightly in the hands of the British colonists, the question immediately arose—which colonists? The land between the Connecticut River and Lake Champlain was a wild no-man's land that was immediately claimed by two competing interests, the newly formed colony of New Hampshire to the east, and the lands of New York, which had succeeded New Netherland to the west. Starting in the 1750s, the ambitious governor of New Hampshire, Benning Wentworth, began selling grants to the land across the Connecticut in what would become known as the New Hampshire Grants. More than 100 townships were established, including his namesake town of Bennington, hard up against the border of what is now New York.

The governor of that territory, De Witt Clinton, retaliated by demanding that Wentworth revoke his claims, taking the dispute all the way to England's King George III. The king decided in favor of New York, setting the boundary at the Connecticut River and demanding that the owners of the New Hampshire grants pay taxes anew to New York. The settlers of these territories, some 20,000 to 30,000 strong, were loath to serve their new master, who employed a manorial land system that was foreign to the freemen who had come out of the town meeting system in Massachusetts and Connecticut. The first stirrings of Vermont identity began with meetings of the leaders of these territories at a tavern in Bennington. "The gods of the valleys are not the gods of the hills," defiantly stated one of their leaders, the towering giant Ethan Allen. Losing their fight in court, Allen and the other rabble-rousers took up arms to form a militia called the Green Mountain Boys, ridiculing the flatlanders from New York and stirring up riots against New York sheriffs that were known as the Anti-Rent wars. By 1773, the Green Mountain Boys were burning houses, beating rent-collectors, and publicly humiliating New York sympathizers. The skirmishes culminated in a courthouse riot in the town of Westminster in 1775 that left two Vermonters dead—the so-called "Westminster riot." The incident helped galvanize public support on the side of the Green Mountain Boys, solidifying resistance to the New York overlords. By this time, however, world events had been set in motion that would have a much greater effect on the course of history in Vermont—eventually making it independent of any master.

WAR AND REVOLUTION
The Road to Revolution
Even a decade before the outbreak of the

THE NAMING OF VERMONT

Despite their long-time presence around Lake Champlain, the French don't seem to have used any variation on the words "green mountains"— or *les montagnes vertes*—to describe their region. Rather, evidence suggests that the name of the state was a Frenchification of the English, and not the other way around. In fact, the term Green Mountains was not in widespread use until nigh 1772, when the Green Mountain Boys were starting their rampage against the New Yorkers. When, several years later, the men of the New Hampshire Grants decided to form their own republic, they first took the name New Connecticut, because leaders such as Ethan Allen had originally hailed from that state.

It was Allen's boyhood friend, Philadelphia doctor and self-taught scholar Thomas Young, who originally suggested the change to "Vermont." Young sent a copy of the Pennsylvania constitution as a model for the new republic and at the same time recommended the name. It's anyone's guess why he suggested a translation into French—perhaps his personal love of that country or a renewed admiration for the nation as the "enemy of my enemy" (Great Britain). Over the years, some historians have criticized Young's choice of words as improper French, as it departs from the literal *montagnes vertes*. In truth, such criticism is unfounded. While not commonly used now, the French word *mont* is an older word for "mountain." Furthermore, the switching in word order of noun and adjective is a well-established naming convention in French (such as in Beaumont or Belmont), and in other French names, such as Verdon, the *t* in *vert* disappears. Thus, the naming of Vermont is on solid linguistic ground, even if the why of it all remains a mystery.

Revolutionary War, few American colonists even considered independence from the Crown. Relations with England, while sometimes tense, were mutually beneficial for both parties, giving the colonies protection and a ready market for their goods, and giving England a source of raw materials and income. The French and Indian War directly benefited not only the burgeoning territory of Vermont, but also the larger colonies of Massachusetts, New York, and New Hampshire, who could now trade without competition from the French or fear of raids from the Algonquin or Mohawk tribes. Millions of words have been spilled over what caused the quick snowball to war, but it essentially comes down to one: taxes.

Saddled with debt from its mammoth military undertakings, England decided to levy taxes on the colonies to pay for the war. After all, the Crown reasoned, hadn't the colonies been the ones who benefited the most from the defeat of the French and Indian tribes? Unfortunately for England, the colonists saw

things differently. When the British Crown levied a series of taxes directly on the colonies starting in 1765, the American colonists reacted with violent protests, including the famous Boston Tea Party of December 1773, when colonists dumped 90,000 pounds of tea into Boston Harbor. From there it was only a matter of time until overt hostilities broke out, starting with the Battles of Concord and Lexington in April 1775 and followed by the much larger battle of Bunker Hill in Boston two months later. The British lost more than 1,000 men at Bunker Hill, while the colonists only lost half that, showing the world that the American Revolution was definitely *on*.

As for Vermont, well, from the beginning the Green Mountain Boys threw in their lot with the Revolutionaries—making a short rhetorical leap from resistance to the tyranny of New York to resistance to the tyranny of England. Just a month after the Battles of Lexington and Concord, Ethan Allen and his men were planning an attack on Fort Ticonderoga.

Only at the last minute were they joined by a Connecticut colonel named Benedict Arnold, who had been charged with an identical task by the militia of that state. While accounts differ, it seems Arnold and Allen agreed to a hasty joint command, taking the fort with a scant 80 men and not a shot fired. A consummate boaster, however, Allen made sure he got most of the credit for the raid. The incident made him an instant hero, bolstering his image throughout the colonies and granting new legitimacy to the Boys' fight for independence.

Shortly thereafter, a second group of Green Mountain Boys, under Allen's able second Seth Warner, captured Crown Point. Soon, however, Allen got his comeuppance after a botched raid on the British town of St. John—and then an even more harebrained scheme to capture Montreal with 100 men in September 1775. Captured by the British in the engagement, Allen was held as a prisoner of war in England for the next two and a half years. Control of the Boys passed to Warner, while larger preparations for the defense of Lake Champlain were overseen by Arnold. Whatever ignominious deeds Arnold would perpetrate later in the war, he is still remembered as a hero in the Champlain region for his noble defense of the lake.

Throughout the summer of 1776, he worked his men feverishly to build a ragtag flotilla of some 15 gunboats to defend the lake against an imminent attack down the lake from British general Richard Montgomery. The fateful battle took place in October off the shore of Valcour Island, where Arnold had set an ambush for the much larger British fleet. After a daring nighttime escape through the British line, all but four of Arnold's ships were destroyed. He was able to escape, however, and the British retreated back up the lake to repair and resupply, delaying their conquest of the lake for another year. That year would give the Americans precious time to raise troops

and prepare their defenses, ensuring that the Revolution wasn't over before it began. As far as turning points of history go, Arnold's defense of Champlain may just have saved the United States.

Despite the war, however, Vermonters hadn't forgotten their own struggle for independence from the hated New Yorkers to the west. With Ethan Allen's capture, leadership of the struggle went to his younger brother Ira, who was both shorter in stature and shrewder in politics than his brother. With Ira's urging, delegates from the New Hampshire Grants met several times in the town of Dorset, where they agreed to form a political entity removed from jurisdiction of both New Hampshire and New York. In January 1777, the assembly officially declared itself an independent state they called New Connecticut—changed to "Vermont" that June upon the recommendation of a Philadelphia doctor.

Even as the delegates were ratifying their new constitution in Windsor, however, the hounds of war began barking again across the state. A new British army under General John "Gentleman Johnnie" Burgoyne was moving down the valley with some 10,000 troops—and this time, he wouldn't be turning back.

Mount Independence and Hubbardton

When colonial militias took over Fort Ticonderoga on the New York side of Lake Champlain early in the Revolutionary War, they immediately encountered a problem. The fort had been built to fend off invasions from the south during the French and Indian War, but would be of little use in countering the anticipated British thrust down Lake Champlain from Canada. General Philip Schuyler, who took command of the northern theater for the Americans, attempted to solve the problem by building a massive fortification on the high ground of the Vermont side of the lake to protect Ticonderoga and defend against a northern attack. Begun right after the signing of the Declaration of Independence on July 4, 1776, the breastworks were jubilantly named after the new document as Mount Independence.

In the summer of 1776, more than 12,000 defenders lived there, making it the largest military city in the New World at the time. By the time of the British attack the following summer, however, many troops had been pulled away to defend New York, and those at the forts numbered less than 3,000, too few to adequately protect against outflanking by the British. General Arthur St. Clair, who was commanding the forts after Arnold's departure, woke up in Fort Ticonderoga on the morning of July 4, 1777, to find that the British were scaling the heights of Mount Defiance on the New York side of the lake with cannons and would soon command an invincible position over his troops. In the dead of night, he ordered retreat of the entire garrison across a floating bridge between "Fort Ti" and Mount Independence.

As St. Clair fled south, he was pursued by British troops under General Simon Fraser. The Redcoats eventually caught up with the Americans on a hilltop outside the little town of Hubbardton. There, St. Clair had placed his most experienced men, a regiment of Green Mountain Boys under colonel Seth Warner, who executed a brilliant set of maneuvers to temporarily delay the British in the short but bloody Battle of Hubbardton. Despite the heavy death toll—354 American casualties to 183 British—the brave rear-guard action allowed St. Clair to escape with the bulk of his troops. Many of them would return a few months later to best Burgoyne at the Battle of Saratoga in upstate New York, the eventual turning point of the war.

Before that crucial victory would take place, however, there were still Gentleman Johnnie's

men to reckon with. That showdown would occur a scant few weeks after Hubbardton during the Battle of Bennington. The battle would prove to be the first in which the Americans beat the British in combat, a fact that more than any other, perhaps, gave Vermont the legitimacy it needed to finally become its own independent republic.

The Battle of Bennington

Fresh from victory at Fort Ticonderoga, Burgoyne was marching down the Hudson River Valley to meet up with British troops from New York. The plan was to cut off New England from supplies and reinforcements from the rest of the colonies, thereby setting it up for easy capture. Feeling the pinch of lack of supplies himself, however, the general made a fatal mistake when he decided along the way to capture a large storehouse of food and munitions in the small town of Bennington, Vermont.

Under command of the German colonel Friedrich Baum, Burgoyne sent some 500 troops—including several hundred dreaded Hessian mercenaries—to raid the town. Unbeknownst to him, however, the American colonel John Stark had previously set off from New Hampshire with 1,500 troops of his own. On August 16, Stark took the battle to the enemy, swarming up a ridge along the Wolloomsac River to attack Baum's position. In a short but vicious battle, his militiamen killed Baum and captured many of his men. Certain of victory, the excited Americans began pursuing the enemy, but they were surprised by a relief column of another 600 Hessian soldiers under Lieutenant Colonel Von Breymann. Stark was pushed to retreat back toward Bennington. The tide of the battle turned once more, however, with the arrival of Warner and 300 of his Green Mountain Boys, who had marched from Manchester, Vermont. In the second engagement, the Germans were routed and fled back to the Hudson, while the Americans claimed victory.

The battle was an embarrassing defeat for Burgoyne, whose army suffered some 900 casualties to Stark's 70. At a time in the war when American morale was low, the battle also proved once again that backcountry farmers and militiamen could defeat the most disciplined troops of Europe. Just two months later, with his forces depleted and short on provisions, Gentleman Johnnie was forced to surrender at Saratoga, and the continued existence of a new United States was all but assured.

The Vermont Republic

As any history book will tell you, the Revolutionary War was won not by the Americans, but by the French and Spanish, who entered the war after the victory at Saratoga and blockaded American ports against the British, swinging the tide of battle in favor of the newly independent republic. In 1783, a full decade after the Boston Tea Party, British general Charles Cornwallis surrendered at Yorktown, leaving 13 newly independent states.

Vermont was not among them. Despite the bravery of its militiamen in the early years of the war, Vermont was simply too much of a hot potato for the shaky new Continental Congress to touch. New York still refused to release its claim on the land, and later, southern slave-owning states objected to the admission of another free state into the Union. That left Vermont in the unique position of being an independent republic from 1777 to 1791, when it was finally admitted as the 14th state in a compromise that also admitted Kentucky a year later.

In the intervening years, Vermont conducted all of the affairs of a sovereign state, electing its first governor, Thomas Chittenden, in 1778, printing its own money, and even asserting its right to enter into a separate peace treaty with England. In fact, Ethan and Ira Allen

went so far as to make overtures to England to bring the republic back under control of the Crown—though to this day it remains unclear how much it was an honest tender and how much it was a ruse to force the United States to act to bring Vermont into the fold. The Allen brothers continued to throw a long shadow over the state from their new home base near Burlington, where they became rich as land speculators through their new Onion River Trading Company. Whatever was going on politically in the state, residents were now freed of control of both England and New York, and many were elated about their new ability to control their own destiny. With a rich store of natural resources, they set about doing what Yankees did best—making money.

19TH AND 20TH CENTURIES
Boom Times

After Vermont finally became a state in 1791, a boom of speculators descended on the state. In 20 years, its population more than doubled to 217,000 in 1810. Pasture was cleared for sheep and cattle, and as the trees came down, business boomed in lumber and potash. While the economy was primarily agricultural, new technologies also spurred the production of woolen and cotton mills on the state's fast-flowing rivers. As the industrialists began amassing wealth, they turned toward educational and cultural pursuits. Two universities, the University of Vermont and Middlebury College, were founded in 1791 and 1800, respectively.

From the beginning of Vermont's statehood, the state was split politically between the Federalists, who aligned themselves with business interests and strong federal government and held sway on the east side of the Green Mountains, and the Democratic-Republicans, who favored a more agrarian economy with a strong interest in states' rights and dominated in the Allens' strongholds west of the mountains. Gradually, the latter group lost support

THE WILL TO SECEDE

Vermont started out as an independent republic, and some want it to end up that way. Led by citizens angered by what they consider the country's post-9/11 tightening of freedoms, the state's secessionist movement is getting plenty of attention—and followers. "Vermont did not join the Union to become part of an empire," argues the group, known as the Second Vermont Republic. Attracting everyone from descendants of old Vermonter stock to New York transplants, the plucky group explains it this way:

Vermont seceded from the British Empire in 1777 and stood free for 14 years, until 1791. Its constitution—which preceded the U.S. Constitution by more than a decade—was the first to prohibit slavery in the New World and to guarantee universal manhood suffrage. Vermont issued its own currency, ran its own postal service, developed its own foreign relations, grew its own food, made its own roads, and paid for its own militia. No other state, not even Texas, governed itself more thoroughly or longer before giving up its nationhood and joining the Union. Over the past 50 years, the U.S. government has grown too big, too corrupt, and too aggressive toward the world, toward its own citizens, and toward local democratic institutions. It has abandoned the democratic vision of its founders and eroded Americans' fundamental freedoms.

The group held a convention at the Vermont State House in September 2012 and is aiming to gain enough support to hold a statewide vote on independence.

as the state assembly joined the rest of New England in supporting the Federalists, and the Allen brothers and their Green Mountain Boys eventually saw their political sway slip away.

Nationally, the Federalists reached their apogee when John Adams was elected president in 1796. A backlash, however, soon found the southern agrarians in power under Virginian Thomas Jefferson, and the influence of the Federalists waned. Vermont joined with the other New England states in opposing the War of 1812 (thankfully, a push to secede and form the New England Confederacy around this time failed). In spite of that, Vermont wasn't spared the fighting. In a case of déjà vu all over again, 10,000 British troops, this time under General George Prevost, set out to march down the Champlain corridor, against only a few thousand American militiamen. Vermont was saved from battle by the heroics of naval commander Thomas MacDonough, whose flagship—felicitously named *Saratoga*—outdueled the British fleet and pounded the land positions, forcing them to retreat.

Social Ferment

The War of 1812 signaled the end of Vermont's big boom, even though industry continued to expand steadily through the next several decades. Renewed competition with British goods caused Vermont industry to suffer. At the same time, favorable tariffs for wool led to a rush of sheep grazing, changing the character of many farms from crop to livestock production. More than anything else, however, the times between the War of 1812 and the Civil War were ones of intense social change, as old ideas gave way to new ones.

For several decades, Vermont saw a wave of religious revivalism brought on by missionaries from Massachusetts and Connecticut who were determined to "civilize" their bumpkin cousins up north. As in the rest of the country, thousands of people gathered to see holy-rollers who toured the state as part of the Second Great Awakening.

As religious fervor waned in the 1830s, a new cause shook the state—abolitionism. Vermont, in fact, was one of the first states to write anti-slavery laws into its constitution, even before it was a state. One of the first articles in its constitution of 1786 expressly forbid ownership of slaves. Now, spurred on by the fiery speeches of Massachusetts abolitionist leader William Lloyd Garrison and escaped slave Frederick Douglass, the cause was taken up again all over the state. By 1850, the state was nearly universally in support of abolitionism, and its leaders in national politics were increasingly outspoken in their condemnation of slavery.

No amount of speechifying, however, could prevent the inevitable political clash of the Civil War. While none of the actual fighting of the war took place in Vermont, the state answered the call for troops, fielding 17 regiments by war's end and participating in all of the major battles in Virginia, Maryland, and Pennsylvania. In fact, the Second Vermont Brigade played a decisive role in the battle of Gettysburg, when it came to the aid of the Army of the Potomac after the devastating Pickett's Charge threatened to break the back of the army. At that crucial moment, the Vermonters executed a series of military maneuvers to outflank the Confederate line and cause the rebels to rout, thus saving the day for the Union and ensuring a victory in the battle that spelled the beginning of the end for the Confederacy—another turning point for which the country has Vermont to thank.

Civil War to World War II

The time after the Civil War was a period of flux for the state. The railroad had arrived in Vermont in 1850, transforming patterns of settlement and trade. "Urban" centers grew as rural areas remained static, and new industries emerged that changed the character of the state.

The development of granite quarrying in Barre brought immigrants from Scotland, Italy, and French Canada to the state to cut stone, creating a highly skilled and prosperous workforce. At the same time, the discovery of marble in the Valley of Vermont enriched the town of Rutland and created the fortune of Redfield Proctor, who would become governor and U.S. Secretary of War. But friction with workers over wages led to labor strife and strikes into the first part of the 20th century.

By the early 20th century, Vermonters were already idealizing their agrarian past. Poet Robert Frost captured the public's yearning for a simpler era in verse—even if his poems held deeper, darker meanings below the surface. Frost lived in Shaftsbury from 1920, and brought many writers to the state with the Breadloaf Conference in Ripton. What he did in verse, artist Norman Rockwell would do with images, painting many of his neighbors into illustrations of idealized country life for decades from his home in Arlington.

Vermont's misty optimism came to a crashing halt after World War I in the Great Flood of 1927, a natural disaster that destroyed thousands of homes and decimated herds of livestock throughout the state. As the Great Depression hit, Vermont struggled with an economy that lagged behind the rest of the nation and was increasingly dependent on federal programs such as the Civilian Conservation Corps, which created 30 camps employing some 10,000 Vermonters to help build the state's park infrastructure.

At the same time, the Olympic Games at Lake Placid in nearby New York in 1932 spurred a winter sports craze throughout the state—starting with a rope tow on a small hill in Woodstock and spurred on by forestry chief Perry Merrill, who encouraged the development of ski resorts all over Vermont over the coming decades. As World War II came and went, that development more than any other would point the way to Vermont's economic rebirth.

Modern Times

By the mid-20th century, Vermont was undeniably struggling. Factory farms in the Midwest were making it difficult for Vermont's smaller farms and dairies to compete, and many went out of business or fell victim to consolidation. At the same time, cheaper textiles from the South spelled the end of Vermont's industrial mainstay. As the state entered the 1960s and 1970s, however, it found that the state's lack of commerce and industry added to its appeal as a tourist destination. With the development of the Federal Interstate system, more and more travelers flocked to Vermont to drive its mountain roads and explore its unspoiled villages. While the state first focused on summer tourism, it would actually be winter tourism in the form of ski resorts that would spell the biggest boon for the state. Not everyone welcomed the influx of visitors, of course, with long-time residents grousing about the "summer people" and "resortification" that threatened to upset the very balance that made Vermont such a popular destination to begin with. On the whole, however, Vermont has entered the 21st century gracefully, with a steady influx of visitors injecting cash into the state, and with a well-educated workforce able to succeed in the new knowledge-based economy.

Government and Economy

GOVERNMENT AND POLITICS

It's been said that democracy was founded in Greece and perfected in New England. When the Puritan settlers came to Vermont from Massachusetts and Connecticut, they brought with them the tradition of participatory democracy, wherein every free man was required to attend meetings that had legal standing to determine all the important matters in the town. While most Vermont towns are now run by an elected board of selectmen, the tradition of the town meeting still continues in the annual Town Meeting Day, which occurs each year on the first Tuesday in March. Then residents in each town gather to debate issues ranging from snowplowing to war in Iraq and to vote directly on binding resolutions by hand vote or secret ballot.

Like the rest of the states in the northeast, Vermont is reliably to the left of the aisle politically—its recent status as the first state in the nation to approve civil unions for gays and lesbians (and later the first state to approve gay marriage by an act of the legislature rather than a decision of the courts) is a good indication of that. Its politics are more complicated, however, than such easy stereotyping might suggest. From the first days of the Green Mountain Boys, Vermonters have held independence up as their watchword. On social matters, they've always evinced a live-and-let-live philosophy that has survived to the present day despite periodic revivals and temperance movements. Religion is not something that most people here wear on their sleeves, and tolerance toward people of different race, gender, and sexuality is par for the course. (Though some might argue that as it's one of the whitest states in the nation racial tolerance is rarely actually put to the test.)

On economic issues, however, the beliefs and practices of voters are much more conservative—part of the reason that Republicans dominated politics here well into the 1970s. Vermont's traditional independence has led at times to strong anti-tax sentiment and a resistance to "big government" handouts. That changed somewhat in 20th century, partly through the vision and leadership of Senator

© MICHAEL BLANDING

the Vermont State House

George Aiken, who defined the progressive wing of the Republican Party for more than 30 years, charting a moderate course toward land use and regulation that selectively supported elements of Franklin D. Roosevelt's New Deal. That tradition continued into modern times with Senator Jim Jeffords, a Vermont Republican who switched parties to become a Democrat in protest against the conservative excesses of President George W. Bush.

In the past 30 years, however, the state has swung toward the more liberal end of the Democratic Party. Current Senator Patrick Leahy was aggressive in challenging the Bush Administration on its civil rights record, being one of only 10 senators to vote against the USA Patriot Act and leading hearings into National Security Agency wiretapping. Former governor Howard Dean launched a fiery presidential campaign in 2004 that galvanized grassroots Democrats with a fervent opposition to the Iraq War. In the end, his campaign was sunk by a too-passionate speech after losing the Iowa caucuses to his Massachusetts neighbor John Kerry. Since then, however, he has achieved success for the Democrats as Democratic National Party Chair, pushing forward a 50-state strategy that paid off in Democrats gaining both houses of Congress in 2006. Finally, there is Vermont's most cherished politician, Bernie Sanders, who was representative for 15 years before succeeding Jeffords as senator in 2006. Former anti-war activist and avowed Socialist, Sanders is a leading proponent of labor rights, climate change legislation, and gun control, and has been an outspoken opponent of the war in Iraq. Despite such liberal credentials, however, he has always run as an Independent—keeping alive the streak that has animated Vermont politics for 200 years.

ECONOMY

Since its founding as a state, the Vermont economy has been underpinned by agriculture—especially beef, sheep, and dairy farms. Over the years, farming and logging enterprises have gone through times of boom and bust, with only dairy farming surviving as a major source of income for the state. Even that industry has seen its share of decline over the years—decreasing from more than 10,000 farms 60 years ago to fewer than 2,000 today. At the same time, however, milk production has actually increased due to technological innovations. Today, only 3 percent of the state's working population is engaged in agriculture, many of them involved in production of artisan and organic foods, specialty cheeses, and of course maple syrup. Vermont supplies more than one million gallons of the sweet stuff annually and is the top producer in the country, with more than a third of national production. In the record year of 2011, the state's maple syrup harvest skyrocketed to 1.7 million pounds.

Over the decades, Vermont also developed a healthy manufacturing sector, starting with the textile mills and gristmills of the 19th century and continuing with marble and granite quarrying and machine tool manufacturing into the 20th century. While manufacturing has declined in Vermont, as it has across the country, granite quarrying is still big business in Barre. Starting in the 1980s, Vermont also developed an active technology center, with computer company IBM setting up shop in Essex Junction outside of Burlington. The company now accounts for more than a quarter of manufacturing in the state and is a major employer, despite layoffs in 2002. With technology creating more freedom than ever, the state has seen a new influx of independent knowledge workers and start-up technology companies in the past two decades. Vermont's gross state product was still only $26 billion in 2010—making it the smallest economy in the country (ranked per capita, however, it comes in a respectable 30th).

The state's largest industry is the one you picked up this book for—tourism. Driven by the big-name winter ski resorts—Killington, Mount Snow, Stowe, Sugarbush, and Stratton—as well as busloads of visitors who come every fall to view foliage—tourists directly spend $1.4 billion on goods and services in the state, contributing $200 million in tax and fee revenue to the state. Of 13.7 million "person-trips" to Vermont each year, half are overnight visitors coming from out of state. The industry directly supports some 33,000 jobs, 11.5 percent of the state's total.

People and Culture

When famously taciturn president Calvin Coolidge, a native of Vermont, was once approached by a socialite, the story goes that she said to him: "Someone bet me that I couldn't get you to say three words in a row." To which, it is said, he replied: "You lose."

The tales about the traditional Old Vermonter personality are indeed no joke. Like most New Englanders, Vermont citizens tend to be much more stoic than your average American. But those who call Vermonters "cold" just haven't spent enough time with them. It's true that hellos and good days may not be as forthcoming as in the South or the West, but Vermont residents make up for a lack of superficial friendliness with a straightforwardness that lets you know exactly where you stand in their hearts. And if you do find your way into those hearts, you'll find an intense loyalty and camaraderie that is as surprising as the surface flintiness can be off-putting.

Equally embedded in the population's cultural consciousness is an unshakable sense of independence—which goes back to its beginnings as an independent sovereign republic and is still manifested today in a faction calling for secession.

Generally economically conservative and socially liberal, Vermonters are staunch protectors of their environment, passing laws like the 1968 Billboard Law, which bans billboards from highways, and the Beverage Container Law, which keeps bottle and can litter to a minimum. And that's one thing that's as true of the state's growing number of newcomer citizens (known as flatlanders), who arrive from New York and Boston, as it is of Old Vermonters.

STATISTICS

Vermont is home to 626,000 people. That's roughly the same number of residents who live in Boston, New England's largest city. The state's largest city, by far, is Burlington, with just 42,000 residents, bolstered by three of its surrounding suburbs, Essex (19,000), South Burlington (18,000), and Colchester (17,000). Outside the Burlington area, the only substantial population centers are Rutland and Bennington, each with about 16,000 people, and Brattleboro with 12,000. The state capital, Montpelier, has a scant 8,000 souls.

Annual median household income is $51,841, about equal the U.S. average. Meanwhile, the unemployment rate is 5 percent—lower than the national average of 8 percent.

Vermonters are highly educated, with 90.6 percent of the population having received at least a high school diploma, and 33.3 percent at least have a bachelor's degree. In terms of marital status, 55 percent of Vermonters are married, 27 percent remain unmarried, and 10 percent are divorced.

ETHNICITY

According to census figures, Vermont averages far higher than the rest of the country in its number of Caucasian residents—95.5 percent

compared to the nation's 78 percent. The next-largest ethnic groups in the state are Hispanic residents (1.6 percent), Asian residents (1.3 percent), and African-American residents (1.1 percent). Persons of American Indian descent number only 0.4 percent.

CULTURE

Two major strands of culture typify the region: the thriving rural culture that keeps alive farming, fishing, and livestock traditions, and the educated, intellectual culture that flows out from the colleges and universities. The most typical Vermont towns contain evidence of both: county fairs that still generate excitement in the populace, and cultural institutions such as museums, theaters, and art galleries that can be found in even the most remote corners of the region.

RELIGION

Christianity is far and away Vermont's most dominant religion, practiced by approximately 83 percent of residents. Judaism, by comparison, is practiced by only about 1 percent.

Within the Christian population, the Catholic Church claims the devotion of between 25 and 35 percent of Vermont residents, depending on which survey you consult. Behind that, about 5 percent of the population consider themselves United Methodist Church. Other churches, though not found widely, are the Episcopal Church, Northern Baptists, and the Church of Jesus Christ of Latter-day Saints. Vermont also has a healthy share of nonbelievers; about 11 percent of people consider themselves nonreligious, while another 1.2 percent call themselves agnostic.

LANGUAGE

English is by far the most widely spoken tongue in the state—94.6 percent of the people speak only English—which is not surprising in a state with such a small immigrant community. Only

1.1 percent of the population speaks Spanish; another 3.3 percent speak other Indo-European languages.

That said, Vermont English does have a few of its own distinctions: The early presence of the Algonquin Mohawk and Iroquois tribes in Vermont has resulted in common use of Native American words for place-names around the state. What's more, Vermont's dialect differs from that of some other New England states in its pronunciation of the final *r* in many words.

THE ARTS

A love of music and the arts has dominated New England's cultural scene for centuries, and thanks to the legacy of the Boston Brahmins (those blue-blooded families who ruled the region's society and industry in the 19th century) and the enterprising, artistic spirit embraced by Vermonters today, there are plenty of places to appreciate it—from Brattleboro's Art Museum and summer music festivals to the independent art galleries of Burlington.

But much of the culture found in this area of the country is just as easily found in its streets, pubs, and colleges. A thriving rock and folk music scene dominates the nightclubs and bars around the University of Vermont (which spawned the band Phish) and Middlebury College (birthplace of Dispatch). A strong handful of contemporary music composers (from Peggy Madden and Jon Appleton to Lian Tan) also call Vermont home and give regular performances all over the state. And no matter how far afield you go, it seems there's always an independent artisan practicing a craft in a welcoming studio—be it glassblowing, painting, or sculpture.

SHOPPING

What Vermont lacks in designer boutiques and department stores, it more than makes up for in unique, artistic, independent shops and galleries. The proliferation of crafts here is impressive—from blown glass and pottery to hand-stitched sweaters and handcrafted specialty foods. (Can anyone ever have enough maple syrup in their pantry?) Find all of it in the many country stores that anchor the centers of many Vermont towns, or visit the artists' studios directly; they can be found everywhere, from centrally located town greens to the mountain roads.

Meanwhile, bargains are also on the horizon. Antiques collectors and dealers have long known the deals to be had in Vermont's country antiques shops—from inexpensive, charming bits of Americana to big-ticket 18th-century armoires. Then there are the designer outlets offering significant discounts on brand names; they line the streets of Manchester, attracting hordes of shoppers from all over the state, not to mention fashion lovers from Boston, New York, Montreal, and beyond.

HOLIDAYS AND FESTIVALS

Rather than waiting for the weather to cooperate, Vermonters make their celebrations a year-round activity; even in the coldest temperatures, winter festivals abound. January's Stowe Winter Carnival, for example, features snow golf, snowshoe racing, ice carving, snow volleyball, hockey, and parades.

Spring is sap season, and the Vermont Maple Festival in St. Albans does it justice in April with maple exhibits, food contests, antique and craft shows, fiddlers show, pancake breakfasts, and an epic parade.

In summer, county fairs abound—one of the biggest is the Vermont State Fair. It all but takes over Rutland, with rides, tons of food, rodeos, horse pulls, arts and crafts, and farm animals galore.

Autumn is the region's prime time for tourism (and arguably its most beautiful season), so it's no wonder the festivals hit during those months. The Killington Foliage Weekend gets going every September, with

VERMONT ON FILM

The kaleidoscopic foliage and picturesque church spires of New England have proven irresistible to filmmakers over the years. Since the 1920s, more than 100 movies have been filmed in Vermont. Here are 10 favorites.

- *The Trouble with Harry* (1954): One of Alfred Hitchcock's stranger films is a black comedy about a dead body that shows up in a small New England town, much of it filmed in Craftsbury Common in the Northeast Kingdom. Shirley MacLaine has her first film role.

- *Terror Train* (1979): A campy horror film with Jamie Lee Curtis and David Copperfield—playing a magician—makes a stop at the station in Bellows Falls.

- *The Four Seasons* (1980): Alan Alda directed a story about three couples going through various midlife crises against the backdrop of foliage and ski slopes in Vermont. It was partly filmed at Edson Hill Manor in Stowe.

- *Baby Boom* (1986): For everyone who ever wanted to leave the rat race, there's this film, in which Diane Keaton has a baby and leaves a yuppie existence in Manhattan for the laid-back Vermont farmhouse. The movie was filmed in the village of Peru, outside Manchester.

- *Beetlejuice* (1987): Though it takes place in Connecticut, all of the exterior shots for this paranormal black comedy were shot in East Corinth. Michael Keaton and Winona Ryder star in the movie.

- *Ethan Frome* (1993): The stark Northeast Kingdom landscape of Peacham lends a dramatic backdrop to this adaptation of Edith Wharton's masterpiece about an unfortunate farmer, played by Liam Neeson.

- *The Spitfire Grill* (1996): Peacham takes another star turn in this film, a dark sleeper hit about a woman out of prison who finds work at a restaurant in a small New England town.

- *A Stranger in the Kingdom* (1997): Though set in the Northeast Kingdom, this adaptation of Howard Frank Mosher's tale of small-town race and retribution with Martin Sheen was filmed in the central Vermont towns of Chelsea and Vershire.

- *Me, Myself & Irene* (2000): The Farrelly brothers' dark comedy about multiple personality disorder starring Jim Carrey features shots in Burlington, Middlebury, and Waterbury, including a cameo of Ben & Jerry's ice cream factory.

- *The Cider House Rules* (2003): Even though John Irving's novel is set in Maine, the adaptation starring Tobey Maguire, Charlize Theron, and Michael Caine was filmed just about everywhere else in New England, including the Scott Farm apple orchard in Brattleboro and the train station in Bellows Falls.

a Brew Festival and gondola rides. The holidays get started early in South Burlington, which around Thanksgiving hosts the largest and oldest juried show of Vermont artisans, the Vermont Hand Crafters & Art Show, with 160-plus booths selling enough crafts to fill the space underneath even the biggest Christmas tree.

ESSENTIALS

Getting There and Around

Vermont is easily accessible by road, rail, and air (and even sea if you are coming by ferry from New York). While Burlington International Airport is the most obvious destination, in some cases it can be cheaper to fly into airports in neighboring states. Amtrak's rail network isn't very extensive, but it does connect to several major cities. Those that aren't on the train routes are accessible by bus or car.

BY AIR

With 650,000 passengers flying out annually, **Burlington International Airport** (1200 Airport Dr., South Burlington, 802/863-1889, www.btv.aero) offers competitive rates to Vermont from many major American cities, including Cleveland, Chicago, Detroit, Newark, New York, Orlando, Philadelphia, and Washington, DC, and one international flight from Toronto (Porter Airlines). It's worth checking, however, to see if you can get a cheaper or more direct flight to the much larger **Boston-Logan International Airport** (1 Harborside Dr., East Boston, MA, 800/235-6426, www.massport.com/logan). The largest transportation hub in the region, it is

only a two-hour drive from Brattleboro, so it can provide an even quicker trip to southern Vermont. The airport serves nearly 30 airlines, of which a dozen are international, including Aer Lingus, Air Canada, Air France, Alitalia, British Airways, Iberia, Icelandair, Japan Airlines, Lufthansa, Porter Airlines, SATA, Swiss, TACV, and Virgin Atlantic Airways. International flights arrive in Terminal E.

Several of New England's smaller regional airports also provide cheaper flights or quicker travel times to parts of the state. **Bradley International Airport** (Schoephoester Rd., Windsor Locks, CT, 860/292-2000, www.bradleyairport.com), located halfway between Springfield, Massachusetts, and Hartford, Connecticut, is only an hour-or-so drive from Brattleboro along I-91. In addition to a half dozen major domestic carriers, Bradley is also served by Air Canada. In New Hampshire, **Manchester Airport** (1 Airport Rd., Manchester, NH, 603/624-6556, www.flymanchester.com) competes aggressively with Logan in the areas of price and convenience. It's an hour and a half from Brattleboro and two hours from Killington. Manchester is served by Delta, Southwest, United, and US Airways.

Another option is to fly into the **Albany International Airport** (737 Albany Shaker Rd., Albany, NY, 518/242-2200, www.albanyairport.com), which sits just over 60 miles away from Brattleboro and has car rentals and several convenient bus routes out of its terminal. It is served by most major domestic airlines as well as Air Canada.

BY RAIL

Amtrak (800/872-7245, www.amtrak.com) runs frequent trains along the aptly named **Vermonter** route, which runs to St. Albans from New York (10 hr.) and Washington, D.C. (14 hr.). Along the way, it passes through Brattleboro, White River Junction, Montpelier, Waterbury, Burlington, and other locations.

Also, Amtrak's **Ethan Allen** route offers once-a-day service to Rutland from New York City (10 hr.). Connecting to that route at Albany, New York, Amtrak's **Adirondack** route offers service to Rutland from Montreal, Quebec (15 hr.).

BY BUS

While not the quickest way to travel, the bus can be an attractive alternative for those on a budget or traveling to more rural or remote regions not served by rail or air. Vermont is accessible from many domestic and Canadian locations via **Greyhound Bus Lines** (800/231-2222, www.greyhound.com). Buses stop in several major cities, including Burlington, Brattleboro, Montpelier, Rutland, and White River Junction. Hours to Brattleboro from major cities are as follows: New York (5.5), Philadelphia (9), Montreal (6.5), Washington (13), Buffalo (14), Toronto (15), and Cleveland (16). Plan on an additional 3–4 hours for Burlington—except from Canadian locations, from which you should subtract the same amount.

For those who really want to leave the driving to someone else, Vermont-based **New England Vacation Tours** (802/464-2076, www.sover.net/~nevt) offers a set of custom tours for foliage and ski seasons.

While it's possible to visit most Vermont areas by public transportation, the state's bus routes are often slow and cumbersome, with connections in towns out of the way of your final destination. The added expense of renting a car is often worth it for the convenience and freedom of cruising the back roads, especially in foliage season.

The Vermont Agency of Transportation maintains its network of interstate highways, U.S. highways, and Vermont routes, which are fairly well kept and efficient. Then there are those roads that the state terms "Vermont byways"—highways or other public roads with special scenic, historic, or

CAR RENTAL COMPANIES

The following companies all have branches at Burlington Airport, as well as at the other locations listed.

- **Alamo** (877/222-9075, www.alamo.com)

- **Avis** (800/230-4898, www.avis.com): Brattleboro (1380 Putney Rd.), South Burlington (1890 Williston Rd.)

- **Budget** (800/527-0700, www.budget.com): South Burlington (1890 Williston Rd.)

- **Enterprise** (800/261-7331, www.enterprise.com): Barre (1246 Rte. 302), Bennington (96 Northside Dr.), Brattleboro (801 Putney Rd.), Middlebury (1410 Rte.

7S), Rutland (131 S. Main St.), South Burlington (1116 Shelburne Rd. and 1891 Williston Rd.), St. Albans (16 Swanton Rd.), St. Johnsbury (26 Memorial Dr.), and White River Junction (60 Jasmin Ln.)

- **Hertz** (800/654-3131, www.hertz.com): Barre (697 South Barre Rd.), Rutland (1004 Airport Rd.), and South Burlington (1335 Shelburne Rd.)

- **National** (800/227-7368, www.nationalcar.com)

- **Thrifty** (877/283-0898, www.thrifty.com): White River Junction (93 Beswick Dr.)

---

cultural import. These can be meandering and slower, but are often the very definition of the great American drive. Also, thanks to the state's snowstorm-prone climes, road travel can become treacherous in wintertime. Travelers can get roadway information ahead of time by contacting the Vermont Agency of Transportation and State Police; they have teamed up to offer travel information at the telephone number 511, which can be accessed anywhere in the state.

In addition to the bus and train options, each region of the state has its own public bus carrier, though they vary widely in quality and extent of service. In some rural areas, such as the Northeast Kingdom, transport is extremely limited. For more information on service in a particular region, check out the website of the **Vermont Public Transportation Association** (www.vpta.net).

BY CAR

The major auto route into Vermont is I-91, which enters the southeast corner of the state at Brattleboro, 3.5 hours from New York or 7.5 hours from Washington, DC. From the west,

the main route into New England is I-90, also known as the Massachusetts Turnpike (or Mass Pike for short). From there, you can connect to I-91 at Springfield to drive to Brattleboro (1.5 hr.) or take the more scenic route up Route 7 in western Massachusetts to Bennington (1 hr.). From Boston, drive up I-93 to I-89 to enter the state at White River Junction, or drive west on Route 2 to connect with I-91 to Brattleboro; either route takes about 2 hours. From Montreal, take Autoroutes 10 and 35 to Route 133, which connects to I-89 at the border—2 hours total to Burlington.

BY FERRY

Three ferries make the trip across Lake Champlain from New York: Plattsburgh to Grand Isle (12 min.), Port Kent to Burlington (1 hr.), and Essex to Charlotte (20 min.). For more information, contact **Lake Champlain Transportation** (King St. Dock, 802/864-9804, www.ferries.com, late May–early Oct.).

VISAS AND OFFICIALDOM

Visitors entering Vermont from Canada do not require a visa, but do require a valid passport.

In checking through customs, they are asked to provide tickets and documents for their return to Canada or onward destination if traveling by air, rail, boat, or bus. If you are driving a rental car, be sure to bring a copy of the rental agreement, as officials are often on the lookout for stolen vehicles.

Crossing the border requires going through immigration customs both ways, and the process is usually pretty routine, though vehicles are occasionally searched. Visitors who are 21 years or older may bring the following into the United States: 200 cigarettes or 50 cigars or 4.4 pounds of tobacco; one liter of alcohol; gifts worth up to $100. The Department of Homeland Security is changing the rules on crossing borders fairly frequently these days, so it's wise to check with the Foreign Affairs and International Trade Canada office (www.canada.gc.ca) before your trip.

Recreation

The abundance of mountains, lakes, parks, and rivers all over Vermont means there is very little recreation that can't be enjoyed here. Of course, what you do depends on season and geography—in winter, skiers flock to the snowy peaks of the Green Mountains; fall and summer bring hunters, anglers, hikers, and mountain bikers to trails and streams. (Spring, on the other hand, is often far too muddy for any of the latter.) Meanwhile, the widely varied parks and preservation lands throughout the state are excellent grounds for bird-watching, year-round.

CYCLING

Cyclists in rural Vermont are blessed with countless terrain options: Small country towns sport wide and pretty roads meandering through historic villages, and the low-lying trails make for excellent mountain biking (especially during fall foliage season). Even Vermont's cities are small enough to accommodate bicyclists, though a lack of bike paths means that bikers should ride with extra caution.

HIKING AND CAMPING

New Englanders love camping, and they prove it year after year by filling Vermont's campsites in droves—so much so that on holiday weekends, the challenge isn't finding a camping ground (there are plenty all around the mountainous areas as well as by the lakes) but finding one with available sites. On such popular dates, it pays to arrive early in the morning (preferably before the weekend begins) or make a reservation in advance. Also, not all campgrounds offer sites for both RVs and tents; call ahead to be sure. While most state parks provide hot showers and dumping stations for RVs, few provide hookups.

Rates for camping vary by park, but are always reasonable, running from $16–27 per person for tent and trailer sites, and $21–25 per person for lean-tos. Some parks also have cabins or cottages, ranging from $42–46 per day and $490–660 per week. Reservations can be made more than two weeks in advance online at www.vtstateparks.com, or through the central reservation line, 888/409-7578 (9 A.M.–4 P.M. Mon.–Fri.). Less than two weeks in advance, it's necessary to call the park directly. Most campsites require at least a two-night minimum stay. A credit card is needed to secure a reservation; payment is refundable, less a $10 cancellation fee, up until the day before the reservation.

© VERMONTVACATION.COM/DENNIS CURRAN

climbers atop Mount Mansfield

HUNTING, FISHING, AND BIRD-WATCHING

Every season, without fail, droves of dedicated sportsmen and sportswomen descend upon the backwoods of Vermont, seeking to watch, catch, or take home some of its bounty. Local regulations and licensing requirements can be strict; certain animals (specific rules apply to most species for trapping, baiting, shooting, and catching) are protected in certain districts. So be certain to check with the local Fish and Game offices of your area of interest before planning your trip.

Hunting areas are well regulated and plentiful, particularly further north, where animals from woodcock and deer to turkey and moose roam.

Moving-water fishing takes place mostly in summer and early fall. Serious trout and bass anglers gravitate toward the Missisquoi, Batten Kill, and Connecticut Rivers. In winter, ice fishing is popular in many small northern towns—particularly in the area around Lake Champlain. The sport requires hardy enthusiasts to cut holes in the ice above ponds and lakes, and then catch fish as they cruise beneath the hole.

Any time of year, bird-watchers can feast their eyes in any number of wildlife refuges. Some of the best include the Missisquoi and Silvio O. Conte National Wildlife Refuges.

KAYAKING AND CANOEING

Wherever there's water in Vermont, there are usually plenty of places to put in a kayak and head out for a run. Meanwhile, there are river-rafting opportunities for nearly every level of paddler. Highlights include the Class II Batten Kill, which is the best run in the summer and flows under four picturesque covered bridges; Otter Creek, a Class II, north-running river into Lake Champlain; the Class II Winooski River, which runs past stunning natural scenery and small waterfalls; and the

JUST CHUTE ME

To the uninitiated, driving by an alpine slide does nothing more than, at the most, evoke quizzical expressions and, at the least, a blank stare. The sight of the long, usually bright blue chutes descending off of an otherwise pristine-looking mountain can indeed give passersby pause. But to those familiar with the ride (especially if they happen to have children in tow), it's tough not to pull over, buy a ticket, and pile into the wheeled carts that hurtle down the slide all summer long.

Made sometimes of cement, sometimes of fiberglass, the slide itself has a smooth track at its base and high walls all the way down its length. Passengers (usually one, two, or three) sit on a cart at the top of the chute and control the speed of the ride via a hand brake.

Alpine slides are easy to find; most of Vermont's large ski resorts—including Stowe, Killington, Bromley, and Pico—offer them in warm weather.

Lamoille River, which ranges from flatwater to Class III.

ROCK CLIMBING

Northern New England is a veritable playground for mountaineers, who flock in all seasons to the area's challenging rock-climbing faces. Popular climbs are found in Groton State Forest (Gem Boulder), Deer Leap, Shangri La, Eagle Eye near Rutland, and North Duxbury near Waterbury. Farther north, ice climbing is popular at areas like Smugglers' Notch, Ragnarock, and Elephant Head Buttress.

SAILING

Vermont may be landlocked, but residents take full advantage of its lakes by getting out on them in as many ways as possible. On the larger lakes, that includes sailing—particularly on Lake Champlain, where several chartering companies can be found and schooners can be rented for day cruises, and Lake Memphremagog, where a marina serves sailors who make their way to and from Canada.

SKIING AND WINTER SPORTS

Skiing in Vermont is more than a mere sport; it's what makes the winters bearable for many residents. The pastime keeps entire small-town economies revved up from December through March (and for true addicts, April) and pulls many out of their homes and into face-to-face, downhill encounters with nature.

The state's slopes vary greatly in difficulty, but it's safe to say that the state draws some of the region's most serious skiers to top mountains like Stowe, Stratton, Okemo, Killington, and Mad River Glen. Meanwhile, those who prefer to make horizontal tracks will find plenty of ground to cover all over the state; Vermont has 885 miles of well-groomed cross-country trails at the big resorts, at cross-country centers, and in private woods—many of which belong to inns and are open to guests.

In addition to skiing, the majority of resorts allow snowboarding, though some do so in designated areas, and many offer special snowshoeing trails. (The latter can also be found on many hotel properties.) Snowmobiles can be found come winter in many an area state forest; strict regulations, however, require enthusiasts to be careful about where they motor.

Ice skating, too, is a popular winter activity—done in town and city parks and at recreational rinks. Most are open to the public, usually charge a small fee, and are listed with local town halls. Local parks are also full of sledding opportunities.

Accommodations and Food

Throughout the book, accommodation listings include the range of rates for a standard double room in high season (roughly May–Oct.). Depending on location, prices can be much higher during peak times (e.g., foliage or ski season) and steeply discounted in winter and spring. Food listings include the range of prices for dinner entrées, including sandwiches but not salads. Lunch is often significantly cheaper.

LEAF-PEEPERS

Many tourist destinations celebrate their peak seasons in the summer when the weather is the nicest; not so in Vermont. Peak travel here is in the fall, particularly in late September and October when the foliage is at its most dramatic and students are pouring into area colleges. Many hotels jack up their prices by a factor of two or even three during this brief crowded season. If leaf peeping isn't your thing, you can save a lot of money by traveling in late August or early September when the summer humidity has dissipated but hotel prices haven't yet skyrocketed.

B&BS

Along with the rest of the country, Vermont has seen a steady rise in the price of accommodations at all levels, making it difficult to find any bargains among the major-name hotels. Bed-and-breakfasts, especially in more rural areas, can be an attractive alternative; often run by couples or families, they can offer dirt-cheap prices without sacrificing amenities or hominess. Those who prefer the anonymity of a motel will find more bargains (though less consistency) in independent operations. Gone are the days when a Super 8 or Motel 6 offers a

plush accommodations at the Round Barn Farm

COURTESY OF ROUND BARN FARM

the work and learn about the day-to-day happenings of a farm.

LOCAL CUISINE

In general, Vermont fare is a hybrid of time periods—the very traditional dishes of a land-locked New England state, brought into this century with a widespread dedication to fresh, locally and sustainably grown ingredients. That means cornbread made of organic corn from the farm down the road, cheddar cheese made and aged at the town's dairy farm, and maple syrup tapped in the backyard of the restaurant where it's served.

While all-American country dishes (from apple pie and corn chowder to burgers and BLTs) do abound, the state is also peppered with respectable international restaurants; it isn't unusual to find a Thai, Mexican, or Italian eatery in even its smaller villages, while its larger towns like Burlington and Manchester sport a strong handful of global dining options.

That said, the best foods in Vermont are local foods, often those that it excels at creating naturally—springtime fiddlehead ferns found in the forests, brook trout from the rushing rivers, and richly flavored game like venison and duck. Meanwhile, the area's farms are a wealth of palate-tempting prizes: Vermont farmers pride themselves on raising superb cows—many grass-fed and hormone-free—so that steaks have a delicious, slightly earthy taste, and milk and cheeses tend to have more complex flavors than the standard supermarket alternatives.

Cheese, in fact, is an enormous point of pride in these parts: The Vermont Cheese Trail, a collection of small, often out-of-the-way dairy farms, alone includes upwards of 35 artisanal cheesemakers, many of which have won national awards. And of course, maple syrup remains all but a regional obsession; the amber liquid is made not just in large-production

rich harvest at a local farmers market

$39 double—$139 is more like it. By contrast, you can still find a room in the $60 range at places like the Minuteman or Lamplighter. If in doubt, don't be shy about asking to see a room before committing.

COUNTRY INNS

For families, Vermont abounds in large country inns that serve as an economical alternative to the big-name hotels. Often historic properties that have seen slightly better days, they make up in charm what they lack in polish. Beware, however, of properties in high-traffic tourist destinations that have not been renovated since the Revolution. And don't immediately rush to the inn that shares the name of the town—that fact alone can boost prices by 20 percent or more. Also, don't hesitate to consider a farm stay—working farms that operate as B&Bs (and with similarly reasonable prices) offer guests the opportunity to lend a hand in

THE VERMONT FRESH NETWORK

It's unavoidable; you sit down at nearly any restaurant in Vermont these days, and there it is, looking back at you from the menu: "We are a proud member of the Vermont Fresh Network." But what does that mean, exactly? In essence, only good things—especially for someone about to eat a meal reaped from its benefits. The Vermont Fresh Network (www.vermontfresh.net, 802/434-2000) is a statewide group dedicated to encouraging farmers, food producers, and chefs to work more closely together, to build partnerships to support one another, and, essentially, to shorten the time from the moment an ingredient was made to the moment it hits your plate. The network, for its part, helps to promote and publicize those Vermont chefs and restaurants that use Vermont-grown foods. The network also helps educate the public about the nutritional upsides—not to mention the freshness—of eating locally grown foods, as well as the economic impact of supporting local farmers.

sugarhouses, but by hand on small farms across the state.

Because of the state's dedication to responsibly growing and eating healthy foods and supporting local farms, it has created the Vermont Fresh Network, a collaboration between the region's farmers, chefs, and buying public that provides as direct a route as possible from the food's source to restaurant and kitchen tables across the state.

Tips for Travelers

STUDENT TRAVELERS

You'll be hard-pressed to find an area of the country more welcoming to students than New England, and Vermont is no exception to that. The state is home to enough colleges and universities that in some towns, students outnumber the rest of the population. So it's no surprise to find cafes (both those with Internet access and without it) in abundance in college towns, and plenty of discounted tours are offered throughout the state through the tourist boards. Many hotels also offer student discounts with identification cards.

ACCESS FOR TRAVELERS WITH DISABILITIES

Public transportation in the majority of Vermont is wheelchair-accessible, as are most hotels, museums, and public buildings. Many campgrounds are not accessible; in general, the more remote the destination, the greater the

possibility that it will not be. As common sense would dictate, call ahead and plan accordingly.

TRAVELING WITH CHILDREN

With so many attractions for kids, it's no surprise that travel all over Vermont is extremely family-friendly. Most hotels offer cribs in rooms upon request, and public transportation and attractions offer discounted fares for children. The majority of restaurants are happy to offer high chairs, and many have kids' menus. The state also goes further than most in welcoming public breast-feeding for mothers and infants.

The one exception to this rule of family-friendliness is found at the occasional exclusive resort, which usually makes a point of labeling itself adults-only.

WOMEN TRAVELING ALONE

All over Vermont, solo female travelers will feel perfectly at home and can travel safely and without harassment. It is, of course, wise to avoid strolling out late at night, though even in such circumstances, incidents are quite rare.

GAY AND LESBIAN TRAVELERS

At this point in America's social history, few states in the country are friendlier to gay and lesbian visitors than Vermont. The state has significant and thriving gay and lesbian communities, and was the first state in the nation to legalize civil unions of same-sex couples in 2000. In 2009, it crossed a new milestone by authorizing same-sex marriages, identical in every way to opposite-sex unions, by state statute. Up until that landmark law, only three other states had approved gay marriage (Massachusetts, Iowa, and Connecticut), all of them by judicial ruling. The Vermont law was quickly copied by other states, including New Hampshire and New York, soon after its passage.

It should be noted that while civil unions and same-sex marriages afford all the same benefits and protections under Vermont law, they are still not recognized by the federal government. In fact, under the U.S. Defense of Marriage Act (DOMA) of 1996, other U.S. states are not obliged to recognize them.

HEALTH AND SAFETY

In general, there are few safer states to be in than Vermont; the state's rate of crime (both violent and nonviolent property crimes) is a tiny sliver compared to the national average—both in its towns and its rural areas. That said, certain precautions will help you stay as safe as possible. In cities, follow the basic rules of common sense (take precautions in watching your belongings, avoid walking alone late at night, and be aware of your surroundings), and odds are safety won't be a problem.

In the countryside, one of the biggest threats to visitors' safety can be the natural world they seek. When hiking the mountains or canoeing the endless rivers, it is essential to know about the dangers of exposure to the elements. Visit the local tourism offices for specific tips on preparing for an outing, and if you are at all unsure of your outdoors skills, consider hiring a guide to take you on your excursion.

In case of an emergency on the slopes, almost all ski resorts do offer basic medical attention by staff instructors trained in emergency care. Some also have an emergency medical technician and rescue services available on their ski patrols 24 hours a day. But in general, the smaller the resort, the fewer the medical offerings. When serious injuries occur, visitors are brought to one of the state's regional hospitals or medical centers—of which there are roughly 25.

Throughout the state, 911 remains the telephone number for emergencies. The Vermont State Police Department number is 802/244-8727, and the Vermont Department of Health can be reached at 800/464-4343.

Information and Services

MONEY

Vermont imposes a sales tax rate of 6 percent on most purchases, including goods, entertainment, and telephone calling cards. Certain items are exempt, including clothing items of $110 or less, food, and medicine. Taxes on meals and lodging are 9 percent; on alcoholic beverages, 10 percent.

A 15–20 percent tip is customary in all but the most rural areas of Vermont (which are usually accustomed to just slightly lower percentages), in restaurants, bars, and hair salons and spas, if you are satisfied with the level of your service. At hotels in cities, $1 per bag for porters is the norm, doormen usually receive $1 for hailing a taxi, maids usually receive $1–2 per night, and concierges are given anywhere from a few dollars to $20, depending on the services they have provided. For taxi rides, 10 to 15 percent is customary.

COMMUNICATIONS AND MEDIA
Cell Phones

The very thing that often brings visitors to Vermont—pristine, unspoiled nature—is what often causes them to curse the proudly technology-oblivious state. For while cell service is usually available in cities, towns, and most (though not all) villages, it seems to regularly disappear the moment you drive around the backside of a mountain. Venture to complain about it to a local, and you'll usually get a smile and a shrug of the shoulders, at most.

But as the global march of wireless communication advances, that's all changing, even in Vermont. The state government has realized that the image provided by such service gaps might be hurting the state's overall economic development, and it has recently vowed to remedy the situation. That said, even in towns where service is quite healthy, it's wise to keep an eye out in local businesses for the often plentiful signs requesting that you put your cell phone away—particularly in restaurants and cafes.

Internet Access

Cities in the state are peppered with Internet cafes that rent computer terminals (usually in 15-min. increments), as well as regular cafes that offer wireless Internet access (sometimes free, sometimes free only with a food purchase, and sometimes for a nominal fee), to those who bring their own laptops. Outside cities, the availability of Wi-Fi Internet is growing but still limited; local libraries are always a good place to find easy Internet access, as many (if not all) offer free terminal use in varying time increments.

In smaller country towns, finding Internet service can be difficult. Thankfully, more and more lodging options include wireless Internet. It's not just exclusive resorts either—even chain motels and small, historic bed-and-breakfasts often advertise a wireless router as an added perk for their guests.

Magazines

Several regional magazines provide useful information for travelers, including **Yankee Magazine,** for events, festivals, landmarks, restaurants, and tours all over New England; and **Vermont Life,** the quarterly periodical dedicated to all things Vermont. Newspapers of the larger communities include **Burlington Free Press, Rutland Herald, Bennington Banner, Brattleboro Reformer, Barre Times-Argus,** and **Manchester Journal.**

MAPS AND TOURIST INFORMATION
Maps

In these days of GPS and Google Maps, highway maps may seem quaint if not obsolete; however, if you are going to be spending a lot of time in the state or driving to more remote areas, you'll want to pick up DeLorme's *Vermont Atlas and Gazetteer*—the granddaddy of state atlases, with detailed maps of every town in the state. (Purchase one online at shop.delorme.com.)

For help in finding hard-to-find spans on remote country creeks, authors Robert Hartnett and Ed Barna have produced *Vermont Covered Bridges Map & Guide,* with locations and information on more than 100 covered bridges.

For biking, look for *Lake Champlain Region Bikeways Map and Guide* at tourist centers and bike shops (and through www.champlainbikeways.org). Covering more than 1,300 miles of territory, this biking map to the Burlington area is produced by local nonprofit Champlain Bikeways.

For canoeing, the map series *Northern Forest Canoe Trail Maps* (802/496-2285, www.northernforestcanoetrail.org), by a Waitsfield-based nonprofit, covers 13 sections of a 700-mile network of canoeing trips through the northeastern United States and Quebec. Maps for sections 4, 5, and 6 include paddles through Vermont starting in Lake Champlain and passing through the Missisquoi River, Lake Memphremagog, and the Clyde and Nulhegan Rivers to the Connecticut River.

For hiking, we recommend *Vermont's Long Trail Waterproof Hiking Map,* available from the **Green Mountain Club** (802/244-7037, www.greenmountainclub.org). During those rainy days on the trail, hikers will want this durable trail map, produced in conjunction with the Green Mountain Club and covering the entire length of the state's most famous hiking trail.

Business Hours

Business hours vary widely between cities and towns, but most stores and offices in larger towns follow a schedule of 9 A.M. to 5 or 6 P.M. on weekdays; 10 A.M. to 6 P.M. on Saturdays; and noon to 5 P.M. on Sundays. In smaller cities and towns, particularly those in rural areas, expect more erratic weekend hours—or the possibility that they may simply stay closed until Monday. If in doubt, call an establishment in advance to verify hours. Most bars and clubs close their doors by 2 A.M. at the latest (and oftentimes by 1 A.M.).

RESOURCES

Suggested Reading

FICTION AND MEMOIR

Bohjalian, Chris. *Midwives.* New York: Harmony Books, 1998. A meditation on life and death told through the decisions and trial of a Vermont country midwife, this book was an Oprah's Book Club selection and won the New England Book Award for its mesmerizing prose.

Irving, John. Many of the most popular books of this cult Vermont-based novelist are set in New England, including *The World According to Garp,* which takes place in part at a New England boarding school, and *A Prayer for Owen Meaney,* which concerns several generations of a troubled New England family.

Lindbergh, Reeve. The youngest daughter of Charles A. and Anne Morrow Lindbergh moved to Vermont after college and now lives in St. Johnsbury. She's written two novels about country life in Vermont: *Moving to the Country* and *The Names of the Mountains,* as well as a book of thoughtful essays about her adopted home, *View from the Kingdom,* and several Vermont-themed children's books, including *There's a Cow in the Road!* Her latest memoir, *Forward From Here,* comes to grips with the legacy of her often angry and unhappy aviator father, whom, she discovers, secretly fathered seven other children in Europe.

Mayer, Archer. One of the most prolific of all of Vermont's writers, Mayer has been churning out Lt. Joe Gunther mystery novels at the rate of about one a year for more than a decade (16 books at last count). The Brattleboro-based author draws on his own experience as a county medical examiner and investigator for the state's attorney's office to inject a dose of realism into his gritty tales, which are set in villages and towns all across the state.

McMahon, Jennifer. *Promise Not To Tell.* Harper: 2007. A haunting thriller set in Vermont, this debut novel expertly weaves between two child murders: one in the past, one in the present.

Miller, Peter. *Nothing Hardly Ever Happens in Colbyville, Vermont.* Colbyville, VT: Silver Print Press, 2009. One of the foremost black and white photographers in Vermont, Miller opens this book of engaging essays with a joke. Located just downhill from Ben & Jerry's Factory, Colbyville was absorbed into Waterbury years ago. Miller uses the symbol to begin a fascinating examination of how the state has transformed itself from rural subsistence into a tourist mecca—a change he doesn't always consider to be for the better.

Morse, Burr. *Sweet Days and Beyond: The Morse Family, Eight Generations of Maple Sugaring.*

Poultney, VT: Historical Pages Company, 2005. In this recent history, written by one of Vermont's most established—and colorful—maple syrup makers, Morse writes humorously and endearingly about his family farm, which has tapped maples in Montpelier for eight generations.

Mosher, Howard Frank. A former high school teacher turned writer, Mosher captures the quirky spirit of the Northeast Kingdom—and arguably Vermont as a whole—better than any other writer living. His breakthrough novel, *A Stranger in the Kingdom,* about the controversy in a small town when a black minister is charged with impregnating a white girl, is just as powerful now as when it was published in 1989. His latest work, *On Kingdom Mountain,* which is part–love story and part–treasure hunt, displays a writer still on top of his game.

FOOD

Crouch, Andy. *The Good Beer Guide to New England.* Hanover, NH: University Press of New England, 2006. Don't know your Rock Art from your Long Trail? This detailed pub crawl to breweries in New England includes several Vermont favorites.

Hooper, Alison. *In a Cheesemaker's Kitchen: Celebrating 25 Years of Artisanal Cheesemaking from Vermont Butter & Cheese Company.* Woodstock: Countryman Press, 2009. Quite possibly the "cheesiest" book you will ever read, this memoir-cookbook tracks the birth of the artisanal cheese movement in Vermont from one of the pioneers in the field. It also includes plenty of tasty recipes using Vermont Butter & Cheese products.

Lager, Fred. *Ben & Jerry's: The Inside Scoop: How Two Real Guys Built a Business with a Social Conscience and a Sense of Humor.* New York: Three Rivers Press, 1999. If you just can't get enough Chunky Monkey or Cherry Garcia, pick up this book detailing the history of the Vermont local legends.

Lockhart, Betty Ann. *Maple Sugarin' in Vermont: A Sweet History.* Charleston: The History Press, 2008. An encyclopedic recounting of Vermont's famous foodstuff takes in the history of maple syrup, from its earliest discovery by the Abenakis, to its role in the abolitionist movement, to its harvesting by the von Trapp family of *The Sound of Music* fame. The book includes lots of historic photos and excerpts from original sources.

Ogden, Ellen Ecker. *The Vermont Cheese Book.* Woodstock, VT: Countryman Press, 2007. More than just a guide to the varieties of cheese produced in the state, this book takes readers into the farms and kitchens of artisanal cheesemakers to explain the process of how each cheese acquires its unique character.

GUIDEBOOKS

Barna, Ed. *Covered Bridges of Vermont.* Woodstock: Countryman Press, 1996. For the bridge fanatic, this guide gives detailed descriptions and historical information on every bridge in the state, organized into convenient driving tours.

Coffin, Howard, and Jane and Will Curtis. *Guns over the Champlain Valley: A Guide to Historic Sites and Battlefields.* Woodstock: Countryman Press, 2005. This guide takes travelers into the heat of battle, detailing tactics and maneuvers at sites relating to the French and Indian War, the Revolutionary War, the War of 1812, and even the Civil War.

Corbett, William. *Literary New England: A History and Guide*. New York: Faber and Faber, 1993. An excellent guide to sights associated with poets and writers who called New England home, it includes detailed directions to hard-to-find graves and historic sites and houses.

Green Mountain Club. This organization publishes several guides considered gospel by outdoor enthusiasts in the region, jam-packed with no-nonsense directions for hiking and canoeing every inch of the Vermont wilderness. Titles include *Vermont Day Hikes, The Long Trail Guide,* and *360 Degrees: A Guide to Vermont's Fire and Observation Towers.*

Kershner, Bruce and Robert Leverett. *The Sierra Club Guide to the Ancient Forests of the Northeast.* San Francisco: Sierra Club Books, 2004. Despite centuries of human habitation and exploitation, a surprising number of old-growth stands still exist in Vermont. This guide takes you inside their mossy interiors and explains what makes old-growth forests so unique.

Richards, Andy. *Photographing Vermont's Fall Foliage: Where to Find the Iconic Shots.* Portland: BookBaby, 2012. A godsend for leaf-peepers who want to take a bit of fall home with them, Richards' detailed guide for the Kindle includes everything you need to find the best majestic vistas, hidden ponds, and backcountry farmhouses. Specific driving instructions, including routes, landmarks, and even GPS coordinates are included.

HISTORY

Bellesiles, Michael A. *Revolutionary Outlaws: Ethan Allen and the Struggle for Independence on the Early American Frontier.* Charlottesville and London: University of Virginia Press, 2001. One of the better books to explore the enduring popularity and controversy surrounding Vermont's larger-than-life national hero, this book is less a biography than it is a social history of the founding of Vermont.

Cornwill, Joseph D. *Vermont Covered Bridges.* Charleston, SC: Arcadia Publishing, 2004. While more than 100 covered bridges still survive on Vermont back roads, literally hundreds more have been washed away over the years. This up-to-date book tells their stories—both the bridges that survived and those that didn't.

Cronon, William. *Changes in the Land: Indians, Colonists, and the Ecology of New England.* New York: Hill and Wang, 1983. The classic study of early New England history debunks myths and shatters preconceptions about Pilgrims and Native Americans and how each interacted with the landscape.

Duffy, Peter. *Vermont: An Illustrated History.* Northridge, CA: Windsor Publications, 1985. This coffee-table book is full of etchings, drawings, and old photographs, along with a narrative hitting all the high points of state history. It's currently out of print, but if you get your hands on it, you'll find a nice overview of the state without much heavy lifting.

Jennison, Peter S. *Roadside History of Vermont.* Missoula, MT: Mountain Press, 1989. Divided into individual towns along five routes across the state, this combination guidebook and history book provides in-depth depictions of some of the local characters and events that have shaped its history. It's just as useful to read as you travel as in an armchair while you plan your trip.

Naylor, Thomas H. *Secession: How Vermont and All Other States Can Save Themselves from the Empire.* Port Townsend, WA: Feral House, 2008. Not as kooky as it might sound, this book makes a compelling case for why Vermont would be better off alone. The founder of the Second Vermont Republic and professor emeritus at Duke University, Naylor makes his arguments in such reasoned prose that, even if you don't agree with them, at least you'll understand them.

Prince, Cathryn J., *Burn the Town, Sack the Banks: Confederates Attack Vermont.* New York: Basic Books, 2006. A very readable account of the little-known "St. Alban's Raid," the only Civil War battle fought in Vermont. The story brings alive the backdrop of spies, soldiers, and politicians behind the desperate last gasp of the South. The courtroom drama of one of the nation's first "celebrity" trials is almost as exciting as the raid itself.

Sherman, Joe. *Fast Lane on a Dirt Road: A Contemporary History of Vermont.* White River Junction, VT: Chelsea Green Publishing, 2009. Probably the best-written history of the last 60 years of the state, this newly updated book contains everything from the beginnings of the ski industry in Vermont to the fight to approve civil unions.

Sherman, Michael, Gene Sessions, and P. Jeffrey Potash. *Freedom and Unity: A History of Vermont.* Barre, VT: Vermont Historical Society, 2004. Written as a companion to the excellent permanent exhibit of the same name at the Vermont Historical Society Museum, this three-inch-tall tome is an exhaustive resource on everything from the Abenaki people to Bernie Sanders, told in an engaging and analytical style that explores the contradictions of Vermont's oxymoronic state motto.

Todish, Timothy J. *America's First World War: The French and Indian War, 1754–1763.* Fleischmanns, NY: Purple Mountain Press, 2002. This book is an illustrated history of the conflict that predated the Revolutionary War and enveloped Vermont in several violent clashes.

Wiseman, Frederick Matthew. *The Voice of the Dawn: An Autohistory of the Abenaki Nation.* Hanover, NH: University Press of New England, 2001. A story of the Abenaki, from their origins to their conquest by Europeans, draws upon archaeological information and firsthand contemporary accounts from an author who grew up as an Abenaki in Vermont.

NATURAL HISTORY AND ECOLOGY

Albers, Jan. *Hands on the Land: A Natural History of the Vermont Landscape.* Boston: MIT Press, 2002. In a gorgeous oversized book, Albers details the various factors—geological, ecological, and economic—that have transformed the Green Mountain State.

Degraff, Richard, and Mariko Yamasaki. *New England Wildlife: Habitat, Natural History, and Distribution.* Hanover, NH: University Press of New England, 2001. This is a no-nonsense guide to every last species of mammal, reptile, amphibian, and bird in the region, along with seasonal information and distribution maps. Note, however, that the book is limited to land species.

Klyza, Christopher McGrory, and Stephen C. Trombulak. *The Story of Vermont: A Natural and Cultural History.* Middlebury, VT: Middlebury College Press, 1999. Well-written and informative, this landscape history book explores how humans have impacted the landscape and its flora and fauna. The book is split into three sections—one on the early history of the state, one on the transformation of the landscape in the last 200 years, and, finally, one on the current ecology of the state.

National Audubon Society. *National Audubon Society Regional Guide to New England.* New York: Knopf, 1998. The amateur naturalist would do well to pick up this guide, which details many local species of trees, wildflowers, reptiles, and mammals, along with 1,500 full-color illustrations.

Wessels, Tom. *Reading the Forested Landscape: A Natural History of New England.* Woodstock, VT: Countryman Press, 2005. A good read before heading off into the hills, this book helps put features of the landscape in their proper context.

Zielinski, Gregory A., and Barry D. Keim. *New England Weather, New England Climate.* Hanover, NH: University Press of New England, 2005. From nor'easters to Indian summer, this book patiently explains the meteorological underpinnings to New England's famously wacky weather.

REFERENCE

Duffy, John J., Samuel B. Hand, and Ralph H. Orth, eds. *The Vermont Encyclopedia.* Burlington: University of Vermont Press, 2003. Graze like a Jersey cow over this exhaustive compendium of all things Vermont, with 1,000 entries written by nearly 150 authors about the places, people, companies, and attractions that make the state what it is.

Internet Resources

Sandwiched between the slew of websites hawking hotel discounts and vacation packages are some legitimately useful ones, full of updates and resources for planning a trip—from often-comprehensive information to maps and events.

GENERAL REGIONAL WEBSITES

New England Towns
www.newenglandtowns.org/vermont
Read through the history of small Vermont towns, plus little-known facts and statistics.

Ski Vermont
www.skivermont.com
A streamlined but informative guide to the state's best ski resorts, this site allows you to choose your destination by the type of activity (alpine skiing and cross-country to snowboarding), area, or type of terrain you prefer.

Vermont
www.vermont.gov
The official state website includes a comprehensive guide to the area's tourism, environment, recreation, and politics, plus insider information on the education system, employment, and safety. The "travel and tourism" section includes links to regional tourism boards as well as other useful state departments, such as transportation and parks.

Vermont Fall Foliage Report
www.vermont.com/foliage.cfm
Get in-depth and up-to-date foliage reports on each area of the state, starting in early September and continuing throughout autumn. Updated twice per week by the self-dubbed "Leaf Squad," the site tracks and updates Vermont's changing foliage with a color-coded map showing where the leaves are peaking.

Vermont Historical Society
www.vermonthistory.org
Much more than just a portal for the Vermont Historical Museum, the official site of VHS includes an online catalog of its extensive collections of books and manuscripts, lesson plans for teachers, links to local historical societies, and an online store full of books, maps, and other history-related goodies.

Vermont State Historic Sites
http://historicsites.vermont.gov
A one-stop shop to plan your assault on all of Vermont's many reminders of the past, this state-run website has plenty of interactive tools to keep your history straight, including a Vermont Timeline, a map that organizes sites into regions, and detailed write-ups on certain aspects of the past, including Revolutionary War sites and historic homes.

Vermont Vacation
www.vermontvacation.com
As befits a state with such a large tourism industry, the official Vermont tourism site is impressively designed and chockful of information conveniently organized by region. From apple picking and the latest on the fishing season to hotel descriptions and rates, this website covers the gamut of planning your trip.

Yankee Foliage
www.yankeefoliage.com
Another great resource for leaf peepers is this constantly updated website produced by the editors of *Yankee* magazine, which includes an up-to-the-minute foliage map based on reports submitted by readers, suggestions for fall activities, and a blog by *Yankee*'s own foliage expert, Jim Salge.

MAJOR DESTINATION WEBSITES
Attracting visitors by the hundreds of thousands every year, the region's best-known attractions have become increasingly web-savvy. Expect to find basic background information about the destination, plus essentials such as hours, location, entrance fees, driving directions, and special deals or packages currently being offered.

Ben & Jerry's Ice Cream
www.benjerrys.com
Learn about new flavors, current activism efforts, and up-to-date visitor information at this entertaining and animated site.

Cabot Cheese
www.cabotcheese.com
Cheese recipes and pairings, a cheese blog, and, of course, factory tour information are all included on this, dare we say it, very cheesy website.

Killington Chamber of Commerce
www.killingtonchamber.com
Here you'll find information on nightlife and dining, shopping, accommodations, ski resorts, local churches, and businesses, plus help on getting around the area by public transportation and finding local festivals.

Lake Champlain Regional Chamber of Commerce
www.vermont.org
Get general information on Burlington and the surrounding area, including hotel and restaurant information, a scrolling list of events and festival happenings, and business information from medical services to car repair.

Official Guide to Stowe
www.gostowe.com
Find out everything you need to know about the area, including special information on arranging weddings and conferences in the area, and take advantage of the site's interactive travel planner.

Stowe Mountain Resort
www.stowe.com
Snow reports, lodging rates, special packages, and events at the resort are all listed on the site.

Town of Bennington
www.bennington.com
Get the lowdown on events, hotels, and shops in the Bennington area.

The Vermont Country Store
www.vermontcountrystore.com
The state's most beloved (and most marketed) quirky country store sells its hard-to-find stock online—everything from penny candy to sock monkey sheets.

Woodstock Area Chamber of Commerce
www.woodstockvt.com
Information on weather forecasts, local businesses, relocation services, restaurants, weddings, and plenty more is available on the site.

Index

List of Maps

www.moon.com

DESTINATIONS | ACTIVITIES | BLOGS | MAPS | BOOKS

MOON.COM is ready to help plan your next trip! Filled with fresh trip ideas and strategies, author interviews, informative travel blogs, a detailed map library, and descriptions of all the Moon guidebooks, Moon.com is all you need to get out and explore the world—or even places in your own backyard. While at Moon.com, sign up for our monthly e-newsletter for updates on new releases, travel tips, and expert advice from our on-the-go Moon authors. As always, when you travel with Moon, expect an experience that is uncommon and truly unique.

KEEP UP WITH MOON ON FACEBOOK AND TWITTER
JOIN THE MOON PHOTO GROUP ON FLICKR